Praise for Nabokov's Blues

"[Johnson and Coates] have made his posthu[mous] [scien]-tific history into a lucid, wide-ranging narrat[ive of] Nabokov's life and his interest in butterflies [and why their] study is so important to science and conservation efforts...."

—*The London Observer*

"Since Leonardo da Vinci, few thinkers with serious scientific pretensions can be said to have also created great art or vice versa.... Johnson and Coates make good arguments that Nabokov belongs among that elite."

— *Science*

"If Vladimir Nabokov had never written a line of fiction, he would have an honored reputation as a naturalist, and an expert on a large group of butterflies known as Blues. He loved his butterflies as passionately as his literature and both pursuits built the fullness of his life. Johnson and Coates's biological expertise and keen understanding of Nabokov's work allow us to integrate and understand one of the great figures of twentieth-century art – and science."

—*Stephen Jay Gould*

"Readers with a taste for science and literature will love this book, which is both entertaining and polymathically informative – rather like the English/Russian, naturalist/novelist, scholar/artist Nabokov himself."

— *Starred review, Publishers Weekly*

"[S]eeing Nabokov as a scientist gives the understanding of his life and works a whole new dimension."

—*Lancet*

"[O]nly now that Johnson and Coates have put Nabokov's scientific work in lay terms…can we see how the writer approaches his science with a distinctively novelistic mind."

—*San Francisco Chronicle*

"[W]ell worth reading…. It is a smart story about one of the century's towering intellects and his lesser-known passion: entomology."
—*American Scientist*

"A view of Nabokov's science and art that is both eerily evocative and stunningly new, that makes delectable reading without patronizing the reader."
—*Dmitri Nabokov*

"Blues is bound to charm and edify anyone who loves Nabokov, natural history, and especially butterflies."
—*The Washington Post Book World*

"It is an insightful and lively look at science and an extraordinary life, in part, in science."
—*Starred review, Booklist*

"*Nabokov's Blues* tells an astonishing story: a literary genius's scientific discoveries, their fall into oblivion, their rediscovery and extension almost half a century later. Vivid and varied, surprising and thoughtful, wry and poignant, *Nabokov's Blues* will appeal to anyone with a taste for adventure and contrast (a windswept Andean ridge, the hush of a laboratory bench), and an interest in the ironies and accidents of scientific discovery and in our knowledge of biodiversity that seems to be expanding not quite as fast as our planet shrinks."
—*Brian Boyd*

"Johnson and Coates have written an absorbing account of an indispensable side of one of the greatest writers of the age."
—*The Seattle Times*

"This is a grand book: erudite, generous, and wise. It is written with a grace and intelligence worthy of its eponymous subject."
—*The Boston Globe*

NABOKOV'S BLUES

The Scientific Odyssey of a Literary Genius

KURT JOHNSON

STEVE COATES

McGraw-Hill

New York Chicago San Francisco Lisbon London
Madrid Mexico City Milan New Delhi
San Juan Seoul Singapore
Sydney Toronto

McGraw-Hill

A Division of The McGraw·Hill Companies

Previously published in hardcover by Zoland Books.

Extracts from the works of Vladimir Nabokov by arrangement
with the Estate of Vladimir Nabokov.

1 2 3 4 5 6 7 8 9 0   FGR/FGR   0 7 6 5 4 3 2 1

ISBN 0-07-137330-6

Printed and bound by Fairfield Graphics.

This book is printed on recycled, acid-free paper containing
a minimum of 50% recycled de-inked fiber.

To Elizabeth, Alicia, and Ricardo

K.J.

To my parents

S.C.

I found it and named it, being versed
in taxonomic Latin; thus became
godfather to an insect and its first
describer — and I want no other fame.

Wide open on its pin (though fast asleep),
and safe from creeping relatives and rust,
in the secluded stronghold where we keep
type specimens it will transcend its dust.

Dark pictures, thrones, the stones that pilgrims kiss,
poems that take a thousand years to die
but ape the immortality of this
red label on a little butterfly.

> — Vladimir Nabokov,
>   from "On Discovering a Butterfly"

Contents

Preface and
Acknowledgments

Many lepidopterists, past and present, contributed to the completion of the studies of Latin American Blue butterflies that were pioneered by Vladimir Nabokov. As scientists had long realized, given the wellsprings — and scope — of Nabokov's work, its completion was a project beyond the reach of a single person, or even a few. For this reason, although this book is partly an account of the role played by one of its authors, Kurt Johnson, the story is appropriately told in the third person and not through Johnson's eyes alone.

The book itself could not have come about without help from many people, including Stephen Hull of Zoland Books, who first suggested the idea. Much of it could not have been written without the masterly research of Nabokov's principal biographer, Brian Boyd, who was also generous with his time and advice. Attention and comment from Dmitri Nabokov as the book neared completion were greatly appreciated.

Although any errors and omissions are solely the responsibility of the authors, the following people kindly read and commented on the manuscript, in whole or in part. Most made other contributions as well. We extend our thanks to George T. Austin, Zsolt Bálint, Barbara Benham, Dubi Benyamini, Rachel Coates, Robert Dirig, Robert Eisele, Ted Goldman, Jason P. W. Hall, Amy J. Johannesen, Elizabeth Johnson, Greg Kareofelas, Robert M. Pyle, Tomasz W. Pyrcz, Julián Salazar, Arthur M. Shapiro, John Shuey, Andrei Sourakov, and Carol Witham.

The contributions of three colleagues, in particular, are worthy of special notice. They are Gerardo Lamas, Zsolt Bálint, and Dubi Benyamini, whose tireless work both in Europe and South America is fully recounted in the pages that follow.

During the preparation of the book, numerous friends, colleagues, and organizations answered questions or provided other important assistance, advice, support, or encouragement, for which the authors are most grateful. They include the American Ethical Union, Allison V. Andors, Rick Bassett, Susan Borkin, Gary Bradford, Lincoln P. Brower, Laura Brown, Stephanie Capparell, Luis Constantino, Charles V. Covell, Jr., Maire Crowe, Cornelia Dean, Henri Descimon, Julian P. Donahue, Nancy Dooly, John C. Downey, Michael Duckworth, Thomas C. Emmel, Sarah Funke, Sabine Gaal, David Grae, Seth Grae, Alyson Grunder, S. Blair Hedges, John B. Heppner, Ken Hobson, Glenn Horowitz, Artur Jasinski, D. Barton Johnson, David F. Kroenlein, Karl R. Kroenlein, Katherine Koutsis, Zoran Kuzmanovich, Jean François Le Crom, David Matusik, Ed Messer, Jacqueline Y. Miller, Lee D. Miller, the Nature Conservancy, Andra Nicoara, Stephen Jan Parker, Nicholas Pritzker, Eric L. Quinter, John E. Rawlins, Wade Rawlins, Charles L. Remington, Joan Richardson, Frederick H. Rindge, Shari L. Rosenblum, Jerome Rozen, Phillip Schappert, David H. Schmidt, Lester Short, Geeta Sirripaul Singh, Nikki Smith, Judith Tillman, Rodrigo Torres-Núñez, Jesús Velez, François Vuillemier, G. Warren Whitaker, the World Wildlife Fund, Allen M. Young, and Dieter E. Zimmer.

Steve Coates is deeply grateful to his wife, Rachel, and daughters, Charlotte and Katie, who cheerfully made many sacrifices and assumed far more than their fair share of domestic burdens so that this book could be written. Kurt Johnson expresses the same thanks to his wife, Elizabeth, daughter, Alicia, and son, Ricardo. For lifelong inspiration he also thanks his scientific mentors, Charles A. Long, John C. Downey, and Frederick H. Rindge.

In these acknowledgments, and in the mention of scientists throughout the book, we have elected to omit formal academic titles. Although most modern scholars hold some technical degree in their field, usually the Ph.D., this has not always been the case in the history of lepidoptery, nor is it always the case now in all parts of the world.

Regarding nomenclature, we have followed the modern rules of style for scientific names and placed all species and generic names in italics, with generic names capitalized. Categories above the genus level (family, tribe) are capitalized but not italicized. We depart from this form only in quoting Nabokov directly, because his usage predated the modern conventions. Finally, sometimes in lepidoptery scientific names have become standardized as common names, and the reader will see, for example, both *Calisto,* the scientific name for Antillean Satyr butterflies, and Calisto, their unitalicized common name.

PART I

THE AURELIAN

1 ⟨~⟩

The Most Famous
Lepidopterist in the World

> Frankly, I never thought of letters as a career. Writing has always been for
> me a blend of dejection and high spirits, a torture and a pastime — but
> I never expected it to be a source of income. On the other hand, I have
> often dreamt of a long and exciting career as an obscure curator of
> lepidoptera in a great museum.
>
> — *Strong Opinions*

L EPIDOPTERY, the branch of science dedicated to the study of butterflies and moths, has its own legendary figures, and its history is
both long and glorious. But for lepidopterists, as in fact for most
entomologists, the light of celebrity seldom shines outside a narrow but
passionate circle of scientists and collectors.

During the Age of Exploration, when the influx of exotic new plants
and animals from the four corners of a seemingly boundless globe astounded Europe, the study of biology, often a preserve of the well-born,
offered a path to wealth and fame. Sir Joseph Banks, the eighteenth-
century English biologist who accompanied Captain James Cook on his
three-year circumnavigation aboard the British ship *Endeavour*, was a
friend of King George III and one of the most famous men of his day. In
the next century, Baron Alexander von Humboldt, a Prussian nobleman
who pioneered the study of South America's vast flora and fauna, was considered by many of his contemporaries to be, after Napoleon, the most famous man in Europe.

For natural biologists of the twentieth century however, the story takes
on a different complexion. In 1973 the Austrian zoologist Karl von
Frisch shared a Nobel Prize (the only entomologist ever to have won such

recognition) for deciphering the honeybees' intricate food dance, the ritualistic motions a worker bee uses to convey the exact location of sources of nectar, pollen, and water, even miles away, to the rest of the hive. Von Frisch's work caught the public imagination for a while, but today few nonscientists even remember his name. Other researchers, too, have claimed a share of the limelight. Edward O. Wilson, for example, has become a recognizable public-television personality on the strength of his popular writings on ants and his influential work on the biodiversity crisis. And the lively meditations of the paleontologist Stephen Jay Gould on everything from dinosaurs to baseball have enshrined him among the media's most reliable scientific pundits. But for the most part today's entomologists, and certainly the lepidopterists among them, toil along with little public recognition. "Lepidopterists are obscure scientists. Not one is mentioned in Webster," explained one of their number, the novelist and lepidopterist Vladimir Nabokov.

Nabokov himself was a peculiar case. In 1999, the centennial of his birth in St. Petersburg, Russia, Nabokov is known mostly as the Cornell University literature professor who in the 1950s wrote *Lolita,* a serious novel with a salacious reputation and an underaged heroine whose name filled a semantic gap in the English language. But he was much, much more.

In fact, *Lolita* was only a part of a literary career that reached back to the 1920s and across two continents. Along with seventeen novels, he wrote poems, plays, film screenplays, and stories, some in Russian, some in English, but all with the same distinctive flair for language and imagination — an astounding bilingual achievement.

In some ways Nabokov's popular literary reputation reached a peak in the 1960s, but he maintains a passionate and distinguished following, and there are many signs of a resurgence. In academic circles Nabokov is increasingly mentioned in the company of such lights as Marcel Proust and James Joyce. Three scholarly journals are devoted to his life and works. There is a Nabokov web site, called Zembla, after the imaginary kingdom in his novel *Pale Fire.* In the last several years a remake of the film *Lolita* has been the controversial subject of wide media attention. In 1998 the editorial board of the Random House Modern Library, in a highly discussed list, ranked *Lolita* the fourth-best English-language novel of the twentieth century, ahead of anything written by William Faulkner, Henry James, D. H. Lawrence, Virginia Woolf, Ernest Hemingway, or Saul Bellow; according to some of the participants, *Lolita* was actually ranked first by more of the invited judges than any other work. *Pale Fire* occupied the fifty-third spot on the same list. Nabokov's *Speak, Memory* is another masterpiece, one of the most celebrated of modern literary memoirs; it ranked eighth on the Modern Library's nonfiction list, making Nabokov the only author with a book in the top ten of each. Furthermore, some critics believe that *The Gift*, written during the 1930s, is the century's best Russian-language novel. And in the world of scholarship Nabokov's massive four-volume translation of and commentary on Pushkin's great poem *Eugene Onegin*, which he published in 1964, is still the most authoritative.

These are only a few of the highlights of his work, yet as impressive as Nabokov's writings are, his biography is almost equally intriguing. In outline Nabokov's life story seems almost like a fairy tale. His birth into a stupendously wealthy family of Russian nobles and a blessedly happy childhood and youth were followed by the loss of nearly all possessions, expulsion from home, and the violent death of his beloved father. Then came decades of relative anonymity, the precarious struggles of exile, and a demanding career as a college teacher at Wellesley and Cornell, before the great reward in the fullness of years, somewhat incongruously in Nabokov's case, the particular kind of fame that only American popular culture can bestow. And, for the epic touch, his was a life played out against a background of some of the greatest social and political upheavals of the twentieth century: Nabokov was driven out of Russia by the Bolsheviks in 1917 and then, twenty-five years later, out of Europe by the Nazis. These experiences supplied the author with one of his major literary themes: the poignant absurdity of the exile.

Despite the brilliant résumé, for most of his career Nabokov wrote in comparative obscurity, first for the small and fragmented world of the Russian emigration and later for a narrow, though ardent, readership in English. Until 1958, the "year of grace," when *Lolita* was published in the United States, Nabokov was unable to support himself solely on his literary creations. But suddenly the little girl and her creator became international sensations.

A small circle of admirers was already aware of yet another strange and wondrous facet of Nabokov's life: that he collected and studied butterflies and had published articles on lepidoptery in scientific journals; that he was an acknowledged expert on a group of butterflies called Blues, and even that he had held an official position at the Museum of Comparative Zoology at Harvard University. An entire chapter of his memoirs, which were published serially in *The New Yorker* magazine beginning in the late 1940s, had been devoted to his love of butterflies, and *Time*, *Vogue*, and other magazines had sent photographers to capture him at work at his desk in the museum. As word spread that lepidoptery had provided for a steady stream of themes, metaphors, background, and incidental detail of much of Nabokov's literary production, including *Lolita,* his engagement with butterflies became an irresistible sidelight of his fame.

Throughout his literary career Nabokov had reserved lepidoptery as a potential alternative profession. He told interviewers that, if not for the Russian Revolution, he might indeed have been a full-time professional lepidopterist. As it was, even after he became an international superstar of literature, he ranked lepidoptery as one of his three professions, along with teaching and literature. "My passion for lepidopterological research, in the field, in the laboratory, in the library, is even more pleasurable than the study and practice of literature, which is saying a good deal," he told an interviewer in 1966.

This double fascination for literature and lepidoptery took on mythical proportions among his admirers and was interpreted as a reversion to the Leonardo archetype of the scientist-artist, a distinct oddity in the late twentieth century. There was lofty talk of the mystical places where art and science meet. Academics and journalists alike enthusiastically seized on this curious side of the exotic author, and often Nabokov, butterfly net in hand, just as enthusiastically obliged with a collector's pose in cloth cap, shorts and high socks.

In fact, Nabokov seemed to regard himself as a sort of public ambassador of lepidoptery. As early as 1951, when he had already established a modest literary reputation, *Life* magazine asked him for assistance on a projected article about his collecting. Nabokov responded enthusiastically, suggesting suitable quarry and collecting sites in the American West, his favorite hunting grounds:

> All these western butterflies can make wonderful pictures and such pictures have never been taken before. Some fascinating photos might be also taken of me, a burly but agile man, stalking a rarity or sweeping it into my net from a flowerhead, or capturing it in midair. There is a special professional twist of the wrist immediately after the butterfly has been netted which is quite fetching. Then you could show my finger and thumb delicately pinching the thorax of a netted butterfly through the gauze of the netbag. And of course the successive stages of preparing the insect on a setting board have never yet been shown the way I would like them to be shown. All this might create a sensation in scientific and nature-lover circles besides being pleasing to the eye of a layman. I must

stress the fact that the whole project as you see it has never been attempted before.

To be sure, Nabokov no doubt appreciated the latent possibilities for literary self-promotion, but his personal desire to court a wider audience for his lepidoptery was pure and authentic, and it survived to the end of his life, well after any need for the financial rewards that publicity might bring had vanished. Images of him on the hunt are familiar to his readers today. A photograph of an intensely focused Nabokov, age sixty-six, net at the ready, by Philippe Halsman for an article in the *Saturday Evening Post,* taken from the perspective of the invisible prey, has become a literary icon. It is probably the most famous photograph of the author, but it is only one fragment of the evidence of the public's enchantment with his quirky pursuit. Brian Boyd, Nabokov's principal biographer, could write that, by the end of 1959, Nabokov had become the most famous lepidopterist in the world.

Amid the adulation, however, one glaring fact stood out. It was impossible for most people to know what to make of all this. Journalism could offer little guidance, beyond reciting Nabokov's professional affiliations. Lepidoptery, like much natural science, stands outside the experience of most journalists, as of most of the readers of his literature. On one level there was the simple question of how serious Nabokov was about butterflies. For reasons that will become apparent, it was really only in the 1990s that an answer to that question was possible for the large majority of interested readers; one of the many glories of Brian Boyd's two-volume biography, *Vladimir Nabokov: The Russian Years* and *Vladimir Nabokov: The American Years,* published in 1990 and '91, respectively, is that it clears up any doubts about the author's profoundly serious and dedicated attitude. Before that even readers well-disposed to Nabokov had to make of his lepidoptery what they would, as many still do. Most are merely bemused or perplexed. The benevolent are free to see the harmless eccentricity of a crank, while the most uncomprehending critics have detected an elaborate, self-serving literary pose.

Most admirers of his literary works are sufficiently versed in language and literature to make their own judgments about the caliber of Nabokov's literary accomplishments. But while no one who has looked even casually into Boyd's biography can now doubt the seriousness of his science, few have the expertise to judge the work for themselves. Was Nabokov a true scholar of Lepidoptera, or merely a dilettante whose contributions were unremarkable? Many might assume that the answer to that question is a hard and fast one, and that the question could be answered simply by canvassing a few experts. This is not at all the case; his attainments are a matter of some disagreement among scientists, and his reputation in science, like his reputation in literature, has fluctuated over the years. Moreover, in science as in art, the judgments of individuals often reflect personal prejudices, inclinations, and points of view. In Nabokov's case they are also affected to some degree by the social history of science in America.

A cardinal point in many of the discussions of Nabokov's lepidoptery is that, whatever his accomplishments, he attained them without benefit of formal training. He had no degree in biology, and as a lepidopterist he was self-taught, having studied butterflies from the early years of his childhood, a passion he described in incomparable images in *Speak, Memory*. His first published work in English was in fact a slender article about butterflies, "A Few Notes on Crimean Lepidoptera," which appeared in one of his favorite magazines, *The Entomologist,* in 1920, while he was a student of French and Russian at Cambridge University during the first years of his family's exile.

For much of his adult life in Europe, Nabokov had set aside time, when he could, to visit the continent's museums and, more rarely, to collect. Toward the end of 1940, soon after arriving in the United States and despite the exigencies of finding a way to support himself, he wasted no time in heading to the American Museum of Natural History in New York with an unusual butterfly he had taken on the flowery slopes above the village of Moulinet, in the Maritime Alps of France. He was given free access to the collections and helped along in his research.

And then, in 1941, after taking up a lectureship at Wellesley College, he stopped at the nearby Museum of Comparative Zoology at Harvard University to visit the lepidopterological collection. Finding the specimens ill-organized and poorly protected in glassless trays, he presented himself to Nathan Banks, the head of the Entomological Department, and volunteered to straighten up the collection. That association soon turned into a modest formal position, a part-time research fellowship that made him the museum's de facto curator of Lepidoptera. His starting salary of $1,000 a year eventually rose to $1,200, and the job lasted until 1948, when he accepted a professorship at Cornell University.

Although his Harvard contract required Nabokov to work only three half days a week, the research he chose to pursue involved long, grueling hours; at one point he told his friend the writer and literary critic Edmund Wilson that he was spending as much as fourteen hours a day on entomology, all sandwiched between his responsibilities of teaching at Wellesley and the labors of his writing. Yet Nabokov later described those years at the Museum of Comparative Zoology as "the most delightful and thrilling in all my adult life." During this period lepidoptery often seemed to eclipse literature for primacy in Nabokov's heart; according to Brian Boyd, his wife, Véra, more than once had to turn him gently away from entomology and remind him of his other ambitions. It was also during his tenure there that he researched his most elaborate and significant scientific work, upon which his reputation as a professional lepidopterist rests. As in much that involves Nabokov and his lepidoptery, the best description of what he did at the museum is by Nabokov himself, in a letter he wrote to his sister Elena Sikorski in 1945:

> My museum — famous throughout America (and throughout what used to be Europe) — is the Museum of Comparative Zoology, a part of Harvard University, which is my employer. My laboratory occupies half of the fourth floor. Most of it is taken up by rows of cabinets, containing sliding cases of butterflies. I am custodian of these absolutely fabulous collections. We have butterflies from all over the world; many are type specimens (i.e., the very same specimens used for the original descriptions, from the 1840's until today). Along the windows extend tables holding my microscopes, test tubes, acids, papers, pins, etc. I have an assistant, whose main task is spreading specimens sent by collectors. I work on my personal research, and for more than two years now have been publishing piecemeal a study of the classification of the American "blues" based on the structure of their genitalia (minuscule sculpturesque hooks, teeth, spurs, etc., visible only under a microscope), which I sketch in with the aid of various marvelous devices, variants of the magic lantern. . . . My work enraptures but utterly exhausts me; I have ruined my eyesight, and wear horn-rimmed glasses.

The most sublime joy associated with this work came from the butterfly-hunting trips to the West that he took every summer. Nabokov, who never learned to drive a car, estimated that in the glory years, between 1949 and 1959, Véra drove him more than 150,000 miles all over North America, mostly on butterfly trips. Those expeditions have taken on the aura of legend among lepidopterists as well as Nabokov's literary admirers, and such trips were a habit he maintained, with only the geographic scenes shifting, for the rest of his life.

Nabokov was widely acknowledged as a great collector. The several thousands of captures he made between 1940 and 1960, the years he spent in America, are now part of the collections of the Museum of Comparative Zoology (now known as the Museum of Cultural and Natural History), the American Museum of Natural History, the Cornell University Museum of Entomology, and the Carnegie Museum in Pittsburgh, including, he proudly wrote in *Speak, Memory,* great rarities and types (the crucial single specimens by which species are defined). The thousands of butterflies that Nabokov caught in Europe between his move from the United States to Switzerland in 1959 and his death in 1977 are now stored as a unified, independent collection at the Cantonal Museum of Zoology of Lausanne.

As a collector Nabokov was joyfully promiscuous. As a scientist, however, he specialized in Blues, a widespread group of small butterflies known today as the tribe Polyommatini, a part of the lycaenid family. Actually the name Blues is somewhat misleading, because many of them are other colors, including brown, white, and gray. Blues are found on every continent where there are butterflies (that is to say, every one but Antarctica). Historically, they have lacked prestige among both academics and amateur collectors; though certainly never short of a few enthusiasts they do not enjoy the public following of the showy, exotic butterflies like Swallowtails, the iridescent blue Morphos, or velvety green, blue, and orange Birdwings.

Between 1941 and 1952 Nabokov published eight articles on the Blue butterflies of the Western Hemisphere. Written in a highly technical format, they could mean little to nonscientists. Nabokov was right when he remarked later in his career that the articles, per se, could be of interest only to a few specialists. Admirers of his literature had to turn to other sources to learn what his lepidoptery was about. But those sources could be baffling, and for that Nabokov himself and certain aspects of his personality must bear some of the blame. Nabokov the man, like Nabokov the author, was a playful spirit with a twinkle in his eye, a prankster who liked to test the character of the people he met with comic inventions presented seriously, or with straight opinion and unvarnished truth expressed under the protective cover of a wink. He was also well aware of the ludicrous impression butterfly hunters made on ordinary people, and of the absurdity inherent in the sight of a grown man in summer-camp garb swinging a net at tiny insects flitting through the weeds. But if anything he relished the serious pleasure he took in every aspect of lepidoptery all the more for the absurdist mask it sometimes wore, and he exploited this paradox time and time again in his literature and in his relations with the public.

Nabokov's irrepressible humor was much in evidence in June 1959, when Robert H. Boyle, a reporter for *Sports Illustrated*, tagged along with him on a collecting outing at Oak Creek Canyon, Arizona. The resulting article, a notable incidence of genre stretching by the magazine, appeared the following September. Amid other antics, like setting the clock ahead — so he said — to fool Véra into making an earlier start, Nabokov remarked to Boyle: "When I was younger, I ate some butterflies in Vermont to see if they were poisonous. I didn't see any difference in a Monarch butterfly and a Viceroy. The taste of both was vile, but I had no ill effects. They tasted like almonds and perhaps a green cheese combination. I ate them raw. I held one in one hot little hand and one in the other. Will you eat some with me tomorrow for breakfast?" The joking, on this occasion and on others, was an inseparable part of Nabokov's personality, so much so that his biographer Boyd judged Boyle's article "perhaps our finest moment-by-moment image of Nabokov the man."

In the realm of literature, *Speak, Memory,* particularly Chapter 6, is an unforgettable chronicle of the birth of a lepidopterist's passion. But concentrating as it does on Nabokov's youth rather than his mature professional interest, it leaves the door open for misinterpretation of the role of butterflies in Nabokov's adult life, as if they were only a boyish pursuit. And one of its strongest messages is that lepidopterists are a class apart:

> I . . . found out very soon that a "lepist" indulging in his quiet quest was apt to provoke strange reactions in other creatures. . . . Stern farmers have drawn my attention to NO FISHING signs; from cars passing me on the highway have come wild howls of derision; sleepy dogs, though unmindful of the worst bum, have perked up and come at me, snarling; tiny tots have pointed me out to their puzzled mamas; broad-minded vacationists have asked me whether I was catching bugs for bait; and one morning on a wasteland, lit by tall yuccas in bloom, near Sante Fe, a big black mare followed me for more than a mile.

This theme of ostracism also appears in *The Gift*, although that novel contains Nabokov's strongest, most extensive, and most positive literary treatment of lepidopterological themes. The narrator, Fyodor Godunov-Cherdyntsev, a writer and lepidopterist and the son of a great Russian naturalist-explorer, asks:

How many jeers, how many conjectures and questions have I had occasion to hear when, overcoming my embarrassment, I walked through the village with my net! "Well, that's nothing," said my father, "you should have seen the faces of the Chinese when I was collecting once on some holy mountain, or the look the progressive schoolmistress in a Volga town gave me when I explained to her what I was doing in that ravine."

Nabokov was always intensely close to his family, but in all other relationships he was temperamentally a loner. Boyd has noted that lepidoptery was but one of the odd-man-out guises of Nabokov's life, one of the solitary wayside nooks he chose to occupy. Another was the composing of chess problems, an art that calls for a different disposition than playing the game itself, and that the author himself associated with "glacial solitude." In soccer, another of his youthful passions, Nabokov practiced the eccentric art of the goalie, the man set apart from all other members of the team, a discipline "surrounded with a halo of singular glamour."

The marginalization of butterfly hunting carried over into some of Nabokov's interviews and personal and professional relations, too. In 1971, when he and the Australian writer and critic Andrew Field were discussing the possibility of a biography, Nabokov, according to Field, protested: "I told everything about myself in *Speak, Memory,* and it was not a very pleasant portrait. I appear as a precious person in that book. All that chess and those butterflies. Not very interesting."

But here and elsewhere Nabokov showed himself to be a master misleader. He once told an interviewer about butterflies in his fiction: "Whenever I allude to butterflies in my novels, no matter how diligently I reword the stuff, it remains pale and false and does not really express what I want it to express, what, indeed, it can only express in the special scientific terms of my entomological papers. The butterfly that lives forever on its type-labeled pin and in its O.D. ("original description") in a scientific journal dies a messy death in the fumes of the arty gush." That is a far better description of the work of journalists and others who have tried in vain to capture the sense of mystical ecstasy that Nabokov — and only Nabokov — conveyed when writing about lepidoptery.

Nabokov's ironic deprecation of his butterflies might have encouraged Field in his own predilections. Field's book, *Vladimir Nabokov: His Life in Part,* appeared in 1977, the year Nabokov died. This work, the first attempt at a full biography, reflects scant appreciation for lepidoptery, Nabokov's or anyone else's. Field's treatment of this aspect of Nabokov's life is cursory and noncommittal, almost an afterthought to what is in any case an extremely impressionistic biography. In assessing Nabokov's professional achievement, Field was content to quote briefly two unnamed lepidopterists. Each of those sources is quite perceptive, in his own way, but in the end Field failed not only to evaluate Nabokov's entomological achievement with any thoroughness but even to suggest what a significant and time-consuming role it played throughout the writer's career.

To be fair, if Field trivialized Nabokov's lepidoptery as an elaborate literary pose, Nabokov suggested this idea, too — even if only to dismiss it — in a thinly-veiled self-reference in his 1957 novel *Pnin.* In the novel two characters disturb a flock of Karner Blues, remarkable butterflies, and now sadly endangered, that Nabokov himself scientifically named and described. "'Pity Vladimir Vladimirovich is not here,' remarked Chateau. 'He would have told us all about these enchanting insects.' 'I have always had the impression that his entomology was merely a pose.' 'Oh No,' said Chateau."

This is not to say that Nabokov never dealt seriously with questions about lepidoptery; far from it. In the many interviews that he granted in the years after *Lolita* and for the rest of his life, there were routinely one or two de rigueur questions about lepidoptery, although they were seldom followed up with any perception. Nabokov hated live interviews, so he was in the habit of demanding that all questions be submitted in advance, to be answered in writing. The collective results are a basic source for understanding his mature attitude toward lepidoptery, but they remained scattered here and there until 1973, when many were collected in *Strong Opinions,* a book of Nabokov's interviews, reviews, and letters to the editor. And even here a careful reader must not take everything he says strictly at face value. In an interview in 1962, despite abundant and overwhelming proof to the contrary in *Speak, Memory,* in his fiction, and elsewhere, Nabokov could insist with a straight face that this interest in butterflies was "exclusively scientific."

In the atmosphere of incomprehension that surrounded Nabokov's lepidoptery, another misapprehension about his work came to distort the public's perception: the idea that there was some innate, perhaps psychological, connection between Nabokov's study of butterfly genitalia — a thoroughly routine technique crucial to the identification of many of the species he worked with — and the sexual content of his novels. This idea reared its head in a widely read article in the July–August 1986 issue of *Harvard Magazine,* "Nabokov's Blue Period," by Philip Zaleski. Zaleski employed the suggestive notions of "dismemberment" (more commonly

known as dissection) and "impalement" (that is, the mounting of specimens) and referred to the butterfly genitalia Nabokov worked with at the
Museum of Comparative Zoology as the "ravished limbs of love."

In addition, according to a caption in the article, "the anagrammatical
dance of 'incest' and 'insect' suggests how intensely, for Nabokov, art and
science intertwine at their roots." The novel this refers to, *Ada*, does involve both insects and incest, but in context this anagram passes fleetingly
and can bear none of the weight Zaleski, or his caption writer, assigned it.
Many writers, not just Zaleski, seem unable to resist such neo-Freudian
connections. As distorted and overblown as this sort of thing is, it is widespread and can easily prevent the discussion of Nabokov's lepidoptery
from advancing very far among a public that by and large even now
chooses to treat *Lolita* as a tale of lurid prurience and thinks of Nabokov —
a devoted family man — as a sort of repressed Humbert Humbert, the
monster of the novel.

In the end Nabokov's admirers might expect no more from populariz-
ing accounts of Nabokov's lepidoptery. But nonscientists, who tend to
think of all science as a cut-and-dried craft, might be surprised to learn
that over the years Nabokov's colleagues have shown a comparable ambivalence about his achievement; confused readers seeking easy explanations from that quarter have been to some extent disappointed. Here
again Nabokov's own puckish humor is partly at fault. Clearly, he was considered a rather odd figure by those of his colleagues who did not know
him well, and among the anecdotes about him circulated by lepidopterists, it is the jokes that have become immortal. For instance, the story is
told about how, sometime after the initial success of *Lolita*, Nabokov was
late for a lunch with some old colleagues from the Entomology Department of the natural history museum in New York. Upon arriving he
blithely remarked, "I hope you don't think I had stopped to dally with
some young girls."

But Nabokov's obvious talents were recognized by those lepidopterists
with whom he came into contact. No scientist who has read his research
articles could say that he was not technically competent, even brilliant. For
years that understanding has formed the basis for the most respectful
published judgments of his work, even in Field's biography. According to
one of Field's sources:

> He cannot be called one of the ranking authorities, but his work had
> weight. If he had devoted more time to his work in this field he almost

certainly would have been a major figure. . . . There is general acceptance of his work and admiration for its thoroughness. It is not eccentric. Work in this field falls into a certain mold of reporting facts. If his
treatment were not standard, he would have been thrown out, that is,
his work would not have been taken seriously.

But despite his accomplishments, his published work, his tenure at the
Museum of Comparative Zoology and his descriptions not only of new
species but of new genuses as well (related species are grouped together in
genuses), there have always been professional entomologists willing to
dismiss Nabokov as a gifted amateur. On the one hand, his lack of formal
training is often held against him. And, to be sure, Nabokov's output was
not prolific by most standards. During his career he published some
twenty-two lepidopterological articles, many of which were little more
than notes or newspaper reviews of popular-interest books on butterflies.
By contrast, to pick a couple of examples, Nathan Banks, the man who
welcomed Nabokov to the Museum of Comparative Zoology in 1941, published more than four hundred research papers. So did Norman Denbeigh
Riley, for much of this century the British Museum's Keeper of the Department of Entomology, who wielded great influence in the world of lepidoptery and who, as will be seen, played a regrettable role in the way a
crucial part of Nabokov's work was treated in scientific circles.

In the realm of fiction, although it is fiction informed by thorough appreciation of the history of lepidoptery, Nabokov himself credited the
nineteenth-century explorer-scientist Konstantin Godunov-Cherdyntsev, a
hero of *The Gift* (and to some extent Nabokov's literary-lepidopterological
alter ego) with hundreds of articles in entomological journals, in addition
to a number of monumental multivolume works with names like "Lepidoptera Asiatica," and "The Butterflies and Moths of the Russian Empire."
Nabokov, who was always supremely confident of his place in literature,
was proud of his lepidoptery, and he certainly considered himself a professional, but he had no illusions about his relatively humble standing in
the field at the time he did his work.

Still, those who see Nabokov as an amateur naturally tend to be guarded
in expressing their opinion about an immensely popular writer. Perhaps
the most public instance of such an assessment came in Zaleski's *Harvard
Magazine* article. One of those interviewed for the article, Frank M. Carpenter, an emeritus professor of zoology at Harvard and an acquaintance
of Nabokov, somewhat condescendingly commended Nabokov's enthusiasm for butterflies and described his job at the Museum of Comparative

Zoology as "the first rung of the ladder" and "a bottom position." Carpenter was quoted as saying: "He was seriously interested in butterflies, but the level of his interest was that which we find in the majority of amateurs. Of course, within two or three species of the so-called Blues, he obviously knew what he was doing." Carpenter went on to connect Nabokov's interest with his background. "It's an Old World tradition, particularly in the wealthy families, to become naturalists at the amateur level. Going back a bit in history, almost anybody who had property would have a collection of butterflies. Indeed, if you go back far enough, almost all the work was done by amateurs."

This description of the European aristocratic tradition is essentially valid, and it is possible to see Nabokov as a twilight figure in that venerable line, as Carpenter seems to have been suggesting. Moreover, Carpenter's summation of Nabokov's professional standing isn't that far from Nabokov's own description in reply to the question "You're a professional lepidopterist?" in a BBC interview in 1962: "Yes, I'm interested in the classification, variation, evolution, structure, distribution, habits, of lepidoptera: this sounds very grand, but actually I'm an expert in only a very small group of butterflies. I have contributed several works on butterflies to the various scientific journals."

But in his edition of selected Nabokov letters published in 1989, Dmitri Nabokov, the author's son and the translator of many of his works, took exception to Carpenter's comments, calling them "bizarre" and finding in them evidence of the patronizing envy that he thought could be detected in some of his father's former friends and colleagues after his literary success. Dmitri Nabokov was much more approving of another assessment in the same article, that of Professor Deane Bowers, at the time the curator of Lepidoptera at the Museum of Comparative Zoology, who said that as a lepidopterist, Nabokov remained "at some level an amateur. . . . a professional in that he published in professional journals, but an amateur in that he didn't have a Ph.D. in biology, and didn't work full-time in entomology."

The son might have been far less happy with another statement of Bowers's, in an article published in *The Boston Globe* in January 1988 in connection with an exhibit on Nabokov and his work that she curated at the museum. "Essentially, he was a great amateur collector and a scientific naif," she was quoted as saying.

> He couldn't have taught an entomology class; at the Museum of Comparative Zoology he was a preparator, mounting and classifying specimens. He was instrumental in the conservation of the Lepidoptera

collection — spreading, pinning, and labeling butterflies belonging primarily to the genus *Lycaeides*. Nabokov also worked with incredible patience on the classification of a group of small butterflies within the lycaenid family known as "Blues." He relished the description of minute detail, although his understanding of the broader concepts of biology and evolution was cloudy. In *Speak, Memory*, for instance, he contradicts the known genetic basis of marvelous coincidences of mimicry. His twenty published papers are descriptive, and disclose impressive expertise; he was a unique delineator of lepidopteral detail; however, his scientific contributions never rose beyond the descriptive to the synthetic.

Elsewhere in the article the author maintained, "As a scientist he never demonstrated the essential professionalism (publications and so forth) necessary for recognition. What interested him, aside from the poetry of the insect realm employed in connection with prose patterns, was the link between science and art."

The articles in both *Harvard Magazine* and *The Boston Globe* had the effect of minimizing Nabokov's achievements, at least treating them with less dignity than Nabokov himself would have expected. But in context it seems unlikely that either Carpenter or Bowers meant to disparage him. Rather, both were voicing honest opinions that to some degree reflected the values of academic hierarchy and Nabokov's place in it. It might also be arguable that the difference in these quotations and the opinion of the anonymous lepidopterist quoted by Field is one of tone rather than substance. (Certainly, to be fair, away from the ears of the journalists, there are lepidopterists who say much worse, sometimes incomprehensibly and inexplicably worse. For example during the period of scientific research that led up to this book, one who will remain nameless, a Ukrainian with a substantial reputation and familiarity with lycaenids, expressed the vehement opinion that "Nabokov's work is nonsense; it is like his fiction — but science fiction.") But since Zaleski's article appeared in *Harvard Magazine* and *The Boston Globe* article was so closely connected with an exhibit on Nabokov's work, they seemed to carry an institutional stamp.

More important, the statements by Bowers and Carpenter and the offense taken by Dmitri Nabokov hint at some lepidopterological truths. The first and probably the most important is that Nabokov's scientific career resists summing up in quotable sound bites with little context.

The second is the freight that the word *amateur* can and does bear in scientific circles. For just this reason Nabokov's admirers sometimes justify his claim to professionalism by pointing to his salary at the Museum of Comparative Zoology. But such efforts in themselves suggest the extent to which the meaning of *professionalism* has been reduced to mere semantics, minimizing the complexity of Nabokov's position in the scientific community and skirting the question of the quality of his work. This is particularly so for the 1940s, an era in which the border between amateur and professional was much more fluid than it is in this day of extreme specialization. And, as will become evident throughout this book, the history of lepidoptery to this very day is full of researchers who have made significant contributions to the field without being full-time professionals.

Bowers's observation in *The Boston Globe* that Nabokov's contribution to science never rose above the descriptive to the synthetic raised a related consideration. Nabokov was not, and never tried to be, a theoretical biologist. In the terms of systematic biology he was a taxonomist, a scientist who classifies living things into the related groups on the basis of their physical structure, which in turn reveals secrets of their relationships and evolution; he was not strictly speaking a systematist; that is, a scientist who deals with questions of theory and methodology. (In more casual usage taxonomists can also be called systematists, but their concerns are nevertheless distinct from those of the theorists.) In this era of molecular biology and advanced genetics, taxonomists occupy a generally low status in the world of academic science, although this hasn't always been the case. Some negative judgments of Nabokov's abilities simply reflect this prejudice against the mundane business of classification; rather than judge his work, some scientists judge his line of work. Ironically, beyond slighting Nabokov, this attitude has now come to haunt modern biology. At a time when the world seems to be poised on the edge of a massive extinction of species, a threat becoming widely known as the biodiversity crisis, there so few taxonomists that hundreds of thousands of varieties of organisms seem destined to disappear before they are even described by science.

The note of condescension in Carpenter's words might also reflect some naturally mixed feelings among his fellow entomologists about the attention Nabokov's work was getting, particularly when they compared it with his official place in their proud discipline. No doubt some lepidopterists were simply envious of Nabokov's literary success and of the attention the world began to pay his lepidoptery as a result. But it is fair to say that most had far more complex reactions to the ill-informed fans who suddenly discovered a superficial and passing fascination with their field;

it was galling that the literati might see lepidoptery as interesting, profound, even mystical, but only when practiced by an enormously famous writer of fiction. And sometimes the attention due to celebrity impinged on the world of science itself: no doubt the exhibit on Nabokov at the Museum of Comparative Zoology owed more to *Lolita* than to anything he might have written about butterflies.

In yet another variation on the mood, Dr. Frederick H. Rindge of the American Museum of Natural History, for one, has simply and quite naturally become bored with the endless inquiries about Nabokov over the fifty years he has been a curator of Lepidoptera there.

Even Nabokov's enthusiasm for bringing images of lepidoptery to the public could in some ways be irritating to lepidopterists in the trenches. The famous Philippe Halsman photograph, for example, is not the same joy to scientists as it is to admirers of Nabokov's fiction (and, apparently, to Nabokov, who called Halsman his favorite photographer). It is obviously posed, for one thing, and instead of those invisible butterflies it intends to evoke, some lepidopterists can manage to envision nothing more than Halsman's celebrity-seeking camera pointed up at Nabokov's face. Even sympathetic lepidopterists complain that the net Nabokov is using in the photograph is far too pristine to have been put through a real working life. A proper net would be greenish brown with the juices of plants and insects; the one Nabokov is holding is so white it would frighten the quarry. There are some who detect the same aura of the hammy pose in much of the coverage of Nabokov's work. A small and intangible matter, perhaps, but one that can leave a sour impression.

An example of a lepidopterist's sensitivity can be seen in the reaction of Charles Lee Remington to Brian Boyd's ironic observation that Nabokov was by 1959 the most famous lepidopterist in the world. Boyd had no illusions about Nabokov's standing in the field of professional lepidoptery, and it seems clear that his assessment was meant in terms of the publicity accorded Nabokov's second profession after the success of *Lolita*. But in his chapter on Nabokov's lepidoptery in the *Garland Companion to Vladimir Nabokov*, published in 1995, Remington took Boyd to task for the formulation. "*Famous* may be a saving word," he wrote, "but Nabokov would never have countenanced such a claim to leadership; he knew well that some dozens of distinguished full-time authorities would better be so ranked."

It should be noted that Remington, an emeritus professor of evolutionary genetics at Yale University, was one of Nabokov's closest friends at the

Museum of Comparative Zoology. He rated Nabokov as an "excellent butterfly researcher" and through his own writings and his cooperation with Boyd has done as much as anyone else to put Nabokov's skill and accomplishment as a lepidopterist into proper perspective. Lepidopterists, obscure as their field may be, form a proud caste.

Remington's efforts were crucial in the much more favorable public presentation of Nabokov's lepidoptery that have characterized the 1990s. Above all, his opinions and insights informed the treatment of lepidoptery in the 1,350 combined pages of Boyd's two-volume biography. And Boyd's attitude was a polar opposite from Andrew Field's. For the first time, he not only gave most of Nabokov's work with butterflies a thorough and considered treatment, without a whiff of superciliousness, but also presented it solidly in the context of the rest of Nabokov's life. After Boyd's biography that aspect of the Nabokov riddle — the seriousness with which he approached his second career — could never be held in doubt again.

Remington's contribution to the *Garland Companion* offers a quick primer of his view of Nabokov, pointing out, for example, that while Nabokov was an expert on Blues, he had also sorted out a complex problem of identity in a group of southwestern Satyr butterflies, *Neonympha,* which had eluded American researchers. Nabokov, he noted, was, in addition, able to apply his savvy about European butterflies to North American species. For example, he realized that many species that could usually be found breeding in northern territory were not actually permanent residents there, because they failed to survive the cold winters and had to filter back north from their permanent southern ranges. As for what Remington called Nabokov's "very original studies" on the Blues, he said the author "boldly turned away from the mainstream presumptions of more routine classifiers."

One of the reasons Remington admired Nabokov was that the two had worked side by side at the Museum of Comparative Zoology and sometimes collected together, and Remington therefore perhaps had a less clinical view of Nabokov as a lepidopterist than some others. "His long experience in Europe and now North America, coupled with his brainy approach to everything in life, made him an intuitive, skillful master at field work," Remington wrote. "Successful though his science was, it was clear that he most loved butterfly collecting."

Remington has also stressed that Nabokov's skills as a lepidopterist have to be seen in the context of his other pursuits. Against his somewhat skimpy record of publication, for example, stands the fact that Nabokov was able to devote only a small part of his life to intense and formal study of butterflies. As Remington and the anonymous lepidopterist quoted by Field recognized, Nabokov's professional career, strictly speaking, lasted only six years and was sandwiched between the additional responsibilities of teaching literature and Russian at Wellesley College and of writing. Between his arrival at the Museum of Comparative Zoology and his departure for Cornell, he wrote poems in Russian and English, and undertook the translation into English of poems by Pushkin, Lermontov, and Tyutchev that later became the collection *Three Russian Poets*. He published a number of short stories in *The Atlantic Monthly* and *The New Yorker*, several chapters of what later became *Speak, Memory*, a critical study on Nikolai Gogol, and the novel *Bend Sinister*.

Later in life, too, Nabokov actually worked on or contemplated several major books on lepidoptery. For various reasons, but primarily because of the competition of literature for his time, none was completed, but if even one had been, it might have altered the way his work has been viewed; such large publications tend to bring increased attention to their authors, both inside and outside academic circles. It is impossible to know what Nabokov might have accomplished had he abandoned literature for lepidoptery instead of the other way around. Those readers who are bemused by his lepidoptery, however, might be surprised to learn that there are scientists who genuinely view him as someone who was distracted from a promising career in entomology by his penchant for telling stories.

The back-and-forth on Nabokov's achievement suggests another basic truth of natural science: the validity of his scientific contributions cannot be readily determined by tallying the positive and negative comments of other scientists concerning his writings. Even if the subjective judgments inherent in much of natural science could somehow be eliminated, evaluations would still reflect the trends in systematic biology that are generally accepted at the time they were made. Specific theories and methodologies in science are notorious for their short historical half-lives. Four major schools of taxonomic theory and methodology have succeeded one another since the publication of Nabokov's work on Blue butterflies in the 1940s. The differences in these schools are complex; seen through the lenses of any of them, crucial aspects of Nabokov's work might look quite different. Negotiating them is particularly tricky for nonscientists, since notice of the shifting regimes often doesn't filter into nonspecialist literature.

For example, Dieter E. Zimmer, who has translated many of Nabokov's works into German, is also the author of *Nabokov's Lepidoptera,* a smorgasbord of entomological Nabokoviana that appeared as part of the catalog published by the Cantonal Museum of Zoology in Lausanne for the exhibition *Les Papillons de Nabokov* in 1993 and '94. Zimmer is not a lepidopterist and therefore relied on secondary sources for his account of Nabokov's science. Albeit inadvertently, his discussion reflects almost entirely the views of the "evolutionary" school of taxonomy, a body of systematic theory and methodology that was largely replaced after 1980 by the current "phylogenetic" school. Under the influence of the evolutionary school, Zimmer could not unreasonably maintain that "it must be said that Nabokov did not agree with the species concept of present-day biology." Yet, for reasons that will be explored further in the next chapter, Nabokov's concept of the species seems quite modern to lepidopterists trained in the phylogenetic school. As a result, attempts to judge his approach to lepidoptery on such shifting bases of systematics are by nature ephemeral.

Moreover, of all the specifically identified experts who over the years have been invited to comment publicly on Nabokov's expertise, none has been primarily a taxonomist, and, even more striking, none has been an authority on Blue butterflies. Carpenter, for example, specialized in fossil entomology, Bowers's specialty is evolutionary ecology, and Remington is a butterfly geneticist. As paradoxical as it may seem, Nabokov's formal scientific prose is dense and hard to follow; it is doubtful that nonspecialists have spent much time with that material. Finally, as will be shown, the fieldwork necessary for judging Nabokov's final achievement in the realm of Blue butterflies began only in the mid-1980s and continued into the 1990s; before that it would have been difficult even for an expert in Blues to confidently assess Nabokov's place in lepidoptery.

Of the nine articles on Blue butterflies that Nabokov published between 1941 and 1952, most were short pieces on individual species, but four were more substantial. Their titles ring with the unlikely poetry that Nabokov shared with his fellow lepidopterists: "The Nearctic Forms of *Lycaeides* Hübner," "Notes on the Morphology of the Genus *Lycaeides,*" "The Nearctic Members of the Genus *Lycaeides* Hübner," and "Notes on Neotropical Plebejinae."

All four are works of entomological weight. The first three treat the species of a single genus, *Lycaeides,* a group of Blues with members in North America and Eurasia. "The Nearctic Members of the Genus *Lycaei-*

des," a definitive monograph on the genus's North American species, is the single work on which much of Nabokov's scientific reputation has rested for most of the last fifty years; these are the "two or three species of the so-called Blues" in which Frank Carpenter conceded Nabokov's expertise. The task Nabokov set himself here, through the minute examination of some two thousand specimens, was to sort out the tangle of species and subspecies — many of which had been given multiple names by different authorities — that make up this relatively small but complex group. The results are elaborate, thorough, painstaking, and authoritative, the hallmarks of all Nabokov's entomological work.

In 1958 Nabokov told Robert Boyle, the *Sports Illustrated* reporter: "This work took me several years and undermined my health for quite a while. Before I never wore glasses. This is my favorite work. I think I really did well there." His colleagues agreed. A few years after it was published, Alexander Klots wrote in his widely read *Field Guide to the Butterflies of North America* that "the recent work of Nabokov has entirely rearranged the classification of this genus." This notice meant much to the writer. Alfred Appel, Jr., reported in his *Annotated Lolita* that, when he was visiting Nabokov in 1966, the author took a copy of Klots from the shelf, pointed to this quotation, and said: "That's real fame. That means more than anything a literary critic could say."

Nabokov's masterly rearrangement of the group remains scientifically valid. It was a laudable achievement. But in the larger scheme of things, "The Nearctic Members of the Genus *Lycaeides*" was essentially a good, solid footnote to taxonomic history. Despite Nabokov's justified pride, it is not the kind of work that makes a reputation in lepidoptery.

More recently, however, discoveries in the groups Nabokov pioneered have made it possible to view him in a new and more significant light. But in a twist this work involves "Notes on Neotropical Plebejinae," Nabokov's one major paper that looked beyond *Lycaeides*, with its handful of northern species. This treatise, which appeared in the entomological journal *Psyche* in 1945, was of an altogether different order from anything else Nabokov ever undertook, a pioneering classification of what are known today as the Latin American Polyommatini, a large and diverse group of Blue butterflies with members ranging from the southern tip of Chile through South and Central America and across the islands of the Caribbean.

For anyone familiar with the rest of Nabokov's scientific corpus, there are counterintuitive elements in his undertaking such a task. Not only was it outside his familiar genus *Lycaeides* but it was on an unusual scale. Rather than disentangle a muddle of species and subspecies within a single genus, it established a broad range of genuses, a framework into which subsequent researchers would insert their new-species discoveries. The study also involved what to many of his literary admirers cannot help but seem a prank of devious fate. Nabokov, the consummate collector, caught not a single butterfly described in "Notes on Neotropical Plebejinae." In fact, except in described imagination, he never set foot in any of the exotic regions from which emerged the butterflies that most securely ensure him a lasting share of scientific recognition. The specimens were part of the collections at Harvard or borrowed from the American Museum of Natural History.

It was also a particularly daring study for Nabokov, showing that he was not afraid to climb far out on a lepidopterological limb. The neotropical Polyommatini, whose members live in some of the most inaccessible parts of the Western Hemisphere, were little known during the 1940s, when the study of butterflies was not high on the world's agenda. Only about one-tenth of the species of this group listed today were known to lepidoptery then, and because of the war Nabokov had no access to the important collections of Europe's museums. Even without a war intercontinental travel of that age was time-consuming and expensive, and biologists worked in far greater isolation than they routinely do today. Among other handicaps the situation entailed, it exposed Nabokov to a serious risk of sampling error. There was a strong possibility that the available material might not offer a dependable basis for his revision of the group.

Yet, dissecting and drawing only 120 specimens (compared with the 2,000 in his big *Lycaeides* study), Nabokov proposed what he called "a rather drastic rearrangement" of the Latin American Polyommatini, naming in the process seven genuses of Blues — a reordering so thorough as to link his name with the group forever if his study, preliminary and incomplete as it was, should stand up to reexamination by subsequent lepidopterists. If it failed, however, it would simply wind up as an idiosyncratic footnote of the Nabokov legend, a warning to others not to overreach, and Nabokov's detractors could say I told you so. In an interview for *The New York Times* in 1997, Charles Remington recalled that "eyebrows were raised when Nabokov published his research. A lot of people have been uneasy about how well his work would stand up under the scrutiny of good professionals."

Still, in *Speak, Memory,* Nabokov wrote that "Notes on Neotropical Plebejinae" was one of his three favorite scientific articles, along with his major *Lycaeides* paper. The third item on his list was a short note in which he named an additional species — from the Cayman Islands but sent to him from Oxford — that had been found to fit into his neotropical classification. That addendum and a second one like it suggest that Nabokov was aware of what a can of worms he had opened up and that he planned to follow up in one way or another on what he called his "superficial and incomplete" study — which in fact, for an ordinary lepidopterist, would be a natural course to take.

Nabokov, though, was more than an ordinary lepidopterist, and in 1948 he left his lectureship at Wellesley College and his position at the Museum of Comparative Zoology to become professor of Russian and European literature at Cornell. By then, he wrote, "I found it no longer physically possible to combine scientific research with lectures, belles-lettres, and *Lolita*, (for she was on her way — a painful birth, a difficult baby)." Nabokov never elaborated on "Notes on Neotropical Plebejinae," and for nearly half a century neither did anyone else.

For this there were several reasons, all of which will be explored further in this book. As has already been mentioned, lycaenids have never been given the attention accorded by collectors and academics to larger, showier butterflies. Moreover, the sociology of science has changed radically over the last decades. Far-reaching taxonomic surveys aimed at naming large numbers of species are out of fashion at universities and big research institutes, where emphasis is concentrated instead on more exalted and refined objectives in evolutionary theory and molecular biology. Finally, what was true for Nabokov's era holds true even today: the neotropical Polyommatini are such a large group, dispersed throughout some of Latin America's most inaccessible, labyrinthine reaches, that the project seemed prohibitively difficult. A thorough study of neotropical Blues meant extensive collection efforts and the painstaking examination of historical collections of butterflies on three continents. This may sound like very small potatoes in an age of space travel and particle accelerators. But the late twentieth century has also been an era with little money for such projects; society seems to have lost the passion for natural science that once caught the imagination of Europe, and such collectors as are available for the work — many of them far more "nonprofessional" than Nabokov — most often have to pay their own tickets.

Because of its breadth and the scanty information on which it was based, "Notes on Neotropical Plebejinae" always promised to provide the most substantial measure of Nabokov's abilities. And its fundamentality for the study of a major group of butterflies meant that its validation would inevitably raise his standing in the world of lepidoptery. Yet as a result of scientific inertia, " Notes on Neotropical Plebejinae" has had to take a backseat in all considerations of Nabokov's lepidopterological works. In the *Garland Companion,* Remington could only remark that the status of Nabokov's new Latin American genuses had not been settled; in fact, the question had not been opened.

For more than forty years "Notes on Neotropical Plebejinae," while never proved wrong, was largely ignored, most momentously by the British Museum's Norman Riley, in his *Field Guide to the Butterflies of the West Indies,* published in 1975. In the case of one crucial Caribbean grouping, Riley chose to follow the much older and less sophisticated taxonomy of the classic nineteenth-century German lepidopterist Jacob Hübner, one of the most renowned figures in butterfly nomenclature. (Between 1796 and 1838, Hübner contributed hundreds of names to lepidoptery, including that of the genus *Lycaeides,* which is why his own name appears in the titles of Nabokov's papers.) Riley's view, in turn, was accepted as authoritative by nearly everyone else. His reputation for superb technical scientific work, his impressive credentials, and the wide popularity of his field guide ensured that his would be considered the informed opinion. Those of Nabokov — a celebrity as an author but an obscure lepidopterist — were by and large forgotten. It was a pattern that repeated itself over and over.

It was only in the mid-1980s that new light began to shine on the Latin American Polyommatini, helped along by just the kinds of coincidences and quirks of fate that Nabokov savored — events as apparently disparate as the discovery of an unusual little rain forest in the Caribbean, the fall of the Berlin Wall, and the beginning of the large biodiversity surveys in South America. In the end the thoroughly international task of completing Nabokov's research fell primarily to two men, Zsolt Bálint, a lepidopterist at the Hungarian Museum of Natural History who worked on Latin American Blues for his Ph.D. dissertation, and Kurt Johnson, a research associate at the American Museum of Natural History and one of the authors of this book. Later a third researcher, Dubi Benyamini, an Israeli lepidopterist who lent his expertise on the life cycles of butterflies to Nabokov's Blues, figured indispensably in the work.

Before turning his attention to Nabokov's groups, Johnson had published widely on Hairstreaks, lycaenid butterflies closely related to Blues. On the trail of these creatures in 1985, he spent the first of five seasons collecting insects in a unique biological oasis in the Dominican Republic. New discoveries of Blue butterflies there, including the first new Blue from Nabokov's group to be named in more than forty years, changed the direction of Johnson's professional life in ways he could never have foreseen. They eventually led him, with Bálint, Benyamini, and a score of other lepidopterists, on a path of discovery across Latin America, guided above all by "Notes on Neotropical Plebejinae," that neglected work Vladimir Nabokov had produced sitting on his bench at the Museum of Comparative Zoology in Cambridge, Massachusetts, in 1945.

Their efforts and discoveries resulted in a series of publications between 1988 and 1998, together amounting to a complete reexamination of the Latin American Blues, under far different conditions than those that existed in Nabokov's day. By the time the work was finished, Johnson guessed that 95 percent of all existing species of neotropical Blues had been discovered, far more material than Nabokov had had access to. Such was Nabokov's obscurity as a scientist in the mid-1980s that when Bálint and Johnson began their work he was basically a cipher to them — beyond *Lolita,* neither had read any of his work, scientific or literary. But as time passed they were amazed at how well Nabokov's previously obscure taxonomy accommodated their finds. In fact, they eventually began to refer to their undertaking as the Nabokov project.

This book tells the story of how that project was carried out and attempts to suggest what its results mean for Nabokov's reputation in lepidoptery. It was the first thorough reconsideration of his groups since Nabokov's own in 1945. Unlike Nabokov's fundamental study, however, it was based on enough material to minimize sampling error. The researchers' attitude toward Nabokov himself also has some bearing on their conclusions. Most, if not all, assessments of his lepidoptery, large and small, have worked backward from his celebrity. It is significant that Bálint and Johnson began their research as an outgrowth of their own lepidopterological interests, with no reference to Nabokov until they were made aware of his taxonomy in the natural course of their work. Even then years passed before they realized that their findings might be of interest to Nabokov's literary admirers. Finally, as surprising as it may seem, Bálint and Johnson were the first scientists who were actually experts in the taxonomy of Blue butterflies to comment on Nabokov's work.

There were unexpected ramifications. As the two learned more about Nabokov's science, they also became aware of a great artist whose passion for lepidoptery permeated and shaped not only his writing but his entire life. They increasingly realized that Nabokov, through his fiction, his recorded observations, and his unusual place in the public spotlight, had captured the sense of almost mystical wonder that many lepidopterists feel in their work but few have managed to express, certainly not to a wider audience. Because of that realization as much as his pioneering study, Bálint and Johnson named many new species of Latin American Blues after characters, places, or things in Nabokov's novels and stories. In this they had help from admirers of Nabokov's literature who had followed their work with great interest. Inevitably, *Madeleinea lolita* and *Pseudolucia humbert,* named for the two main characters of *Lolita,* resonate the most, but many readers of Nabokov will find their personal favorites. For Bálint and Johnson it was a fitting tribute, a measure of the extent to which they had come of see the Latin American Blues as Nabokov's rightful territory and "Notes on Neotropical Plebejinae" as a work that would put his stamp on lepidoptery. It was also meant as an indication that Nabokov's work is not a dead end in science, a truncated branch of some remote interest only because it was produced by a literary genius, but something that continues to put forth green branches in modern taxonomy. They would be even more surprised to learn as their research continued that the implications of Nabokov's groups, their diversity and the regions they inhabit, also embrace some of the larger questions that contemporary biologists are asking about evolution and biogeography.

No other branch of modern science boasts a guiding spirit like Nabokov. As a knowledge of butterflies can, to varying degrees, shed light on many of his works, so his life and writings continue to form a rich commentary not only on the project named for him but on lepidoptery in general. There is hardly an aspect of lepidoptery today that his career does not elucidate in some meaningful way. If Nabokov is no longer the most famous lepidopterist in the world, he is still lepidoptery's most irresistible ambassador, as he seems to have so deeply wished.

2 ❦

A Tricky Subject

In itself, an aurelian's passion is not a particularly unusual sickness.
— *Speak, Memory*

THERE ARE GREAT GULFS of sensibility in lepidoptery. With butterflies, as in a handful of other biological subjects, like birds, tropical
fish, seashells, and flowers — above all orchids — the unquantifi-
able appeal of the aesthetic, psychological, and even spiritual dimensions
lures casual admirers, hobbyists, and amateurs, most of whom never make
the great leap into rigorous science. Butterflies and moths, at least many of
them, are gorgeous, as a peek into the most basic illustrated guide will reveal, and it is that fact that determines most people's attitude toward
them. Butterfly motifs have recently become the height of chic in jewelry;
real Morphos, big blue tropical butterflies from South America, have long
been framed and used to decorate houses and their wings cut into sections
and mounted in settings like jewels (a practice Nabokov seemed to find
distasteful and tacky). Butterfly farms supply flocks of butterflies to be released at events like weddings. Butterfly houses at natural history museums and zoos, much like the more familiar aviaries of the past, are
attracting more and more people. Nabokov once wrote that he was always
astonished at how little notice people take of the butterflies around them.
But this is no longer true in many parts of the world, where the destruction of their habitat has made butterflies a less common sight in the lives
of ordinary people. In the 1990s, it is fair to say, butterflies aren't far behind dinosaurs in the public imagination, a rank earned by little but their
beauty.

At the next level is a certain kind of butterfly enthusiast to which lepidopterists with formal training or advanced accomplishment sometimes

refer dismissively as a stamp collector. These hobbyists collect ranks of species merely for their superficial beauty or to fill in blanks in an outline. Among the stamp collectors are many bright children, whose interests might advance if given sufficient time, and infatuated adults, whose fascination has remained childlike, from a scientific point of view anyway.

Yet the most proficient and sophisticated lepidopterists are not immune from the same basic urges, if they are honest, even if they eventually progress beyond them. At different stages of his life, Nabokov enjoyed not only collecting butterflies but possessing his collection as a physical object; in the 1930s, when money was sometimes tight, he and Véra bought a case in which to display some of their finest catches. It is also sometimes said that Nabokov was indifferent to the beauty of butterflies, that he was driven rather by the aesthetic-neutral dictates of scientific inquiry. But it is more accurate to say that on some level the two notions were inextricably intertwined, certainly in Nabokov's case. "I cannot separate the aesthetic pleasure of seeing a butterfly and the scientific pleasure of knowing what it is," he wrote. As he described it in *Speak, Memory,* the desire to possess beauty at once fleeting and exotic marked the "original event"— his first butterfly, taken when he was six years old:

> On the honeysuckle, overhanging the carved back of a bench just opposite the main entrance, my guiding angel (whose wings, except for the absence of a Florentine limbus, resemble those of Fra Angelico's Gabriel) pointed out to me a rare visitor, a splendid, pale-yellow creature with black blotches, blue crenels, and a cinnabar eyespot above each chrome-rimmed black tail. As it probed the inclined flower from which it hung, its powdery body slightly bent, it kept restlessly jerking its great wings, and my desire for it was one of the most intense I have ever experienced.

No one has expressed the enchantment of butterflies better than Nabokov, but he was far from alone in his passion, even if his lepidoptery was more refined and sophisticated than most. Butterflies have exerted a similar fascination throughout the millennia, appearing in motifs carved on stone, tusk, or shell as early as the late Paleolithic Age, before 10,000 B.C., and proliferating thereafter. Nabokov himself, who developed a keen interest in the history of butterfly illustration, pointed out that *Danaus chrysippus,* a danaid butterfly related to the Monarch, was the first recognizable species known to have been depicted in art, with seven specimens shown flitting over Nile papyrus in a tomb painting from the Eighteenth Egyptian Dynasty, now in the British Museum.

The most alluring of insects, butterflies — and moths, too — have symbolized delicacy but also power; their metamorphosis from humble, crawling caterpillar to transcendent flying adult has been a perennial symbol of hope, rebirth, and resurrection. In the realm of early entomology, Jan Swammerdam, a great seventeenth-century Dutch naturalist who pioneered the study of metamorphosis, expressly saw in the caterpillar, pupa, and adult stages of a butterfly a paradigm for the progress of the human soul from earthly life through a postmortem waiting period to resurrection. Nabokov himself eschewed organized religion, and his ideas about an afterlife must be deduced from nebulous evidence. But Brian Boyd suggested that Lepidoptera contributed something to Nabokov's suspicion "that although consciousness might appear to be cut off in death, it could well in fact simply undergo a metamorphosis we cannot see." Nabokov once joked with an interviewer that "I also intend to collect butterflies in Peru or Iran before I pupate." But the crucial word is *joke*. As Boyd put it, "Insect metamorphosis for Nabokov was not an answer to the riddle of death, not an argument, a model, or even a metaphor to be taken seriously." Certainly he seems to have taken pains to avoid these kinds of commonplace associations in his mature literary creations.

But all his life Nabokov celebrated the multidimensional allure of lepidoptery. In an interview in 1964 he distinguished the four main elements of pleasure in butterfly hunting, all of which answered some basic human predilection rather than just the sterile dictates of pure science:

> First, the hope of capturing — or the actual capturing — of the first specimen of a species unknown to science: this is the dream at the back of every lepidopterist's mind, whether he be climbing a mountain in New Guinea or crossing a bog in Maine. Secondly, there is a capture of a very rare or very local butterfly — things you have gloated over in books, in obscure scientific reviews, on the splendid plates of famous works, and that you now see on the wing, in their natural surroundings, among plants and minerals that acquire a mysterious magic through the intimate association with the rarities they produce and support, so that a given landscape lives twice: as a delightful wilderness in its own right and as the haunt of a certain butterfly or moth. Thirdly, there is the naturalist's interest in disentangling the life histories of little-known insects, in learning about their habits and structure, and in determining their position in the scheme of classification — a scheme which can be sometimes pleasurably exploded in a dazzling display of polemical fireworks when a new discovery upsets the old scheme and confounds its obtuse champions. And fourthly, one should not ignore the element of

sport, of luck, of brisk motion and robust achievement, of an ardent and arduous quest ending in the silky triangle of a folded butterfly lying on the palm of one's hand.

The word *butterfly* is a Germanic inheritance: in Dutch it is *botervlieg;* a German variant is *butterfliege;* in Old English the word is *buter-fleoge,* and to Chaucer, it was *boterflye* ("Swich talkyng is nat worth a boterflye"). It's origin is obscure. One guess is that the emergence of the insects in warm weather coincided with butter-producing time. Another is that throngs of yellow Brimstones, one of the first butterflies to appear in the European summer, reminded people of the color of butter. In folklore butterflies, or witches in the shape of butterflies, stole milk and butter. (Nabokov once heard a child say "flutter-by," which he thought might solve the riddle; a good try, he wrote, was "better fly," that is, one bigger and brighter than other flies.)

Other European languages took a different tack, but not without leaving lepidopterological traces of their own. The Latin for butterfly, *papilio* (cognate with the French *papillon*), is the genus name for most Swallowtails and the name given by the eighteenth-century biologist Carolus Linnaeus, the founder of the modern taxonomic system, to his original all-encompassing genus of butterflies. The ancient Greek word for the immortal soul, *psyche,* was also the word for butterfly, which was resurrected as an adult from a kind of death in its chrysalis stage. The Greek personification of the soul, Psyche, was the mistress of Eros and was shown in art with a butterfly's wings or even as a butterfly. This is also the source of the name of the entomological journal *Psyche,* where Nabokov published much of his most important work, including "Notes on Neotropical Plebejinae."

Beyond their widespread irrational appeal, there is more to learn about butterflies than the casual admirer might ever imagine, even more when they become the subject of scientific inquiry. Informed knowledge of the subject, particularly the encyclopedic kind of expertise that Nabokov developed during his life, takes years to accumulate. Butterflies, moths, and skippers (common fast-flying creatures belonging to the family Hesperiidae, which most scientists classify as intermediate between the other two) belong to an immensely diverse group of winged insects that makes up the order Lepidoptera. The name is compounded of Greek words that mean "scale-covered wing," a reference to the microscopic scales that cover these creatures like the shingles of a house and give many of them their dazzling colors. Lepidoptera range in size from the Pygmy Blue butterfly, which has a wingspread of as little as a half-inch, or even tinier micromoths, to the

Birdwing Swallowtails of the East Indies, with a wingspread of half a foot or more, or the giant silkworm moths of China, which can easily exceed a foot.

Structurally, Lepidoptera are similar to all other insects, with a head, a thorax with six legs and four wings, and an abdomen. It is primarily their scales that distinguish them as an order, but they have some other characteristics that set them apart, too. Chief among these is the long proboscis, or feeding tube, that can usually be coiled spirally beneath the head. Charles Darwin once examined an orchid from Madagascar whose nectar was secreted at the bottom of a narrow, foot-long tube; knowing that the flower needed a pollinator, he predicted the existence of a moth or butterfly with a twelve- or thirteen-inch proboscis. Years later a Hawkmoth — now known as Darwin's Hawkmoth — was found there that fit the bill, with a proboscis four times as long as its stubby body.

As with the Hawkmoth, the mouth parts of adult Lepidoptera are adapted for feeding on the nectar of flowers and other organic liquids, the order's primary food. The caterpillar larvae have well-developed mandibles and feed chiefly on leaves, buds, or flowers. Most species have caterpillars that are adapted to eat a very restricted range of food plant, often a single species, or in some cases a specific part of a species; it is important that the adult butterfly lay its egg on just the right sort of plant or its offspring will die. Scent is one way butterflies determine the right plant for egg laying. When the caterpillars hatch they move around on their host plants on what appear to be many pairs of legs. In fact, only the three pairs at the front of the caterpillar's body are structurally legs (the typical six legs of an insect); the rest are organs called prolegs, which evolved to aid in locomotion and grasping but are structurally completely different. For defense many have evolved fearsome-looking physical characteristics — spines, horns, or large spots on the head that give the appearance of being eyes, presumably to fool predators into believing they are dealing with a much larger and more aggressive animal; some adult butterflies use the same trick, with even more elaborate eyespots displayed on the wings.

There are other wrinkles of complexity in the lifestyles of some larvae. It is common knowledge, for instance, that some ants keep "cows," very often aphids, which they protect and tend carefully in return for drops of "honeydew," a nourishing liquid that the aphids produce. This kind of symbiosis, myrmecophily, which often involves the sharing of the ants' nest by the symbiotic partner, is one of the wonders of nature. Some Lepidoptera larvae, including many species of Blue butterflies, have precisely the same sort of relationship with ants. In exchange for the honeydew they produce from special glands, typically at the backs of their heads, they pass part of their life cycles in ant colonies, presumably gaining protection from some kinds of predators. In turn they are given ant larvae to eat, making them, in effect, meat eaters. Other caterpillars, like those of the New World moth *Laetilia coccidivora,* are carnivores, too, feeding on aphids and scale insects; the same is true of the larvae of North American Harvesters, close relatives of Blue butterflies.

Caterpillars are often regarded simply as feeding machines, but they are complex and important in their own right. In recent years scientists have begun to emphasize that the caterpillar and chrysalid stages of butterflies are as biologically important as the more beautiful adults. During his formal career at Harvard, Nabokov, typical of most lepidopterists of his day, concentrated mostly on the dead adult specimens represented in museum collections. However, in later correspondence and in several uncompleted projects later in his life, he too began to stress the taxonomic and ecological importance of studying the creatures' immature stages as well.

Lepidoptera larvae undergo a complete metamorphosis from caterpillar to pupa, or chrysalis, to adult, one of the most astonishing transformations in the biological world. Other groups of the higher insects — like beetles, flies, and wasps — also undergo this transformation, but it is more remarkable in the Lepidoptera because of the striking beauty of the creature that emerges from the comparatively inert and plain pupa. Insect metamorphosis is actually a specialized form of molting. All animals with exoskeletons molt in order to grow; some insects, Lepidoptera among them, take advantage of this periodic casting off of the outer casing to introduce profound physical changes in their bodies. Caterpillars, whose skin will not expand to accommodate their growing bodies, undergo several molts as they become larger. Each of these stages is called an instar. The transformation from caterpillar to pupa is simply a specialized molt, with the pupa forming under the last cast-off skin, and the emergence of the adult butterfly from the pupa is another. The pupa — typically immobile or with limited movement at only two of its intersegmental joints and often compared to a mummy — is uncanny; in the advanced stages the ghostly outline of the adult butterfly, the features of its head and body and the contours and lineaments of its compacted wings ("the lovely flush of the ground-color, a dark margin, a rudimentary eyespot") can be seen eerily embossed on the surface.

As for metamorphosis itself, science fiction has appropriated the process to marvelously sinister effect, and Nabokov, to whom metaphors from lepidoptery came easily, used a wonderful extended description of it to introduce his literature classes to the transformations in "Dr. Jekyll and Mr. Hyde": "There comes for every caterpillar a difficult moment when he begins to feel pervaded by an odd sense of discomfort. It is a tight feeling — here about the neck and elsewhere, and then an unbearable itch. Of course he has moulted a few times before, but *that* is nothing in comparison to the tickle and urge that he feels now. He must shed that tight, dry skin, or die." But Nabokov was also among those who see in the development of the pupa a promise of something wonderful to come. In 1946, replying to the request of Katharine White, his editor at *The New Yorker*, for something for her magazine, Nabokov wrote, "I do have a story for you — but it is still in my head; quite complete however; ready to emerge; the pattern showing through the wing-cases of the pupa."

Again, in an interview in 1977, not long before his death, Nabokov said of this stage: "In certain species, the wings of the pupated butterfly begin to show in exquisite miniature through the wing-cases of the chrysalis a few days before emergence. It is the pathetic sight of an iridescent future transpiring through the shell of the past, something of the kind I experience when dipping into my books written in the twenties."

This phrasing is suggestive of another aspect of pupation in Nabokov: its relation to his "nymphet," Lolita. *Nymphet* — meaning an immature but sexually attractive girl, at least attractive to a certain sort of man — is Nabokov's one clear contribution of a word to the spoken English language, and it annoyed him that his authorship was slighted in Webster's. As often in Nabokov's fiction, a multitude of associations flock around this single word. In Greek mythology and religion, a nymph is a mostly beneficent female spirit of nature that embodies the divine power of the mountains, waters, woods, and trees she inhabits. Nymphs were envisioned as young and attractive, so the word could also mean a marriageable young maiden or a bride. In addition to their close association with specific landscapes, nymphs were fleeting, elusive, and imbued with a divine nature. It is not surprising that nymphs, satyrs, and other figures from the half-magical Greek countryside populate the nomenclatorial rolls of lepidoptery. Nymphs were often pursued and raped by the more powerful Olympian deities, and this web of mythological associations binds Lolita and butterflies closely enough; Nabokov's male counterpart to a nymphet was a "faunlet," a word that sprang from the same Greek fields and forests.

In English, *nymph* in entomological terms most often refers to an immature stage of a hemimetabolic insect, a grasshopper, for example, that, unlike a butterfly, does not undergo complete metamorphosis; insect nymphs by and large resemble adults, except in size. But *nymph* can be used as a synonym for *pupa;* and that *nymphe* is simply French for "pupa" is often overlooked, as Dieter E. Zimmer has pointed out in his discussion of the word in "A Guide to Nabokov's Butterflies and Moths." Typical of the multiple layers of Nabokov's allusiveness, *pupa* is also the Latin word for "doll," which recalls one of Lolita's nicknames, Dolly. In addition to the obvious mythological associations, a nymphet is a creature that has not reached sexual maturity: Lolita's "iridescent future" was irreparably blighted by Humbert Humbert.

For those butterflies or moths not blighted by their own many sorts of roving predators, the climax of the life cycle is to become one of those delightful adults — an *imago* or *image* in the unromantic Latinate terminology of science. As the chrysalis splits open in the creature's last molt, the adult crawls out wet, glistening, and amorphous, its body swollen and its wings crumpled. As it hangs on to or nearby the chrysalis, blood and fluids are pumped from the bloated body through the veins of the wings, which spread the wing membranes into their familiar shape. The veins, when dry and hardened, not only form the prominent structural framework of the butterflies' wings but also serve as a kind of group fingerprint, providing one of the markers by which various kinds of Lepidoptera can be classified together or distinguished one from another. As soon as they can fly, adult butterflies look for mates, and the entire cycle begins again. Once mated most adults live out their short allotted span, their wings becoming worn and bedraggled, a fact that in 1974 gave Nabokov a chance to evade an interviewer's question about the beauty of Lepidoptera: "All butterflies are beautiful and ugly at the same time, like human beings. I let it go when it is old and frayed or if I don't need it for my collection."

Butterflies are the most familiar Lepidoptera, but by classification they form only a small contingent of the order, five to eleven of the forty or so recognized families, depending on the taxonomic scheme preferred; there are some fifteen thousand known butterfly species, compared with ten times that many species of moths, the "legions of night" that dominate the order. The differences between most butterflies — which are known scientifically as Rhopalocera — and most moths — Heterocera — are readily enough apparent, but in some ways the distinction is arbitrary. Most moths fly at dusk or by night, although quite a few fly during the daylight hours; conversely, there are butterflies that fly by night. Moths are usually robust, with fat abdomens, and often have a furry appearance. Most are dingy-colored, although a few well-known day fliers are spectacular. The antennae of butterflies are usually long and slender, with tiny clubs on the ends, while those of moths are usually either feathered or long and slender without the clubs. Butterflies tend to rest with their wings folded together over their backs, whereas moths usually rest with wings spread. The chrysalises of moths are usually wrapped in the web of a spun silk cocoon, whereas butterfly pupae are normally naked and exposed to the elements. Yet with all these familiar differences, there is such variety among both moths and butterflies that no single feature distinguishes the two groups.

Moths also have their sinister associations and conjure a fear of the unknown, the uncanny, or the alien. The Death's-Head moth bred by the killer in *The Silence of the Lambs* played on these fears. (It is an Old World species of Hawkmoth, *Acherontia atropos,* with the eerie outline of a skull on the back of its large thorax; it feeds on the deadly nightshade and squeaks if it is handled.) Common names for the larvae of some moths, like cutworms or armyworms, summon up images of pestilence, and moths account for most of the damage that Lepidoptera cause to crops, although butterflies are not without their own villains, like the White Pine Butterfly, whose larvae have sometimes caused significant damage to the pine forests of the western United States.

The historical age of butterflies is poorly documented. Moths and butterflies evolved from a common ancestor, but few Lepidoptera fossils have been discovered. Most of those that do exist are imperfect imprints in sedimentary rock, or fragments locked in amber. Primitive moth fossils are known from as far back as the Jurassic, from 190 million to 136 million years ago, during the age of the dinosaurs. They were about the same size as today's moths; unlike in some insect groups, there appear to have been no giant forms. The fossil record preserves no butterflies before the early Oligocene, in Cenozoic time, during the age of mammals, some 29 million to 35 million years ago. These are puzzlingly similar to today's butterflies. Accordingly, the geological age of Lepidoptera, especially that of the day-flying butterflies, has been hotly debated, even as other directions of research have pushed the possible age of origin further and further back. The distribution of modern Lepidoptera, the history of continental drift, and the order's close connection with flowering plants suggest that their diversification began late in the age of the dinosaurs or shortly thereafter — along a cusp edging the Cretaceous (130 million to 70 million years ago) and the Cenozoic Eras when, by 50 million years ago, mammals and flowers were already in proliferation.

Such an age might account for the distributional connections of some butterfly groups, including the Blues, between South America and Africa — which were gradually drifting apart during this period. Most biologists agree that butterflies were proliferating as the Cenozoic unfolded and the continents began moving into much the positions in which we find them today.

Altogether the order Lepidoptera is made up of well over 160,000 scientifically named species, not counting myriad others as yet unnamed or undiscovered in the jungles or even neglected in the drawers of the world's great museums. While those numbers might seem impressive in comparison with figures for birds or mammals, they are negligible compared to the numbers of species of other groups of insects, like beetles, which lead the orders in named species. And the numbers would no doubt prove pitifully small compared with the real populations of insects for which scientists have made much less effort to elaborate names, like flies, bees, or wasps, or even more so among the wider world of invertebrates, mites or chiggers.

In the second item of Nabokov's list of the joys of butterfly hunting, butterflies are linked closely, in ways big or small, to geography. Except for Antarctica, butterflies and moths occur on every continent, even at harsh high altitudes and in relatively cold climates. Early biologists realized that butterflies and other life-forms within certain broad geographic ranges, roughly reflecting today's continental landmasses, show physical similarities, and they divided the world into faunal regions that are still used to describe biological distribution in its broadest sense. These are the categories reflected in Nabokov's biological papers: Nearctic butterflies, like Nabokov's northern Blues, are simply those found in temperate North America and Greenland; neotropical butterflies are those of South and Central America and the Caribbean.

There is much diversity within these regions, however; the neotropics, for example, contain not only lowland tropical butterflies of the sorts found in the Amazonian jungle but butterflies of the temperate regions of the Andes and Patagonia. On an even smaller scale, the actual ranges of individual species are affected by many factors, including climate and the availability of specific food plants. Some butterfly species, perhaps isolated by chance in some tucked-away corner of an alpine valley, might exist there and nowhere else.

Different butterflies spend varying amounts of time as eggs, caterpillars, or chrysalises — a reflection of a species's individual survival strategy within its ecosystem. The absence of winter in the tropical lowlands, where living conditions are optimal, is one reason that butterflies are particularly diverse there, but for the same reason many tropical species have short life cycles, perhaps only a few weeks, with the adults often living just long enough to mate. By contrast, butterflies that live in temperate climates, where winter alternates with other seasons, must evolve a strategy for surviving the seasonal cold; it is in the temperate zones that metamorphosis becomes a particularly pronounced survival strategy. Some migrate to warmer climates. Others overwinter in a kind of dormant state, which extends the length of their overall life cycle. Different butterflies overwinter in different stages of the life cycle — as eggs, pupae, or adults. Therefore, the adults of some species live for a considerable time, like the migratory Monarch, whose individuals fly every fall from as far away as Canada to their famous roosting grounds in Mexico and part of the way back in the spring. The Monarch is the only butterfly that migrates annually and makes a return trip, somewhat in the fashion of birds. But other species emigrate — that is, in summer they fly northward from their ordinary ranges and produce one or more broods before the cold weather kills all the emigrants off.

The vagility of butterflies, that is, how far they range, varies as well. In contrast to migrators like the Monarch, which fly across continents or oceans, some butterflies are patrollers, which tend to fly up and down stretches of paths or streams in search of food plants and mates, most no farther than a quarter mile, and many far less than that. So-called perchers make up a third category of flight; these butterflies tend merely to sit on a larval food plant, venturing only the shortest distances away to mate or nectar. Some of them fly little, if at all, preferring to crawl from plant to plant on their legs, presumably as a defense against wind and cold. There are even moths that have no wings.

By any measure butterflies have always been convenient subjects for scientific study, not least because, of all the insects, and probably of all the world's biota, they have been the most collected. Moreover, many are readily reared, and they provide a simple anatomical layout — the head; the thorax, or midsection, to which the wings are attached; and the abdomen, in which variously shaped bony genital structures occur. Butterflies' contributions to our scientific knowledge have been distinctive, and important discoveries from butterfly research are recognized in the fields of genetics, ecology, evolution, and endocrinology.

Because of their stages, short life spans, selective feeding habits, variability, and complex ecological and climatological associations, butterflies are in many ways more complicated to study than the higher animals. As James Scott put it in his *Butterflies of North America:*

> To be sure of observing adults of a particular butterfly species, for example, you must know not only the range of the species and the coloration of the adults (the sexes and even the generations may differ), but also the preferred habitat, the time of year when the adults emerge and fly, the sort of place favored by mate-searching males, the plants favored by females for their eggs, and the kinds of food preferred by male and female adults. To find eggs and larvae, you must know the larval hostplants, where the eggs are laid on the plant, the part of the plant eaten, and — in order to estimate when the eggs and larvae will occur on the plants — the timing and duration of the overwintering stage and the adult flight period.

To understand Nabokov's interest in lepidoptery, it is important to realize that it is this inherent complexity that seizes the imaginations of lepidopterists whose interests progress beyond an aesthetic attraction or a hobby. It is undoubtedly one of the reasons that Lepidoptera sustained the interest of a complex man like Nabokov far beyond a childish attraction. It is also a point Nabokov was trying to make in the BBC interview in 1962, when he responded to a question about his lepidoptery with this multifaceted reply: "Yes, I'm interested in the classification, variation, evolution, structure, distribution, habits, of lepidoptera." Anyone who thinks a generalized mastery of these fundamental topics is child's play simply hasn't tried it themselves; the nearly inevitable confusion that reigns when a casual writer or critic tries to take Lepidoptera by the horns is one of the reasons that Nabokov was so skeptical of attempts to analyze his literary work in the light of butterflies, or so amused when other, less sure-footed writers fell into the trap, confusing, say, a Purple Emperor butterfly with the Emperor moth. ("Lepidoptera, a tricky subject," Nabokov wrote Alfred Appel, Jr. in 1967, urging him not to hazard his own comments on butterflies in his *Annotated Lolita,* but to rely on Nabokov to supply them.)

The dawning of the awareness of this complexity, which came very early for Nabokov, is a crucial and special event for a lepidopterist; nowhere has the joy and wonder of that moment been caught with more insight than in a loving passage of *The Gift*. The lepidopterist-narrator, Fyodor, recalls how his father, a world-famous explorer and entomologist, taught him the secrets of Lepidoptera:

> The sweetness of the lessons! On a warm evening he would take me to a certain small pond to watch the aspen hawk moth swing over the very water, dipping in it the tip of its body. He showed me how to prepare genital armatures to determine species which were externally indistinguishable. With a special smile he brought to my attention the black Ringlet butterflies in our park which with mysterious and elegant unexpectedness appeared only in even years. He mixed beer with treacle for me on a dreadfully cold, dreadfully rainy autumn night in order to catch at the smeared tree trunks that glistened in the light of a kerosene lamp a multitude of large, banded moths, silently diving and hurrying toward the bait. He variously warmed and cooled the golden chrysalids of my tortoiseshells so that I was able to get from them Corsican, arctic and entirely unusual forms looking as if they had been dipped in tar and had silky fuzz sticking to them. He taught me how to take apart an ant-hill and find the caterpillar of a Blue which had concluded a barbaric pact with its inhabitants, and I saw how an ant, greedily tickling a hind segment of that caterpillar's clumsy, sluglike little body, forced it to excrete a drop of intoxicant juice, which it swallowed immediately. In compensation it offered its own larvae as food. . . .
>
> He told me about the odors of butterflies — musk and vanilla; about the voices of butterflies; about the piercing sound given out by the monstrous caterpillar of a Malayan hawkmoth, an improvement on the mouselike squeak of our Death's Head moth; about the small resonant tympanum of certain tiger moths; about the cunning butterfly in the Brazilian forest which imitates the whir of a local bird. He told me about the incredible artistic wit of mimetic disguise . . . about these magic masks of mimicry; about the enormous moth which in a state of repose assumes the image of a snake looking at you; of a tropical geometrid [moth] colored in perfect imitation of a species of butterfly infinitely removed from it in nature's system. . . . He told me about migrations, about the long cloud consisting of myriads of white pierids that moves through the sky, indifferent to the direction of the wind, always at the same level above the ground, rising softly and smoothly over hills and sinking again into valleys, meeting perhaps another cloud of butterflies, yellow, filtering through it without stopping and without soiling its own whiteness — and floating further, to settle on trees toward nighttime which stand until morning as if bestrewn with snow — and then taking off again to continue their journey — whither? Why? A tale not yet finished by nature or else forgotten. "Our thistle

butterfly," he said, "the painted lady of the English, the *'belle dame'* of the French, does not hibernate in Europe as related species do; it is born on the African plains; there, at dawn the lucky traveler may hear the whole steppe, glistening in the first rays, crackle with an incalculable number of hatching chrysalids." From there, without delay it begins its journey north, reaching the shores of Europe in early spring, suddenly enlivening the gardens of the Crimea and the terraces of the Riviera; without lingering, but leaving individuals everywhere for summer breeding, it proceeds further north and by the end of May, by now in single specimens, it reaches Scotland, Heligoland, our parts and even the extreme north of the earth: it has been caught in Iceland! With a strange crazy flight unlike anything else the bleached, hardly recognizable butterfly, choosing a dry glade, 'wheels' in and out of the Leshino firs, and by the end of the summer, on thistleheads, on asters, its lovely pink-flushed offspring is already reveling in life. "Most moving of all," added my father, "is that on the first cold days a reverse phenomenon is observed, the ebb: the butterfly hastens southward, for the winter, but of course it perishes before it reaches the warmth."

Blue butterflies, the ultimate objects of Nabokov's scientific fascination, are members of one of eight subfamilies — to use the most widely accepted modern classification — of the family Lycaenidae. Nabokov knew this subfamily as Plebejinae, but it is more often called Polyommatinae today. The Lycaenidae, in turn, are one of five to eleven families of butterflies generally recognized by biologists. They are distinguished from other butterfly families by a constellation of anatomical characteristics, interestingly, more on their bodies than in wing pattern or color. Fortunately, general wing shape and color are also useful in recognizing them. The vernacular term *Blue* reflects the blue color of the upper wing surface that distinguishes Blues from other closely related groups of lycaenids — Coppers, which are indeed generally copper-colored; and Hairstreaks, which take their name from the short, hairlike tails on the edges of their hind wings. But all these groups have members that are easy to confuse with the others. Some Blues and Coppers have tails like Hairstreaks, some Coppers are colored blue, and some Blues are copper, a fact that confused the taxonomy of the Blues of South America for centuries.

All the lycaenids, along with Metalmarks, butterflies with bright metallic wing patches that make up the family Riodinidae, are generally small, most no more than an inch, and they are often secretive in their habits; some scientists today prefer to include the riodinids in the family Lycaenidae. Excluding the more primitive Skippers, the remaining families of butterflies are comparatively large and showy, more vagile, and certainly better known, among scientists as well as the public. Nabokov mentioned representatives of them all in *Speak, Memory:* the Pieridae, or Whites and Sulphurs, named chromatically like the Blues; the Papilionidae, or Swallowtails; and the Nymphalidae, a group that includes many of Nabokov's favorite literary vernacular names, including Tortoiseshells and Fritillaries, his Red Admirables, Camberwell Beauties, and Peacocks. Their splendid names recommend these creatures for literature as much as anything else about them. Some other butterflies Nabokov mentioned — Browns, Ringlets, and Nymphs — were in his time universally included in a family called Satyridae. Today, however, many scientists do not recognize the satyrids as a separate family and merge its members with the Nymphalidae.

The Lycaenidae — also known as the Gossamer Wings — provide fertile ground for discovery, and there are possibly more species of lycaenids than of any other butterfly family. More than four thousand have already been named worldwide, and recent studies in Brazilian rain forests suggest that unknown lycaenids compose up to 70 percent of the unknown butterfly faunas there. Even if the specific numbers can be argued, it is without doubt among the Blues, Hairstreaks, Metalmarks, Skippers, and other small butterflies that explosive diversification has occurred in the tropical regions and unnamed species abound. Thus, his specialization in the family Lycaenidae abetted one of Nabokov's earliest and most cherished dreams, the discovery of new species.

Nabokov's focus on Blue butterflies in his major lepidopterological writings, from the viewpoint of his overall interest in lepidoptery, appears to have been largely serendipitous, a choice driven by the circumstances of his career. His first serious attempt to name a new species, in 1941, involved a peculiar Blue butterfly that he had captured on the flowery slopes above the French village of Moulinet in the Maritime Alps in 1938, which he called *Lysandra cormion* Nabokov. This discovery may well have given him an instrumental push toward Blues. But neither in *Speak, Memory* nor in any of his other nonscientific writings did he betray a particular favorite among butterflies.

Moreover, he was quite well-informed about moths, distinctly more so than the average professional lepidopterist specializing in butterflies today, and the Hawkmoths in the countryside around Vyra, the Nabokov family estate near St. Petersburg, flit in and out of *Speak, Memory* like guiding spirits. A few highlights of Nabokov's career with moths will suffice for illustration. "Sugaring" for moths — that is, setting out pungent bait to attract them, which Fyodor mentions in the previously quoted passage of *The Gift* — was one of Nabokov's passionate lepidopterological pastimes; as unlikely a picture as the possibility may have presented, he once tried to interest his friend Edmund Wilson in having a go: "Try, Bunny," he wrote. "It is the noblest sport in the world." Walking in a Berlin neighborhood during the 1930s, he recognized a rare moth sitting on a tree and was able to sell it to a local dealer in Lepidoptera; some rare Pug moths he caught in France were among the handful of specimens that he was able to rescue from his European collection and bring to the United States at the outbreak of World War II. In 1943 Nabokov collected a series of unfamiliar Pugs at Alta, Utah, for J. H. McDunnough, a prominent entomologist he had met at the American Museum of Natural History; one of these McDunnough named *Eupithecia nabokovi* in honor of Nabokov, who was the only one of McDunnough's sources to have caught it, and he wrote: "A fine lot of material collected recently by Mr. V. Nabokov of Cambridge, Mass., in Utah, has been most helpful in augmenting my series in many cases, and I am very grateful for the opportunity of studying this collection." Finally, one of Nabokov's short lepidopterological notes, "Sphingids over Water," published in *The Lepidopterists' News* in 1947, recorded his observation of a Striped Hawkmoth of the genus *Celerio* hovering over water with its proboscis immersed.

Despite his eclectic interests, though, the Blues were the only group of butterflies or moths in which Nabokov explicitly claimed to be an expert, and various subgroups of Blues were the subjects of his most important lepidopterological papers. Even here, as penetrating as Nabokov's studies of Blues were, their worldwide diversity and his concentration on the genus *Lycaeides* meant that he actually touched on only a tiny fraction of the fourteen hundred or so species of Blues known today.

Compared with many other butterfly groups, whose members can show strong differences in size, shape, and color, Blues are remarkably uniform in overall appearance. This is particularly true in the temperate zones that dominate most of Eurasia and North America, which were the regions Nabokov primarily covered in his scientific work and in which he did all his collecting. In tropical regions they become slightly more experimental in their external features but not extraordinarily so. Everywhere Blues are small, mostly between a half inch and an inch in wingspread, and the wing shape is most often gently rounded, lacking the audacious angles, scallops, or incised shapes that other butterfly families often boast. But Blues have a distinct, perky — some would say noble and dignified —

profile which Nabokov, a proficient illustrator of butterflies, caught perfectly in some of his drawings. When their flashier cousins are set distractingly alongside them, it is clear that they aren't the most eye-catching of Lepidoptera, but it is unfair to say they are drab. Their beauty is rather of the subtle sort, invented by nature in one of her understated moods. They are, perhaps, an acquired taste but one well worth acquiring.

Despite their name, many Blues would better be described as brown, copper, gray, silver, or even white. As Nabokov explained to Alfred Appel, Jr., "When a lepidopterist uses *Blues*, a slangy but handy term, for a certain group of Lycaenids, he does not see that word in any color connection because he knows that the diagnostic undersides of their wings are not blue but dun, tan, grayish etc., and that many Blues, especially in the female, are brown, not blue."

If the upper surfaces of the wings aren't of uniform color, usually some iridescent blue or violet, they sport margins of dark brown or black, often quite narrow. Some species also have black or black and orange macules, or spots, arranged individually or in bands. The blue itself is not a pigmental color like those of white, yellow, brown, or orange butterflies; it is instead a structural color, produced by very fine laminations in the wing scales refracting the light, so the beholder sees a shimmering iridescent blue, like that in a rainbow. The brilliant blue color of the large tropical Morpho butterflies is produced in the same way.

The iridescence is believed to aid in the butterflies' "flash and dazzle" escape mechanism. When threatened, a Blue butterfly flashes its dazzling blue, shifts position, and brings its wings together over its back, now with only the dull ventral surfaces of the wings showing. The search image of a predator (often a bird or lizard with a brain smaller than a pea) becomes hopelessly confused. The undersurfaces of the wings of Blues also tend to uniformity, usually with a ground color of white, light gray, or light brown covered with patterns of spots, bands, or combinations of both. These markings are usually plain black or brown, although they can be lined and accented by some white or, in exceptionally flashy Blues, by orange or red. Nabokov himself grouped all the ventral wing patterns (his "diagnostic undersides") of the Blues known to him into only two categories — catachrysopoid, which is seen as a group of spots, and itylloid, which is best described as banded. As Nabokov recognized, the underwing patterns are in themselves no doubt protective in nature, the overall pattern mimicking the flower head on which the insect might sit or sleep, with some of the macules imitating dewdrops, or the eye of a lizard or bird, or the eye of the butterfly itself. As Nabokov also noted, the blue color of the males is in addition epigamic; that is, it serves to attract females of the appropriate species, one of the most important evolutionary functions of the gorgeous colors of most butterflies.

In the high-altitude temperate zones of the so-called tropical regions, like the Andes Mountains and Patagonia — the home of many of Nabokov's Latin American Blues — they become slightly more unusual in color, a few quite splendidly so, with hues of gold and silver and pattern elements outlined in more spectacular bands of burnished bronze or purple. But by and large high altitudes also favor the phenomenon of discoloration. There many Blues become a uniform brown, the darker color thought by many to be an adaptation for regulating temperature in these inhospitable climes, because darker colors retain more heat. Only in parts of New Guinea and Borneo do some Blues take another tack entirely, boasting a larger size and sporting white and black patterns, ceasing to look like the usual run of Blues at all.

The general physical resemblance of most Blues, though, has complicated the job of classifying them and explains why taxonomists who concentrate on them seem to spend so much time on observational minutiae. In his *Lycaeides* studies Nabokov meticulously counted under a microscope and recorded the numbers of rows formed by the scales of a butterfly's wing and the numbers of scales — each much smaller than the head of a pin — in the several rows. His primary interest in these wing patterns and their origins came from his interest in speciation. That is, if the taxonomist is using characteristics of wing pattern to differentiate species, how do these relate to ancestry and descent? To put it another way, he was looking for reliable new sets of characteristics that might be used in distinguishing species that look very much alike and was also interested in explaining how the differentiation arose.

Some highly respected contemporaries, particularly William Comstock of the American Museum of Natural History, thought Nabokov's scale counting represented a taxonomic advance. Like his work on American Blues, this line of inquiry was not widely followed after Nabokov's time, but Yale's Charles Remington has expressed the belief that it may become more common in the future, and perhaps resolve the question of whether this part of Nabokov's science was innovative.

In fact, there is at least one modern study on the origins of wing patterns, by H. Frederik Nijhout, a biologist at Duke University. It focuses primarily on the Nymphalidae and is tailored around genetic and evolutionary concepts that were not available in Nabokov's day. Nijhout ties butterfly wing patterns directly to genetics, generalizing how the patterns emerge as symmetry systems, that is, how the mirror-image bands and markings on the wings emerge under the direction of certain genes. Although Nabokov knew nothing of the genetics of butterfly wing patterns, he too treated the band and macule systems as emerging symmetrical patterns tied to phylogeny — which is to say their ancestry, a notion equivalent to modern genetics. From this point of view, several passages from "Notes on the Morphology of the Genus *Lycaeides*" have an intriguingly modern ring to them.

Toward the other end of the life cycle, the caterpillars of Blue butterflies are small, slug-shaped, and often but not always furry. Their colors can vary spectacularly, often adapting to the background of the flower or leaf on which they feed — green, orange, or even purple. The caterpillars most often feed on flowers or the soft tissues of flower buds, and the larvae of individual species can be finicky. Some are in fact monophagous, feeding off a single species of plant. But there are Blues whose larvae are oligophagous and can feed off related species within a genus, and others that are polyphagous and feed off many plant varieties. Much modern research involves the extent to which butterflies and their specific food plants have evolved together over the millennia.

Blue butterfly chrysalises are brown and bulletlike, most often dropping to the ground to be buried in detritus during the period of hibernation. In different groups of butterflies, different stages in the cycle of metamorphosis are designed to overwinter, and in the case of the Blues, it is the chrysalid. Despite the somewhat misleading classification Neotropical, many Latin American Blues inhabit temperate or even colder climates. In such regions adults tend to have short lives, generally a week or two. Adulthood is in some ways the most vulnerable stage of a butterfly. Adults can be easily frozen, drowned in rain, or blown away by the wind. Caterpillars of Blues, by contrast, can estivate, or go into a state like hibernation, if conditions become unfavorable, and resume development when the weather is better. For this reason adult Blues tend to emerge in "pulses," determined by the weather. There are one, two, or three broods a year, again depending on the species.

Behaviorally, Blues are gentlemen, dainty and polite compared with many other groups. Few are fast fliers, and still fewer are particularly inquisitive or pugnacious — yes, some butterflies can be very territorial and will buzz intruders, including humans, in much the way some birds do; a nymphalid butterfly known as the Baltimore is notorious for this. Another group, Hackberry butterflies, love human sweat and will fly from their perches in hackberry trees and taste you if you happen to walk by. But most Blues are "flutterers," flitting demurely from flower to flower looking for nectar. Some sit so stupefied by the nectar's sweetness that they can easily be plucked from the plant with the fingers. Decorum seems to be a natural part of their makeup: even when they congregate in shoals at communal mud puddles, a common behavior, Blues appear to line up civilly and take turns drinking.

The diversity of Lepidoptera, like that of other large groups of living organisms, is reduced to manageable, meaningful order by classifying them into a hierarchy, which in today's universal conception reflects real biological family relationships. This process, in its widest scope, represents yet another conceptual leap in lepidoptery; as many enthusiasts who begin as "stamp collectors" never advance further, many lepidopterists, including skilled field collectors with a "naturalist" bent, never become experts in the finer points of scientific classification. Instead of sunshine, grassy, open fields, and blasts of fresh air, classification inhabits a more restricted world of naphthalene, the laboratory, and, to a degree, abstract theory. Nabokov, however, loved both worlds, and it is impossible to understand his lepidoptery without some knowledge of the field.

Classification involves two related functions: systematics, which deals with questions of organizational theory and methodology, and taxonomy, the codification and application of rules to govern biological classification. Systematics as a whole is concerned with the larger, primarily theoretical, questions of biological process. It is a wide discipline that includes taxonomy but goes beyond it to cover the entire arena of questions concerning evolution and how it works. The premises and methodologies of systematics are matters of constant debate in the scientific community as part of the advancement of the science and knowledge of evolution.

Nabokov was by choice and natural inclination a taxonomist; as he put it himself, he was a lepidopterist of an analytic rather than a synthetic bent. The notion of choice is important, because today there is an assumption that a taxonomist is someone incapable of grasping or advancing the presumed complexities of systematic theory and thus settles for a "lower" calling. And in one way the practical nature of taxonomy arguably relates it to the wider field of systematics in somewhat the way accounting relates to economics. Taxonomy is a realm that exalts the specific over the general and requires much attention to minute detail and shrewd perception of differences. Although they were of little significance to his own entomological career, Nabokov did, however, think about the broader aspects of systematics, and his notions, though never fully elaborated, were more sophisticated than he is sometimes given credit for. But it was with taxonomy that Nabokov was most concerned in his major publications.

The broadest result of systematics and taxonomy is a family tree of life. Most people, perhaps, associate this tree with high school biology, and a little reminding can refresh their memories of the tree's main branches, known in taxonomy as the obligatory categories — categories into which every classified organism must be officially assigned. The organization works something like a filing system, starting from the broadest category — which for a Blue butterfly would be the Animal Kingdom — and working downward to the most specific, the species. Along the way the butterfly would be registered into a phylum (Invertebrata, animals without backbones); a class (Insecta, six-legged invertebrates); an order (Lepidoptera, insects with scaled wings); a family (Lycaenidae); a genus (for example, *Lycaeides,* the genus Nabokov studied so intensely), and a species (let's say *Lycaeides melissa,* the Orange-Bordered Blue, also known as the Melissa Blue). There are also conventional intermediate stages between some of these groups, such as subfamilies, subgenuses, and subspecies (once also called forms or races), with which Nabokov was so concerned in his *Lycaeides* papers. These are often convenient for classifiers and reflect real questions of genealogy, but under current rules of classification organisms need not be assigned to any of them (hence the contrasting obligatory categories).

As most interested people are aware, a species actually goes by two Latin names. The first of these is the genus designation, which a number of species typically share. In addition to *Lycaeides melissa,* for example, there is a species called *Lycaeides argyrognomon.* The second element of the name is the species itself, sometimes called the species epithet. Under current rules genus names are unique — since *Lycaeides* is recognized as the name of a certain group of Blue butterflies, it may not be assigned as a genus name for any other group of organisms; the species epithet, by contrast, can be freely used — there is nothing to stop a species of fish, or bird, or fly from being called *melissa.* But together an organism's two given names readily distinguish it from any other organism, whether it is closely related or distantly separate. Finally, in formal usage the name of the author — the person who discovered and named the species — and the date

of that authorship is traditionally appended to the binomial construction; looking at those names attached to butterflies in the lavishly illustrated lepidopterological volumes he read as a youth seized Nabokov's proud imagination; in later life it offended him to see the author's name, with its rich historical associations, omitted from the species name in works on butterflies. To return to our Melissa Blue example, its full formal name would be *Lycaeides melissa* (Edwards) 1873, named by its discoverer, William Henry Edwards.

This so-called binomial system of classification was first proposed in 1758 by the Swedish naturalist Carl von Linné, better known by his Latin nom de plume Carolus Linnaeus. This is a very different convention than the biblical "one name" system, familiar from everyday life, in which an animal is a lion, a tiger, a gazelle. Linnaean nomenclature is hierarchical — the first of the two names is actually a category and is able to contain one or more members going by a second name, just like the surname of a family in English. If we think of scientific naming as roughly equivalent to the "last name first, first name last" convention, it is easy to understand its utility to the scientist, who is interested in grouping organisms genealogically according to their biological relationships — that is to say, phylogenetically.

The broadest of the obligatory categories are uncontroversial. Most organisms fit easily into a kingdom, a phylum, a class, or an order. From the family level on down, however, groups are to a large extent arbitrary; only the species has a particular definition, and that definition itself is one of the trickiest topics in the classification of living organisms. On a number of levels, no question has caused more division among taxonomists, though the species is the penny currency of their trade. In theory nothing could be simpler: species are, to use the words of Ernst Mayr, a contemporary of Nabokov's at Harvard and the American Museum of Natural History, and an early proponent of this conception, "groups of actually or potentially interbreeding natural populations, which are reproductively isolated from other such groups." That is, a species is a group of organisms that breed in nature, or could breed, within an exclusive group. This is called the biological species definition, and while it seems concrete enough, it is obviously difficult for the workaday taxonomist to apply in the laboratory, faced as he or she is with only dead specimens. The modern foundations for the biological species definition were laid by Mayr and Theodosius Dobzhansky, famous contemporaries of Nabokov, whose work he followed with critical interest.

The goal and function of taxonomy is nomenclatorial: from the point of view of scientific "bookkeeping," a species need be little more than a convenient label for something. Indeed, as Nabokov derisively pointed out, in his day and for nearly a century before him, the meaning of a "species" might go no further than a name casually tagged onto a specimen by one of the early European dealers. Under these circumstances the taxonomist, for purely practical reasons, needs to establish an independent set of criteria for distinguishing species in the laboratory. For Nabokov, and for taxonomists today, these criteria were based on form and structure — or morphology — that could be quantified, objectified, and analyzed in a laboratory. Thus, for years the concept of species has actually fulfilled two functions, a practical one and a theoretical one, which are sometimes at odds with each other.

This conception is important for understanding Nabokov's lepidoptery, because his attitudes toward species — specifically, his ideas about biological species definition — have sometimes been viewed as not only fatally out of date from the point of view of modern science but stubbornly and obtusely wrong even according to the science of his day. Many biologists who know Nabokov only by reputation have the mistaken impression that he rejected the notion outright. This supposition, in turn, stems largely from his criticism of the practical limitations of Mayr's species definition and from his insistence on a definition that is underpinned by observable anatomical differences. "I do not object to the concept of the biological species," he wrote. "My objection is its being used as a primary method."

Nabokov explained his point of view in a talk presented to the Cambridge Entomological Club on October 10, 1944, and various prepatory and lecture notes have survived among his papers. It is a technical presentation for a technically minded audience of professionals, but Nabokov's acceptance of an abstract notion of the species is fairly clear:

> Up to here I have mentally agreed with myself that a "species" is something that actually . . . exists and thus lends itself to a general definition to which it will always conform. I still believe that such a definition *can* be found although I am not satisfied either with those in current use or with those that I can supply myself. The idea of interbreeding is better left alone, not alone because nothing is definitely known whether say, a race of *Agriades pheretes* from the Swiss Alps will breed with a race of the same species from China, but also because the gap between the abstract idea of species and its concrete form as a "collection of individuals" remains most clumsily unbridged. . . . If a species cannot be based

on morphological data, the concept must be dropped altogether insofar as it is linked up with the nomenclature and classification in use and some new kind of classification evolved.

Nabokov found several concrete problems with Mayr's attempt to detach the definition of species from structural concepts. For example, when Mayr included *potential* interbreeding in his definition, Nabokov asked how such potential would even be suspected without relying on structural evidence — i.e., it is only because the organisms appear to be so similar that the ability to interbreed might be presupposed. For this reason he saw the logic of Mayr's definition as circular. Moreover, while the notion of interbreeding seems a concrete matter, easily ascertainable, in the case of insects, butterflies included, it is far from easy to determine interbreeding populations. Under Mayr's definition, which stresses breeding *in nature,* it won't do simply to bring live specimens into the laboratory and see if they can be made to breed. Mayr's own specialty was birds, and Nabokov believed that insects, beyond Mayr's expertise, were exceptions to many of his ideas.

But by and large Nabokov's objections were practical, made from the point of view of the taxonomist in the laboratory, who needed concrete criteria to work under the accepted system of classification. This same practical view is reflected in an observation that is often wrongly cited as evidence for Nabokov's scientific naïveté regarding modern genetics. In an overwhelmingly favorable 1970 review of Lionel C. Higgins and Norman Riley's *Field Guide to the Butterflies of Great Britain and Europe* — a review written not as a technical treatise or even for a scientific audience but for *The Times* of London — Nabokov said, "In a few cases, however, the authors seem to have succumbed to the blandishments of the chromosome count. *For better or worse our present notion of species* in Lepidoptera is based solely on the *checkable* structures of dead specimens, and if Forster's Furry cannot be distinguished from the Furry Blue except by its chromosome number, Forster's Furry must be scrapped" [our italics]. His own tentative definition of a species, prepared for that talk in Cambridge in 1944, was as follows: "A species is a relative category, at its tangible best represented by a number of interbreeding organisms which constantly differ in structure from and do not interbreed with any other organism inhabiting the same area." This definition involves structure not instead of but as well as reproduction.

Counting chromosomes in particular proved to be an unreliable method of determining species of butterflies; many species that clearly do not interbreed, for example, have the same number of chromosomes. More sophisticated science of a much later age, including an understanding of DNA mapping, helped to explain the inconsistencies, but as far as merely counting chromosomes, which can be seen under a microscope, Nabokov turned out to be quite right. Modern insect taxonomy still depends almost entirely on anatomical considerations, as did taxonomy in the 1940s and in 1970. Despite impressions to the contrary, even the most up-to-date, sophisticated, and advanced methodologies, like genetics and molecular biology, have failed to solve the debate on the definition of a species. Modern methods deriving from the perspectives of so many subdisciplines appear in fact only to have increased the number of ways it is possible to disagree about the notion.

DNA analysis, which was only developed to any level of sophistication after Nabokov's death, requires specialized training and equipment that is not yet widely available. Thus, genitalic examination under a dissection microscope is still fundamental for basic "alpha" taxonomy today. Though promising in the long run, universal replacement of simple microscopy by DNA sequencing appears unlikely in the foreseeable future. It is more likely that the two will work in tandem, with the older method used to "red-flag" subjects for the more sophisticated technology, just as in the first half of the century the study of wing-pattern detail red-flagged specimens requiring anatomical study under the microscope.

Other aspects of Nabokov's sophistication with notions of the species will be considered later. For now it must be stressed that his systematics grew out of his experiences as a classifier, a taxonomist. Rather than the thin air of abstract theory, Nabokov was most comfortable breathing the rich atmosphere of practical, basic taxonomy. It is far more relevant to the understanding of Nabokov's lepidoptery to grasp classification at quite another, fundamental level. For his purposes a species had to be recognizable by a distinctive set of physical characteristics, or characters, that allowed it to be readily differentiated from another species. His overriding concern was to recognize such characteristics and to group his specimens accordingly. As already suggested, for butterflies like Blues, many of which appear much the same externally, one of the most important of these characters is the genital anatomy.

It surprises many nonscientists to learn that what constitutes characteristics sufficiently distinctive to define a species is often a judgment call of an individual. This is, if anything, even more true of a genus, a concept notoriously hard to pin down. There is, in fact, no definition of a genus beyond the general idea that it is a group of related species with a common ancestor. But if there are twelve butterflies, all clearly related in some way yet with some differences, too, should there be one genus to contain all twelve, or should there be, say, three genuses reflecting those differences? And what differences, precisely, should be the determining ones? The answer will necessarily remain to some extent subjective, left within a degree to the individual scientist; as Nabokov put it: "The idea of 'species' is the idea of difference; the idea of 'genus' is the idea of similarity. What we do when trying to 'erect a genus,' as the saying goes, is really the paradoxical attempt to demonstrate that certain objects that are dissimilar in one way are similar in another."

Depending on how finely tuned they believe the distinguishing characters should be, taxonomists generally divide into two philosophical camps, lumpers and splitters. Lumpers tend to minimize the significance of variations they encounter and so group large numbers of specimens into relatively small groupings, genuses and species, for example. Splitters — and most entomologists, friend and foe, have looked upon Nabokov as one of these — accord more significance to variation and would designate a larger number of groupings for the same specimens. The two camps often agree only in each believing that the other is fundamentally wrong.

Historically, the tension between lumpers and splitters stemmed from the realities of everyday institutional research. Dead, dried, or otherwise preserved specimens were the only tools available to workers at early museums or in private collections. Especially during the colonial era, when specimens often came from great distances, the home-based scientist was unable to make judgments about subjects based on their behavior in nature. Although modern biology has significantly increased the size of collections available to laboratory workers and workers often have the chance to observe organisms in the field, nothing has reconciled the lumpers and splitters.

This venerable notion of lumping and splitting, particularly at the level of the genus, is in most ways more germane to Nabokov's lepidoptery than any higher considerations of broad systematics. In the introduction to "Notes on Neotropical Plebejinae," Nabokov wrote that his detailed work on Nearctic Blues had spurred him to delve into their relatives in the south. It was on this excursion into the Blues of the New World tropics and their vast diversity in South America's western mountain chains that

Nabokov, who made no secret of his desire to discover and name new species, found the treasure trove he had so long sought. In fact, the biological riches he encountered there compelled him to limit himself to naming the broader, generic groups and to defer the descriptive process that would be required for individual species. There were several reasons for this. As Nabokov wrote, the delightfully unexpected results of his initial inquiries led him to publish "Notes on Neotropical Plebejinae" "despite its rather superficial and incomplete nature." He was also probably sensitive to the small number of his samples and believed he might return to the project in the postwar years, when far more ample material was sure to be available.

Nabokov named seven new genuses in "Notes on Neotropical Plebejinae" and redefined two others. Practically speaking, this involved above all finding the determining physical characteristics that would define each one. Each genus, in turn, held rich potential for the discovery of new species within its boundaries. It was, so to speak, the tip of a taxonomic iceberg; it is largely this fact that makes this work so central to Nabokov's legacy in entomology. By describing a seminal taxonomy for a group whose diversity vastly exceeded his own knowledge or expectation, he stood to put an indelible mark on the field, a mark far more lasting than if he had continued solely with the tedious elaboration of subspecific names (subspecies, forms, and so forth) that typified his work on *Lycaeides* and much of the European taxonomy of the time, where the territory had been covered again and again. By defining and naming the genuses of all the Neotropical Blues, he assured that his name would be attached to the whole group. He would be "the first reviser," the inventor of the fundamental classification into which all the region's species of Blue butterflies would fit. Not only would he be "godfather to an insect" (as he so proudly called himself in the poem "On Discovering a Butterfly," which provides the epigraph for this book) but he would in a sense be godfather to hundreds. It was the kind of fame he craved.

In 1945 Nabokov offered definitive opinions, based on the physical characteristics of the limited amount of material at his disposal, on the relationships of the Neotropical Blues. How would those opinions fare when applied to the complex mix of tropical lowlands, mountainous terrain, and scattered island ecologies that make up the vast neotropical biological region? Fifty years passed before other researchers took up Nabokov's project and began to provide answers to that question.

3

A Legendary Land

I confess I do not believe in time. I like to fold my magic carpet, after use, in such a way as to superimpose one part of the pattern upon another. Let visitors trip. And the highest enjoyment of timelessness — in a landscape selected at random — is when I stand among rare butterflies and their food plants. This is ecstasy, and behind the ecstasy is something else, which is hard to explain. It is like a momentary vacuum into which rushes all that I love.

— *Speak, Memory*

IN THE EARLY 1980s some new light was shed on the Latin American Polyommatini, turning up the first chance clues that led to a reevaluation of Nabokov's legacy as a lepidopterist. It was then that Albert Schwartz, a research associate at the Milwaukee Public Museum, began to report on rare species of butterflies that he had discovered in a remarkable little biological jewel box called Las Abejas, a remote and isolated rain forest hidden in the mountains along the Dominican Republic's southern border with Haiti. Among his finds were two of the rarest butterflies in the Western Hemisphere, *Battus zetides,* a black-and-yellow Swallowtail so seldom observed that its first scientific illustration — by none other than the British Museum's Norman Riley — omitted the long black-and-golden tails gracing its delicate hind wings; and *Anetia jaegeri,* a spectacular milkweed butterfly related to the common Monarch but so rare that before Schwartz's discovery, it was known by only a handful of specimens in the British Museum labeled merely "Haiti."

Although Schwartz reported on primarily these larger, showy butterflies, it was clear from the quantity and rarity of his captures that he had stumbled onto a lepidopterist's Shangri-la. There was little doubt that this biological oasis would also harbor a wealth of smaller species, like Hairstreaks and the related Metalmarks and Blues. Nabokov, of course, never visited the Antilles, or any of the Latin American sites that harbored the Blue butterflies he described in his seminal study. But he likely would have been captivated by their unexpected magic and timeless aura. The profound impression the little forest has made on scientists who have visited it is only intensified by its ecological vulnerability and the well-grounded fear that it may not survive far into the twenty-first century.

One comes upon Las Abejas abruptly, as if a curtain had been pulled back on the arid mountainous pines, lowland desert growth, and thorny mesquite that make up the characteristic face of the Sierra de Baoruco mountains in Pedernales Province in the southwestern Dominican Republic. A trail along the edge of the dry upland pines follows a short decline around a mountain bend and opens up to reveal, from above, the canopy of a dense subtropical forest stretched out along the fingers of lower-lying ravines and canyons. With its broadleaf deciduous trees, it is the Caribbean version of a rain forest, although it is dwarfed by its more famous counterparts in South and Central America. Rather than the continuous, uniform expanse of those giants, the luxuriant ravines at Las Abejas form a small, isolated world of humidity, an unexpected and breathtaking contrast to the surrounding pine forest and desert. The rich biological diversity of this upland region is intensified by the irregular interplay of the galleries of deciduous forest, weaving along the gullies and ravines of the escarpments, and the drier pine forests above. One instantly notices big tropical Swallowtails, soaring in groups of ten or more over the ravines, back and forth from the high trees on one side to those on the other, marking the ecological boundaries of the subtropical forest.

Because it lacks their constant heavy rains, Las Abejas is drier than the great South American forests. Its verdant growth is kept moist by the thick nighttime dews and runoff from sporadic but torrential downpours, which the loose soil immediately soaks up. When darkness falls after a sweltering day, amid the din of nocturnal birds, insects, and reptiles, the temperature drops dramatically; by morning the leaves drip with the dew wrung out by the nighttime cold. This is primarily how the forest sustains itself: there are no standing bodies of water in this biological oasis and no permanent streams, a condition that has prevented permanent human habitation.

Las Abejas means "the Bees," a name that is conceptual as much as geographic: for the solitary migrant farmers who have wandered across the region for decades, it is among other things an excellent place to gather honey. A Dominican aluminum-mining concern, Ideal Dominicana S. A., formerly the Alcoa Exploration Company, appropriated the name as a transect designation for a sector of proprietary land on the south slope of the Sierra de Baoruco that includes both the broadleaf subtropical forest and the mountainous desert landscape around it. Colloquial speech sometimes prefers the singular, La Abeja, and on some local maps the area is labeled Fondo de Abeja, or Abeja Bottom, but Schwartz and his co-workers established the usage Las Abejas in their work for scientific journals, and subsequent researchers have followed his lead.

Ownership of the entire area reverted to the Dominican government in 1985, and it has been designated a national conservation zone, the 97,000-acre Sierra de Baoruco National Park. But it remains under the direct guardianship of Ideal, and in 1987 no employee of the Dirección Nacional de Parques had apparently ever been there or could even describe the place or how to reach it. The park, whose boundaries have been marked only from the air, is still ringed by the Dominican Republic's mining reserve, which in turn is closed to the public. The only maps with any detail are kept secret by the military, concerned with the country's security along the Haitian border. For this reason, and because of its irregular shape, it is impossible to say precisely how large Las Abejas actually is.

The Sierra de Baoruco itself — a chain with jagged peaks rising abruptly to seven thousand feet and crossing the southernmost stretch of the border with Haiti — is a confusing maze of tracks and trails running off in every direction, with innumerable forks, twists, and bends; without maps the zone of subtropical forests is hard to find. The last two or three miles of the journey must be made on foot. Schwartz, who specialized in the fauna of Haiti and the Dominican Republic, was led into Las Abejas by employees of Ideal Dominicana, eager amateur naturalists who informally watch over the park for the government from a former Alcoa aluminum exploration base at Cabo Rojo, near the town of Pedernales, some forty-five arduous miles from the broadleaf forests. Their help has been crucial in every step of the exploration of the broadleaf forests; in fact, without their support no research could have been conducted there at all.

Immediately after his first exploration of Las Abejas in 1981, Schwartz began sending specimens to Kurt Johnson at the American Museum of Natural History for identification. But in the interest of protecting his discoveries and that wonderful patch of forest, Schwartz never published the exact location of Las Abejas and was initially hesitant to discuss it with other researchers. David Matusik, a burly field associate of Chicago's Museum of Natural History, first read of Schwartz's discovery of Las Abejas in 1983. On foot and by truck, Matusik crisscrossed the Sierra de Baoruco without finding the upland subtropical forests. In 1984, however, the Ideal naturalists led him to what they remembered as the spot Schwartz had explored. Matusik reported the location to the Museo Nacional de Historia Natural in Santo Domingo, and under their auspices, and with support from institutions in the United States, an increasingly elaborate series of expeditions to Las Abejas was launched by Matusik, Johnson, and other American and Dominican scientists. Even so, they were never satisfied that Schwartz's Las Abejas and the collection site Johnson and the others called by the same name were in fact the same place; each group caught butterflies the other never saw. What was certain was that everyone involved had reached subtropical bottomland forest teeming with a spectacular array of rare and unknown butterflies and other insects, including the first new species of Nabokov's Blues to be recorded in forty years.

When he went to Las Abejas, Schwartz was looking for biological remnants of a lost world. Paleogeography is the study of landmasses in the earth's past, and by its lights Hispaniola, which comprises the Dominican Republic and Haiti, is the most fascinating of the Caribbean islands. It now occupies a central position in the Greater Antilles, between Puerto Rico on the east, Cuba on the west, and Jamaica to the southwest. But originally it was two distinct landmasses — a North Paleoisland, which lay closer to Cuba, and a South Paleoisland, aligned along Jamaica, with which it shared close biological affinities. In the history of continental drift, the North and South Paleoislands piled together along the Cul-de-Sac de Neiba, a stretch of desert, much of it below sea level, that cuts across the south of both Haiti and the Dominican Republic. Despite a chain of lakes there, a mixture of saline and freshwater, the plain is hot and dry.

Biologically, areas on either side of this depression have little in common. Nearly all of what was the South Paleoisland now forms the Tiburon Peninsula of Haiti, a country whose desperate poverty has turned it into an ecological disaster area. Recent estimates suggest that less than 1 percent of Haiti's original forests survive. Photographs of the Haitian-Dominican border, like the ones published in the November 1987 issue of *National Geographic* magazine, show a sickeningly abrupt transition between the green forests of the Dominican Republic to the east and the brown, denuded landscape of Haiti undulating westward. But a small part of the South Paleoisland also makes up the Peninsula de Barahona in the Dominican Republic, whose central physical feature is the Sierra de

Baoruco. Thus, Las Abejas, in its geographic isolation, is also an oasis in time: its dense subtropical forests harbor most of what is left of the ancient plant and animal species that evolved on the South Paleoisland. Many of the species that occur in the Sierra de Baoruco National Park can be found there and nowhere else. In addition to endemic butterflies and moths, nineteen bird species live only in the park, and some 20 percent of its 166 orchid species are also endemic. Two endemic Dominican mammal species, the only native land mammals to have survived there into modern times, and now extremely endangered, are also known to have lived at Las Abejas. One is the Hispaniolan solenodon, a hairy insectivore fifteen inches long with short legs and a narrow, turned-up snout; the only other known species lives in Cuba. The other, an insect-eating rodent of about the same size, is the hutia. By the mid-1980s neither of these nocturnal creatures had been reported in the Las Abejas area for a decade, according to the Ideal naturalists. It may already be too late for them there. If the Sierra de Baoruco National Park cannot be maintained, many of its species face extinction.

Schwartz's discoveries caused a sensation in the world of lepidoptery. When Matusik led staff members of the Museo Nacional de Historia Natural into Las Abejas after his first trip there in 1984, they and officials of the Dirección Nacional de Parques were eager for further biological studies of the area to support conservation efforts. The American Museum of Natural History Theclid Research Fund supported the work of Johnson and Matusik in the area in 1985 and 1986, and when they returned with a treasure trove of the elusive *Battus zetides* and *Anetia jaegeri,* the Carnegie Fund for Invertebrate Zoology and the Carnegie Museum of Natural History in Pittsburgh sponsored a larger expedition to collect from all groups of nocturnal and diurnal insects from the South Paleoisland.

Every trip to Las Abejas paid enormous dividends in discovery, but the expedition of 1987 stands out. The rich harvest of specimens, the large number of new species captured, and the laboratory work that arose from it all marked a new beginning for the study of Nabokov's arrangement of the Latin American Polyommatini. In other ways, though, 1987 followed more or less the same routine as previous expeditions. Having rented a truck in Santo Domingo from a company that would never have consented to the deal had they known where it was being taken, Johnson and Matusik set out with another lepidopterist, John Rawlins, the head of Invertebrate Zoology at the Carnegie Museum, who specializes in moths, and Robert Davidson, the Carnegie's coleopterist, or beetle specialist. To-day the two-hundred-mile journey from Santo Domingo to the town of Pedernales takes some four hours over new roads, but in 1987 it was eight or nine hours, a long and wearing trek.

In Pedernales Province, the truck left public-access roads behind and passed first through an Army checkpoint into the Dominican mining re-serve and then through another, manned by both the Army and Ideal Do-minicana security personnel, that guards the road to the company's seaside administrative facility at Cabo Rojo. Among other courtesies pro-vided by the company, its regional mineral exploration headquarters — surrounded by desert and perched dramatically on the cliffs over the Caribbean — was to be the base for exploring Las Abejas. Johnson and Matusik always came out in early July, timing their arrival to the emer-gence of lycaenid butterflies. As usual for the two weeks of the 1987 expe-dition, a fairly typical-length stay, the two traveled by truck each day from Cabo Rojo, across the desert and mesquite to the foot of the Sierra de Baoruco and then upland through the pine forests for about ten miles on the access track to Ideal's most remote open-pit mine, a near-surreal moonscape. From the edge of the mine, they carefully chose the correct one of the dozens of radiating jeep trails that eventually, high up in the pines, dwindled to donkey paths, impassable to motorized vehicles. The final three miles or so they covered on foot, carrying their gear and choos-ing paths by the landmarks picked out on earlier trips — a scorched tree trunk, an abrupt turn in a track, a big patch of loose, sandy soil that was hard to walk through. The team was able to follow Schwartz's landmarks to a point on this stretch, a sinkhole about the size of a Volkswagen that had obliterated that part of the trail. But after that they could not agree on the right path to the "real" Las Abejas. In retrospect, they have always thought that Schwartz might have veered left somewhere after the hole, whereas they turned right, a touching sort of lepidopterological parting of the paths so far from home.

The trail down into the Las Abejas ravine passes through three distinct levels, each with its characteristic fauna and physical features, which the expedition called upper, middle, and lower Abejas. The three levels to-gether extend from an altitude of about 3,800 to 4,100 feet. On the heights near the rim of the canyon, pines suddenly give way to the broadleaf for-est, and the highest part is sunny, warming butterflies enough for them to be active by nine in the morning. The area is also scattered with flower-ing blackberry bushes, a rich source of nectar for an array of Lepidoptera, including Hairstreaks and Skippers, which could be caught in relative profusion as they fed.

The trail then descends over the rim along a precipitous incline. The slippery, claylike soil on the path made it next to impossible to keep even footing, particularly after a rain, and the climbers eventually just accepted the inevitable falls and spread out to limit the damage. *Anetia jaegeri* flocks in such profusion along the shrub-strewn path that it was dubbed Jaegeri Alley. Arriving at upper Abejas in the early morning, the researchers watched these large, gorgeous butterflies, seldom seen in any collection, often dew-covered, crawling up from the lower stalks of plants like *Gyrotaenia,* where they had rested for the night. After sunning themselves for a quarter of an hour, they would take flight.

Farther down, in the middle reaches of the ravine, the trail flattens out across 65-foot stretches of stair-step tablelands that sink to an elevation of 3,900 feet. Middle Abejas is more interspersed with subtropical understory growth, and the succession of flat steps opens numerous gaps in the canopy between 150 and 300 feet below the pines. *Battus zetides* can be seen here in its high, soaring flight as the sun begins to penetrate into the forest. It feeds on a flowering vine that climbs the highest forest limbs.

Still descending, the trail enters lower Abejas at 3,800 feet, at the base of the steep slopes. This is the wettest part of Las Abejas, where the vegetation is the most lush; the area is covered with dense forest except for a few small clearings. Outside the clearings the forest growth is anchored by the taller trees, which spread a broad umbrella over everything else. It is this canopy that sustains the cooler, wetter environment of the subtropical forest, forming the conditions for collection and retention of dew; without the big trees the sun would beat down incessantly and prevent the growth of life less tolerant of the dry heat.

Beneath the canopy grows a second layer of trees, about one-third to one-half their height and with a much less dense leaf covering. The ground is then typically covered with thick shrub or brush, ranging from about one to seven feet high and often impenetrable even to the eye. This triple layer of vegetation is common in tropical forests, but at Las Abejas the steep profile of the ravines offers an unusual perspective: standing at the edge of one of them, one could peer through the forest at several levels, including the higher reaches of the tall trees, where the branches are farther apart and butterflies could be seen moving around. Sometimes individual butterflies, canopy dwellers, could be captured as they strayed toward the ravine edge.

Here and there in the lowest level of Las Abejas are small clearings, and the trail ends in the largest of these, shaped like a bowl and overflowing with flowers. The sun constantly penetrates into the bowl, and on a good day butterflies bubble over its rim. *Zetides* is by all lepidopterological standards a rare butterfly, but it is not rare here. Beyond the left edge of the bowl, the ravine drops yet again, into a tangle of dense undergrowth beneath the wall of majestic trees towering between forty and sixty feet and trailing moss and vines from their lower limbs.

What turned out to be the first Nabokovian discovery at Las Abejas came in 1987 deep in the bottomlands in the undergrowth beyond the bowl, an unexpected place for Blue butterflies. Blues are sun lovers, and are more often found in desert, chaparral, or savanna. In Las Abejas, Johnson and Matusik had never collected a Blue in the moist bottomland; in their experience, and from what they learned from Schwartz, Blues at Las Abejas were upland xerophiles — that is, adapted to hot, dry regions — occurring in the dry pinelands above the ravine and only invading the canyon along its rim. But there are woodland Blues in all the major biological realms of the world, and a notable one in Jamaica, the ancient sisterland of the South Paleoisland of Hispaniola: *Leptotes perkinsae,* or Miss Perkins's Blue, is a little-known forest-edge species that William J. Kaye named in 1931 for Lilly Perkins, a local woman who was one of its earliest collectors.

On previous trips to Las Abejas, Johnson and Matusik had made some of their rarest captures in the bowl at the bottom end of the trail, but they had never tried to collect in the thick tangle in the ravine beyond. For one thing the understory there is so dense that it is hard to move a net. Also a migrant farmer had built a lean-to hut there, and it was impossible to be sure whether the squatter — typically a Haitian or Dominican moving through the forest planting beans and bananas to pick up on some future trip back through — was friendly or whether he was armed.

The farmers often plant small crops among the existing growth, but they also slash and burn the forest to make clearings. The pine woodlands are in no danger, because they grow on rock-on-rock substrate that is unsuitable for cultivation. Still, the migrants' destruction of the hardwood forest is the most serious threat to Las Abejas. Matusik first saw significant deforestation from their activities in 1984. In 1987 he and Johnson noticed that about five acres of canopy near lower Abejas had been destroyed and the ground planted over. Farther down the drainage larger areas had already been cleared, and on several days in both 1986 and 1987, lower and middle Abejas were filled with smoke from burning in nearby fingers of the forest. Schwartz wrote that in a single day traveling on the Alcoa access road in 1986, he and a companion could see as many as ten fires on the adjacent range.

Johnson and Matusik were troubled by the moral dilemma the burning presented, one repeated throughout Latin America. In some parts of Asia or North America, the destruction of habitat is arguably a direct function of corporate greed, but the men who were destroying Las Abejas were clearly just trying to earn a subsistence living. Still, in 1987, after Ideal had sent Johnson and Matusik's photographs of forest destruction to park officials in Santo Domingo, an Army patrol came into the area and temporarily cleared it of squatters. Illegal intruders, the team was told, are taken to jail in Pedernales, but not for long; when released they eventually return, resentfully, to the forest. Johnson and Matusik had no desire to bear the brunt of their anger; Las Abejas would be an easy place to dispose of a body.

In the end a large population of *Calisto chrysaoros,* the first Johnson and Matusik had ever seen, flitting out of the bowl and into the undergrowth, lured them inexorably on. Calistos belong to a group of butterflies known as Satyrs for the way they appear to romp through forest understory, grass, or shrublands, flying slowly and disappearing to perch within the thick growth. They seldom fly higher than one or two feet off the ground. *Calisto* is a Caribbean genus unique to the Antilles, and Hispaniola appears to be the center of its spectacular diversity. Schwartz had named nearly a dozen new species of Calistos from the South Paleoisland and the nearby Sierra de Neiba since 1983, many from the area of Las Abejas. Matusik and Johnson had discovered another in the Central Cordillera of the Dominican Republic in 1985. What caught their attention now was a species with a striking silver stripe slashed obliquely across its brown hind wing. Many years ago the famous biologist and pioneer on the Cuban fauna Dr. Marston Bates had named it *chrysaoros* on the basis of a few tattered museum specimens. Schwartz had written of this silver-striped species, but Johnson and Matusik had never seen it. It was Bates's Calisto that finally drew them into the dense bottomland.

A descent of more than sixty feet beyond the bowl brought them into dense understory. Brown Calistos with the characteristic stripe of *chrysaoros* flitted rapidly and erratically from stem to stem of the undergrowth around them, but the scientists could hardly move a net in the tangle. Now, in addition to Calistos, they could see bright little flashes of metallic gray, as if someone had tossed up a handful of silver coins, the mark of a lycaenid butterfly, a Hairstreak or a Blue. Occasionally the gray would deepen and the flash appear to be azure, an indication of a Blue and a sign that Nabokov must have trained himself to see well.

The gray flashes were familiar in Las Abejas, where the small but spectacularly blue-gray Hairstreak *Nesiostrymon celida,* another creature so rare that it lacks a common name, appears in greater numbers than are to be found in all the museum drawers of the world. But *celida* flocks only in the early morning, just as the sun is high enough to begin to filter through the canopy. That it was noon on a sweltering day, hot enough to bring out the fast-flying Skippers and large yellow-and-orange Sulphurs, offered the promise of a lycaenid that had not previously been collected at Las Abejas, perhaps something rare or unknown.

Fortunately, given the impenetrable undergrowth beyond the rim of the bowl, there is more than one way to net a butterfly. The classic movement is the sweep, a calm but deliberate motion that aims to catch the quarry in midair, followed by a flick of the wrist to close the fabric. (In case of a miss, most lepidopterists, with nothing to lose, will try a quick backhand.) The other method is the trap, in which the net is simply suspended in position in the hope that a butterfly will pass underneath. Tedious and totally dependent on luck, it requires no real motion, so it was the only option amid the tangle. Johnson's luck was good enough for one surprising catch — a Blue, and indeed a find of great interest. For when he and Matusik removed it from the net with a light forceps and pinched its thorax, they saw that it displayed but a single spot on the hind wing — the character of Miss Perkins's little Blue from far-off Jamaica. Audaciously marked by that single spot, it would ultimately have its abdomen dissected under a microscope at the American Museum of Natural History in New York. A comparison of its internal anatomy with that of its relatives was likely to reveal much more about its identity and place on the family tree of biology than the study of its wing patterns alone.

The obvious possibility of the Las Abejas Blue being one of Miss Perkins's pets, or a near relative, concerned tantalizing questions that go far beyond lepidoptery to summon up visions of islands adrift in the sea and the very creation of the modern geography of the Caribbean. If the Las Abejas expedition had come so far to find a Miss Perkins's Blue, and it had been seen nowhere else in Hispaniola, how had it gotten there? And why were its nearest relatives found more than three hundred miles away on yet another island, Jamaica? Questions like these, some on a worldwide scale and even more perplexing, are the realm of biogeography, which seeks to explain the distribution of the earth's varied life-forms. Arguments over the answers have been raging since the early part of this century.

Many biologists of Nabokov's generation, accepting that era's gospel of a stable earth, would have invoked transoceanic flight by the little butterfly. Indeed, some migrating butterflies, like the Monarch, are famously vagile — that is, they can fly for great distances. Many types of pierids, the group of mostly white-and-yellow butterflies that includes the common cabbage butterfly, are highly vagile migrants and thus wonderful colonizers; many Caribbean pierids undoubtedly reached distant islands that way. But many lycaenids, including Miss Perkins's Blue, are perchers, relatively sedentary butterflies that tend not to venture far from their food plants. The Las Abejas Blue would barely be able to fly out of the tangled understory of bottomland forest breaks deep in the Sierra de Baoruco, much less three hundred miles across an ocean.

A variant on the idea of colonization supposes other means of transoceanic dispersal, that sedentary butterflies might have been transported between islands by an accident of nature, for example, as inadvertent passengers on a clump of vegetation. Such movement remained merely a theoretical possibility until an astounding documented case in 1995, which happened to take place in the Caribbean. In October of that year, fifteen green land iguanas, traveling on a waterlogged clump of trees blown into the water by a hurricane, appeared to have completed a monthlong, two-hundred-mile sea voyage from Guadeloupe to Anguilla, where none of their kind had lived before. And although all were dehydrated and some were injured, there are signs that the population has established itself in its new home. Despite this amazing piece of evidence, however, it is far from clear how large an overall role such accidents might have played in the spread of life-forms. Certainly reptiles like the iguanas are far, far better physically equipped to survive such journeys than butterflies, and unlike butterflies, whose survival is often tied to a single specific type of plant, omnivorous reptiles would also be far more likely to survive in their new surroundings.

Some scientists, like George Gaylord Simpson and P. J. Darlington, guiding lights to a generation of biologists who worked at Harvard in the years after Nabokov's departure — had tried to explain such far-flung relationships as evidence of old land bridges or corridors: somehow, fingers of land had previously existed, and living things had used them to traverse what now appear to be impossible distances. Such a hypothetical corridor was thought of as a filter if a comparatively large number of plant and animal species had been able to make the journey, each handicapped or advantaged by its own way of life or environmental tolerances. If, however, only one or two species out of thousands had managed the crossing, the passage was called a sweepstakes, as if survival was the result of winning a lottery. True to his era, Nabokov entertained these notions, asking in "Notes on Neotropical Plebejinae" what the center of origin of his Blues might be, as if the places where they had once been absent acted like vacuums into which they were in some way drawn, an idea actually called the vacuum theory in the scientific conception of the 1940s.

At around the same time Simpson and Ernst Mayr had also advanced the important concept of allopatric speciation, the idea that species can originate through the geographic separation of populations. Such populations, now isolated from one another, follow separate paths of evolution, which eventually lead to their no longer being reproductively compatible and thus to the creation of different species. But neither Simpson nor Mayr completely grasped a fundamental biogeographical aspect of this notion: that biota, Blues included, could be distributed geographically after the breakup of once contiguous pieces of the earth's crust. If environs were, in fact, cut up and displaced over time, their biotas would move with them in situ — a dispersal mechanism known as vicariance — a concept very different from the hypothetical corridors over which the animals and plants were believed to have moved themselves.

The mechanism that broke up once-contiguous landmasses became clear only decades later, with the appreciation of continental drift: the realization that over the millennia the land itself was moving, pieces of the earth's crust (the plates of modern plate tectonics) floating on a viscous mantle. Such movement created today's world map over hundreds of millions of years, at infinitesimally small yearly rates, measurable by a few inches at most. Geophysicists discovered how continental drift occurs in the 1970s: the continual upwelling and cooling of magma on the sea floor at one end of a plate, and the subduction and remelting of crust at the other, a cataclysmic process that pushed up gigantic mountain ranges in folds like butter pressed off the side of a knife.

While the theory of continental drift came eventually to mainstream biology through the back door of geophysics, the global distribution of many living organisms had called out for such an explanation for decades. Indeed, the evidence of the process had its isolated champions even earlier. The geologist Alfred Wegener proposed a theory of drifting continents in 1915, and beginning in the 1950s the biologist Leon Croizat detected intercontinental relationships in the distribution patterns of related organisms that seemed to repeat themselves across diverse groups of plants and animals. Croizat, a Venezuelan, concluded that various continental landmasses, such as South America and Africa, had once been contiguous. But these ideas were at first derided by a large segment of the scientific world. In fact, had Croizat not had a wealthy wife willing to finance the publication of his works, his views might have gone unrecorded, and it is arguable that part of the reason they were so long ignored is that they were written in Spanish, not at that time a prestigious language in the world of science. If one looks for villains in the long journey of acceptance of the theory of continental drift, one might argue that Nabokov's own Harvard was a fortress occupied by the last holdouts against what now appears so obvious that it is accepted as dogma.

But scientists react to evidence, and even Simpson, Darlington, and Mayr eventually applied their encyclopedic knowledge of organisms to the theory of continental drift. Suddenly the question of centers of origin, at least for many biotas, became less meaningful. There was not a center, there was a whole, whose pieces had simply ended up in different places. Of course, it is important to realize that, as pieces drift slowly apart, the life-forms aboard evolve in different directions and what were once the same species become differentiated. The longer the drift, the greater the differentiation. Thus, big differences between species on a far-off island and their counterparts on the mainland from which they have drifted imply long-term ancient drift; on an island closer to the mainland, smaller differences would be expected. Even on the far island, recent transoceanic flight dispersal might also be at play in some species, complicating the picture. There are innumerable complexities in the actual distribution of life-forms, but in some specific cases diagrams showing evolutionary development of certain plants and animals fit like a glove over maps of plate-tectonic drifting.

One way to look at vicariance is to think of a unified landmass as a vast set of enormous filing cabinets, the blocks of drawers filled with biotas. Some small groups may occupy only a few drawers, but more widespread life-forms will fill countless numbers. If giants take a notion to rearrange the cabinets randomly, the blocks of drawers that hold a particular life-form become separated, and the organisms begin to evolve independently. The result of such a shuffling would be very confusing, but if there were some way of knowing which drawers had been next to each other before the giants began their work, the biologist would often know where to go to find the drawers that hold related species. Such provisional maps of the old cabinets at various stages of their rearrangement have been suggested by geologists and paleographers. Conversely, if biologists undertake general inventories of all the drawers as they find them, they can test the geologists' maps and sometimes provide maps of their own.

For Nabokov's Blues in the Caribbean region, one has only to envision an ancient Central America breaking into pieces at a time well after the age of the dinosaurs and into the age of mammals, the Eocene period, about 50 million years ago. The pieces rafted out into the Caribbean as the West Indies, and the gap left was bridged again, some ten million years ago, by a new Central America, formed from the persistent volcanic activity of the time. Jamaica and the South Paleoisland of Hispaniola, once one biological entity, had in turn drifted apart and, with them, the ancestors of *Leptotes perkinsae* — Miss Perkins's Blue of Jamaica — and its sister species, found deep in Las Abejas. In the plate-tectonic terms of biogeography, such wholesale rafting of landmasses came to be called a Noah's Ark if entire floras and faunas were carried along for the ride on a substantially large island or a beached Viking ship if the vessel was smaller and its riders' chances of survival thus more tenuous. (The Indonesian island of Celebes, for instance, seems to be made up of nearly twenty fused fragments from various places.) Some biologists believe the South Paleoisland of Hispaniola was a Noah's Ark, slamming into the North Paleoisland along the Cul-de-Sac de Neiba and bringing with it its complement of butterflies and other precious living cargo.

When the Las Abejas team traveled to Hispaniola, they held a geological map of what appeared to be the old arrangement of the biological filing cabinets of the Caribbean. It suggested that a drawer that had once been next to Jamaica had been moved by the plate-tectonic giants to that little corner of the Dominican Republic. The researchers had high hopes of finding what was left of the contents of that drawer deep in Las Abejas. Sure enough, the broadleaf forest of the South Paleoisland shows many unmistakable biological links with Jamaica, among them the splendid *Anetia jaegeri* and a handful of newly discovered Hairstreaks; for Johnson, one of the most stirring is that little Blue from the bottom of Las Abejas that they were to name *Leptotes idealus.*

But biogeography is subject to innumerable complexities, and there are other puzzles in the bigger picture. Geological evidence suggests that even the highest parts of Jamaica were submerged for long durations some forty million years ago, during the Oligocene period, just when the island was on its voyage from Central America to its present position. If that is true it becomes hard to see how Blue butterflies and other creatures could have survived that part of the journey. One possibility is that parts of the original landmass are submerged now but were above sea level in the distant past, so that the original biota always had someplace to perch. Another, related solution might be that an older biota exists on what is actually a younger island, as in Hawaii, where islands continually submerge and rebuild, with the biota moving the relatively short distances from older island to younger by what is called a biogeographic escalator.

In any case Jamaica is a curious place in other ways, too. In their authoritative 1994 study of Antillean butterflies, David Spencer Smith of the Hope Entomological Collections at Oxford University and Lee D. and Jacqueline Y. Miller, a husband and wife from the University of Florida, noted that, of all the Caribbean islands, Jamaica appears to have the largest contingent of species that occur either nowhere else or at some seemingly odd or far-flung place. The nearest apparent relative of one Jamaican species, *Cyanophrys crethona,* a beautiful cyanine-colored Hairstreak with broad reddish borders on the underside, lives high atop ancient South American crustal blocks along the north rim of the Amazon Basin, indeed in the same geological formation from which Venezuela's Angel Fall, the highest waterfall in the world, tumbles for an astonishing 3,296 feet. William P. Comstock, Nabokov's mentor during his tenure at the American Museum of Natural History, was the first to point out this surprising Jamaican relationship, in a paper written with his colleague E. Irving Huntington in 1943. Johnson and Smith later named the butterfly *Cyanophrys roraimiensis,* after the Mt. Roraima plateau, on the border between Venezuela and Brazil, one crustal block on which it occurs.

On a still larger scale, the genus *Leptotes,* which includes Miss Perkins's Blue, is itself an extremely enigmatic biogeographic group. The wide transoceanic distribution of this genus, whose members are often called Zebra Blues because of their black-and-white-striped underwings, is hard to explain by any single theory. There are Zebra Blues in Africa, in South and Central America, on islands in the Caribbean, and in both the Atlantic and Pacific Oceans, including one species on the Galápagos Islands. Much of this distribution might relate the oldest crustal blocks of the Caribbean to the ancient supercontinent Gondwanaland, which in the age of the dinosaurs comprised the modern continents of Africa, South America, Antarctica, and Australia. Several other groups of modern butterflies and other biotas with close relatives in both Africa and South America seem to reflect the same plate-tectonic scenario, including yet another Blue butterfly grouping, *Brephidium,* a genus of three tiny species, two in the New World and one in Africa. But the oceanic island distributions of *Leptotes* do not reflect any well-known pattern of continental drift and are hard to explain without falling back on the extremely problematic notion of transoceanic dispersal by direct flight or accidental transport; all that can be said with confidence is that *Leptotes* is a very ancient line, tracing its ancestry to before the breakup of Gondwanaland.

All these mysteries, and others like them, are intrinsically fascinating and hot topics in biology. But several of their elements also bear directly on the question of Nabokov's scientific legacy and how he should be viewed in the realm of lepidoptery. First, the development of the theory of continental drift, now fundamental to discussion of biological distributions, took place after Nabokov had given up his professional career as a biologist. Before the geological mechanism of plate tectonics was discovered, many formidable scientists ridiculed the notion that continents could move. It would be misleading and anachronistic, therefore, to suggest that because Nabokov did not grasp this concept as it is understood today he was an incapable or naïve lepidopterist.

In fact, there are indications in "Notes on Neotropical Plebejinae" that he was uncomfortable with some of the assumptions about distribution that the conventional ideas of his day forced on him, particularly that all Old World butterflies must have arrived in the Western Hemisphere over the well-known Bering Strait land bridge. Regarding some lycaenids, including the African-American *Brephidium,* he wrote in his idiosyncratic way that "the difficulty of making them take the Bering Strait route is very great, but in the case of Plebejinae, the discontinuity and distribution is not so disconcerting, and I find it easier to give a friendly little push to some of the forms and hang my distributional horseshoes on the nail of Nome rather than postulate transoceanic land bridges in other parts of the world."

These are not the qualms of a naïf, and in the inevitable game of what if? in any assessment of the unfulfilled potential of Nabokov's truncated career, one might venture to say that he would have been among the first to utter a magisterial aha! when he saw what neat solutions to his reservations continental drift had to offer. If this principle of seeing Nabokov's career in the context of the time and environment in which he worked is respected and applied generally — not just to continental drift — it will be clear that he was a far more capable and sophisticated scientist than has too often been supposed. The period from the late 1940s to the early 1960s saw the introduction or development of a string of concepts that play a fundamental role in the conception of modern biology: revolutions were under way in the understanding of genetics, biogeography, evolution, taxonomy, and ecology, to name a few. By a quirk of fate Nabokov's formal scientific career was largely over by 1948, when he left the Museum of Comparative Zoology at Harvard to become a language professor at Cornell.

Yet another aspect of the discussions of continental drift is pertinent to Nabokov's legacy: the groups that he pioneered in "Notes on Neotropical Plebejinae" are increasingly involved in questions of "big science." That is, they are regularly viewed as evidence for the more sweeping questions of biogeography. Many well-studied groups can be and are used in this way, but Blue butterflies promise to become particularly important for answering major questions for parts of South America; for example, what was the origin of the life-forms in the High Andes? Often those who are the first to sort out the relevant groups take on an exalted status among the researchers who follow in their footsteps and build on their accomplishments. This kind of renown, very familiar in traditional lepidoptery, is perhaps a sort of reflected glory, but it is nevertheless well-deserved by someone whose work has proved to be a steady foundation for posterity.

"Notes on Neotropical Plebejinae," which dealt with only genuses whose members were restricted to Latin America, omitted *Leptotes*, which contains Miss Perkins's Blue and her relatives around the world. It was an arbitrary decision, though, one intended more than anything else to establish a convenient study group; Latin American *Leptotes* have long evolved alongside Nabokov's Plebejinae. Had he continued his formal scientific career and been able to elaborate on his work in the kind of course his research might have been expected to take, sooner or later he would probably have dealt with *Leptotes* as well; Bálint and Johnson, in fact, did so as a natural part of their research, and they eventually assigned three additional species to *Leptotes*, two of them named in honor of Nabokov.

After their morning flight in lower Abejas, lycaenid butterflies take shelter from the intense midday heat, but in the late afternoon they reemerge briefly to make a second foray for nectar. Only then did the lepidopterists begin the return journey out of the Las Abejas ravines, a steep uphill walk much more demanding than the morning trek in, and all the more exhausting because of the torrid sun. Here the lepidopterist's drive to solitude asserted itself, and although it was a little dangerous in the sweltering heat, the group usually walked out individually, each at his own speed, early arrivers waiting for the others at the truck. Some chose to make the trip hurriedly and then rest. Others went slowly, and once out of the dense subtropical forest they would stop from time to time to catch their breath in the meager shade of the narrow pine trunks. Years later they all remembered resting among the pines.

At one spot along the high ridges about two miles from Las Abejas, an immense blackbird rookery set up a constant din, which could be heard from hundreds of yards away. Paradoxically, this bedlam, a mix of thousands of frantic screeches and the churn of wind in the surrounding pines, never failed to induce in Johnson, as he rested from his climb, a sense of perfect tranquillity. It was a feeling of being utterly alone yet somehow comforted by the birds' chatter, as if on another plane of natural consciousness. Although he now thought of himself as an atheist, Johnson had spent five years in a monastery earlier in his life, and up on the trail by the blackbirds he often mused on whether it was possible to believe in a God. Perhaps God had set this complex universe in motion and then walked away; that would explain the faults of humanity and the degradation of the natural world. But as his head cleared Johnson could only laugh at himself: this notion was simply classical deism, a view that had gone out of style in the late eighteenth century.

On this same track year after year the lepidopterists often saw an old gray-white horse with a misshapen foreleg, obviously abandoned but surviving well on the abundant grass and frequent rain along the margin of the lush bottomland forest. He always kept his distance, off in the undergrowth where the subtropical forest joined the upland pines. Once the researchers tried to approach, but when he showed signs of bolting, they decided to spare him the fear. A couple of times they gathered grass in bunches and left it in piles on the trail, thinking he might wander over later and get an easier meal than he could forage for himself. Perhaps he did. Years later when Johnson read of the mare that followed Nabokov and his net through the wasteland near Santa Fe, he couldn't help thinking of the Las Abejas horse as a sort of puckish Nabokovian spirit marking his progress through this far outpost of the Latin American Blues.

Unlike Johnson and Matusik, Rawlins and Davidson collected insects by night. At the spot where the truck was parked, near the rim of the ravine, they had set up a base camp that provided a place to sleep out of the Las Abejas dews but still gave them relatively easy access to the bottom.

The camp also offered plenty of collecting opportunities, and its location has now been granted a certain kind of lepidopterological immortality by the minute printed letters on hundreds of labels at the American Museum of Natural History and the Carnegie Museum (18 degrees 10' N, 71 degrees 37' W, 1600 m, circa 4 km from upper Abejas). For Matusik and Johnson, however, the comfortable beds and hot showers at Ideal headquarters made the long daily drive worthwhile; by way of recompense they regularly hauled supplies out to the base camp for the night shift.

Out of the hardwood forest, Johnson and Matusik met Rawlins and Davidson at the camp, just loading up their heavy car batteries (for the ultraviolet light traps) and other equipment onto two-man shoulder poles. They would lug this paraphernalia down the trail, often slippery from the afternoon rain, by early evening, leaving plate-size water traps along the way to catch night-roving insects and spiders. And they would set a Malaise trap (named after the Frenchman who invented it), a long, fine net strung across a major flyway, like a stream or steep ravine, to catch hordes of small insects that fly into it. There was little time for small talk, only the request by the night team that their previous night's catch, laboriously pinned into small cardboard boxes, be taken back to Ideal for storage. This would keep ants or roaches, which can destroy a box of specimens overnight, from feasting upon the ranks upon ranks of wasps, bees, pinned moths, and beetles, which when studied in detail might provide vivid comment on the natural history of this enigmatic island.

Fifty miles away, back at Ideal headquarters at nightfall and after an ice-cold beer from Ideal's locked cooler (to which the company had kindly provided the key), Johnson and Matusik looked at their new forest Blue, with its large Perkins-like eyespot. At the time it was impossible to know exactly what they had. The catch might well prove to be a Miss Perkins's Blue, or something new, but either possibility was good to sleep on. Falling asleep after working in places like Las Abejas, one sees tokens of a long day of hard work, vivid blobs of green floating before half-closed eyes, much as drivers who have driven all night before taking rest are used to seeing the line of the road continue to pass before their eyes as sleep overcomes them.

Some environmentally minded people feel unease when large numbers of insects are taken by collectors, and some groups, like the North American Butterfly Association, are increasingly encouraging butterfly watching as opposed to collecting. But aside from a few specific instances, most conservationists agree that collecting in environmentally healthy areas, whether by science professionals or hobbyists, doesn't put a dent in fast-multiplying insect populations. Nabokov realized this, and although he was always careful to obtain the required permits, he chafed at restrictions on butterfly collecting in United States National Parks. "Here is a line of behavior," he wrote in 1953 in a letter to *The Lepidopterists' News*.

> Collect whatever insects you want wherever you go. When a Park official (they are all very nice fellows) dutifully remonstrates, just point to the nearest series of parked cars. Let him count the number of butterflies that the radiators have collected while passing through the Forbidden Zone. Have him talk to these motorists, take their license numbers, compute how many cars pass daily through and how many "bugs" they accumulate per day. Ask him when he has last seen any one with a butterfly net. If no cars are in sight, draw his attention to the millions of endemic insect larvae, mostly undescribed, fed to imported fish by imported fishermen. Tell him he has just destroyed a new species of mosquito on his cheek.

It is in fact the collecting work of scientists that enables conservationists to identify areas that merit legal protections as parks and preserves. One of the goals of the Las Abejas expedition was to help the Dominican museum of natural history and the country's parks service define what was unique about Las Abejas and why it should be protected. The real threat to butterflies is the destruction of habitat. Despite the official protection it has received, the future of the Sierra de Baoruco National Park and particularly that of Las Abejas is far from certain. When Johnson left there for the last time in 1988, he believed that the broadleaf forest wouldn't last for another decade; when Matusik returned in the summer of 1989, most of upper Abejas had been cut down. The entire team felt that the specimens they brought back could well offer science the final opportunity to study many Las Abejas species before they were driven extinct; for this reason they came back with specimens from all groups of insects and spiders. If they couldn't be saved from extinction at least these specimens would be rescued from scientific oblivion. Pathetically, this seemed to be the only available choice.

But in the Dominican Republic as a whole, the remnant of the South Paleoisland is far from alone in danger. At the end of the 1987 season at Las Abejas, the Carnegie expedition took a detour before returning to Santo Domingo, up the Sierra Baoruco by jeep trail and down across the Cul-de-Sac de Neiba — where they quickly contacted the local police to assure them that they had not arrived laterally through Haiti — then northward toward Hispaniola's Central Cordillera. Here the island's majestic uplands reach altitudes higher than 10,400 feet at Pico Duarte and nearby Loma la Pelona, a region known as the Switzerland of Hispaniola. But disappointment awaited, the cumulative effect of years of human activity. What were once isolated villages had become boom towns; deep ravines where subtropical forest species typifying the North Paleoisland had once been collected had been obliterated by giant earthmovers; small desert oases with their own unique faunas were now burgeoning with irrigated crops. Thus the two-edged sword of progress, here reflecting what had happened decades earlier in the United States.

In 1985 Johnson and Matusik had collected native species, including one that was new, literally outside the doors of their hotel in the town of Jarabacoa; but on this trip the expedition had to drive over fifty miles from the same hotel to find natural vegetation in which to do follow-up sampling work. That distance was etched in John Rawlins's mind because he had watched the mileage gauge simply out of disgust. Not far away Matusik knew one of the few spots in the Central Cordillera with a population of hard-to-find Clearwing butterflies — odd, fragile, shade-loving creatures with elongated, transparent wings, they look more like damselflies than Lepidoptera; their weak flight and reluctance to leave cover make it probable that their distribution in the Antilles is due entirely to vicariance. The Central Cordillera Clearwings lived in a ravine abutting a cemetery, which the expedition used as a landmark to find them. But when they crossed the cemetery they discovered that the entire ravine had been filled in and leveled by the earthmovers that are obliterating the natural landscape of the country.

At the base of another ravine where the expedition finally pulled up well after dark and amid the mountain coolness, they saw thousands of eerie lights from deep in the canyon bottom. The lights were dying fireflies caught in the silken webs of tropical black widow spiders. As they were driving back that night along a weaving road some five thousand feet above the valley below, a different light pervaded, that of the scattered towns that a decade before had had no electricity — a silent, twinkling witness to the accelerating transformation occurring throughout Latin America. In areas where soils are fertile or there is some other exploitable attraction — mountain havens or beautiful beaches — new access roads can transform the landscape in a matter of months. Electricity and piped water come first, then regularly arriving payloads of trucked-in goods.

Dirt paths are transformed to paved roads, and houses spring up along the lines of the new sewers, followed soon by restaurants and hotels.

For the local people, this is essential progress; for the scientists who return every year or two, it is a startling lesson in exponential change. Where one year it is impossible to find a bed or a meal, one now has the choice of two or three hotels, a restaurant, café, or pizzeria, perhaps even a movie theater, each marked with bright neon. But for the student of nature, there is always shockingly less than there was before.

One of the scientists who has been working in the Dominican Republic more recently is Andrei Sourakov of the California Academy of Sciences, like Nabokov, a Russian emigrant. Following up on the work of Schwartz, Matusik, and Johnson, Sourakov adopted Hispaniola's brown Calistos as his specialty. He was particularly interested in learning to what extent the populations of this genus of Satyr butterfly, spread out across the island, were separate species or disjunct pockets of the same species isolated by continuing ecological deterioration. In the course of his travels in 1996, Sourakov decided to seek out an eccentric American biologist, David Kenneth Wetherbee. Once the youngest man ever to be the curator of Harvard University's ornithological collection, Wetherbee, now seventy-six, had retired to a remote area of Hispaniola's Central Cordillera a decade before. In the small mountain village of Restauración, in Dajabón Province along the Haitian border, he had spent the years patiently pecking out on his typewriter a series of studies of Hispaniolan natural history.

Arriving at Restauración on a flatbed truck that served as a public bus in the remote mountains, Sourakov found Wetherbee living in a small peasant shack. The only objects on the dirt floor were two beds covered by mosquito netting, a careless pile of books and papers on biological subjects, and a locked wooden chest to protect his food supply from casual pilfering by village children. Wetherbee's doorway was full of them when Sourakov arrived, but he himself sat in a corner, reading and writing, and paying them no attention. Some had recently broken his only remaining aquarium. "There goes my chance to study the life histories of the local fish," lamented Wetherbee, who in a sense was living amid a multitude of last chances.

The biologist volunteered to take Sourakov on a hike toward Guayajayuco, a village near the Haitian border where he knew of a surviving population of the rare silver-striped *Calisto chrysaoros*, the butterfly that had enticed Johnson and Matusik into the tangled bottom of Las Abejas in 1987. As they approached, Wetherbee pointed to evidence of the tremendous pressure on the land. At the site itself nearly all the remnants of natural vegetation had been cleared away, replaced by some potato plants, parched and nearly dead in the hot sun. As Sourakov surveyed one side of a closely cropped ridge for any signs of what he hoped would be a few remaining *chrysaoros*, a man with a machete was clearing all that was left of the native plants on the other side. The *Calistos* here were destined for extinction.

On the way back the two men fell in with a group of indigent Haitians who had crossed the border to beg for money and food. Wetherbee said that he was saddened by this and that he saw more of it every year. Sourakov learned later that Wetherbee had died a few months after his visit.

"After six trips to the Dominican Republic," Sourakov wrote to Johnson,

> I almost feel at home. My English-speaking intellectual friends in Santo Domingo think of me as an odd fish when I tell them about the places that I visit on their island. "Don't you have anything better to do than torture yourself with bad hotels, old pickup trucks, and sleeping next to a fire on the cold ground? Our island has so many nice resorts like Samaná, Boca Chica, and Puerto Plata." How can I explain to them that I might be one of the last visitors to the interior of the island who can appreciate the biodiversity once found everywhere, but which now only survives because of the inaccessibility of a few godforsaken places. Every peasant shack I pass during my journeys has four or five friendly young faces (the future of the country) looking out to greet me. When this future grows up, it will demand land to live and raise food on, and the current weak protection of the national parks will not then stand a chance.

Another day in the Sierra de Baoruco eventually brought Matusik and Johnson face to face with two contradictory views of Caribbean Blues — the first proposed by Vladimir Nabokov, a little-known lepidopterist whose work seemed to have been passed over by science, and the other by Norman Riley, the enormously prestigious and influential keeper of the Department of Entomology at the British Museum.

By 5:30 A.M., as usual, the two were up and ready to walk the quarter of a mile across the cactus-strewn desert between Ideal's seaside corporate residences and the company's breakfast cantina. The buildings, on the cliffs about fifty feet above the Caribbean, form a shelter from the strong winds that blow from landward in the late afternoons, and butterflies find it convenient to take refuge there — enough of them to support a large population of fat green spiders. Here in 1986 Albert Schwartz's team found a Maesites Hairstreak (*Chlorostrymon maesites*), a brilliant violet, fingernail-size Caribbean Hairstreak, the first ever recorded in Hispaniola, dead and entangled in a spider's web.

Schwartz had often visited the site over the years, but he had never seen the Maesites Hairstreak before; in 1986, after that first chance find, he and a colleague caught twenty-three others, all but one from that single spot at Cabo Rojo, despite many hours spent looking for them elsewhere in the region. Johnson and Matusik, for their part, failed to find a single specimen on any of their Dominican Republic trips (although afterward Johnson made checking spiderwebs part of his ordinary field routine, and was well rewarded; it was a trick with which Nabokov was familiar). The reason for this puzzling pattern is a central feature of the life cycle of butterflies — the adults of many species tend to emerge simultaneously in waves, or pulses, often in response to specific environmental factors. *Speak, Memory* tells how a Hawkmoth chrysalis Nabokov had kept for seven years hatched in the overheated railway car during a train journey. One effect of this kind of cycle is that it can create a misleading impression about the rarity of a given butterfly, particularly in remote, inaccessible areas where there are no year-round local collectors. Unless transitory outsiders are lucky enough to appear on the scene at precisely the right moment, they will find nothing on the wing, but that doesn't mean that their quarry is rare — the entire population is simply in another, harder-to-detect stage of development, waiting to burst out when conditions are right.

Pulses can be spectacular. The previous night it had rained, an infrequent occurrence in the region around Ideal headquarters, and the desert was alive with butterflies. Here, for the only time in any of the Las Abejas expeditions, appeared the Swallowtail butterfly *Protesilaus zonarius,* a two-by-four-inch, gorgeously green-and-black-striped species, an exotic cousin of the familiar black-and-white Zebra Swallowtail of North America. With their characteristic wispy, hummingbird-like flight, throngs of the butterflies were hovering just above the surface of the thousands of mud puddles made by the recent rain. Johnson and Matusik made a point of capturing many of the Swallowtails that day because, as they well knew, no American collection had more than a handful of these insects, and those were from old collections, most often labeled only "Haiti." There was no risk of endangering these butterflies, coaxed by the rain from their chrysalises and covering every puddle in sight. It was a familiar phase in the desert life of the region, a day that had occurred regularly over the millennia, el Día de las Mariposas — the Day of the Butterflies.

This was also a day to bring supplies to the Las Abejas base camp; the extra time needed for that chore limited the day team's hunting to the pine forests around the camp. It was a fascinating area, where Schwartz had collected two new Calistos, common in the forest there but known from nowhere else. Blues and Hairstreaks frequented the blooming legumes that dot the sandy open areas here, which, as one could tell by the deep black scars on many trees, had been burned over years before by a terrible fire. Other rare butterflies also frequented these hot, sunny clearings, including a fast-flying, fist-size, vividly blue-and-black species known as the Royal Blue, although it is not a Blue at all but a member of the nymphalid family, and at the time known from only a handful of specimens, and a suite of dry-forest Skippers recently discovered by Schwartz and his colleagues.

"Who knows what else is up there?" Matusik wondered as he popped the clutch to get the truck out of Ideal's parking lot past the gate guard. Every day the researchers drove through the gate, shouting, "Las Abejas," to the guard, so he would know where to tell the authorities to look if the team did not return by nightfall. That day dense clouds were rising above the mountains, dense enough to have prevented the trip had not the night team at the Las Abejas camp needed water and other supplies. There was nothing more frustrating than making the fifty-mile truck ride and three-mile hike only to find Las Abejas shrouded in clouds. Butterflies are cold-blooded and need the sun to bring them out; without it collecting is abysmal. Unlike in Argentina, where a team of a dozen lepidopterists went years later in pursuit of more of Nabokov's Blues, in these relatively low-lying mountains one can't drive high enough to escape the clouds.

By the time the men reached Ideal's last open-pit mine — where the truck had to maneuver around behemoth earthmoving equipment and huge mounds of earth that shifted from day to day in the course of the mining work to find the track toward Las Abejas — the clouds were boiling up and burning off magnificently. Amid a confusion of gray and white, the sun was working furiously to resurrect the day for collecting. At the Las Abejas base camp, it was shining gloriously.

It may seem incredible that at a distance of thirty feet a lepidopterist in a moving vehicle might realize that there is something he has never seen before fluttering in the air beside the road. But despite the chance of making a fool of oneself, it is a chance worth taking, and it is not unusual for lepidopterists to stop and jump out after spotting some likely quarry in the roadside brush. (In the 1970s the Panamanian lepidopterist Gordon Small tried this trick and put his foot on a Bushmaster, a well-known cautionary tale among lepidopterists; it was a long trip to the hospital, but Small made it in time to save his life. Hispaniola has no known poisonous snakes.) As he pulled into the camp, Matusik spotted something unusual, slammed on the brakes, and was out of the truck, net in hand, instantly.

The Blues that normally frequent the sunny breaks in the Sierra de Baoruco pine forest are Miami Blues, or *Hemiargus thomasi* (named from specimens from the region by Nabokov's friend Harry Clench in 1941); they have profusely spotted underwings with an orangish margin. But Matusik's informed eye caught a flash of uniform gray, and almost before Johnson could react, he had the butterfly in his net. From what was known at the time, Matusik's catch was immediately recognizable as a member of the genus *Hemiargus* but not apparently of the usual species *thomasi*, and in fact it had peculiarities that no one had seen before. It was whitish gray on the undersurface of the wing, with five big, well-defined black spots. Matusik carefully placed it in a small glassine envelope and popped in a label precisely noting the locality. He and Johnson then took the time to collect a longer series of *thomasi*.

Many butterflies congregate at mud holes or wallows, attracted by the moisture and by liquid animal wastes on which they can feed. Blues go mud-puddling with particular passion, and Nabokov fondly referred to this well-known habit in *Speak, Memory*. In the region around the base of the Sierra de Baoruco, there are many large cattle wallows around watering troughs, where Blues, Hairstreaks, and other butterflies gather by the thousands. The Las Abejas expeditions traditionally visited a large wallow on the road to the base camp, at a place called Las Mercedes, nothing more than a cattle-watering site and the quarters of some transient herders, surrounded by profuse thickets of thorny acacia bushes. Here dozens of Blues could be caught with a single swipe of the net, and it was easy to sort through the common species — like *Hemiargus thomasi* — and occasionally find a very rare *Pseudochrysops bornoi*. Nabokov himself, in "Notes on Neotropical Plebejinae," had set up the genus *Pseudochrysops* for this one species, which is easily recognized by the little tails on its wings. The expedition tried to obtain enough specimens of *P. bornoi* for its anatomy to be studied in some detail in relation to the equally rare populations in Puerto Rico and Cuba. Researchers wanted to know whether such far-flung groups indeed represented one species or whether a similar outward appearance belied several, a phenomenon known as hidden diversity, with which Nabokov was well-acquainted.

Among their equipment Johnson and Matusik carried a huge net, its open mouth a full yard in diameter, mounted on a twenty-foot extension handle. Under the right conditions it could be used for catching huge quantities of swarming specimens at one swipe — mud-puddling species, which will usually sit until the net is thrown over them, or those known for bursts of swarming behavior, like some of the desert Whites and Sulphurs. Alternatively, it could be used in the rain forest to extend a lepidopterist's reach in situations in which accuracy was problematic. Matusik, however, who is built powerfully, was the only one strong enough to wield it effectively in this fashion, and he regularly used it here over the wallows.

Along with the specimens of *Pseudochrysops bornoi* he was able to catch, he scooped up many *Hemiargus thomasi* to use in comparative anatomical studies back in New York; again, there was no way to know it immediately, but unrecognized among the *thomasi* lurked a special kind of treasure ready to reveal its surprise. As with the Miss Perkins look-alike and the Blue Matusik took at the base camp, though, some time would pass before the significance of these studies could be realized. The Las Abejas expeditions reaped so much material that some of it has not been digested to this day. In 1987 alone, some 20,000 specimens were taken from the Sierra de Baoruco region, among them 6 new species of butterflies, 150 new moths, and as yet uncounted numbers of probable new species from other groups of insects.

In all the lepidopterists visiting Las Abejas had netted twelve new species of butterflies: three Blues, four Hairstreaks, three Satyrs, and two Skippers, one of these last so unusual it has still to be named.

In a laboratory in New York, the internal anatomy of common Blues would be compared with that of Matusik's two unusual catches; if the anatomies proved similar, it would suggest that Matusik's black-spotted Blue might be merely a genetic aberration. But if the anatomy of the find differed significantly from that of *thomasi*, and from those of other known species of *Hemiargus*, it could well be a species new to science.

In the end Johnson discovered it was that and quite a bit more: not only a new butterfly but one that came with a mystery attached that it took Vladimir Nabokov to unravel.

4

Lumpers and Splitters

My work enraptures but utterly exhausts me. . . . To know that no one before you has seen an organ you are examining, to trace relationships that have occurred to no one before, to immerse yourself in the wondrous crystalline world of the microscope, where silence reigns, circumscribed by its own horizon, a blindingly white arena — all this is so enticing that I cannot describe it.

— *Letter to his sister Elena Sikorski, 1945*

RESEARCH BIOLOGISTS SAY that natural history museums, together with their laboratories, are like libraries, except instead of books they hold specimens. For taxonomists the dissection of a specimen is the equivalent of opening one of the books and reading it. Butterfly morphology, the study of the internal structures of Lepidoptera, specifically the genitalia, is tedious and exacting labor. It is also exhausting; willingness to tolerate the drudgery is a requisite for most laboratory taxonomists, for Nabokov no less than others. But the search for hidden information is the kind of detective work that brings rich rewards and reveals an unorthodox beauty. It is also the key to the third item on Nabokov's list of the joys of lepidoptery — the possibility of exploding an old taxonomic classification, upsetting the old scheme, and, as Nabokov put it, confounding its obtuse champions.

Nabokov knew of genitalic dissection by the 1930s at the latest, since he mentioned it in *The Gift,* and he appears to have been introduced to its practice at the American Museum of Natural History soon after arriving in New York City as a refugee in 1940. In the first paper he published in America — the study of his *Lysandra cormion,* the Blue butterfly he caught in the Maritime Alps of France before the war — Nabokov thanked his mentor at the museum, William P. Comstock, for dissecting the genitalia of his specimens. But he clearly learned fast. Morphology was the basic tool of classification in his more ambitious papers written at the Museum of Comparative Zoology at Harvard in the 1940s, including "Notes on Neotropical Plebejinae." His detailed drawings of the internal anatomy of butterflies became a hallmark of those studies. Nabokov was one of the first lepidopterists to emphasize the anatomy of the female butterfly in this kind of work; remarkably, though as useful for identifying species as the males, females were often ignored at this time, no more perhaps than a curious reflection of the era's cultural chauvinism. Nabokov was also among the first researchers to make more than a single genital illustration for each species; instead, particularly in "Notes on Neotropical Plebejinae," he illustrated series of specimens, the multiple illustrations buttressing his hypotheses concerning ranges of variation in one species and the hiatuses, or breaks, in those characters that distinguish different species.

Nabokov's emphasis on the overriding importance of morphological study was particularly important for Blue butterflies, because individuals of different species, and different genuses, too, often appear quite similar in overall appearance and generalized wing patterns. "I am guided among other things by the belief that the systematist may fare better when keeping to the all-important morphological moment," he wrote in his 1944 work on *Lycaeides*. His insistence on this point surprised even Nabokov's peers — some of whom seldom ventured beyond the wing markings for identification — but he felt so strongly about it that a reference to its origins found its way into *Speak, Memory*. During his boyhood, he wrote, great upheavals were taking place in lepidoptery. The Germans, led by Otto Staudinger, who was also the head of Staudinger & Bang-Haas, Europe's largest firm of insect dealers, had dominated the field in the nineteenth century. But while they remained content to classify butterflies by features visible to the naked eye, English-speaking writers were beginning to introduce taxonomic changes based on the microscopic study of organs. "The Germans did their best to ignore the new trends and continued to cherish the philatelylike side of entomology," Nabokov wrote. "Their solicitude for the 'average collector who should not be made to dissect' is comparable to the way nervous publishers of popular novels pamper the 'average reader' — who should not be made to think."

Insects, having no internal skeleton, rely on bonelike, or sclerotinal, structures, which are actually inward developments of the exoskeleton, to fulfill the function of hard internal body parts, most importantly those that maneuver the genitalia during mating. Because these genital structures are intricately varied and, unlike the rest of the butterfly's body, rigid and extremely well-defined, they are crucial to identifying specimens and determining their relationships to one another. These organs are complex, with variously shaped appendages, extremities, and attachments, which Nabokov described as "minuscule sculpturesque hooks, teeth, spurs, etc. visible only under the microscope." He was in fact much more inventive than the common run of lepidopterists in his descriptions of genitalic parts and shapes. To note only a few, he compared the shapes of various organs to a buffalo hump, a beheaded dromedary, and an elephant. Another, he wrote, surrounded the front of the male butterfly's penis "in the manner of a stiffly bulging waistcoat, too ample as it were for the body it encloses."

Common sense suggests that the structure of the sexual organs of butterflies corresponds to some degree with mating compatibility among individuals and species. This is one of the reasons that Nabokov had serious difficulties in accepting a species definition for Lepidoptera that involved interbreeding but not structure, as Ernst Mayr had urged. It also led to the rather Victorian-sounding notion, common in Nabokov's time and earlier, of a lock-and-key mechanism; according to this theory, within an interbreeding group, presumably a species, only the male's key (the penis, or aedeagus) could open the lock on the corresponding genitalia of the female. It is clear that this idea was an oversimplification, and Nabokov reached that conclusion early in his work. "A certain harmony, as yet rather obscure, seems to exist between a particular type of male armature and a particular female one," he wrote in "Notes on Neotropical Plebejinae."

> The impression I have formed so far that with "natural genera" specific differentiation in these organs is more marked (or at least easier to observe) in the male, may be due to insufficient investigation, but anyway I cannot find any *exact* correlation between female lock and male key. In what manner and to what extent the sclerotized parts of the sexes in Plebejinae fit each other during copulation is not clear, but I doubt whether the valves, the termination of which is evolutionarily the most vulnerable part, come into any direct contact with such structures in the female organ that might lead to some intersexual adaptation.

As this observation makes clear, the precise function of many parts of the sexual anatomy of a butterfly was mysterious in Nabokov's time, and it remains so today. In fact, a substantial number of genital parts have specific names, mostly incomprehensible to the nonspecialist, not because of the role they play in mating but only because they are so useful in taxonomy. A lepidopterist with routine access to extremely sophisticated equipment could make a splash by running a CT scan or NMR imaging on a pair of copulating butterflies, which would yield more precise information about the mechanics of mating. But no one has done this, and the focus on the mating habits of Lepidoptera in modern science has shifted away from mere mechanics to the study of the interaction of minute sensory stimuli, of the powerful chemical communicators known as pheromones, and of finely tuned correlations between reproductive isolation and ecological conditions.

In any case, the many components of butterfly genitalia and their functions in mating vary greatly among families, genuses, and species. Some structures share names but not true biological function or evolutionary affinity, since in various groups some genitalic parts developed from different segments of the insects' abdomens. While this extreme differentiation is what makes butterfly genitalia so useful to the taxonomist, it also makes generalized discussion of their structure problematic. But there are some common denominators.

The male genitalia are made up of a sclerotized ring, the vinculum, within which is mounted a rodlike penis, the aedeagus. The ring anchors the muscles that move the penis. Along its ventral, or bottom edge, the two halves of the ring are joined by a strong tab, called the saccus; a structure called the labides fills the same function on the dorsal edge of the ring. The ring also bears a number of clasping organs, which physically connect the male genitalia with the female during mating. In nature mating takes place soon after the adults emerge from the chrysalis, sometimes preceded by elaborate courtship dances or mutual stroking of the wings. Copulation occurs with the partners facing opposite directions, the tips of their abdomens joined; many species, though not all, copulate while locked together in flight, with both partners, or sometimes only one, active, again depending on the species. The principal clasping parts of the male are the clasper (or valvae, or valves), mounted ventrally on the ring, and the tegumen and uncus, both mounted dorsally on the ring.

In Blues the valves are the foundation for many smaller structures with names like rostellum, mentum, and ostia; collectively they are called terminalia. These structures are the ones traditionally used in taxonomic classification, and Nabokov dealt with all of them in his work. Likewise, on the tegumen/uncus are other structures he frequently mentioned, like the falces and labides. Another distinguishing characteristic of Blues is a quite stout and complex penis, with numerous specialized structures, compared with a more simple and elongate organ in most groups. Blues also offer supporting struts and other subsidiary features that do not occur in other groups, even in other lycaenids.

Historically, it was the male genitalia, particularly the clasper, that formed the basis of morphological comparisons. Females were less commonly studied, though, as suggested, this was largely the result of convention. The female genitalia in most butterflies are made up of a sclerotized tube, the ductus bursae, which receives the penis. The inner end of the tube leads to a sperm sac, the corpus bursae. Inside the corpus bursae are structures called signa, which perhaps act like little hooks to hold sperm sacs, although this is a matter of dispute. Female butterflies can store sperm to fertilize eggs well after mating has taken place; for this there is a separate sac, connected to the corpus bursae by a seminal duct. It is usually attached right at or near the juncture of the ductus bursae and the corpus bursae. The terminal end of the ductus bursae, which actually receives the penis, often has lips called lamellae, or structures called superior and inferior genital plates that may have reciprocal clasping abilities of their own.

Female Blues share relative genitalic complexity with their mates. Often instead of a simple tubelike ductus to receive the penis, they have a membranous duct leading to the sperm sac, and, in lieu of the elongate tube, more complex structures at the terminus called the henium and mentum, which function like lips or plates. In addition, two flaps protrude from the female at the end of the terminalia, the papillae anales, which may also provide clues to the butterfly's taxonomy.

As Nabokov mentioned in *Speak, Memory,* it had been the English pioneers of morphology who recognized that these structures consistently differed in shape from species to species and that they thus offered tremendous utility for taxonomy. But Nabokov took this principle further than most lepidopterists of his time, who tended to consider only the general features of the clasping parts of the male organ. Instead, Nabokov stressed the multiple differences in all the parts of the genital anatomy, in females as well as males. And by being extremely specific about the shapes of the various structures along the contour of the male clasper, as well as many other organs, he introduced many new structures into the study of Blues, the names of which, he noted proudly, found their way into biological dictionaries.

"Humerulus, alula, bullula, mentum, rostellum, sagum, surculus, Bayard's Angulation or Point, Chapman's Process — are terms I invented thinking them up as I went," he wrote in a letter to the lepidopterist Alexander Klots. This is part of the taxonomist's unceasing attempt to find "new characters" for species identification, and such innovation is never without controversy; an amused reference in the same letter refers to the genitalic work of the Frenchman Henri Stempffer, which Nabokov obviously considered less punctilious than his own: "'Stempffer's Process' is really a euphemism: it is something he saw (a projection of the uncus in *shasta* [a kind of North American Blue butterfly]) and I did not. I think it was merely a hair scale that had got involved in his preparation (he had another mistake in one of his first papers on these things: leaving his falces for too long a period in a corrosive solution which caused structurally not existing serrations which he dutifully figured)."

Another of Nabokov's intriguing innovations, originating in his 1944 work on the northern genus *Lycaeides,* involved what he came to call his "magic triangles." He was very proud of this straightforward but novel analytical method and recommended it to colleagues. It seemed to impress them, too: the margins of Klots's personal copy of Nabokov's 1943 study of *Lycaeides* contain doodles of magic triangles alongside Nabokov's text. It was a simple method: inside two-dimensional outline drawings of a series of similar genitalic structures, Nabokov would draw a triangle; the base of the triangle was the length of the structure, and the apex represented its maximum width. The resulting shapes of the triangles measured the relative dimensions of parts, offering an effective way to compare the overall shapes of a series of genitalic structures. Nabokov believed that relationships among species could be traced through this examination of their structural prototype, or ground plan.

Although qualitative techniques like the magic triangles have been largely replaced today by more exacting quantitative statistical analyses, there was a larger significance to this method. Linking the progression of changes in the triangular ground plan from group to group, Nabokov suggested directions of evolutionary development within a group of related species. This approach closely approximates the modern phylogenetic practice of looking for "direction" or "polarity" in evolution — from the most primitive of characters to the most advanced — precisely the kind of information that yields a true genealogy. Nabokov came remarkably close to this modern idea, for instance, writing in his 1944 work on *Lycaeides:* "I view evolution in *Lycaeides* as . . . its general graduation from the most primitive structures to the most specialized ones." His magic triangles represent a concrete expression of that very modern idea.

With Nabokov's studies of wing markings thrown into the mix, it was clear that no one else was applying such detailed analysis to Blue butterflies in the 1940s. Indeed, studies of such depth were relatively uncommon anywhere in lepidoptery. But while Nabokov's work on *Lycaeides* had relied heavily on details of wing pattern, he put this method aside in "Notes on Neotropical Plebejinae," which was predominately an anatomical study. This turning away from the wing spots was perhaps a reflection of the study's small sampling of Latin American specimens and of its concentration on genuses rather than species. Historically, anatomy had been shown to be less variable and thus more reliable in establishing those broader groups of butterflies.

It was, then, his dissection of genitalia, at the Museum of Comparative Zoology, that led to Nabokov's "rather drastic rearrangement" of the Neotropical Blues in 1945. Based not on any new discoveries per se but on the museum specimens that were more or less available to any interested researcher, Nabokov's work thoroughly transformed the conventional taxonomy of the Blue butterflies of the Neotropics. The Blue butterfly species known from around the Caribbean basin and Central America, for example, had simply been lumped into Hübner's 1818 genus *Hemiargus*. Nabokov, however, recognizing four distinct generic groupings here, named three new ones — *Pseudochrysops, Cyclargus,* and *Echinargus* — and "restricted" *Hemiargus;* that is, he retained Hübner's name but used it to cover only a fraction of its former species. Thus, to distinguish the different usages of the same name, taxonomists might use Latin to refer to "*Hemiargus sensu* Nabokov," meaning Nabokov's conception of the genus, or "*Hemiargus sensu* Hübner," for Hübner's very different one. (Except for *Echinargus*, which Nabokov knew from Mexico and Trinidad, all these are Antillean groups.)

In South America, where little taxonomic work on Blue butterflies had been done since the Age of Exploration, nearly all the Blues with which Nabokov concerned himself were mistakenly placed in a genus of Copper butterflies called *Lycaena,* an error that stemmed from most South American species' orange-tinged coloration; the rest were in a genus that the German Max Draudt had named *Itylos* in 1919. Nabokov, however, from his genitalic studies in 1945, distinguished five natural groupings from South America that he considered genuses: four new ones that he named himself — *Parachilades, Pseudothecla, Pseudolucia,* and *Paralycaeides* — and the now restricted *Itylos* (*sensu* Nabokov). In the end he had named seven new genuses of Polyommatini and restricted two others.

This sudden and extensive transformation in the taxonomy of Blue butterflies, the admittedly small sample of specimens on which it was based, and Nabokov's modest standing and reputation in the wider world of contemporary lepidoptery go far to explain Charles Remington's remark that the rearrangement "raised eyebrows" when it was published. It should have been just the sort of thing to set off the taxonomic polemics that Nabokov would have relished. In the aftermath other lepidopterists might have been expected to consider his arguments and either reject his findings in favor of another scheme or begin following his results in their own work, lending them currency among biologists. Eventually, the winners in this competition for shelf space would see their work taken up by the writers of more popular and widely read regional butterfly books or field manuals. The losers would be marginalized or forgotten. This market system of academic consensus was the way reputations were made in Nabokov's day, and to some extent the same is true today.

But Blue butterflies, particularly Neotropical Blues, were a backwater, and there were not many immediate ramifications to Nabokov's paper, in part because it was the victim of bad timing. His treatise in fact appeared shortly after two influential general studies of the Lycaenidae of the Caribbean. The first, "Lycaenidae of the Antilles," published in 1943, was a collaboration of Nabokov's former mentor, William Comstock, and E. Irving Huntington, a successful businessman-lepidopterist and research associate at the American Museum of Natural History. The second study, which appeared in 1944, applied this taxonomy to a wildlife survey of Puerto Rico, a long-term project of the American Museum of Natural History. Unlike Nabokov two years later, Comstock and Huntington brought nothing new to the general taxonomy for the region; in the case of the Neotropical Blues, they deviated little from Draudt's rudimentary arrangement of 1921.

Yet these works, by well-known authors, were considered authoritative by most general lepidopterists for years after their publication. Both were published by the New York Academy of Sciences, a prestigious organization at the time and one that typified many aspects of the scientific culture of the World War II era. Members of the academy, whose numbers included wealthy amateurs and interested businessmen as well as professional scientists, met weekly at the American Museum of Natural History for informal discussions on cross-disciplinary and specialized topics, and for the fellowship of mutual interest. Later the organization's importance dwindled, a reflection of the growing sophistication within scientific disciplines and the increasing emphasis on specialization that was driving science.

The irony of the situation is that Comstock seems to have viewed his protégé and former student of morphology as the authority for the Neotropical Polyommatini; in 1953 he helped name a species that fit into one of Nabokov's Neotropical genuses, *Echinargus huntingtoni* (after his old coauthor). Had the timing been different he might well have recognized Nabokov's entire classification in his regional book on the Antilles, and Nabokov's place in lepidoptery would have looked very different over the last fifty years. As it was, Comstock's book, written too early to consider Nabokov's groupings, continued to exert influence over other lepidopterists.

In 1964, in a synopsis of Antillean Lycaenidae, Nabokov's friend and fellow researcher from Harvard, Harry Clench, by then associate curator at the Carnegie Museum of Natural History in Pittsburgh, called "Notes on Neotropical Plebejinae" a work "of particular significance," praising Nabokov for bringing "an intimate knowledge of Palaearctic and Nearctic groups to bear on the Neotropical fauna, where this knowledge was peculiarly valuable." Clench lent some credence to Nabokov's anatomical distinctions, but in the end he decided to view his colleague's Caribbean groups as subgenuses under *Hemiargus*. And, somewhat puzzlingly, he still considered the 1943 work by Comstock and Huntington "the basic reference" on the Neotropics, probably for no reason other than the utilitarian one that it treated both Blues and Hairstreaks, whereas Nabokov's work was less comprehensive.

The tendency to view Comstock and Huntington's work as authoritative was monumentally confirmed in 1975, when Norman Riley of the British Museum published his popular *Field Guide to the Butterflies of the West Indies,* an elaborate volume that followed his already successful *Field Guide to the Butterflies of Britain and Europe,* prepared in 1970 with his British Museum colleague Lionel C. Higgins. Both of these radiantly colorful books followed the format of the famous field guides to birds pioneered by Roger Tory Peterson, which became popular best-sellers in America. In his later years Nabokov was in demand as a reviewer of such works, because of the appeal that celebrity added to his expertise and enthusiasm, and he wrote a very positive notice of *Field Guide to the*

Butterflies of Britain and Europe in the *Times Educational Supplement* (London) in 1970.

Riley was an immensely influential figure throughout his career. Among his many other positions, he became in 1924 the editor of *The Entomologist*, one of Nabokov's favorite journals, and held that post for forty years. He joined the British Museum staff in 1911, at age twenty-one, and in 1932 was named head of the museum's insect collections or, in its imperial-sounding nomenclature, Keeper of the Department of Entomology. As such Riley held a good deal of sway in entomological circles around the world, particularly after World War II, a crucial period in taxonomy when an international commission was formed to standardize the rules of classification. Riley had published some four hundred technical papers on butterflies by the time he died in 1979; he was eighty-four when *Field Guide to the Butterflies of the West Indies* went to print.

Unsurprisingly, Riley's book was extremely popular and influential, and, unfortunately for Nabokov, the view he adopted for Caribbean Blues was very different from that outlined in "Notes on Neotropical Plebejinae." Riley accepted *Pseudochrysops,* a genus name Nabokov had erected for a unique Blue butterfly with tailed wings, known in Nabokov's time only from the desert areas around Las Abejas and Haiti. Perhaps the physical appearance of this butterfly, with such obvious wing distinctions, made it easy for Riley to accept it as a separate biological entity. But Nabokov had placed nearly all his remaining Caribbean species into the two genuses *Hemiargus* and *Cyclargus* on the long-neglected basis of genital differences. The species in question were externally similar, with their blue upper sides and speckled undersides, a configuration that Nabokov termed the catochrysopoid pattern. In his book Riley backpedaled, ignored Nabokov's *Cyclargus,* and left Hübner's *Hemiargus* intact.

This view, coming from such a formidable source, was adopted by virtually everyone else. The average reader of Riley's book certainly had no idea of a competing history for *Hemiargus;* Riley didn't even mention Nabokov's name. Moreover, it is unusual to refer to morphology in a popular work, and Riley's field guide was no exception; reviews of the time praised the book, and, outside scattered references in technical specialist literature, Nabokov's classification was by and large forgotten.

In the ten or so major field guides or regional treatments on the butterflies of North America and the Caribbean region that appeared between 1945 and 1995, two recognized his new genuses as subgenuses of *Hemiargus,* but the rest reverted wholly to *Hemiargus sensu* Hübner. And, ironically, the one new Nabokovian genus that Riley did use, the flashy *Pseudochrysops*, was also sunk back into *Hemiargus* in the books of Riley's successors. In nearly every case the reason given for the classification adopted was that a previous field guide or regional treatment had used it. In what might be interpreted as the ultimate affront, a review of Caribbean butterflies published by the Academy of Natural Sciences of Philadelphia in 1978, three years after the appearance of Riley's field guide, not only failed to mention Nabokov's name but erroneously credited authorship of the single genus it recognized, *Pseudochrysops*, to Comstock and Huntington. For fifty years none of the general writers who touched upon Caribbean Lycaenidae appears to have returned to the empirical evidence of morphology, instead being content to take the word of a predecessor. Had they done otherwise Nabokov's classification might have been much more prevalent in the literature of the time.

How had the world of lepidoptery conspired to eclipse Nabokov's most important scientific work? This was the question Kurt Johnson found himself asking soon enough. The answer he eventually found was that the destiny of "Notes on Neotropical Plebejinae" had little to do with any reasoned reaction it raised at the time, or with the level of its expertise. Indeed, what happened is instructive for understanding that in lepidoptery, and no doubt in all branches of study, the quirks of fate and happenstance sometimes determine whether a piece of research flourishes or fades. In addition to bad timing and the follow-the-leader instincts of writers of general books on butterflies, Johnson discovered that Nabokov's Latin American taxonomy seems to have been the victim of cumulative bad luck: one colleague in a hurry, another with an aversion to the drudgery of morphology, slipshod printing, and Nabokov's own unwieldy format and style.

Because of the prevalence of Riley's view of *Hemiargus*, the task facing the scientists returning to the United States from Las Abejas in 1987 seemed straightforward if laborious: dissection of the unidentified Blues among the expedition's catches and comparison of the results with dissections of known members of the long-established genuses *Hemiargus* and *Leptotes*, the latter a genus that Nabokov did not deal with directly in his 1945 study but that contained Miss Perkins's Blue. The discovery of significant anatomical divergence might reinforce the external differences already apparent in the wing patterns of some of the new captures; if so, a strong case could be made that the Las Abejas catches constituted unknown species under the rules of the International Code of Zoological Nomenclature, known by taxonomists as the Code. Since Johnson, like nearly everyone else, took Riley's conception of the Antillean butterflies for granted, it did not immediately occur to him or any of his colleagues that they might be dealing with unknown, or at least unfamiliar, genuses as well, or that their catches might not fit into what they understood to be the standard classification.

To name a new species under the Code, a taxonomist must be able to state clearly how it differs from all the others. This fundamental defining statement of what a new species is, as it appears in a journal laying claim to the new species, is called a diagnosis. Not so important for science in its broadest sense, perhaps, but certainly crucial for the researcher who wants to be given credit for a discovery, are other procedural steps — technicalities of the Code — also required for the naming of a new species:

1. A physical description must be provided. For Blue butterflies, this would include a detailed account of wing patterns and genital anatomy.

2. The individual specimen on which the diagnosis and physical description are based must be designated. This is known as the type specimen, or holotype. From now on this one specimen will define the new species. (Such specimens are important and confer a kind of scientific immortality on the specimen and then its first describer; in museums they are specially marked with red labels, as in Nabokov's poem, "On Discovering a Butterfly").

3. The whereabouts of the type specimen must be listed.

4. Any other information that is known about the natural history and life cycle of the new species must be provided.

5. A scientific name must be chosen in accordance with the rules of the Code, and its meaning, or etymology, must be accounted for. As inconsequential as it may seem, this technicality may well prove to be instrumental in preserving a part of Vladimir Nabokov's entomological legacy, the species names for Neotropical Blues Kurt Johnson and his co-workers based on Nabokov's fiction.

When completed, such a formal description is submitted to a scientific journal and undergoes scrutiny by other researchers in an anonymous peer-review process. But still the name is not considered valid until it is actually published, or "made available" in the jargon of taxonomy; it is then listed in an annual publication called *The Zoological Record,* a kind of Social Register for the biological world.

Johnson began work on the material from Las Abejas at the American

Museum of Natural History, Floor 5, Section 13, Room 76, where Nabokov worked under Comstock in the early 1940s. This room was Comstock's office from 1910 to 1953 and later was office to a string of research associates, all of whom had in one way or another a significant connection with Nabokov or his legacy: F. Martin Brown, a prolific lepidopterist and historian of lepidoptery who set up the archives at the museum that now contain much of Nabokov's scientific correspondence with his colleagues there; Cyril F. dos Passos, author of the official list of synonyms of North American butterflies and a frequent correspondent with Nabokov on the much-disputed subject of subspecies; and finally, from 1980 until 1993, Johnson himself.

The method of dissection, much the same as the one Comstock taught Nabokov back in 1941, is classic: the abdomen is snapped off the specimen with a forceps and soaked overnight in a caustic solution of potash, or potassium hydroxide. This softens the muscle, fat, and other membranous tissue but doesn't harm the sclerotized genital structures. Next, the abdomen is placed under a binocular microscope, in alcohol, with the outer wall of the abdomen carefully removed to expose the internal organs to more intricate examination. Unidentified or unfamiliar specimens call for meticulous care at this stage, because it is impossible for the researcher to know the precise location of the genitals in the abdominal cavity; carelessness can lead to inadvertent damage of parts that, in a unique specimen, are irreplaceable. The genital structures are then teased out of the abdominal tissues with microinstruments. The size of butterfly genitalia varies, but in the male Blue, the relevant parts might be the size (and sometimes have the appearance) of a flea; the job demands a microscope of about ten to fifty power. After extraction the genitalia are rinsed with alcohol or acetic acid to neutralize the potash and cleaned up with a camel's-hair brush. The same procedure is carried out on the type specimen of a given species. When it is over the genitalia are placed in a microvial and attached to the pin on which the specimen, now without its abdomen, is stored. This is the reason that specimens seem in many photographs to have stubby bodies. They are in fact missing their abdomens.

For the sake of a full comparison, Johnson also carried out dissections on a large selection of specimens of every known species of *Hemiargus* and *Leptotes*, not only from the immediate area of Las Abejas but from all over the Caribbean. These dissections acted as a kind of control on the work and allowed comparisons to a large number of potential relatives. Because of the overriding interest in the ties between Las Abejas and

Jamaica, Johnson turned first to the male Perkins-like Blue from deep Las Abejas, comparing its anatomy with those of two males of Miss Perkins's Blue, *Leptotes perkinsae,* from the Blue Mountains of Jamaica and two males of *L. cassius,* a common Caribbean species. Another ready source of comparative reference for the Perkins-like Blue was the unique genitalia of a new *Leptotes* from Cuba that Johnson and Albert Schwartz were in the process of naming. This species, *L. hedgesi,* was the first Cuban Blue named in about a hundred years.

The results of the *Leptotes* dissections were straightforward and rewarding. Just on the basis of the male clasping organ, the little Blue butterfly from the tangle of lower Abejas differed from all the others with which it was compared, not only in overall shape but in the number of attached specialized appendages. It was clear that a new species of *Leptotes* had been discovered from Las Abejas; as the researchers suspected, it had close affinities to Miss Perkins's Blue and Jamaica.

However, the dissections of what everyone knew as *Hemiargus* — including the little five-spotted Blue butterfly that David Matusik had leapt from the Jeep to snatch on the canyon rim above Las Abejas — were perplexing. In most respects Matusik's Blue was similar to the Miami Blue *H. thomasi,* but it also differed significantly, enough certainly to merit new-species status. That was exciting news for the Las Abejas expedition, but there were surprising difficulties with the *Hemiargus* specimens being used as controls. If the genus indeed consisted of close biological relatives, their genital structures would be expected to show at least some rudimentary similarity. Yet in many cases, except for a vague resemblance in the terminal shape of the male clasping organ, there was none. Genitalia from some of the species were so different from one another that it was impossible even to identify generalized structures in common. There was no structural coherence to the sample, even though all were supposedly in the same genus. It was like looking at a parking lot full of Cadillacs, Volkswagens, and dune buggies that a car dealer had assured you were all alike. Something was greatly amiss with Riley's long-accepted view of *Hemiargus.*

Johnson called John Rawlins in Pittsburgh and Matusik in Chicago with the news. The conundrum was sure to complicate the meeting that the Las Abejas research team had scheduled for later in 1987 at the Carnegie Museum to discuss plans to publish their findings. It was gratifying, to be sure, that the Las Abejas material included what were clearly two new species of Blues on top of four new Hairstreaks and two as yet unidentified, and quite possibly new, Skippers. But no one could write a species description for the new five-spotted Blue from Las Abejas if it couldn't be satisfactorily compared with its congeners, that is, a species from its own genus.

As Johnson spoke with Rawlins, it suddenly occurred to him that some work on Latin American Blues had been published by Vladimir Nabokov and that Nabokov might have had something to say about the Blues in question. Johnson promised Rawlins he would check Nabokov's publications and report back if they shed any light on the problems with *Hemiargus.*

Johnson had initially heard of Nabokov's work when studying in a master's degree program under John C. Downey, first at Southern Illinois University and then at the University of Northern Iowa. Downey became a prominent specialist on Blue butterflies during the 1960s, but his connection with Nabokov began with an oddly Nabokovian coincidence that has become part of the writer's legend. As a teenager in the late 1940s, driving a truck for the Forest Service in the Wasatch Mountains of Utah, Downey happened to encounter a man with a butterfly net walking along a canyon highway, naked to the waist, in shorts, and wearing a knotted handkerchief for a cap. Downey stopped and offered the man a ride, explaining that he was a lepidopterist himself, but he was covered with the dust from the coal he was hauling and the stranger seemed wary. Then a butterfly flashed across the highway, and the stranger pointed and asked, "What's that?" Downey identified the butterfly, and then two more in rapid succession, by their scientific names. Finally won over, the stranger put out his hand and said, "Hello! I'm Vladimir Nabokov."

At the time the Nabokovs, on one of their storied expeditions to the western states, were staying in the ski resort of Alta, and Nabokov would walk down from there every day into Cottonwood Canyon. He and Downey met several times after that when Nabokov returned to Utah to collect and Downey was a student at the University of Utah. Downey says his acquaintance with Nabokov influenced his own concentration on Blues, beginning with his doctoral studies at the University of California at Berkeley. His particular specialty was the western members of Nabokov's adopted genus *Lycaeides,* their relationships with their host plants, and the complexities of their evolution in the vast Rocky Mountain regions. In the early 1960s he published several copiously detailed studies of the western *Icaricia* (a genus named by Nabokov) and its complex assemblages of species and subspecies, a subject that had fascinated Nabokov.

Downey hoped to base an extensive multivariate analysis on this work. A multivariate analysis is a kind of computer-aided study extremely in vogue in the 1960s and 1970s; because it is not hierarchical — that is, it has nothing to do with genealogies, or true evolutionary relationships — this type of study is now outdated. But as part of his overall research strategy, Downey had already published, in the journal *Ecology* and elsewhere, pioneer research on the complexities of the members of *Icaricia* and their food plant usages, a study in coevolution, which treated the plant species as islands on which the butterflies evolve. As Downey says, Nabokov had put the study of North American Blues on a strong taxonomic footing, and the work he had produced had created a context for researching the evolution of this group in the complex environs characterizing the Rocky Mountains and Great Basin regions. Because of his specialty and their acquaintance, Downey followed Nabokov's morphological work perhaps more closely than any other lepidopterist.

The two men continued to correspond even in the 1960s, when Nabokov was living in Switzerland and entrenched in his literary work and Downey was coming into prominence as a scholar. Downey's accomplishments by this time had resulted in his being recruited to contribute to the sections on Blues for Doubleday's *Butterflies of North America,* being edited by the renowned butterfly artist William H. Howe. It was a complicated project that took a decade to complete and was published in 1975. Downey, who greatly admired Nabokov's talent for anatomical analysis, took pains to share his work with the author and asked for advice on the status and validity of available names from the groups Nabokov had studied. Nabokov's response was to send Downey the card catalog of his genitalic dissections. This catalog was actually a set of index cards on which Nabokov had kept his notes and drawings of specific genitalia. (This was a common practice in scientific research, but Nabokov seems to have adapted it for fiction composition; *Lolita* and many more of his novels were written on similar cards, and his fictional poet John Shade uses the same technique in *Pale Fire.*) According to Downey, Nabokov replied that he was too busy with literary work to write a detailed response to Downey's questions and that the cards would save a great deal of time.

Downey often spoke of Nabokov and his work in discussions with students and colleagues. At the University of Northern Iowa in 1969, while Kurt Johnson was Downey's student, the two were preparing a study of the North American Blue genus *Everes* for the Iowa Academy of Sciences. Faced with a ticklish question about the differentiation of two species,

Johnson suggested to Downey that perhaps they should write to Harry Clench, Nabokov's fellow researcher at Harvard. Downey snapped, "Clench wouldn't know! Nabokov might know, but Clench wouldn't know!" As Downey was obviously well aware, Nabokov had done hundreds of genitalic preparations during his studies of the northern genus *Lycaeides* and his pioneer study of Latin American Blues, but dissection was not one of Clench's strong points.

It was this incident that had impressed Nabokov's name on Johnson's mind. Although he had never seen Nabokov's work on Blues himself, Johnson had a reasonable hope that Nabokov might have had something useful to say about *Hemiargus* in his treatise on Latin American Blues. To check Nabokov's research Johnson had simply to walk across the hallway at the American Museum of Natural History. This room, 82, had always been the office of the museum's curator of Lepidoptera. Since 1949 the curator has been Frederick H. Rindge — a winner of lepidoptery's coveted Jordan Medal for his research on moths and the man who became so bored with inquiries about Nabokov's lepidoptery. Rindge had come to the museum just as William Comstock was falling into poor health, in time to help Comstock finish one of his most famous works, a mammoth picture book on the sprawling tropical nymphalid genus *Anaea*, a fascinating group whose species look so much like leaves that they amaze even the most jaded trained eye.

Rindge's office was, and is today, where the museum's Lepidoptera reprint collection, a huge file of offprints and copies of individual articles arranged alphabetically in boxes under the authors' names, is kept. The system saves researchers looking for a single article the trouble of combing through the scattered journals where lepidopterological research is published. In the box labeled with a big letter *N,* Johnson found a sheaf of papers about a half-inch thick containing copies of most of Nabokov's published scientific writings on butterflies. Some of the reprints were clearly from the author's original mentor at the museum, Comstock himself, for on the upper-right corners of the covers they bore the inscription, in india ink and laboratory pen, "For William P. Comstock, with best wishes, from the author." The style is unmistakable, the same as Nabokov used on his specimen labels — the old-fashioned, hand-dipped, metal-tipped pens make a heavy stroke and bifurcate if pressed too hard. The reprints were tattered and already yellow with time: Nabokov's papers had gathered some dust.

Nabokov's approximately twenty-two published articles, notes, or reviews on butterflies vary greatly in character, depending on his intended audience. Of his four major works, the largest and last, "The Nearctic Members of the Genus *Lycaeides* Hübner," published in 1949 in the *Bulletin of the Museum of Comparative Zoology,* was missing. Perhaps it had never been put into the box; perhaps it had been taken and never replaced. Still there, however, was "*Lysandra cormion,* a New European Butterfly," his 1941 paper in *The Journal of the New York Entomological Society* in which Nabokov made a reluctant claim of species status for the Blue butterfly he had captured on the slopes above Moulinet in 1938. So was "Butterfly Collecting in Wyoming, 1952," an evocative and colorful account, in *The Lepidopterists' News,* of a summer's expedition; Nabokov thought it of sufficient literary interest to include in *Strong Opinions,* a collection of his essays and interviews. But there was no copy of Nabokov's first contribution to lepidoptery, "A Few Notes on Crimean Lepidoptera," an account of his captures during the eighteen months his family spent in the Crimea after being driven from St. Petersburg by the Bolsheviks, published in *The Entomologist* in 1920, while he was a student at Cambridge University.

It took Johnson only a few seconds to find "Notes on Neotropical Plebejinae" and only a couple of minutes more to recognize the drawings of the genitalia he had been dissecting. Some were listed under Hübner's *Hemiargus,* and nearly all the rest were in one of the genuses Nabokov himself had erected, *Cyclargus* Nabokov 1945. Johnson then read the text in detail and saw that Nabokov had clearly shown how his *Cyclargus* differed from Hübner's *Hemiargus:* except for that slight similarity of shape at the end of the male's clasper, virtually all the rest of the genital structures in the two groups were different. After Johnson reviewed his own dissections under the microscope, there was no room for doubt. While dissections of species like *hanno, ceraunus,* and *ramon* clearly put them into a group — which Nabokov called *Hemiargus* — others, like *dominica, ammon, woodruffi, thomasi,* and the little five-spotted Blue from the rim of Las Abejas, with their substantially different genitalia, clearly belonged to Nabokov's *Cyclargus;* the two groups simply did not share the same structures. It was obvious that the *Hemiargus* of Riley's field guide, and of Comstock and Huntington before it, was really two distinct groups. Nabokov had gotten it right.

That raised a puzzling question. Nabokov's work on these two groups had succeeded Comstock and Huntington's but was not recognized by Riley; the taxonomic situation was unequivocal and amply explained in Nabokov's treatise. How, then, had Riley gotten it wrong? There are several possible explanations, none of which suggests that Riley actually found fault with Nabokov's taxonomic science.

First, a simple error caused by the old-fashioned, unwieldy format of "Notes on Neotropical Plebejinae," which separates not only the text from the illustrations but also the illustrations from their captions, may have been to blame. The captions themselves are very long, written to stand on their own and printed in small type. In his text Nabokov addressed the issue of possible genitalic confusion between *Cyclargus* and another of his new genuses, *Pseudochrysops*. But he didn't bother to do so for *Cyclargus* and *Hemiargus*, simply because no such possibility existed.

It is likely that Riley, preparing an illustrated field guide that was published when he was in his mideighties, looked first to the butterflies' external similarity. Having recognized *Pseudochrysops* as distinctive, he would then have compared the species he ended up placing in *Hemiargus*. They all share the spotted ventral pattern Nabokov called catochrysopoid. Then Riley would have checked the illustrations of the male claspers to back up his initial impression; it is possible that Riley, a traditionalist, would have looked at only that one feature. Here, since Nabokov illustrated a number of genitalia and genitalic details in isolation, absent attention to the captions (which are placed eight pages earlier) and a keen eye for the "coxcomb" at the tip of the clasper in *Cyclargus* (the teeth of which are less than a millimeter in length in Nabokov's crowded illustrations), Riley may have concluded that the clasper tips were alike. There is a certain visual similarity, but anatomically they are clearly not the same structure.

Any good lepidopterist — and Riley was surely one of the best — would usually check primary sources for such a work as his field guide. But it is possible that Riley had never looked at Nabokov's study at all but was satisfied to follow Clench's 1961 synopsis of Antillean Lycaenidae. Oddly, a crucial table in Clench's work is marked with numbers for footnotes that never appear, and one of the numbers is set beside the entry for *Cyclargus*. It is very likely that the footnote would have explained Clench's view of that genus; if so, this would have been the place for his statement of why he decided to group Nabokov's *Cyclargus*, *Echinargus*, and *Pseudochrysops* as mere subgenuses under *Hemiargus*.

In broad terms this need have been nothing more than a classic face-off between a lumper, in this case Clench, and a man viewed as a splitter by temperament, Nabokov. (The lepidopterist John Franclemont, an emeritus professor at Cornell University who was friendly with Nabokov during his years there, liked to joke about his colleague's predilection as a splitter:

"I told him, after his *Lycaeides* paper, that if he carried his methods to their logical conclusion, butterflies would become their own phylum." The argument would come down to whether the distinctions Nabokov saw between his various groups were significant enough to merit full genus status.

But beyond lumping and splitting, there were additional crucial differences between Nabokov and many other lepidopterists of his own era and even later, including Clench, Downey, and to some extent Riley. The fundamental goal of modern systematics, which Nabokov shared, is to reconstruct biological lineages, to ascertain the genealogy of evolution. In this it differs fundamentally from a view of relatedness based merely on physical similarity, the dominant paradigm not only when Linnaeus introduced his system in the eighteenth century, but in Nabokov's time as well, and even into the 1970s. This approach to taxonomy, now generally discredited, is known as phenetics, and its practitioners took the utilitarian view that taxonomic genealogies, the evolutionary relationships between various organisms, could not be established and, thus, taxonomy should be based to a large extent on organizational convenience.

These two distinct views lie at the heart of Nabokov's Neotropical groupings and how they were treated by others. Nabokov believed that the distinctions he saw in his genital dissections proved that his genus groups were monophyletic, that is, their members were descended from a single ancestor: his *Hemiargus* and *Cyclargus* were two distinctly different things, even though they looked alike on the outside. But pheneticists believed that these ancestral lineages could not be discovered, so *Hemiargus* was in fact a preferable grouping to them because it was more convenient. This helps explain why so many writers of guides and books ignored Nabokov's genuses. Nabokov was taking a sophisticated specialist approach to his Blues, asking refined questions of what was related to what. The guide authors, by contrast, were taking a generalist or regionalist approach; for organizational purposes it was almost always easier and more convenient for them to follow phenetically influenced groupings.

In preparing his own field guide, Riley operated under the same cast of mind; it was easy for him to see the exotic tailed Blue *Pseudochrysops* as a distinct genus, because on the outside it looked like one. *Hemiargus* and *Cyclargus*, equally distinct in Nabokov's eyes, were harder for him to accept. The disjunct between specialist knowledge and the needs of general writers is as strong as ever today. John Burns, a specialist on Skippers at the Smithsonian Institution, once complained to Johnson that "I get so tired of going to all this effort in my technical papers to work out detailed anatomical relationships and place the many similar-looking Skippers where they belong, only to find that the next field guide or regional book has simply put them back where they used to be, or placed them anywhere else they like depending on what the wings look like." After Johnson and his colleagues realized Nabokov's classification was so accurate, they took pains to keep generalist writers informed so history wouldn't repeat itself.

There was another, perhaps related, difference between Nabokov and Clench. In contrast to Nabokov's diligence with dissection, it is likely that, in the case of the Antillean Blues, Clench failed to carry out dissections at all. In earlier studies he had admitted a dearth of dissections, which he complained were wretchedly time-consuming; in his paper on the Antilles he had clearly dissected only a few Hairstreaks. In retrospect Johnson realized that this was the point of Downey's exclamation: "Clench wouldn't know!"

One reason Clench found dissection so cumbersome was a reflection of the scientific methods of the time. After examination the dissection needs to be preserved for later reference. In the first half of the century, dissected genitalia were mounted on a microscope slide, covered in resin, and permanently capped with a flat glass slide cover, essentially allowing only one view of the specimen and sometimes distorting the features of the dissection. The process took much time, and if it was done incorrectly, say, if air bubbles became trapped in the resin, the specimen would have to be rinsed and the process begun again. Ten slides a day would have been remarkable speed with this method.

In some institutions the same procedure was employed into the 1970s; Nabokov used it at times, too, but he also took advantage of the relatively new technique of popping the loose specimen into a small vial of glycerin, an inert material that prevents the specimen from drying out or deteriorating. "I prefer keeping [genitalia dissections] in vials," he wrote to a fellow lepidopterist in 1944, "because the 'elbow' of the falx is liable to be a little distorted by the pressure of the cover, and sometimes the 'spur' of the valve tends to be furled when mounted." Not only is this fast but the specimen can be removed later, placed in a watchglass — a Pyrex microscope glass with a rim — and treated like a fresh dissection under the microscope; the researcher is not limited to what ends up viewable on a permanent resin-mounted slide. (Today's tiny microvials are plastic, with silicon stoppers; the primitive versions Nabokov used were glass with tiny cork stoppers, which were harder to work with.) The procedure helped Nabokov to become one of the first researchers to complete relatively large numbers of dissections and to be one of the first to illustrate series of dissections to show ranges of variation.

Another factor that might have played a role in Nabokov's being overlooked in the lepidopterological tradition will disappoint or even shock many of his literary devotees. Nabokov wasn't merely being modest when he once told an interviewer that his formal scientific papers could be of interest to only a small group of specialists. His most important works are extremely difficult to read, in places nearly impenetrable. Aside from a few telltale flashes, there are few signs of the lucid, graceful, charming author loved by so many. And this is not simply because of the technical material presented though that is an obvious factor, but in the way it is presented. Here is a passage as illustration, chosen more or less at random from "Notes on Neotropical Plebejinae." It discusses Nabokov's conception of the term *Plebejinae:*

> In spite of the work accomplished since 1909, by Tutt and Chapman in England and by Stempffer in France, entomologists in this country employ the term *Plebejinae* simply as a euphemism for the "Lycaena" of German authors, or "Blues," and *Plebejus* is used for a number of heterogeneous Nearctic species only *one* of which (*saepiolus* Boisduval) belongs structurally to the genus of which the Palearctic *Plebejus argus* Linnaeus is the type. In a way the initial blunder was Swinhoe's who while correctly giving a subfamilial ending to the group which Tutt's intuition and Chapman's science had recognized ("tribe" *Plebeidi* which exactly corresponds to the *Plebejinae* of Stempffer) as different from other "tribes" (i.e., subfamilies) within the *Lycaenidae,* failed to live up to the generic diagnoses which he simply copied from Chapman's notes in Tutt and tried to combine genitalic data he had not verified or did not understand with the obsolete "naked v. hairy eyes" system (which at Butler's hands had resulted in probably the most ludicrous assembly of species ever concocted, see for example Butler 1900, Entom. 33:124), so that in the case of several Indian forms which Chapman had not diagnosed, Swinhoe placed intragenerically allied species in different subfamilies and species belonging to different Tuttian "tribes" in the same subfamily.

Nonspecialist readers aren't the only ones to be baffled by such dense thickets, which Nabokov himself once accurately described to a colleague as "entangled in subordinate clauses and brackets." More recently Lionel C. Higgins, Norman Riley's coauthor in *A Field Guide to the Butterflies of Britain and Europe,* responding to a correspondent's question about papers by Nabokov and Jon Shepard, another specialist in the genus *Lycaeides,* said that while both papers were "invaluable," Shepard's is "comprehensible but unconvincing," whereas Nabokov's "of course is incomprehensible but not without great interest." Higgins saw himself as a rival to Nabokov's view of *Lycaeides* and might be considered a hostile witness, but Nabokov's allies had the same complaints, albeit made more gently. "Your paper is somewhat hard reading because of your almost telegraphic expression," Comstock wrote him in March 1945. "I suppose this was necessary to keep the cost down in these war days but nevertheless I think it a detriment because everyone is busy and they are apt to pass over a paper if it is hard to read."

Comstock's letter suggests one plausible reason for Nabokov's style: he felt he had to pack a lot into his allotted space; today much of the material that Nabokov strung together might be presented in a table or other sort of graphic for ready comprehension. From a different time and in a less formal but related "scientific" vein, his "Butterfly Collecting in Wyoming, 1952," contains some of the most beautiful writing on butterflies ever printed. But whatever the reason behind Nabokov's chosen style in his more formal presentations, Comstock was right. There is a good chance that some authors of general works on butterflies, who had to review large volumes of primary research for their books, took a look at his prose and quickly moved on.

Beyond David Matusik's five-spotted Blue, *Cyclargus* held other surprises from the Las Abejas region: among the several hundred common Blues taken in the nearby desert was another new species, although it was recognized as such only after the research team had returned to the United States, too late to try to collect additional specimens. Luckily the location of its capture had been well-documented: it turned up among the series of twenty-five *thomasi* (which Johnson and the others were now calling *Cyclargus thomasi*) taken at the Las Mercedes cattle wallow and dissected for comparison with the unknown five-spotted Blue from above Las Abejas. It is quite possible that, if not for this stroke of luck, the species would never have been recognized at all. Not that it couldn't be distinguished from *thomasi* by its wings: on the upper surface of the hind wing there are two black spots rather than one. The problem is that *thomasi* is so common — "dirt common" is the phrase in lepidoptery — that no one really made the effort to look closely; many museums have so many *thomasi* in their collections that they don't take the time or space to add specimens. The attitude is: if it looks like a *thomasi,* then it's a *thomasi.*

Even among the dissections that distinguished *Cyclargus,* the genitalia of the Las Mercedes specimen looked so divergent that Johnson wondered at first whether some mistake had been made in sorting out the abdomens for dissection. The male clasper had a huge hump along its inner margin, covered with spikelike projections unlike anything in any of the other dissections. This remained a mystery until Johnson again turned to Nabokov. The hump, or setate lobe, was an extreme development of the inner margin near the widest point of the valvae, the feature Nabokov called Bayard's angulation. This inner margin at Bayard's angulation was so narrow in the other species he dissected and illustrated for "Notes on Neotropical Plebejinae" that he never emphasized it in his illustrations. Since his drawings were external views, and the lobe appeared on the inside, the much smaller lobe of the other species was shown in Nabokov's drawings as a dashed line to indicate a feature beneath the surface of the drawing.

The rediscovery of *Cyclargus* complicated the findings from Las Abejas immensely. The Carnegie Fund for Invertebrate Zoology had supported the 1987 Las Abejas expedition and expected results to be published within a reasonable time; a target date was set for the fall of 1988. Matusik and Johnson, therefore, had a good deal of work to do. The naming of new species from the forest would require extensive diagnostic and comparative work, in the lab and then in technical printed format. Each new species had to be discussed and illustrated in relation to others. This was a formidable task, given that a computer-based genealogical analysis (a so-called cladistic analysis) was to be carried out on two of the Hairstreak species. Matusik and Johnson also wanted to return to Las Abejas during the summer of 1988 for some follow-up fieldwork before publication. In addition, they had agreed to contribute a report on a new Hispaniolan Hairstreak to *The Butterflies of Hispaniola,* a book being readied independently for publication in 1989 by Albert Schwartz. Matusik and Johnson had shared information from their Las Abejas expeditions with Schwartz and his co-workers and were cooperating with him on his book, which showed Hispaniola as the most lepidopterologically diverse island in the Caribbean.

But correcting old errors and restoring Nabokov's *Cyclargus* to taxonomic usage was of a different order from the other work. It was a revisionary problem, requiring specific taxonomic procedures and compliance with the complex rules that govern classification. The initial Las Abejas report, appearing in *Annals of the Carnegie Museum* in September 1988, included the new name of the male Perkins-like Blue from lower Abejas: *Leptotes idealus,* in gratitude to the staff at the Ideal headquarters for their many kindnesses during the expeditions' visits to the Sierra de Baoruco. That same year Matusik and Johnson, returning to Las Abejas, captured the first known female. Like that of the male, its anatomy supported the sister-species relationship with Miss Perkins's Blue from Jamaica. But because of the complexities involved, the write-up of *Cyclargus-Hemiargus* and of the two new Nabokovian species from Las Abejas — both of which provided valuable biogeographical insights for the Caribbean — would have to be postponed; Johnson and Matusik planned to deal with these as separate issues as soon as possible.

Matusik chose to name the five-spotted Blue *Cyclargus kathleena* after his wife, Kathleen. The existence of this very local Blue — together with the unique Hairstreaks, Skippers, and Satyrs also discovered at Las Abejas — supported a view, first voiced by Schwartz, that significant speciation had occurred in the mountainous regions of the South Paleoisland of Hispaniola. The little Blue from the Las Mercedes cattle wallow was to be named *Cyclargus sorpresus,* from the Spanish word for surprise. This butterfly, which had turned up only in the comparative dissections used to study *C. kathleena,* eventually proved to share an otherwise unique clasper with the Jamaican species *C. shuturn,* which Johnson and Zsolt Bálint named in 1995, yet another clear indication of the close biological relationship between Jamaica and the South Paleoisland.

Despite the fact that the new Nabokovian discoveries couldn't be immediately published, by the time the initial Las Abejas report came out, word had spread of what the expedition had confirmed: that Riley's *Hemiargus* was clearly made up of two separate groups, just as Nabokov had concluded. But Johnson was eager to see the work in print so Riley's old error would not continue to be replicated. It would be poor science to knowingly publish a classification that in terms of the Code was paraphyletic, that is, one that made two groups falsely into one, particularly when the correct arrangement had been presented in the scientific literature in 1945. Nevertheless, lepidopterists who had lived comfortably with Riley's version for so long wanted to see the modern study, with the drastic changes it entailed, put through peer review. Authors working on wide-ranging butterfly books like regional or national studies need official specialist publications behind them. When the University of Florida published Albert Schwartz's *Butterflies of Hispaniola* in 1989, it included

Leptotes idealus, but Schwartz, always the cautious scientist, was unwilling to incorporate Nabokov's *Cyclargus,* and all the species that properly belonged there were wrapped up under the usual catchall genus *Hemiargus* Hübner.

Johnson did not want to see the same thing happen in another important book, *The Butterflies of the West Indies and South Florida* by David Spencer Smith, Lee D. Miller, and Jacqueline Y. Miller, a successor volume to Riley's 1975 guide to the Antillean butterflies. This attractive, generously proportioned book would represent a quantum leap in sophistication from Riley's portrayal of butterflies in the region because of significant advances in knowledge of the Antillean fauna, including a new appreciation of the biogeographical implications of continental drift, discoveries in existing museum collections, and a wealth of new material from extensive fieldwork in the Caribbean by Schwartz and others.

Among these new advances would be a development that lent further weight to Nabokov's 1945 study. Field-workers had found representatives of *Pseudochrysops,* the little tailed Blue that the Carnegie expedition had worked so hard to find at Las Mercedes, in both Cuba and Puerto Rico. Because of its distinctive appearance, Riley had easily accepted its status as a separate genus, which Nabokov had recognized. Ironically, it was modern science, reluctant to establish genuses that contain only a single species, that was more likely to question the validity of *Pseudochrysops.* After all, the pattern of speciation as it is now understood is like the branching of a tree; seldom, except in cases of extinction, does anything stand by itself. *Pseudochrysops* was a good candidate for origin by continental drift. It was extremely doubtful that *P. bornoi,* the little desert Blue so hard to find in the hot and dry climes of western Hispaniola, could have found its way to the island by transoceanic flight. The discovery of *Pseudochrysops* members on other Caribbean islands, whether one wished to view them as separate species or not, established it as an ancient lineage with several branches, certainly worthy of genus rank.

In 1987 *The Butterflies of the West Indies and South Florida* was already in preparation for Oxford University Press, and Johnson kept in close touch with the authors, Smith, a curator at the Hope Collections of Entomology at Oxford University, and the Millers, a husband-and-wife team from the Allyn Museum of Entomology in Sarasota, Florida. Their book would show Nabokov's Latin American research in an intense and favorable light, as long as the editors and contributors could complete their work in time to meet the publishing schedule. Johnson and the Millers decided that the safest way to be sure that Nabokov's genus names and the names of the new *Cyclargus* discoveries would be available would be to have the relevant documentation published by the Allyn Museum, where the Millers could shepherd its progress.

But fate seemed still to be working against Nabokov. Soon after the paper on *Cyclargus* had been prepared and reviewed, budget cuts at the museum held up its publication, a not-so-gentle reminder of taxonomy's humble place in the world. By 1991 the situation was desperate. The plates for the new Caribbean butterfly book had been made up and most of the text had been written, all reflecting the new Nabokovian discoveries, but the names were still not officially available. As a last resort Johnson and Matusik decided to include the relevant material under the cover of another work that Johnson had written on Elfin butterflies, close relatives of the Hairstreaks, for the University of Wisconsin. Because of space constraints, however, most of the detailed textual explanation supporting Nabokov's original view had to be stripped away, and readers were simply referred to "Notes on Neotropical Plebejinae." In 1992 the bare descriptions appeared with the new names *C. kathleena* and *C. sorpresus,* supported, though, by rather fine anatomical drawings, intentionally rendered in Nabokov's characteristic style to simplify comparison with his original work.

This expedient at least allowed *The Butterflies of the West Indies and South Florida,* which was published in 1994, to adopt Nabokov's revived Caribbean classification, making it the first book to do so. The definitive discussion of the taxonomic reinstatement of *Cyclargus* and the consequent restriction of *Hemiargus* did not appear for yet another year, in 1995, exactly fifty years after Nabokov had completed his groundbreaking work. By then much of Johnson's work with two new colleagues, Zsolt Bálint and Dubi Benyamini, on the Neotropical Blues of South America, had already seen print. Despite the clear superiority and sophistication of his Caribbean classifications, it had taken half a century for Nabokov to upset the old scheme and confute some of lepidoptery's obtuse champions.

5 ❧

A Life in Lepidoptery

I have hunted butterflies in various climes and disguises: as a pretty boy in knickerbockers and sailor cap; as a lanky cosmopolitan expatriate in flannel bags and beret; as a fat hatless old man in shorts.

— *Speak, Memory*

"WHY THE BUTTERFLIES?" It is a question many people who know Nabokov only from the point of view of his literature feel compelled to ask. The underlying assumption is that while a love for literature calls for no explanation, a love for butterflies does. Nabokov understood this cultural prejudice and was patient with those who displayed it. But he also believed that an interest in nature was as desirable a human trait as fascination with great books, and as a teacher he was often shocked to be reminded how little his students knew about the birds, insects, and plants around them. If, from the point of view of literature, his interest in butterflies is sometimes painted as an eccentricity, as a lepidopterist he was firmly mainstream: Nabokov found the same appeal in butterflies that millions of others have felt. He was an extraordinary person in many ways, including his social background and literary genius. But his lepidopterological interest was unexceptional in and of itself.

Nabokov fundamentally differed from other talented lepidopterists, both amateur and professional, in that he also had a genius for literature. No one else has come close to him in so richly describing lepidoptery's allure and delights. But his passion is one that was widely shared in his time and is very common among lepidopterists today. Moreover, as Kurt Johnson learned in the months after his discovery of "Notes on Neotropical Plebejinae," almost every stage of Nabokov's entomological career can be understood in terms of his culture, his environment, and the circumstances that shaped him.

The butterflies, of course, were only one aspect of an exceedingly complex life. Nabokov was born in St. Petersburg, the westward-looking capital of czarist Russia, on April 23, 1899. His family were Russian aristocrats, possessors of significant political influence, fabulous wealth, and intellectual distinction. Nabokov himself became independently wealthy at age seventeen, when he inherited Rozhdestveno, an estate that belonged to his uncle. But except for a few jewels hidden in a box of talcum powder, it was only the intellectual inheritance that survived the seizure of power by the Bolsheviks in 1917. There followed two decades of exile in Western Europe — in England, Germany, and France — filled with intellectual ferment and literary creativity but also with insecurity and fear for the future. During these years, under the pseudonym Sirin, Nabokov turned himself into the major writer of the Russian diaspora. He enjoyed the sort of invigorating if claustrophobic celebrity possible in the tightly knit European communities of Russian refugees, but he was also forced to endure the cold indifference of foreign bureaucrats, and his family sometimes depended on the charity of friends and relief agencies to make ends meet.

In 1940 Nabokov, his wife, Véra Evseevna Slonim, and their son, six-year-old Dmitri, fled yet another group of tyrants, this time the Nazis, and sailed to a new life in America, the country they proudly adopted as their own. In the United States, undergoing an astounding linguistic metamorphosis, Nabokov led an exhausting and comparatively obscure life of writing — now in English — college teaching, and lepidoptery until 1958, when *Lolita* brought him immense fame; if the wealth she also brought could not compare with what his family had enjoyed in prerevolutionary Russia, it was still enough to provide him with the leisure and freedom to give up teaching and devote himself completely to his writing. Then, despite Nabokov's sense of allegiance to his new country, what began as a temporary sojourn in Europe in 1959 turned into a permanent residence in Switzerland, where he and Véra lived at the Montreux Palace Hotel until his death in 1977.

In some respects then, as he himself noted, Nabokov led four distinct lives, one after the other, of roughly twenty years each, in circumstances that could not have been more dissimilar. But Nabokov was supremely self-sufficient; although he hated tyranny and political oppression, he held himself famously aloof from the fragmenting currents of practical politics. Despite his family's fall from fortune, the precarious existence of the refugee, and the personal dislocation and tragedy of exile (one of his brothers died in a Nazi concentration camp), many powerful threads run true through the hectic patchwork: his cult of memory — literary and personal — his deep devotion to his wife and son, and his total commitment to literature come easily to mind; lepidoptery provided another strong unifying force in his life.

Like many amateur and professional lepidopterists, Nabokov discovered butterflies as a child and always associated them with childhood happiness. In an interview in 1971 he maintained that the most delightful and thrilling years of his adult life were those he had spent behind a microscope at the Museum of Comparative Zoology at Harvard University. "Incredibly happy memories," he wrote in *Speak, Memory,* "quite comparable, in fact, to those of my Russian boyhood, are associated with my research work at the MCZ, Cambridge, Mass. No less happy have been the many collecting trips taken almost every summer, during twenty years, through most of the states of my adopted country."

Though not without its share of typically misleading Nabokovian irony, Chapter 6 of *Speak, Memory* is Nabokov's nostalgic ode to youth, sunshine, and butterflies, the most complete account of his youthful passion; reading it is essential for anyone who wants to understand what lepidoptery meant to him. A butterfly's ghost lurks even in the title: until dissuaded by a cautious and sales-minded editor, Nabokov had wanted to call the book "Speak, Mnemosyne." Mnemosyne is Remembrance, the mother of the Greek Muses, but she is also a Parnassian butterfly, *Parnassius mnemosyne,* a drawing of which graces the endpaper maps of the revised version of *Speak, Memory,* and which, along with the Hawkmoths that flit through the book, presides over it as a sort of tutelary deity.

Although the family spent much of their time at their town house on Morskaya Street in St. Petersburg, *Speak, Memory* unforgettably celebrates the summers at Vyra, his family's expansive country estate fifty miles south of the city. A rambling two-story wooden mansion with spreading verandas, Vyra sat amid its own gardens and parks, which in their turn gave way to fields of flowers and forests of birch and fir, reaching the banks of the Oredezh River. Here the Nabokovs lived a life of high society, waited upon by their fifty servants. Nabokov was the oldest of five, two girls and three boys, and his siblings considered him spoiled. The children lived on a floor apart from their parents, with a succession of foreign tutors and governesses. It was a life of tennis, gazebos, and elaborate family fetes under the trees, with seasonal journeys on elegant trains to the resorts of Europe. It is crucial, however, to the understanding of Nabokov to realize how thoroughly he rejected the appeal of merely material possessions. His lifelong nostalgia for his boyhood home and Russia had to do with what he called "unreal estate": powerful memories, his family, the beloved Russian language. During the family's years in America, friends of the Nabokovs were often shocked at their spartan lives, now more a matter of choice than of economics, typically with only a few sticks of furniture and scarcely any decoration on the walls.

Despite the grotesquely false impression created in some quarters by *Lolita,* Nabokov was intensely devoted to his family, and he consciously associated his love of butterflies with many of those closest to him — his mother, Elena, who taught him to spread his first catches, and above all his father. Vladimir Dmitrievich Nabokov was nothing less than a Russian Renaissance man. Under the czars he risked his career and his life through his support of European-style liberalism and a constitutional monarchy. To Nabokov's everlasting pride his father was one of the original founders of the Constitutional Democratic Party and a member of Russia's first elected legislature, or Duma, convened in 1906 as a czarist concession to reform amid the riots and strikes of the so-called first Russian Revolution. In the aftermath of the Duma's dissolution, its leaders, V. D. Nabokov among them, were stripped of political rights and imprisoned for a time. Barred from politics until the Romanovs abdicated, he turned to journalism, serving on the editorial staff of the liberal-left review *Pravo.* A man of culture and a promoter of a wide range of the arts, V. D. Nabokov was at various times a jurist, a criminologist, a journalist, a statesman, and the author of many articles and books, including "The Provisional Government," a primary source on the short-lived post-Romanov Kerensky regime, in which he served as chancellery minister.

V. D. Nabokov was also a butterfly collector, having been introduced to the pursuit, like his son, in his boyhood; lepidoptery was a family tradition. "There was a magic room in our country house with my father's collection," Nabokov once wrote in notes for an interview, "the old faded butterflies of his childhood, but precious to me beyond words." One of Vladimir's prized specimens, handed down to him by his father, was a Peacock butterfly, rare in the woods near St. Petersburg, which a tutor from Germany had helped V. D. Nabokov capture on August 17, 1883; a quarter century later, on the same spot, along a trail called the Chemin du Pendu on Batovo, another family estate near Vyra, eight-year-old

Vladimir netted a Hawkmoth at the western edge of its territory. There were also other memories. Nabokov recalled one summer afternoon when his father "burst into my room, grabbed my net, shot down the veranda steps — and presently was strolling back holding between finger and thumb the rare and magnificent female of the Russian Poplar Admirable that he had seen basking on an aspen leaf from the balcony of his study."

In 1908, when his father was jailed for three months because of his political activities, Vladimir sent him a butterfly, and V. D. Nabokov wrote Elena, "Tell him that all I see in the prison yard are Brimstones and Cabbage Whites."

Other family connections came into play. In *Speak, Memory* Nabokov linked the scientific writings of Nikolay Kozlov, his mother's maternal grandfather, the first president of the Russian Imperial Academy of Medicine, with his own lepidopterological works. Dr. Kozlov's daughter, who had a room reserved at Vyra for her chemical laboratory, hired a noted university professor to give her own daughter, Nabokov's mother, private lessons in natural history. Elena Nabokov, for her part, spread her son's first butterfly and had an equivalent passion for boletic mushrooms. Her joy in the solitary hunt was akin to Nabokov's own.

Elena's lessons were also the ultimate source of some gloriously attractive illustrated volumes on Lepidoptera that Nabokov carried down from Vyra's attic when he was eight years old, a precious advantage of the family's wealth that made a deep and lasting impression on him. Some were as old as the eighteenth century. From the nineteenth century were Edward Newman's *Illustrated Natural History of British Moths* and *Illustrated Natural History of British Butterflies;* Ernst Hoffman's *Die Gross-Schmetterlinge Europas;* the nine volumes of *Mémoires sur les Lepidoptérés* on Asian butterflies and moths by the Grand Duke Nikolay Mikhailovich, with painted figures that Nabokov thought "comparably beautiful," and Samuel Hubbard Scudder's "stupendous" *Butterflies of the Eastern United States and Canada.* Nabokov also said that by 1910 he had dreamed his way through the first volumes of Adalbert Seitz's *Die Gross-Schmetterlinge der Erde,* a comprehensive work on the earth's Lepidoptera that Nabokov called a "prodigious picture book." Seitz's book, which became a great classic, was published in installments beginning in 1906, with the final volume appearing in 1954. It was within Seitz's work that his co-worker Max Draudt had presented, in a volume of 1919, one of the first arrangements of the world's lycaenids.

It would be hard to exaggerate the impression these lavish productions must have made. Early illustrated books of Lepidoptera are works of art in themselves, and Nabokov was always sensitive to their beauty; anyone who wants to understand his youthful attraction to butterflies should seek out and enjoy some of these volumes, although doing so may not be such an easy undertaking. They are true antiques, with hand-painted color plates, and they tend to be fragile. To consult something of the sort in the rare book archive of the American Museum of Natural History, one must wear a surgical mask and nylon gloves, and even then a trained archivist sometimes supervises the turning of the pages.

V. D. Nabokov took care to see that his children were exposed to a wide range of European cultures; Nabokov was fluent in both Russian and English from infancy, and he added French not long afterward. As a child he kept his notes on butterflies in English, with terms borrowed from *The Entomologist*, an English journal that he always admired and that published his first lepidopterological papers, beginning in 1920. Art lessons later came in handy for drawing Lepidoptera in his work at the Museum of Comparative Zoology at Harvard.

A charming passage from *Speak, Memory* is one of several that illustrate Nabokov's perception that Lepidoptera, or, perhaps more accurately, the splendors associated with the hunt for Lepidoptera, formed a kind of gentle passage between his magical childhood and his life as an adult. When the family's janitor caught that first Swallowtail butterfly that had thrilled the boy at age seven, Vladimir's governess popped it into a wardrobe, expecting the mothballs to kill it overnight. But the next morning when the door was opened,

> my Swallowtail, with a mighty rustle, flew into her face, then made for the open window, and presently was but a golden fleck dipping and dodging and soaring eastward, over timber and tundra, to Vologda, Viatka and Perm, and beyond the gaunt Ural range to Yakutsk and Verkhne Kolymsk, and from Verkhne Kolymsk, where it lost a tail, to the fair island of St. Lawrence, and across Alaska to Dawson, and southward along the Rocky Mountains — to be finally overtaken and captured, after a forty-year race, on an immigrant dandelion under an endemic aspen near Boulder.

The idyll ended abruptly, in 1917, when the Nabokovs fled to the Crimea to escape the Revolution, only to have it catch up with them two weeks later. Vladimir, sent ahead with his younger brother Sergey to avoid conscription into the Red Army, was annoyed to have arrived in such a fascinating lepidopterological region after the collecting season had passed.

The sixteen months the family spent there was Nabokov's first taste of exile and the slightly unreal life of the postrevolutionary Russian diaspora. Amid the changing fortunes of war, the Crimea was occupied in shifts of Bolsheviks, Germans, Tatar nationalists, and, closing the circle, Reds again. Under them anti-Bolshevik officers were shot and beaten, and the Nabokovs had to disguise their identity. Baron Yuri Rausch von Traubenberg, Nabokov's cousin and best friend, died charging a Bolshevik machine-gun emplacement. Moreover, the family had long disdained the idea of foreign bank accounts as unpatriotic, and financially they were ruined. That handful of jewels, smuggled from St. Petersburg in a talcum powder box, was all they had preserved of their fortune.

Amid the undercurrents of confusion and occasional fear, anti-Bolshevik Crimea was the scene of a lively, even boisterous, social life among the exiles, with Vladimir developing into quite the libertine. "Many young people were always around," he wrote in *Speak, Memory,* "brown-limbed braceleted young beauties, a well-known painter called Sorin, actors, a male ballet dancer, merry White Army officers, some of whom were to die quite soon, and what with beach parties, blanket parties, bonfires, a moon-spangled sea and a fair supply of Crimean Muscat Lunel, a lot of amorous fun went on."

But despite this somewhat distracting background, Nabokov managed plenty of butterfly collecting on the peninsula, whose southern ecological ambience seemed exotic in comparison with the northern climes of St. Petersburg. The involuntary sojourn, in fact, offered a measure of compensation for an entomological expedition that Vladimir had dreamed of taking beyond the Urals into Asia in his time between school and university. There were few insects of interest in the parks and gardens of the coast, where the family stayed near Yalta. Most of Nabokov's collecting was done nearby, on the rocky southern slopes of the mountain Ai-Petri and the hilly pastures of the Yayla region beyond. Nabokov also made several expeditions to the central and northern reaches of the Crimean Peninsula, visiting on one of those excursions Chufutkale and Bakhchisaray, the ancient seat of the Tatar Khans, whose fountain provided the title for two famous poems by Pushkin. On another, along a path above the Black Sea, he was stopped by a Bolshevik sentry who tried to arrest him for signaling to a British warship — with his net, the man said. (The next day, convinced of the innocence of his pursuit, the soldiers brought as an offering a clumsy assemblage of local butterflies.) In all Nabokov collected about two hundred species of butterflies and moths, material for his first publication in lepidoptery (and his first in English, as well), "A Few Notes on Crimean Lepidoptera," which appeared in *The Entomologist* several years later.

In March 1919 the Nabokovs and other opponents of the Bolsheviks sailed from Sebastopol for Constantinople and on to the Piraeus on a small, filthy Greek cargo ship. Along with everything else left behind in Russia were Vladimir's treasured collection at Vyra and his captures from the Crimea. Nabokov told his first biographer, Andrew Field, that he could conceive of his Crimean collection as having fared better than his more important specimens at Vyra, and ending up among the holdings of some Soviet museum: imagining another life for himself, Nabokov speculated that he could have lived quietly, and perhaps with distinction, as an entomologist attached to such an institution.

The family stopped in Greece, where Vladimir admired the Parthenon but had abysmal luck with Lepidoptera. They made their way to London, where V. D. Nabokov's brother, Konstantin Nabokov, was chargé d'affaires at the Russian embassy, in the precarious position of representing a government that had been abolished a year and a half earlier. Vladimir's father vainly hoped to find a post from which to influence opinion in Britain to continued opposition to the Bolsheviks. It was decided that Vladimir and Sergey would attend university, and, partly because of Vladimir's interest in entomology, he was steered toward Cambridge, which had a good reputation in science.

These years mark what might be considered a fork in the road for Nabokov, because after a couple of terms he dropped the study of biology, opting for French and Russian instead. Had he followed another course, his career might have taken an entirely different turn. With a degree in biology from Cambridge, he would certainly have avoided the misleading label of amateur that followed him insidiously through the rest of his scientific career. Still, it was not as if Nabokov had given up his interest in entomology. As a Trinity College undergraduate he published his paper on Crimean Lepidoptera (in which he recalled a "handsome grey-marbled moth, *Smerinthus tremulae* . . . which, in happier days, I used to find at the foot of aspens in the neighbourhood of Petrograd"). And in a later list of things he "went in for" at Cambridge, entomology kept company with "practical jokes, girls, and, especially, athletics." In 1921 he wrote a poem called "Biology," which celebrates the joys of dissection and the microscope.

But aside from his article it is unclear how Nabokov exercised his interests in butterflies at Cambridge. In a letter to his father in 1920, he spoke with puzzling dismissiveness of "the most unbelievable propositions" he had been presented for earning summer money, one of which was to be an "assistant entomologist" in Ceylon; at other times during his life, Nabokov dreamed of just such a trip. It was, in fact, soccer that "remained a wind-swept clearing in the middle of a rather muddled period," as Nabokov wrote in *Speak, Memory,* a role that lepidoptery might have been expected to occupy.

Nabokov was racked by homesickness. Besides the soccer and the girls, his own Russian poetry was his central concern, and it has been pointed out he could take his Cambridge degree in French and Russian with little effort, while pursuing his own interests — few of which were directly related to his studies. "The story of my college years in England is really the story of my trying to become a Russian writer," he wrote in *Speak, Memory.* Scores of his poems, stories, and other works were beginning to appear in various Russian émigré periodicals, particularly in *Rul'*, a daily Russian-language newspaper of which V. D. Nabokov was now an editor. Toward the end of 1920, finding London a dead end, V. D. had moved the family to Berlin, which for reasons geographical and financial became the center of the Russian diaspora. There he helped set up what eventually grew into the largest Russian-language publishing house in Berlin, Slovo. The firm was owned by the large German publisher Ullstein and managed by Joseph Hessen, a friend and colleague of Nabokov's father. Slovo also turned out *Rul'*.

It was by chance that Nabokov, on a break from Trinity College, was in Berlin on March 28, 1922. At a political lecture in Philharmonia Hall, two assassins, members of the extreme right wing of the Russian diaspora, tried to shoot Paul Milyukov, one of the senior Nabokov's rivals in the Constitutional Democratic Party. V. D. Nabokov, who was sitting on the stage with Milyukov, had managed to restrain one of the assassins when the other pumped three bullets into his body. Two struck his spine, the third pierced his heart. He died almost instantly.

The murder was the most devastating event in Nabokov's life. In a fragment of his diary transcribed by his mother and reproduced in Brian Boyd's biography, there is a lucid and moving account of how word of his father's death was brought to the family. But Nabokov's first biographer, Andrew Field, found him unable or unwilling to discuss it decades later. The theme of assassination and death through mistaken identity burned its way into *Pale Fire,* which was published in 1962.

After the murder Nabokov's mother moved to Prague, where she was

eligible for a small pension. But Nabokov stayed on in Berlin after graduation, and his development as a writer can be traced through verse, drama,
short stories, and excerpts from the early novels published in *Rul'* from
1921 until the paper closed in 1930. Nabokov lived in Berlin until 1937, but
he remained aloof from German culture. Although as a child he had nav-
igated German butterfly books with the help of a dictionary, he made no
effort to learn the language. Even before the Nazi horrors Nabokov found
Germany repulsive, and in time he came to despise it utterly. But from the
early 1920s, during the years of the Weimar Republic, Berlin was the hub
of Russian émigré life, eclipsing centers in Paris and Prague. Here, professionals and intellectuals led a sort of shabby-genteel communal life, in
many ways completely independent of the Germans around them, chron-
icled in many of Nabokov's early novels and stories, including *Mary, The
Eye,* and *The Gift.*

Nabokov — as a youth a playboy and a ladies' man, another mirrorlike
inversion from his adult self, a picture of steadfast faith — had flirted with
marriage several times, but something had always snapped. In 1923 he met
Véra Slonim, a fellow exile from St. Petersburg, at a charity ball, and they
began to see a lot of each other. Nabokov played chess with her father, of
whom he wrote: "He understands so well that for me the main thing in life
and the sole thing which I am capable of doing is to write." Véra evidently
understood that as well, for with their marriage in 1925, she dedicated her
life to Nabokov's work, becoming his companion and at various times his
secretary, teaching aide, entomological assistant, and, after his death, literary executor. In his address at her funeral in 1991, Dmitri Nabokov said
that "even in her eighties, she helped with the preparation of many editions of her husband's works, wrote an introduction for a Russian edition
of his poems, assisted in the compilation of a collection of his letters,
[and] dedicated immense effort to the Russian translation of *Pale Fire.*"

By 1930 Nabokov, under the pen name V. Sirin, was widely recognized
as one of the leading lights of the emigration, the best writer of his generation, as an older exile, the Nobel Prize–winning poet and novelist Ivan
Bunin, was of his. Yet, as impressive as his output became, Nabokov was
unable even at the peak of his career as a Russian author to earn a living
solely through writing, and he had to look for other ways to survive —
anything from translation to giving lessons in French and Russian, tennis,
boxing, and poetry. Nabokov had an early affinity for the movie industry.
He and Véra, who lived in a succession of rented rooms or with Véra's
cousin Anna Feigin, managed to attend the cinema fairly regularly in

Berlin, and both occasionally found work as film extras in the city, which at the time was second only to Hollywood as a center for movie production. Nabokov also worked on a series of film scenarios, although none was ever produced. A translation of his short story "The Potato Elf" was brought to the attention of a well-known Hollywood producer, the Russian-born Lewis Milestone, who in 1930 had directed *All Quiet on the Western Front*. Milestone showed interest, at one point suggesting that Nabokov come to Hollywood, but Nabokov's subsequent offering, "Camera Obscura," which later became the novella *Laughter in the Dark,* was judged too erotic, and Hollywood had to wait until 1962, when Stanley Kubrick produced his version of *Lolita*.

In time Nabokov began to make money from literary readings, as the guest of literary clubs or universities in Germany and other parts of Europe. As Sirin's reputation grew, this European version of the lecture circuit replaced the giving of lessons as a supplementary source of income. Throughout the 1930s he read in Dresden, Antwerp, Brussels, Paris, and Prague, where he was able to visit his mother, who lovingly stacked copies of *The Entomologist* on the table beside her bed.

In some ways the 1920s and early 1930s set a familiar pattern for Nabokov's later life: the rented quarters, the consciousness of being foreign, the constant struggle both to support himself and his family and to continue with his writing. But of all the periods of his life, his childhood included, the years of the "lanky cosmopolitan expatriate" seem the most remote from the familiar image of the eccentric professor or the reclusive celebrity that stuck to Nabokov during his years in America and Switzerland. The peculiar pressures, schisms, and political divisions of the Russian emigration are obscure to most people today, and Nabokov, who plunged vigorously into the intense literary disputes of the 1930s, mellowed as he grew older.

In the introduction to *Strong Opinions,* he wrote: "The present body of my occasional English prose, shorn of its long Russian shadow, seems to reflect an altogether more agreeable person than the 'V. Sirin,' evoked with mixed feelings by émigré memoirists, politicians, poets, and mystics, who still remember our skirmishes of the nineteen-thirties in Paris. A milder, easier temper permeates today the expression of my opinions, however strong; and this is as it should be."

Nabokov had little time for butterflies during those tumultuous years. But his passion never left him; he had friends who were lepists, and he paid casual visits to museums when he could. In 1926 Nabokov and Nikolay Kardakov, an entomologist friend, traveled to the outskirts of Berlin to visit the Entomological Institute at Dahlem. There he met a famous lepidopterist, Arnold Moltrecht, "who spoke so wonderfully, so touchingly, so romantically about butterflies, that tears came right into my eyes," as Nabokov wrote to his mother. "I fell utterly in love with this old, fat, red-cheeked scientist, watched him with a dead cigar in his teeth as he casually and dexterously picked through butterflies, cartons, glass boxes, and thought that only two months ago he was catching huge green butterflies on Java. . . . I will go back and bliss out again in a few days." In the years that followed, Nabokov returned to the museum occasionally to classify rare butterflies, "moving and exciting work," he wrote.

Visiting his mother in Prague in 1930, Nabokov went to the museum there, accompanied by still another lepidopterist friend, Nikolay Raevsky. "They showed me their excellent collections," he wrote to Véra, "not of course as full as in Berlin, but you can't say that to the Czechs." Raevsky once related that, as they spoke of the tropics, he told Nabokov that it was probably a good thing for Russian literature that he had no money, or else he might have died prematurely in some place with wonderful butterflies but a dangerous climate. With "rapturous enthusiasm," Nabokov replied that he did indeed dream of traveling to New Guinea, French Equatorial Africa, or, perhaps, the Solomon Islands. "The climate is vile in all these places," he is reported to have said, "but I am young, healthy, fit, so maybe I'd stay alive to bring back fabulous collections."

The serendipity that played such a role in Nabokov's fiction often seemed to visit him in life, too, sometimes in the form of Lepidoptera. During the Berlin years he wrote to his mother of "an enchanting, utterly sweet adventure" that had happened one morning in Berlin on his way to give some lessons. "I found on a linden tree near Charlottenburg station a wonderfully rare moth — the dream of German collectors (it's rather large, with soft-emerald forewings marked with brown). I immediately took it off to the owner of a butterfly shop on Motzstrasse. He was amazed — and really it is a great rarity — and offered to spread it himself." (Although Nabokov didn't say, the creature may well have been the large and splendid Moon moth, a European relative of North America's luminescent green Luna moth.)

At last, in 1928, Ullstein paid Nabokov enough for the German rights to his second novel, *King, Queen, Knave,* to finance a substantial butterfly expedition to the Eastern Pyrenees of Southern France the following year. The four months he and Véra spent in Le Boulou and Saurat yielded more than a hundred species and subspecies, which he listed in his second lepidopterological publication, "Notes on the Lepidoptera of the Pyrénées-Orientales and the Ariège," which appeared in *The Entomologist* in 1931, ten years after his first. Among the unorthodox delights admitted by the journal's easygoing format was the recounting of a dream that Nabokov, eager for the hunt to begin, had on the night train from Paris. In his dream someone offered him "what looked uncommonly like a sardine, but was really a tropical moth, the mimic — mirabile dictu — of a flying fish."

In the windy mountains here Véra first learned to catch butterflies, and Nabokov collected images and characters to be transformed to literature, in *Despair* and in *The Defense,* on which he worked during the trip, foreshadowing a pattern he would continue for the rest of his life: restful and invigorating lepping expeditions on which he would catch butterflies during the day and write in the evenings or during bad weather.

A photograph Véra took in their hotel, the Éstablissement Thermal du Boulou, on February 27, showing Nabokov intensely at work on *The Defense,* is reproduced in *Speak, Memory.* "Seldom does a casual snapshot compendiate a life so precisely," he wrote. Before a background of family photos propped against the four volumes of Dahl's Russian dictionary, Nabokov's "writing hand partly conceals a stack of setting boards. Spring moths would float in through the open window on overcast nights and settle upon the lighted wall on my left. In that way we collected a number of rare Pugs in perfect condition and spread them at once." The Pugs and his other catches from this trip were the basis for a "wonderful" collection of Southern European Lepidoptera, which, like his earlier ones, was not to survive for long.

Now with their son, Dmitri, who was born in 1934, the couple stayed in Berlin far longer than many of their fellow exiles and certainly long after the bloom had faded from émigré culture there. In May 1936 General Biskupsky, a right-wing White Russian resented by most of the diaspora, was appointed to run the department of émigré affairs under Hitler, and, to Nabokov's revulsion, Biskupsky's second in command was none other than Sergey Taboritsky, the man who had killed Nabokov's father. When all Russian émigrés in Germany were required to register with the government, Nabokov began a concerted campaign to find any reasonable work related to literature in any corner of the English-speaking world, bombarding friends and acquaintances with letters. Some had the tone of desperation. None bore fruit.

Nabokov set out on a reading tour in early 1937, with stops in Paris (where an audience included James Joyce), Brussels, and London, and he used the occasion to take his leave of the Germans and Germany for good. Before he and Véra settled in Paris late in 1938, they stayed in various locales in the South of France, including the village of Moulinet in the Maritime Alps. The place was not a frequent haunt of butterfly collectors but was renowned, Nabokov later wrote, for some remarkable lycaenids. There, on the twentieth and twenty-second of July, amid the strong winds and steep, flowery slopes at an altitude of four thousand feet, Nabokov netted two male specimens of an unusual type of Blue butterfly. They were clearly different from the other Blues in the area, and they fascinated him for years. During another speaking engagement, in London in 1939, Nabokov visited the British Museum, but a search through its collections revealed nothing comparable. Those butterflies would become the basis for his first American scientific article, in 1941.

Paris seemed gray and gloomy to the Nabokovs when they settled there. They were among friends from the emigration, including Ilya Fondaminsky, whose journal, *Sovremennye Zapiski* (or *Contemporary Annals*) had published Nabokov's mature Russian novels in their first, serialized forms, from *The Defense* (1929–30) to *The Eye* (1930), *Glory* (1931–32), *Kamera Obskura* (1932–33), *Despair* (1934), *Invitation to a Beheading* (1935–36) and *The Gift* (1937–38). To Nabokov, Fondaminsky, who was to die in a Nazi prison camp, was "a saintly and heroic soul who did more for emigré literature than any other man."

Money remained a serious problem, and Nabokov fell back once again on giving language lessons while continuing to look for academic work abroad. In 1939, with war with Germany already declared, salvation came in the guise of an offer from Stanford University to teach a summer course in Russian literature, an opportunity almost lost through the excruciating ordeal of having to obtain exit permits from corrupt officials, and threatened further by the now-advancing Germans. Throughout his life Nabokov found anti-Semitism detestable, a position only reinforced by his marriage (Véra was a Jew). This attitude was in part inherited from his father, who at great risk to his own career had attacked anti-Semitism in a widely read article after a murderous pogrom in the Russian city of Kishinyov in 1903. Remembering that and other such principled stands, HIAS, a Jewish rescue organization in New York, offered half fare to V. D. Nabokov's son and his family on a refugee ship to America. Friends chipped in, and the Nabokovs slipped out of France at the end of May 1940, three weeks before German bombs destroyed the building in which they had been living.

Some of Nabokov's specimens, including his rare Pug moths and the Blue butterflies he had taken above Moulinet, shared the journey to America, but he had stored the bulk of his European butterfly collection, together with some private papers, in the basement of Fondaminsky's apartment building. When the Nazis ransacked the basement, the butterflies were destroyed. It was the third collection he had lost to political turmoil; for much of the rest of his life he preferred to donate his specimens to whatever institution he happened to be associated with at the time — the American Museum of Natural History, the Museum of Comparative Zoology, or Cornell University. The European specimens he managed to save, however, constituted the first impression he was to make on his new country: one of the customs men to greet him at the dock, he recalled, became interested in his collection, "and even suggested one kind be called 'captain.'"

From the first the Nabokovs embraced America as they had no other place since leaving Russia. While fellow émigrés had warned him against the provinciality and cultural backwardness of Americans, Nabokov vehemently disagreed. "This is a cultured and exceedingly diverse country," he wrote in 1941 to his friend George Hessen, himself about to emigrate from Europe. "The only thing you must do is deal with genuine Americans and don't get involved with the local Russian emigration." Nabokov in fact did not abandon his Russian friends, but there was a fundamental change in his relationship with the Russian diaspora: the émigré period of Russian literature was over, and without its emotional and near-to-the-heart political distractions, Nabokov soon began to spin all the threads of what Brian Boyd called the strange triple life of lepidoptery, writing, and teaching that he led for most of the 1940s.

As Nabokov waited for the details of his lectureship at Stanford to be worked out, he still hoped for a permanent position in academia, but work was not easily forthcoming. For a time he gave lessons, this time in Russian, and also received some support from the Literary Fund, a Russian organization that assisted writers. But with the help of Edmund Wilson, Nabokov began his American literary career as an occasional reviewer for *The New Republic, The New York Times,* and *The New York Sun.* Wilson, who became profoundly interested in things Russian during the war years, raved about Nabokov's work, and the two began one of the most notable literary friendships of the century. (It eventually deteriorated into one of the century's most bitter literary enmities, which can be traced in its demoralizing stages through the correspondence of the two men, which was eventually gathered and published.)

Because of the war America was growing more interested in things Russian, and Nabokov had hopes of working in academia as a lecturer in Russian literature. With the help of Mikhail Karpovich, a Harvard history professor he had met in Prague in 1932, Nabokov was signed up for lecture engagements under the auspices of the Institute of International Education. His first lecture was at Wells College in Aurora, New York, where his cousin, the composer Nicolas Nabokov, taught music. Another talk, at Wellesley College in 1941, led to a position there that lasted for seven years.

Lepidoptery had been on the back burner for Nabokov in Europe. But in America, despite the usual worries about money and employment, he wasted surprisingly little time in turning to Lepidoptera. He wrote almost immediately to Andrey Avinoff, a Russian lepidopterist at the Carnegie Museum in Pittsburgh, asking about American butterflies. And his lifelong dream of lepping on another continent was soon fulfilled through the hospitality of Karpovich, who invited the family to spend much of the summer of 1940 as guests at his Vermont farmhouse.

Soon after his arrival in America, Nabokov also paid a visit to the American Museum of Natural History, hoping to check his puzzling Moulinet catches. Eventually he made friends with a number of scientists there: Comstock, his mentor; the transplanted Canadian J. H. McDunnough, for whom he was to catch that series of Pug moths; and the research associate Cyril dos Passos. Comstock gave him access to research material and dissected the genitalia of his two specimens from Moulinet, a technique Nabokov knew about but had apparently never performed himself. In what for all intents and purposes was his equivalent of graduate school, Nabokov worked as a volunteer at the museum during the fall and winter of 1940 and 1941, and published two short papers in the *Journal of the New York Entomological Society* — his most sophisticated to date — including the one on his Moulinet rarities, the only European butterfly he ever formally described.

With misgivings Nabokov offered it as a new species, *Lysandra cormion*, although he suspected that it was a natural hybrid, the offspring of two other sexually compatible strains, *Lysandra coridon* and *Meleageria daphnis*. "Some of the Blues have been suspected of unconventional pairings," he wrote. (This is not an exception to the biological definition for a species, because the offspring of such successful matings are themselves sterile.) Yet he took the plunge because he doubted that he would ever have the opportunity to revisit the place to see if the line could still be found there or had died out in a single season. In *Speak, Memory* he lovingly reproduced photographs of his *cormion* and wrote, "It may not rank high enough to deserve a name, but whatever it be — a new species in the making, a striking sport, or a chance cross — it remains a great and delightful rarity." In years since Nabokov's reservations have proven well-grounded: *Lysandra cormion* is clearly not a separate species but a naturally occurring hybrid that has also been produced in the laboratory by mating *L. coridon* and *Meleageria daphnis*. Except in the annals of Nabokoviana, where it carries resonant associations, *L. cormion* is therefore an "unavailable" name.

In the summer of 1941, traveling to Stanford to take up his summer lectureship, the Nabokovs, armed with a permit issued by the American Museum of Natural History, stopped to collect butterflies at the Grand Canyon. In the canyon itself and on its rim, they captured several specimens of what he believed was a new species of the Satyr *Neonympha,* the fulfillment of Nabokov's lifelong dream. He named his discovery *Neonympha dorothea* after Dorothy Leuthold, a student who had volunteered to drive the family west and whose foot had kicked up the new butterflies from beside a trail. Nabokov had *Lysandra cormion* in mind in December 1942 when he wrote the poem "On Discovering a Butterfly," but *Neonympha dorothea* was the first to make him truly "godfather to an insect" in the way he intended it. "Pleasingly called by lepidopterists 'Nabokov's Wood Nymph,'" as he put it, it is still recognized as a distinct geographic entity, though now a subspecies, with the name *Cyllopsis pertepida dorothea* Nabokov.

Back East after his summer in Stanford, having rented an apartment in Wellesley, Nabokov traveled to Harvard's Museum of Comparative Zoology to check his Grand Canyon catches against its collection. There he found some of the material in disarray, and his offer to straighten it up as a volunteer was accepted. In 1942, after he had completed "Some New or Little Known Nearctic *Neonympha,*" on his Grand Canyon discoveries, Nabokov was appointed to the part-time position of research fellow in entomology at the museum for the 1942–43 academic year, at a salary of $1,000, raised to $1,200 a year later. Since his preparator had gone off to war, Nabokov was now the museum's de facto curator of Lepidoptera. The position would be renewed annually until he left for Cornell in 1948. In

September the Nabokovs moved to Cambridge, close to the MCZ, and he commuted to Wellesley.

Nabokov's years at the Museum of Comparative Zoology, the most important in his lepidopterological career, were the reflection of an era, and it is important to consider the historical and cultural context in which they occurred. During the war and in subsequent years, gaps in academic manpower were filled with available workers without strict regard to their professional training. What today would be considered the standard requisite of doctoral-level training for a career in systematic biology was quite rare in the 1940s. To name just one among many, Harry Clench, Nabokov's friend and contemporary at the MCZ, became a renowned expert on Hairstreaks, although he too never had a Ph.D. In fact, at the major American institutions with active Lepidoptera collections, fewer than 10 percent of curators had doctoral degrees. Nabokov was fortunate to live during a time when an intelligent and motivated individual without professional training could gain access to scientific collections and have opportunities to publish. A part-time worker would not be able to achieve such an important role in lepidoptery today.

According to Charles Remington, Nabokov, in his first years at the museum, was not particularly close to his fellow entomologists on the staff, "which included leading authorities on lacewings, parasitic and hunting wasps, ground beetles, flies and social wasps, ticks, and fossil insects, but not the butterflies which were his sole concern." But as the war came to an end, two lepidopterists, Remington and Clench — whose father was the museum's curator of mollusks — arrived in Cambridge to provide a more collegial atmosphere.

Nabokov's relationship with Clench produced a classic anecdote, recounted in the Lepidopterists' Society's twenty-fifth anniversary commemorative volume, in 1977. Like other such tales it features Nabokov's character as a practical joker. "Harry had agonized over a small *Thecla* [i.e., a Hairstreak] from southern Brazil," the volume records, "and his frustration was well known to Nabokov. One evening Harry left the specimen in a box on his work bench, and went home; the following morning when he returned, Nabokov was nowhere to be seen, but the specimen had a neatly printed determination label on it from Nabokov proclaiming it to be "*Thecla caramba* Hewitson." One has but to know how many Neotropical Theclinae Hewitson described to imagine Harry's frantic search through the literature to find the original description of "*Thecla caramba.*" It is a tribute to Nabokov's puckish sense of humor that Clench never found the description he sought, because Hewitson wrote no such description. Harry, however, liked the name and adopted it. It now stands as the valid name of a Neotropical thecline, despite the admonition of one of the elder Clench's Latin American graduate students: 'You shouldn't use that name, Harry, it is just like calling your butterfly *Thecla* hell!'"

Yet, in contrast to this pervasive image of Nabokov as a joker and to the sometimes unflattering assessments that have been offered, there is little to suggest that he was considered anything but a serious lepidopterist by his colleagues in Cambridge and elsewhere. He was duly elected to the Cambridge Entomological Society, in which he was an active participant; it was one of the few clubs or groups to which Nabokov, never a joiner, consented to belong. His correspondence with Comstock, dos Passos, Alexander Klots, Cornell University's John G. Franclemont, and other renowned lepidopterists, during these years and for the rest of his life, certainly does not suggest that any of his correspondents looked on him as an inferior.

Nabokov also applied himself with particular diligence, often to the point of exhaustion; despite the obvious joy he derived from Lepidoptera, his uncertain professional future and the workload he took up made his years at the MCZ a period of great physical and mental stress. There were stretches of time when he spent six, ten, or even fourteen hours a day behind his microscope, far more than his contract called for, a labor that in later years he claimed had ruined his eyesight. He was also conscious that his attention to his butterflies, as pleasurable as they were, was hurting his writing career. "The appalling condition of my purse," he wrote Edmund Wilson, "is my own fault, i.e., I am devoting too much time to entomology (up to 14 hours per day) and although I am doing in this line something of far-reaching scientific importance I sometimes feel like a drunkard who in his moments of lucidity realizes that he is missing all sorts of wonderful opportunities."

Throughout his life Nabokov felt the opposing tugs of literature and Lepidoptera to varying degrees, an ambivalence that found expression in a much-quoted pair of contradictory remarks. In 1966 he told an interviewer, "The pleasures and rewards of literary inspiration are nothing beside the rapture of discovering a new organ under the microscope or an undescribed species on a mountainside in Iran or Peru." Five years later, explaining that literature had been keeping him from science, he maintained that "the miniature hooks of a male butterfly are nothing in comparison to the eagle claws of literature which tear at me day and night." Yet if there was one period when lepidoptery seriously threatened to eclipse literature in his devotion, it was during his tenure at the MCZ. In January 1944 he wrote to Edmund Wilson: "Véra has had a serious conversation with me in regard to my novel. Having sulkily pulled it out from under my butterfly manuscripts I discovered two things, first that it was good, and second that the beginning some twenty pages at least could be typed and submitted. This will be done speedily."

In fact, Nabokov worked on the novel — *Bend Sinister* — off and on from 1941 to 1946. While he was at the MCZ, he also wrote his book on Gogol and short stories for *The Atlantic* and *The New Yorker,* some of which became part of *Speak, Memory,* and he had his classes at Wellesley to prepare for and teach. Particularly with that in mind, his scientific production during his years at the MCZ was extraordinary in every respect. But that came to an end when he moved to Cornell University.

For some entomologists Nabokov's lack of formal training has unreasonably tainted his work. But he had no graduate work in literature to his credit either, and this caused some foreboding before his hiring at Cornell, according to Morris Bishop, the man in charge of the university committee appointed to find a professor of Slavic literature. In a volume of essays published in honor of Nabokov's seventieth birthday, Bishop, a professor of Romance languages who was impressed by Nabokov's fiction in *The Atlantic Monthly,* wrote that a committee was "charmed by his person and impressed by the range of his knowledge and the acuteness of his judgments." On the strength of that, as well as his fiction and his critical study of Gogol — which was considered brilliant but eccentric — the committee offered the position to Nabokov over other candidates with more conventional qualifications.

Nabokov, reluctant to give up his post at the Museum of Comparative Zoology, informed Wellesley of the offer in the hope of having his lectureship made permanent. But Wellesley declined, and in 1948 Nabokov moved to Cornell, for a salary of five thousand dollars a year. It was the end of his best years as a research entomologist. Although he was gratified that Cornell's biological facilities in Comstock Hall seemed to offer a recompense for his bench at the MCZ, the uneasy balance Nabokov had struck for so many fruitful years between entomology and writing now tilted against the butterflies, if not in the field and in Nabokov's heart, at least in the laboratory. In 1974 he told an interviewer, "Since my years at the Museum of Comparative Zoology in Harvard I have not touched a microscope, knowing that if I did I would drown again in its bright well."

Indeed, most of his scholarly works on biology published after his move to Cornell were little more than notes. But his years at Cornell, where he was very popular, were productive ones in terms of literature, despite the heavy pressures of teaching. Between 1948 and 1959 he wrote numerous poems and stories for *The New Yorker*, much of *Speak, Memory, Pnin*, and, of course, *Lolita*. He also produced his academic masterpiece, the monumental four-volume translation of and commentary on Pushkin's *Eugene Onegin*, which runs to twelve hundred pages and took five years to complete. While much is made of Nabokov's successes in the disparate fields of literature and entomology, Brian Boyd points out that one must go back a century to A. E. Housman, the poet and classical scholar, to find a figure of comparable stature in both scholarship and literature, although Housman's literary output was tiny compared with Nabokov's.

Nabokov understood that his career as a lepidopterist would be judged by his scientific writings based on his work in the laboratory. But in his list of the pleasures of lepidoptery, he also distinguished other facets of that career, including the hunting of butterflies in the field. As Remington recognized, butterfly hunting was arguably more personally important to Nabokov than his scientific publications, not an uncommon feeling among lepidopterists. If his move to Cornell effectively put an end to his laboratory studies, his fieldwork continued gloriously unabated. After 1948, no matter what Nabokov's workload, there were few summers when the family, with Véra driving, failed to bundle into whatever automobile they owned at the time — Nabokov remembered a Plymouth, a Buick, a Buick Special, and an Impala, in that order — for what became their legendary rambles west on the track of Lepidoptera. Nabokov once claimed that he disliked travel unless it involved butterflies; American literature thus owes some of its best-observed pictures of the 1950s landscape of roadside motels, motor lodges, and ranch accommodations to those same butterflies. In particular *Lolita*, the most quintessentially American of Nabokov's works, owes a profound debt to these summer lepping odysseys:

"Every summer my wife and I go butterfly hunting," he wrote in the afterword to the American edition of *Lolita*. "The specimens are deposited at scientific institutions, such as the Museum of Comparative Zoology at Harvard or the Cornell University collection. The locality labels under these butterflies will soon be a boon to some twenty-first-century scholar with a taste for recondite biography. It was at such of our headquarters as

Telluride, Colorado; Afton, Wyoming; Portal, Arizona; and Ashland, Oregon, that *Lolita* was energetically resumed in the evenings or on cloudy days."

Better than almost anyone else, Nabokov, an immigrant, mastered the uniquely American milieu of *Lolita,* because of what he termed purely utilitarian grounds: from a motor court or ranch lodge, places with names like the Lazy U Motel, the family could walk out the door straight into an aspen grove, into a meadow full of lupines, or onto a rough mountainside. They would ordinarily spend only a day or two at each place, sometimes longer if the catches were good. In 1972 Nabokov explained to a *Vogue* reporter how his captures from those trips were stored in little glazed envelopes, which were labeled with the exact locality and date of the capture, data duplicated in small notebooks. The examples he offered in illustration speak for themselves of the territory he covered and clearly suggest that just such lists of the American places he had visited held for him a kind of poetry:

> Road to Terry Peak from Route 85, near Lead, 6500–7000 feet, in the Black Hills of South Dakota, July 20, 1958.
> Above Tomboy Road, between Social Tunnel and Bullion Mine, at about 10,500 feet, near Telluride, San Miguel County, W. Colorado, July 3, 1951.
> Near Karner, between Albany and Schenectady, New York, June 2, 1950.
> Near Columbine Lodge, Estes Park, E. Colorado, about 9000 feet, June 5, 1947.
> Granite Pass, Bighorn Mts., 8950 feet, E. Wyoming, July 17, 1958.
> Near Crawley Lake, Bishop, California, about 7000 feet, June 3, 1953.
> Near Gatlinburg, Tennessee, April 21, 1959.

Nabokov felt mysteriously familiar with the western states, where the montane butterflies were adapted to harsh winters and short summers, much as were those in the vicinity of St. Petersburg. "Some part of me must have been born in Colorado," he wrote to Edmund Wilson, "for I am constantly recognizing things with a delicious pang."

Those summer treks are now a staple of Nabokov lore, and friends and colleagues had proud memories of meeting the Nabokovs on some leg or another of their journeys. In the decade before he died, Nabokov was planning a second volume of memoirs, perhaps to be called *Speak, America,* and he intended to devote a chapter to these expeditions. But the account was never written. Nabokov was once asked what scenes from the past he would have liked to have filmed. His answer included: "Shakespeare in the part of the King's Ghost. . . . Herman Melville at breakfast, feeding a sardine to his cat. Poe's wedding. Lewis Carroll's picnics." One of his western expeditions would be a worthy addition to this list of delicious literary scenarios. Lacking that, Nabokov's own essay "Butterfly Collecting in Wyoming, 1952" and Robert Boyle's playful *Sports Illustrated* portrait of him in 1959 at the serious work of lepidoptery capture the volatile mixture of charm, humor, and profundity that he brought to butterfly hunting. Boyle's article is lent an added poignance because it records part of the last expedition the Nabokovs took in America.

The success of *Lolita* in 1958 allowed Nabokov to resign his post at Cornell, which brought him relief from the physical and mental burdens of teaching. But another move was more surprising to many people given the Nabokovs' professed devotion to their adopted country. A triumphant voyage to Europe, where Nabokov was to be feted by his publishers in England, France, and Italy, turned out to be the beginning of a permanent move, the final great sea change in his life. They left New York on September 29, 1959, and although they would return to the United States from time to time for reasons of business — for example, to work on the screenplay of the film version of *Lolita* in 1960 — they never settled there again. At first the couple told themselves the move was temporary, so they could be near Dmitri, who had begun a career as an opera singer in Milan, but almost imperceptibly the relocation became permanent.

In 1961 they moved into the Montreux Palace Hotel on the shore of Lake Geneva; the place perfectly fit Nabokov's ideal of the grand hotel: "absolute quiet, no radio playing behind the wall, none in the lift, no footsteps thudding above, no snores coming from below, no gondoliers carousing across the lane, no drunks in the corridor." The Palace became Nabokov's home until his death in 1977. During their first year of residence, the couple lived in a suite of rooms on the third floor of the hotel's older wing; the next year they moved to a set of cramped, modestly furnished, but soothingly tranquil rooms on the sixth and topmost floor, with a view of the lakefront and without risk of the overhead footsteps that Nabokov found so irritating. That Nabokov, now a wealthy man again, would choose to live in a hotel struck the proper eccentric note; the lines of journalists and scholars making their nervous pilgrimages to Montreux to speak with the great man became yet another part of the Nabokov legend.

Above all, it was a place where Nabokov could continue his writing without distraction and where the family could finish their work on his enormous literary legacy, the translations in and out of English and Russian and into many other languages, the letters to the editors, the endless interviews, introductions to new revisions of old work. There were reminiscences of his years as Sirin, as new battles had to be waged: a financial one with Maurice Girodias, the owner of Olympia Press, which had published *Lolita* in France in 1955, years before an American or British publisher would touch it; a literary one with Edmund Wilson over Nabokov's work on *Eugene Onegin;* and with Andrew Field over long-running disagreements about his biography.

The mountains around Montreux, like the American West, harbored the alpine butterflies that appealed to Nabokov the most. The resort of Zermatt was one favorite spot; Nabokov loved to take the chairlift, the closest thing to a magic carpet, to his favorite meadow trails. Moreover, the Nabokovs' annual butterfly expeditions continued with scarcely a break. After 1957, when Nabokov was tied up with his *Eugene Onegin* commentary, the couple hunted every summer until 1976, the year before Nabokov's death. The list of their European collecting sites, often chosen in hopes of finding specific rare butterflies, rivaled their American travels: Corsica in 1963; the hills around Lago di Garda in Italy in 1965; the Portuguese coast near Praia da Rocha in 1971; Amélie-les-Bains, a resort in the Pyrénées-Orientales near the site of their 1929 expedition.

In accordance with Nabokov's wishes, their catches from these years — 4,323 specimens — are preserved in the Cantonal Museum of Zoology of Lausanne, remarkably, in a single intact collection, something a larger museum would be reluctant to do. The butterflies were the subject of a special exhibit in 1993 and 1994, "Les Papillons de Nabokov," displayed in the lobby of the Lausanne cantonal library and grouped by locality, an arrangement the museum said "allows one to follow Vladimir Nabokov on his European peregrinations." Keeping his last great collection together in this way is a wonderful tribute to Nabokov, and perhaps some recompense for the three that were taken from him by history.

At the same time that he continued his avid collecting, Nabokov planned two massive lepidopterological studies. One was to have been a complete, color-illustrated catalog of the butterflies of Europe west of Russia, and the other was to be called "Butterflies in Art."

Nabokov agreed to put "Butterflies of Europe" together for Weidenfeld, a British publishing house, in 1962, and, typical of much of his work, the plans grew in complexity and scale over the next few years. By June 1965 they called for 346 species and about 800 subspecies represented by some 3,000 specimens on 128 plates, beginning with Linnaeus's original butterfly genus, *Papilio.* It would have been an enormous project. Nabokov was to provide an introduction and notes on classification, habitat, and behavior. For the first time since the 1940s, Véra was concerned that her husband's interest in butterflies was cutting into his time for his literary projects, like the English translations of his Russian novels, now in demand after the success of *Lolita;* the translation into Russian of *Lolita* itself; and the early stirrings of his latest novel, which turned out to be *Ada.* But the publishers began to have misgivings about the cost of the project, and despite having completed much of the work and received the resulting offer of a tidy advance, Nabokov canceled the whole arrangement rather than live with the uncertainty surrounding the book's publication.

Even while working on "Butterflies of Europe," Nabokov, ever the optimist, was researching yet another lepidopterological project that had sparked his interest as early as 1942, when Florence Read, the president of Spelman College in Atlanta, presented him with an enlarged reproduction of some butterflies on an Egyptian fresco. Nabokov saw the new project, planned for McGraw-Hill, as a purely scientific pursuit. He hoped to solve such problems as "were certain species as common in ancient times as they are today? Can the minutiae of evolutionary change be discerned in the pattern of a five-hundred-year-old wing?" Many of his subjects — in background detail painted by Old Masters like Hieronymus Bosch, Jan Brueghel, Albrecht Dürer, Paolo Porpora, Daniel Seghers, and many others — were in out-of-fashion still lifes that had to be tracked down to obscure crevices in the museums of Europe, and visiting picture galleries in Italy and elsewhere came to take up a great deal of the Nabokovs' time. They tramped through the Vatican Museums only to find a single painting with a butterfly, "a Zebra Swallowtail, in a quite conventional 'Madonna and Child' by Gentile, as realistic as though it were painted yesterday." Much of what Nabokov learned on these excursions wound up among the many paintings in *Ada,* but the eagle claws of literature ensured that, like "Butterflies of Europe," "Butterflies in Art" was never finished.

These books recall two projects that Nabokov had considered earlier in his career. During his years at the Museum of Comparative Zoology, he thought about rewriting W. J. Holland's *Butterfly Book,* a standard treatment of all North American butterflies that was first published in 1898 and reprinted in updated versions for the next half century. Nabokov thought the illustrations, though not the text, excellent. The other book was suggested to him in 1956 by Jason Epstein of Doubleday. As Nabokov described it, "It would contain my adventures with leps in various countries, especially in the Rocky Mountain states, the discovery of new species, and the description of some fantastic cases of adaptation. I think I could achieve a perfect blend of science, art and entertainment."

Any of these four high-profile volumes, had it been completed, might have significantly changed the way in which Nabokov's lepidoptery was regarded, bringing him more exposure than could the obscure realm of pure taxonomy. (Though incomplete, Nabokov's drafts for "Butterflies of Europe" are soon to be published.) It is arguably in the case of these books that his reputation in lepidoptery suffered from his devotion to literature.

In 1975, alone on a collecting outing in the mountains of Davos, Switzerland, Nabokov, a vigorous seventy-six, slipped on a steep slope, losing his net in the fall. As he tried to retrieve the net, he fell a second time and found himself unable to rise. Brian Boyd's account of the episode is one of the most moving in his biography. "He laughed at his predicament . . . and waited for the cable car to glide overhead. Seeing him laughing as well as waving, those on board assumed there was nothing wrong. Only when the cable car operator noticed the tanned old man in shorts still in the same spot as they skimmed past again did he realize he needed help, and at the end of his run sent two men down to carry Nabokov out on a stretcher. He had had to wait two and a half hours between his fall and his rescue."

Nabokov seemed not to be seriously hurt. There were no broken bones, and he resumed his work. But some people close to him believed that he was never the same again and saw the beginnings of an eighteen-month decline in his health during which he was subject to infections and fevers. He died on July 2, 1977, of fluid buildup in his lungs. In the days before, Dmitri Nabokov had visited his father in the hospital, the second to last time he would see him alive. At the end of the visit, Dmitri said, he gave his father his customary good-bye kiss on the forehead, only to see his eyes well with tears. "I asked him why," Dmitri wrote. "He replied that a certain butterfly was already on the wing; and his eyes told me he no longer hoped that he would live to pursue it again."

PART II

THE SEARCHERS

6 ❧

Scientists and Strategy

Only common butterflies, showy moths from the tropics, are put on display in a dusty case between a primitive mask and a vulgar abstract picture. The rare, precious stuff is kept in the glazed drawers of museum
cabinets. As for pursuit, it is, of course, ecstasy to follow an undescribed
beauty, skimming over the rocks of its habitat, but it is also great fun to
locate a new species among the broken insects in an old biscuit tin sent
over by a sailor from some remote island.

— *Interview with Robert Robinson, 1977*

THE VINDICATION of Nabokov's taxonomy of Caribbean Blue butterflies was a satisfying advance for those who recognized the seriousness of his commitment to lepidoptery and his scientific skill.
Clearly he had been denied his due when his carefully described categories
were passed over by Norman Riley and others. But at about the same time
that Nabokov's Caribbean accounts were being settled, independent developments elsewhere also made it possible to reconsider the part of his
work that covered a much more imposing and biogeographically significant area — the continent of South America.

There the issues involving Nabokov's lepidoptery were of an entirely
different nature than those in the Caribbean, in part because of the sheer
scale and inaccessibility of the landmasses in question. The total land area
of the Antilles is less than 91,000 square miles, and the region is often
treated by lepidopterists as a biological unity, as in Riley's field guide or
The Butterflies of the West Indies and South Florida, the 1994 book by David
Spencer Smith, Lee D. Miller, and Jacqueline Y. Miller in which Nabokov's
Caribbean research was taken into account for the first time. In contrast,
the regions of South America that provide homes for Nabokov's Blue
butterflies — above all the temperate zones of the Andes Mountains and

Patagonia — amount to more than 3 million square miles of territory, much of it remote and difficult to explore. This terrain is very diverse, too, and the study of its Lepidoptera tends to proceed country by country, with centers such as Argentina, Chile, and Peru. Yet in the late 1980s research on the Blue butterflies of South America had hardly advanced beyond Nabokov's little-known study of 1945. There had been no regional or national lepidoptery volumes that required any kind of evaluation of his work, nor had anyone tried to check its accuracy or follow it up in any other context.

Nothing illustrates this state of affairs better than a benchmark work on the biology of South America published in 1986 by Oxford University Press, *High Altitude Tropical Biogeography.* This was a study of the origins of High Andean plant and animal life compiled by several authors, among them the French scholar Henri Descimon of the University of Marseilles, who contributed a chapter on temperate butterflies. More than most lepidopterists, Descimon, an authority on Europe's mountain butterfly faunas and a veteran of fieldwork in the Andes, had a foot in both the Old and New Worlds. His chapter, one of the first comprehensive accounts of the region's Lepidoptera, concentrates mostly on pierids — Whites and Sulphurs — because considerable progress had been made in the study of those groups. When it came to Blues, however, Descimon could only cite Nabokov's obscure 1945 article, with little comment. This was not because "Notes on Neotropical Plebejinae" wasn't relevant to his considerations or because it had been superseded by other research. Rather, it was because the study was so strictly taxonomic that little could be made of it for the purposes of biogeography. Like most others Descimon could simply note how few Blue species seemed to roam the continent's temperate zones. Nabokov, by default the only authority, knew of a mere ten species organized into six of his genuses — *Parachilades, Pseudothecla, Pseudolucia, Paralycaeides, Itylos,* and *Echinargus* — all summarized and illustrated in a few short pages of type. As late as the early 1990s this paucity of Blue butterfly species was unquestioned wisdom among biogeographers and other biologists. In fact, eighty species of Nabokov's Polyommatini are known today, sixty-seven of them from temperate South America — a radically different picture.

But to Descimon in 1986, Nabokov's groups merely represented a field that remained to be explored. For the same reasons Charles Remington, in the 1995 *Garland Companion to Vladimir Nabokov,* could say only that the status of his Neotropical genuses had not been settled. Nabokov, with a modest profile in the world of lepidoptery and a reputation as an extreme splitter, was not someone whose genuses would be automatically and unquestioningly adopted. His Caribbean categories had been wrongly rejected or passed over. In South America his work existed in a state of uneasy limbo. And while the Caribbean puzzle had been resolved almost in passing by a pair of researchers who were for the most part concentrating on other groups of butterflies, assessing Nabokov's South American genuses would take concerted efforts by many scientists — which in the late 1980s showed no signs of being made.

A letter that arrived at the American Museum of Natural History in early December 1990 changed all that, however, and set off the chain of events that eventually brought the study of Nabokov's Latin American Blues to a level that the Las Abejas researchers had never anticipated. The letter, addressed to Kurt Johnson, was from Zsolt Bálint, a lepidopterist studying at the Hungarian Museum of Natural History in Budapest. Before becoming involved in lepidoptery, Bálint was a cellist, with a master's degree in music from the Liszt Ferenc Music Academy in Budapest. He had been a member of the progressive group Kis Zenei Studio, which under Communist rule somewhat daringly played many pieces by American composers; Kis Zenei Studio was itself the forerunner of the well-known Group 180, the first Eastern European ensemble to play Steve Reich's *Tehillim* and works by other progressive composers. As a musicologist, Bálint had published several papers on the traditional dance music of Transylvania and Moldavia and adapted a series of liturgical pieces by Heinrich Schütz.

Bálint still performs in Budapest's most beautiful churches as part of a liturgical group supported by the city. But in 1991, pursuing an interest in entomology under the old Communist system, he petitioned for a doctoral student's position through the Hungarian Academy of Sciences and was assigned to the Hungarian Museum of Natural History. He was in the middle of his studies and had already published several technical papers on Eurasian Blue butterflies when Mikhail Gorbachev's administration in the Soviet Union introduced glasnost and the Eastern Bloc began to disintegrate.

As Nabokov's interest in North American Blues led him southward, Bálint's widening knowledge of Eurasian Blues eventually caused him to wonder about their Latin American counterparts. The few Neotropical Blues from Eastern European collections that he had been able to dissect had further piqued his curiosity. He had heard of the lepidopterist Vladimir Nabokov but didn't realize that he was the same man who had written a novel he had recently read, *Pale Fire,* which was less diligently suppressed behind the Iron Curtain than *Lolita.* The Hungarian Museum of Natural History was more fortunate than most Eastern European institutions (which could not be expected to have complete sets of Western scientific literature) in that it had not only *Psyche* but offprints of Nabokov's articles sent there by the author himself, apparently after the war. But Bálint, concentrating on Eurasia, had not read any of them. He had noted Descimon's brief reference, but, despite his passing interest in Latin America, Eurasian Blues held Bálint's attention in 1989. And when the Berlin Wall fell he eagerly took advantage of his new freedom of travel and arranged a trip to the Natural History Museum in London to further his research.

Located on Cromwell Road near Kensington Palace and the Royal Albert Hall, the Natural History Museum has recently reclaimed the splendid ocher and blue of the tiles of its ornate Romanesque facade; before a decadelong face-lift in the 1980s, the grandly turreted structure was black, caked with a century of industrial grime. The museum's holdings, which originated in the collections of Sir Hans Sloane, bought for the nation in 1753, include what is arguably the world's most significant historical assemblage of Lepidoptera, specimens gathered over centuries from the remote corners of Great Britain's far-flung empire. Many of its acquisitions recall a time when Europe's wealthiest people collected butterflies as avidly as they did art, antiques, and orchids. Over its long history it had received incomparable bequests, including the collections of many lepidopterists who had been the major sources of scientific names in the eighteenth and nineteenth centuries, men like William Chapman Hewitson, Hamilton Herbert Druce, Arthur Gardiner Butler, and Hans Fruhstorfer; much of this material had been donated in turn by philanthropists like the Rothschilds, Frederick Godman, Osbert Salvin, and J. J. Joicey. The museum was also the recipient of the collections from the famous Biologia Centrali-Americana expeditions to the New World between 1857 and 1907; financed by a group of wealthy benefactors, these expeditions alone brought more than 100,000 tropical butterflies to London's collections, and the sponsors bought another 20,000, including an array of type specimens, many formerly in the collections of the pioneer lepidopterists Henry Walter Bates and Otto Staudinger, material of unparalleled importance in the history of taxonomy.

As a result of this splendid history, the museum owns so many specimens recognized as types by the rules of the International Code of Zoological Nomenclature that few studies of worldwide Lepidoptera can be completed without reference to its collections. This can be a problem for scientists who for economic reasons cannot travel to Britain, a common plight among taxonomists from Latin American countries. And, of course, it was a handicap for Eastern European lepidopterists before the 1990s. In 1939 Nabokov himself paid a brief visit to the museum, known then as the British Museum (Natural History), to research the unusual Blue butterfly he had captured near the French village of Moulinet the year before. But he had had no opportunity to study its holdings of Latin American Blues when he wrote "Notes on Neotropical Plebejinae" in 1945.

On the last day of his own visit, Bálint, exhausted after a week of intense study on Eurasian Blues, decided to relax and treat himself to a look farther down the museum's long rows of cabinet columns into those representing the New World. Here he saw a more extensive collection of Blue butterflies than he had imagined existed. Moreover, he was amazed at the haphazard state of the New World polyommatine collection. In contrast to other families of Lepidoptera there, even the equally humble Hairstreaks, the Latin American Blues were poorly organized; only a few had labels. During World War II, unlike most of the museum's holdings, the little-understood Blues had never been completely sorted for emergency removal to the museum's Tring annex outside London; the huge collection was largely uncharted territory.

As he scanned the rows Bálint saw many Latin American Blues that were unfamiliar to him and, he assumed, to most lepidopterists. Short of time, he resolved to return the next summer to concentrate on them alone. In the meantime, his curiosity whetted, he could visit other museums more accessible to Budapest and try to find out what further material might be found in the United States. This led to a flurry of letters to this country, among them the one to Johnson at the American Museum of Natural History.

Johnson, whose specialty was Hairstreaks, was not then known as an expert on their close relatives the Blues. But among the many papers Johnson had published was the foundation of a generic nomenclature for New World Hairstreaks, just the sort of study that "Notes on Neotropical Plebejinae" had been for Neotropical Blues. Bálint had also seen Johnson's 1988 paper naming *Leptotes idealus* from Las Abejas, an indication of interest at least. If nothing else, Johnson would be able to tell him how many Latin American Blues were in New York. To Bálint's regret, far fewer American lepidopterists were interested in Blues than in Hairstreaks, mostly because of the assumption that the New World fauna of Blues was small. In contrast, there was a large scientific literature on Hairstreaks; given their explosive diversity in lowland tropical habitats, their numbers were known to be large. Rain forest studies in the 1990s estimated that Hairstreaks might comprise up to 70 percent of unnamed butterfly faunas in certain tropical regions. South American Blues, by contrast, are barely represented in the lowland rain forests, the kind of terrain ordinarily thought of as tropical. In Nabokov's groups in particular the term *Neotropical* can be misleading for nonbiologists; despite its balmy associations, the word refers to the entire geographic zone of South and Central America and the Caribbean. In South America, Nabokov's Neotropical Blues are denizens of the continent's temperate zones, including the Andes Mountains and the Southern Cone of Patagonia, not the rain forests of the Amazon Basin.

Bálint's letter took Johnson aback somewhat. There was very little relevant material in New York, and most of that had been summarized by Nabokov in his 1945 paper. But how much other material Johnson was aware of was another matter. He was just completing extensive research on Hairstreak butterflies of the mountainous areas of Latin America. Bálint had read part of this, a study of Elfin butterflies published in the *Pan-Pacific Entomologist*. Elfins, which exhibit dull or cryptic coloring, are actually Hairstreaks without the characteristic tails, so they sometimes look like Blues. Elfins and Blues also live in the same high-altitude habitats. Over the years Johnson had been sent a large number of Blues by Latin American field researchers who recognized lycaenids but couldn't necessarily distinguish Blues from Elfins; the Blues always stirred Johnson's interest, but since he was already busy with a group made up of dozens of genuses and hundreds of species, he had had little choice but to set them aside.

Johnson's role in the field of Latin American butterflies was unusually broad, and the network of contacts he had established was pivotal in bringing the study of Nabokov's Neotropical Blue butterflies to completion. For years, in conjunction with his work on Hairstreaks, he had been traveling regularly to the Natural History Museum in London and the Muséum Nationale d'Histoire Naturelle in Paris for anatomical research on the historical specimens on which most of the South American Hairstreak names were based. Since Johnson freely shared this information, there was finally a way for Latin American lepidopterists to begin to accurately identify specimens they had collected and to distinguish new discoveries. Johnson had recorded the definitive material in Paris, but the London collections, because of their sheer quantity, had to be approached a little each year. Given the scale of modern science as most people understand it, Johnson's efforts may seem unremarkable. But because South American lepidopterists were so poorly funded and because no one else had made the effort to obtain for them the fundamental information they needed, basic studies in South American Hairstreaks had long been hindered.

Johnson had also been invited by several institutions to participate in biodiversity surveys in Argentina and Chile, both temperate countries in South America's Southern Cone rich in Blue butterflies. As a lycaenid specialist, he had been recruited by two lepidopterists working on competing national butterfly books for Chile — José Herrera and Luis E. Peña — to try to sort out the classification of Chilean Blues, a crucial step in their projects; while the country's other butterfly families had enjoyed remarkable progress in recent years, virtually all that had been published about Blues in the modern era was "Notes on Neotropical Plebejinae." Herrera, then at the Metropolitan University in Santiago, was Chile's best-known professional lepidopterist while Peña was its most notable amateur. Both had been working separately toward the same goal for most of their lives, and the competition had taken a toll: the two were far from friends. Neither was a lycaenid specialist, and each had been sending unfamiliar specimens to Johnson. When they first asked for his help, Johnson agreed to perform the morphological work their specimens required, making it clear that, in the interest of science, he would provide both of them with full reports on all the lycaenid material he received, no matter who had sent it to him. By 1989 Johnson had nearly completed the work on Chilean Hairstreaks that would be reflected in the final book — whoever its author turned out to be.

At the same time Johnson was cooperating with two Argentine missionary-lepidopterists, the Revs. Roberto Eisele and Bruce MacPherson, in tying up some of the loose ends of that country's Lepidoptera. Inevitably, that meant lycaenids, beginning with Hairstreaks: Blues, as usual, were at the end of the line. But Johnson was intimately familiar with Eisele's and MacPherson's collections and had many of their "unknowns" in his hands at the American Museum of National History. Among those were many Blues, specimens that had already suggested questions about the status of Nabokov's names for biotas on the Argentine side of South America's continental divide. He was also looking forward to a long-planned expedition to the high Andes of western Argentina, where Eisele and MacPherson had prepared a long list of promising biomes, or habitats, they had learned about in their combined thirty years of collecting in the region but had never had a chance to sample in detail.

Against this background Bálint's line of inquiry appealed to Johnson immediately, and he tried to describe as well as he could what material he knew to be on hand. If Bálint was interested in some kind of formal study of Neotropical Blues, there might be advantages for Johnson, too. Most immediately, a link with Bálint might be the most practical way of getting the Chilean Blues identified for Herrera and Peña. After all, Bálint was a specialist on Blues, whereas, aside from the technical papers on the Las Abejas *Leptotes* and the genus *Cyclargus,* the sum of Johnson's familiarity with Blues amounted to his dissections for the Chileans.

One misconception in Bálint's letter Johnson was able to dismiss at once. Bálint had noted that most biogeographers considered the Latin American fauna of Blues quite small; if this was the case, he suggested, the simplest way to proceed might be to deal with one group at a time. For example, Nabokov's genus *Pseudolucia* appeared to be easily manageable, he said, with only five or so species (Nabokov had known of only two); that group might be a good point of departure for a broader study of Latin American Blues. In fact, Johnson knew immediately of at least a dozen unnamed species of *Pseudolucia* from the material that had been sent to him by lepidopterists in the Southern Cone. He also knew of a potential wrinkle within the genus: at least one group, whose external markings were virtually identical to those of the blue-and-orange species *Pseudolucia collina,* which was known to Nabokov, revealed very different structures internally. Johnson was already well aware of the problem of such hidden diversity in the Hairstreaks, and after his experiences with the Caribbean genuses *Hemiargus* and *Cyclargus,* hardly distinguishable from the outside, he suspected that a similar phenomenon might be widespread in the South American Blues.

Johnson's reply reached Bálint at the end of 1991, and Bálint's follow-up, a mixture of elation and disbelief, was almost immediate. The wealth of recent material was wonderful news, but it also meant that there was potentially a prodigious amount of work to be done. If Bálint could see the new butterflies from Latin America before his planned trip to London the coming summer, he would be in a position to compare the new collections with the old and with the many unidentified museum specimens. He was also willing to assist Johnson with a technical paper on Chilean Blue butterflies to help advance the Chilean national butterfly book. In February 1992, with permission from Peña and Herrera, Johnson forwarded to Bálint a dissected pair of each butterfly that his initial microscopic studies had indicated was different, along with his microscopic drawings.

Bálint was amazed at the new diversity among the Blue butterflies of Chile, and this made him more eager than ever to return to London. If this much additional diversity was to be found in the recent collections, what might he discover at the Natural History Museum? Johnson proposed that the interim be used to ship the remaining material from Herrera and Peña to Hungary and that the two of them pursue Bálint's short-term suggestion — to prepare the technical paper on the material from Chile, much of it involving the genus *Pseudolucia*. Then Bálint's summer journey to London could be used to verify the Chilean identifications from the historically definitive material unique to the London collection, and, if fortune smiled on the trip, additional data from the historical material there might be added. This focus could serve the purposes of everyone — Bálint, Johnson, and the Chileans.

Bálint now felt that, whatever the results of his research, he was at least no longer working in isolation. Armed with the new specimens being gathered by field-workers in South America, together with the historical collections of Europe, he might well be on the verge of painting a picture of the Neotropical Blues far different than anyone might have expected at the time. Now, feeling the prickles of anticipated discovery, Bálint returned to the columns of drawers he had only begun to open the year before, and, by this time familiar with "Notes on Neotropical Plebejinae," he noticed Nabokov's name almost immediately. One of the museum curators, perhaps Norman Riley or perhaps his colleague, G. E. Tite, had labeled a number of specimens, apparently trying to follow Nabokov's 1945 classification. It had probably been no easy task, since "Notes on Neotropical Plebejinae" featured no illustrations of the butterflies themselves. Without dissection the meaning of his names would have had to be deciphered from the written descriptions alone, an extremely problematic undertaking among a sample as large as that in the collections, which included many entities beyond those Nabokov had been able to include in his seminal work.

The specimens that Nabokov used for "Notes on Neotropical Plebejinae" were simply those he had on hand at Harvard, augmented by others supplied by William Comstock from the Museum of Natural History in New York. Bálint realized that Nabokov had never studied the quantities of material in London, or in other major collections, and this gave reason for pause. It meant that the conception of Nabokov's South American Blues really existed in three separate worlds, two almost entirely unexploited by scientists, including Nabokov. First, there was Nabokov's study itself, which also took into consideration all the old scientific species names available from the illustrated lepidopterological works of the nineteenth century, or from later works that had in turn borrowed from them. As surprising as it may seem, the names and specimens recorded by these kinds of sources not only formed the basic body of knowledge that Nabokov drew upon for "Notes on Neotropical Plebejinae" but also served as the basis for nearly all taxonomic and biogeographic work on Latin American Hairstreaks and Blues as late as the 1980s and '90s. All this material together yielded those ten species that Nabokov himself had been able to study and to arrange in his genuses, the tip of an iceberg in relation to the other two bodies of data.

One of those was made up of the new discoveries from the field, the sort of material passed on from Chile to Bálint through Johnson in New York. And since there had been no continentwide effort to survey Blue butterflies, there was likely to be a significant number of species that existed in the wild but had never before been captured; to exploit this resource thoroughly would be a vast undertaking. The second neglected source was the old European collections, most of which had been put together between 1890 and 1920, which clearly included unknown, uncataloged, or insufficiently studied specimens.

Receipt of the Chilean material had given Bálint time to prepare. He was now familiar with the Nabokovian names and through dissection had come to share Johnson's realization that some considerable part of Blue butterfly species diversity lay hidden inside butterflies of similar external appearance. As he made his way through the rows and rows of butterflies, starting first with the rudimentary determinations made by others before him, he knew that he was on a leading edge of natural history. These specimens, along with what he had recently seen from Chile, were going to change both the accepted complexion of New World Blues and what Nabokov and others had made of them.

True to expectations, Bálint found that the London collection was rich in undescribed Latin American Blues. Not only did he see older specimens of some of the species that Johnson had sent him but he also found ample new species, in the genus *Pseudolucia* as well as in other Nabokov groups. It seemed to him incredible that, nearly half a century before, Nabokov had published a seminal nomenclature for such a huge group of butterflies but that no one, Nabokov included, had ever continued the research. It was, in a sense, a commentary on the problems in the taxonomy of Lepidoptera in general: too few trained workers, even fewer jobs, and a tendency for modern natural science to skip from fad to fad instead of completing the basic, tedious work of classification. It was even more incredible that unwarranted conclusions about the New World Blues, such as their supposedly low numbers of species, had been drawn by biogeographers based on such incomplete data.

But it is the truth in entomological taxonomy: the postwar years, with their relatively simple methodological procedures, should have been the time for much basic work to be completed, but instead, by the time *Sputnik* had pushed American science into today's far more sophisticated realms, it simply went undone. Modern biogeographers and students of evolutionary genealogy, armed with sophisticated mathematics and high-speed computers, were in some cases still relying on estimates of diversity published near the turn of the century. As for the butterflies of the temperate regions of South America, Descimon had complained in 1986 that biogeographers had little choice except to follow the order that Max Draudt had established in his contributions to Adalbert Seitz's *Macrolepidoptera of the World* in 1921; despite its defects it was the only general arrangement available. It makes one wonder what all the graduate students and new Ph.D.'s were doing between 1926 and 1986, and particularly between 1948, when Nabokov left the Museum of Comparative Zoology at Harvard to teach Russian literature at Cornell, and 1991. They were, in fact, mostly involved in science's further sophistication, not wrong in itself but in some ways out of balance with the fundamental need for furtherance of the basic work of natural science.

His discoveries, however, failed to satisfy Bálint. What he had seen on this second visit to London — which he was now sure could not be his last — made him realize that the plans he had suggested to Johnson, the elaboration of the Chilean Blues, mostly species of *Pseudolucia*, did not go far enough. He eventually decided to compile a taxonomic catalog of the Latin American Blues found not only in London but in all the old European collections. That project, with the new species it recorded, both provided a broader basis for comparison with recently captured specimens and formed the foundation of Bálint's doctoral dissertation, itself a significant contribution to the field of Latin American Blue butterflies. But even more important, he now decided that the effort finally had to be made to bring Nabokov's 1945 project to completion.

Although Bálint wasn't thinking in such terms at the time, his suggestion in effect aimed at the heart of Nabokov's lepidoptery. It meant that his most important piece of work would have to be scrutinized in a way that it had never been before, in a context far more broad and far-reaching than any of his other papers had involved. That was because in terms of the taxonomic Code, Nabokov's work on the Neotropical Blues had been that of a first reviser — the first person to arrange an entire group into a comprehensive classification. In this, "Notes on Neotropical Plebejinae" is different from all the rest of Nabokov's scientific work, substantially more significant in its taxonomic and geographic breadth.

From a historical perspective, taxonomic work is never carried out in isolation. It is a continuing process involving successive generations of scientists who make new discoveries of their own and review and revise the work of their predecessors. The work of the first reviser becomes the baseline study for the group in question (in this case, the Neotropical Polyommatini) and to one degree or another will exert an influence on the classification of all subsequent discoveries. But at the same time scientists working with the first revision continually test their results against it; if for some reason it proves inadequate or erroneous, it is modified or, in principle anyway, even completely discarded. As we have seen, Nabokov understood this, relishing the competition implied if a classification is "pleasurably exploded in a dazzling display of polemical fireworks when a new discovery upsets the old scheme." He would no doubt have found it less pleasurable if the old scheme happened to be his own, but he faced even that possibility realistically. Describing his "Notes on the Morphology of the Genus *Lycaeides*," to Edmund Wilson in 1944, he said, "It is going to remain a wonderful and indispensable thing for some twenty-five years, after which another fellow will show how wrong I was in this and that. Herein lies the difference between science and art."

Something as comprehensive as Nabokov's 1945 study demanded evaluation on several levels: for their purposes Bálint and Johnson would have to scrutinize every aspect of "Notes on Neotropical Plebejinae" in the light of their new discoveries, and it was clear there would be many. One of the matters under consideration would be a purely technical one: the study's concordance with the modern rules of zoological nomenclature. These had evolved since Nabokov's time, something which he could not have foreseen but which could nevertheless be decisive in determining whether his classification would be accepted or rejected. Several facets of Nabokov's ability as a scientist would also be tested, including his historical scholarship — for example, how well he had assessed and assimilated the work of those who came before him and his acumen in identifying natural groups of Blue butterflies through his dissections — the basic work of taxonomy.

There were other factors too. First, more than forty years had passed since "Notes on Neotropical Plebejinae" had been published and then, for all practical purposes, put into a drawer. Johnson had been impressed with its treatment of Caribbean butterflies, but otherwise there was no reason to assume that something written so long ago and completely untested would prove valid for the whole of South America. Today Bálint and Johnson speak easily of "completing Nabokov's project," but at the time their intention meant simply offering the first thoroughly researched, modern study of the Latin American groups he touched upon.

Also, as has been pointed out, because of the restrictions under which he worked, Nabokov's study was based on an extremely small sample — 120 specimens, mostly from the collection at the Museum of Comparative Zoology — and thus was vulnerable to sampling error, as he well knew. This could profoundly affect its merit as a regional study in light of subsequent scientists' work on the world's Lycaenidae. If establishing a taxonomy for Latin American Blues could be compared to putting together a jigsaw puzzle, the task facing Bálint and Johnson over the next several years was in part to gather up enough of the pieces — sample specimens and representative species — to form a meaningful, accurate picture of the Blue butterfly fauna of South America, something that Nabokov might not have been able to do with his 120 specimens.

Finding new butterflies in, say, the natural history museum, or in the field, is something like an art historian's discovering a large stash of previously unknown but original works by Titian or Michelangelo: in the latter case there is the potential for centuries of art history and criticism to be stood on its head, particularly if it has been based on faulty premises or mistaken conclusions drawn from what was after all an incomplete body of work. To put this point at its most basic for the classification of butterflies, if the few species of Latin American Blues known to Nabokov were just the tip of a taxonomic iceberg, what was the rest of the iceberg like — how many species of Latin American Blues remained to be discovered? And how well would Nabokov's skeleton taxonomy — his new South American genuses — accommodate those discoveries?

Together the answers to all these questions would to a large degree offer what is probably the only possible objective measure of Nabokov's formal lepidoptery. They would determine whether Nabokov would continue to be seen as a marginal expert in a handful of northern species or as the capable pioneer reviser for a large, scientifically significant, and geographically widespread subfamily of butterflies. In terms of a lepidopterological reputation, the difference is profound. Moreover, how Bálint and Johnson set about finding those answers sheds light not only on Neotropical Blue butterflies and "Notes on Neotropical Plebejinae" but on the ways lepidoptery has changed from Nabokov's day.

To begin with, there were several reasons the questions were being asked only now. The lack of interest in South American temperate butterflies, particularly lycaenids, was one. But in addition, as Bálint and Johnson immediately realized, only recently had a set of circumstances arisen that allowed interested lepidopterists in Europe, the United States, and South America easily to bring their combined efforts to bear. The contacts that Johnson had made in South America and, now, Bálint's exploration of the historical material in Europe finally meant that all the untapped resources could be exploited reasonably easily: there would be an incomparably larger sample of specimens than Nabokov had had, from both old and new collections. And attention could be paid to the historical type specimens, which was required under the rules of modern taxonomy. In the years immediately after Nabokov published "Notes on Neotropical Plebejinae," individual workers, isolated in Europe or North or South America, might have had one or another of these elements at hand, but the fact that potentially interested scientists had been unable to line all of them up prevented any effective follow-up to Nabokov's original work.

As hard as it is to remember in this era of instant communication and easy travel, the world's oceans have historically formed difficult boundaries to scientific interchange. In many areas of human endeavor it was only after World War II that the concept of international cooperation became widespread. And even as politics and economics began to aim in this direction, science was not always quick to follow. In fields such as physics and chemistry, much work was intentionally kept secret for military or economic reasons, but in the biological sciences lack of cooperation was in large part a result of the lack of awareness that the biotas of the separate continents were inextricably intertwined in their histories and destinies. Taxonomy in particular resisted internationalization, with genuses and other higher taxonomic categories often tailored to fit the organisms within given shores. Against the background of these assumptions, few taxonomists felt the need to keep in close touch with colleagues across the oceans, even when it was possible to do so. And even without the concrete political barriers that hindered the movement of people and information until the end of the Cold War, the views and goals of both individuals and institutions were by and large parochial.

This circumstance had various reflections in Nabokov's career. As Charles Remington noted in the *Garland Companion*, Nabokov's background allowed him to find similarities between European and American butterflies that Americans typically failed to notice. On another level is a letter written to Nabokov in 1944 by Austin Clark of the Smithsonian Institution, to whom Nabokov had sent a copy of one of his *Lycaeides* papers, which involved some speculation on Asian-American connections: "What a joy it is," Clark wrote, "to find that there is someone interested in our American butterflies who does not subconsciously entertain the concept that Bering Strait [*sic*] is an impassable line separating the fauna of North America from that of Asia!" (This letter, incidentally, also shows that some colleagues thought Nabokov more advanced in some respects than the general run of lepidopterists of his time.)

The inability of many South American lepidopterists to travel to foreign museums is a handicap in the formal study of Neotropical butterflies even today, given the voluminous old museum material scattered around in the world's collections, particularly in Europe. Four imperial nations — Great Britain, France, Spain, and the Netherlands — had colonies in the New World, and Germany made up for its direct lack of access through its enthusiasm for entomological acquisition. There is a long list of museums that had managed to acquire old South American specimens through the commercial trade.

One of the reasons these museums are so important is that they contain so many of the type specimens on which almost all taxonomic research must be based under the modern rules. It might seem an odd convention to nonscientists, but a type specimen — a single, designated specimen — serves as the definition of a species. Just as a meter is technically defined in science as the length of a certain platinum rod kept at the United States Bureau of Standards, the Code requires a scientist who first names a new species to designate a particular specimen as the standard, or type, of that name. This type specimen becomes the basis for all subsequent comparisons — external, anatomical, geographic, and so forth — that have any bearing on the formal meaning of that name. Type specimens were de rigueur in Nabokov's day as well, and he treated them as precious and rare, as poetically symbolic of a kind of immortality, both for the insect concerned and for the scientist who named it. But, unlike today, in 1945 there were no universal rules that required direct reference to the type specimen during revisionary work like what Nabokov carried out. He was free to study references and descriptions of the type in secondary printed material — which were often extremely slipshod — and make what amounted to his own best-guess inferences.

The advantage of this for Nabokov was that he was not obligated to travel to Europe to view type specimens for his study (or else to obtain descriptions from others on which he was willing to base the legitimacy of his work, not a likely prospect). The disadvantage now — under rules that were made after Nabokov carried out his work but that nevertheless are retrospectively applied to it — is that any errors Nabokov made in interpreting these materials, whether his own fault or the fault of his sources, could conceivably lead to the disqualification of his genuses. In any case the lack of easily available information on a broad range of type specimens was a particular hindrance to lepidoptery and other branches of natural science. Developments in communications and travel after World War II, and, in the case of Nabokov's Latin American Blues, the collapse of the Iron Curtain, radically changed the environment of taxonomy.

But as Bálint was discovering, the old museums are important for a more surprising reason: they are repositories for huge numbers of specimens of undescribed butterflies. Since the 1970s Johnson had been making regular twice-yearly trips to Europe for his own research on Hairstreaks, and he knew there were at least fifteen old European museums whose holdings demanded attention for anyone studying South American lycaenids. He had found, as did Bálint after him, that the specimens relevant to his studies were often either labeled "unidentified" in curated collections or left completely unsorted in unaccessioned backlogs.

In places like the Natural History Museum in London, the condition of the unaccessioned material in particular runs completely counter to the usual idea of well-ordered rows of specimens in intensely studied collections. Specimens are typically packed in Schmidt boxes — wooden containers not unlike cigar boxes — and scattered haphazardly in hundreds of storage cupboards. These corners of chaos are far from unusual: in fact, they typify the old museums. Looking through the storage boxes of unincorporated butterflies in such collections, searching for surprises or important specimens that might have been overlooked, is known to lepidopterists as treasure-hunting. (This is what Nabokov meant by the sailor's "old biscuit tin" in the epigraph to this chapter.)

This material typically includes specimens as old and as many in number as those recorded in the historical literature, and sometimes entire historical collections that have gone astray. As far as Johnson knows today, to whatever extent previous workers in lycaenids had ever studied this material, until his work on the Hairstreaks none had published any of it. While the popular idea of butterfly discoveries almost exclusively involves places like Las Abejas, with scientists wielding nets in the jungle — which is obviously important — the unaccessioned material in the old European museums has been the source of the majority of the new-species discoveries in lycaenid butterflies, particularly Hairstreaks and Blues, since the 1970s.

Both Bálint and Johnson began arranging their schedules to facilitate further visits to the European collections through 1992. In addition to Bálint making the rounds of the continent's smaller institutions, both made trips to places like the Natural History Museum and the Muséum Nationale d'Histoire Naturelle in Paris. Johnson's primary duties in London, connected with previous commitments, were to rearrange its specimens of Andean Hairstreaks according to the new classification he had devised and then to begin work on groups of lowland Hairstreaks. Johnson spent much of his time treasure-hunting for Hairstreaks, and since he was plowing box by box through both accessioned and unaccessioned materials anyway, he told Bálint he would sort out all the strange-looking Blues as well. He would then leave anything unusual he found for Bálint to study upon his arrival.

Simultaneously, they spent the year preparing the new material for scientific publication. As in Nabokov's day it was a long, tedious physical process, hard on the eyes and spirit. And even when such work has been drafted and submitted for review, there are commonly lags of a year or more before it sees print. Taxonomists often complain that their work is 10 percent discovery and 90 percent drudgery. The proportions explain why some lepidopterists with rich hauls, even professionals, never go further than arranging their new discoveries in their own collections, sometimes lost to science.

But if the timing of their trips worked out and the scientific papers on the *Pseudolucia* of Chile and Argentina could be drafted at the same time, Bálint and Johnson would be well on schedule to publish the first fruits of their research by the end of 1992 and begin getting the follow-up of Nabokov's great project into the official scientific record. By that year they knew that the extent of the riches in the Natural History Museum alone meant that the museum's sortings easily eclipsed the numbers of both species and specimens of Blue butterflies that had been collected by Herrera and Peña; for scientists in the know, the whole complexion of the group had already changed; Bálint and Johnson were looking at at least twenty additional species of just *Pseudolucia,* the genus the two had agreed to sort out for Peña and Herrera.

Because of this wealth Bálint and Johnson realized early on that if they tried to complete the study of Nabokov's Latin American Blues, they would be naming many new species. Some spectacularly marked specimens had already been labeled as unnamed species by Peña and Herrera, and they were among the first to be brought to Bálint's and Johnson's attention. In recognition of Nabokov's historical contribution to the taxonomy of Latin American Blues, the two had often discussed using a particularly rich source of new names — his own life and writings. After all, considering his 1945 contribution and its broad geographic and taxonomic implications, the region was in their eyes already Nabokov's territory, no matter how his genuses were finally evaluated.

As it had so often in the past, chance played a large role in this aspect of the project, now in a visit to the American Museum of Natural History in January 1991 by G. Warren Whitaker, a New York attorney who was also an avid reader of Nabokov and a member of the International Vladimir Nabokov Society, a group for scholars and enthusiasts organized by Stephen Jan Parker at the University of Kansas. Whitaker knew that Nabokov had worked at the museum and had donated specimens, and he was curious to see that material for himself. At the time much of it was kept in cabinets in Johnson's office, which Nabokov had formerly used. Because of Nabokov's celebrity, it was common for the Entomology Department to receive requests for visits; in fact, over the years the curator, Dr. Frederick H. Rindge, had often tired of using valuable research time to attend to them and was more than happy that someone else in the department was now working on Nabokov and his butterflies. So it was Johnson who responded to Whitaker's request.

Despite Whitaker's familiarity with Nabokov's literary writings, he had never seen any of the author's scientific papers, and Johnson was not only happy to show him but also to explain the progress of his continuation of Nabokov's work. While making photocopies of Nabokov's papers for Whitaker, Johnson happened to remark that he and Bálint had always thought it an appropriate gesture to name new species after people, fictional characters, places, and things in Nabokov's life or work but didn't know quite how to go about it. Although he and Bálint had at various times been casual readers of Nabokov, Johnson felt that neither of them had the immediate knowledge, or the spare research time, to do a competent job of researching the etymologies for such names — that is, the explanations of the names, however brief, that would be required by the Code. To Johnson's surprise Whitaker volunteered for the job at once. Thus, quite casually began the practice of giving Nabokovian names to new species discoveries in the Latin American Blues.

Not every new Blue was given a Nabokovian name, however. Like most taxonomists, Bálint and Johnson used a mix of naming techniques. The Code itself recommends three broad categories of etymologies — people, places, and descriptive objects or characteristics. The "people" names can come from just about anywhere, from mythology or history, for example. But sometimes they are those of scientists who have been associated in some way with the butterfly in the past or, more familiarly, names with some personal significance to the taxonomic author, such as those of a colleague or a spouse. Before getting involved in the Nabokov project, Johnson had already named a butterfly for a celebrity, one whose work was in fact much better known among biologists and the general public than Nabokov's. In the early 1990s, he noticed a "Far Side" cartoon, entitled "Butterfly Yearbooks," in which a caterpillar was labeled "Kurt Johnson, Class of '68." That was rather amazing, since Johnson had graduated from the University of Wisconsin in that year, and he immediately began receiving inquiries from his lepidopterist friends around the country asking how he had managed to get into a Gary Larson cartoon. Curious himself, he wrote a letter to Larson, who replied that he had just pulled both the name and date out of the air. But he also mentioned that an entomologist had recently named a louse after him. To this Johnson replied that he deserved better, and suggested an upgrade. Accordingly, in 1991 Johnson gave Larson's name to a colorful Ecuadorian Hairstreak, *Serratoterga larsoni*. Names of places are often based on locales or regions from which the butterflies come.

The final category consists of names reminiscent of the physical characteristics of the butterfly, a source the Code might be interpreted to prefer. Nabokovian names could cut dizzily across all these categories. But most modern taxonomists try to avoid drawing on only one source for their names (particularly the names of family members, colleagues, and friends, a sure route to a reputation for narcissism). However, given Whitaker's ability to prepare reliable and informed etymologies for Nabokovian names, as required by the Code for eventual scientific publication, Bálint and Johnson felt free to start using them for many of the new species they discovered. After being filled in on some of their captures to date, Whitaker immediately provided a brief list of possible names and the reasons he thought they made good candidates.

And the naming could begin almost immediately. Among the discoveries from Johnson's trip to London in May 1992 was a Blue butterfly, a member of the group that Nabokov had known as *Itylos,* that received the name *lolita.* This species was so unusual that it had masqueraded as a Hairstreak in London's Natural History Museum collection. During World War II the most valuable holdings in the museum — the priceless historical types and specimens that appeared to be otherwise unique in some way — were removed to Tring Castle outside London. *Lolita* was sheltered from the German bombs because she fit into the latter category, thought to be an unknown Hairstreak, vaguely similar only to the well-known *Strymon* species *bazochii,* named by the Frenchman Jean Baptiste Godart in 1824.

After the war the little Blue was brought back to Cromwell Road as part of what is now called the World War II Reference Collection. Johnson found it there and left it with the museum's curator, Phillip Ackery, for Bálint to work on the following August. Bálint himself had been unsure whether — with its blue dorsal surfaces, slightly tailed hind wing, and cryptically colored ventral of black, gray, and white, arranged in an angulate, camouflaged pattern — it belonged to any known Latin American genus. These markings and the presence of a large black dot beneath the tail had allowed it to masquerade as a Hairstreak: the dot was of the sort that lepidopterists recognize almost automatically as the Thecla-spot, which typifies Hairstreak butterflies. It was this delicate little Blue, a cross-country traveler with a captivating and enigmatic personality, that took the special name.

But *lolita* was just one of thirteen Nabokovian species names suggested by Whitaker that appeared in Bálint's early 1993 catalog, the first official fruits of his research. Also in London, in Nabokov's *Parachilades,* he discovered three specimens of an oddly marked species whose undersurfaces, instead of having the stripes that typify the genus, showed a fragmented checkerboard pattern. He chose for this species Whitaker's suggested name *luzhin* — after the chess monomaniac in the novel *The Defense.* And a new species of *Pseudolucia* found there had fooled its original captor, the noted turn-of-the-century British collector Henry John Elwes. Elwes, an expert on Asian butterflies who is mentioned in *The Gift,* had labeled it as a member of the Blue genus *Scolitantides.* But G. E. Tite had recognized the error and clearly marked it "sp. n.," the standard notation for "new species." Because of this name change Bálint called it *sirin,* Nabokov's old European nom de plume.

As the point man in Europe, Bálint was also making the rounds of the continent's other institutions, among them the Muséum Nationale d'Histoire Naturelle in Paris, the Naturhistorisches Museum in Basel, and the Naturhistorisches Museum in Vienna, all of which produced important specimens for the study of Nabokov's Blues. Like London they typify the grand imperial era. Nabokov venerated such places for the august lepidopterological history they represented, an important fact to grasp if one is to understand his attitudes toward lepidoptery.

In Paris the premiere butterfly collection of the Muséum Nationale d'Histoire Naturelle had been bought specimen by specimen by an aristocratic patron of science, Aimée Fournier de Horrack. Housed in a special room graced with its original ornate wooden cabinets and with portraits of the grand lady herself, Madame Fournier's collection has produced more than its share of new discoveries since its treasures came to the attention of specialists. The initial beneficiary, before the collection became the property of the museum, was the British entomologist Percy Lathy, whom Madame Fournier hired as its first curator and who named more than fifty new Hairstreak species from its holdings.

This famous collection, however, was not to be Bálint's pot of gold. Instead he turned up a spectacular new *Paralycaeides* while trawling through the museum's other old material, stored in an annex to the main building. Unlike the central structure, the annexes have not had their superstructures cleaned in a century or more. Treasure-hunting in their attics and storage rooms means opening myriad little wooden boxes so covered in soot that at the end of the day the lepidopterist looks like a chimney sweep. Bálint's new *Paralycaeides,* identified on the basis of two specimens labeled "Huancayo, Peru," showed a stubby tail in the hind wing and was red-brown above and golden beneath, with large, blocklike black spots and vivid white highlights, all characteristics never before seen in this genus. He named this flashy species *shade,* after Nabokov's alter ego, the poet John Shade, whose poem in the novel *Pale Fire* was twisted into a brilliant kaleidoscope of pathological fancy by the mad commentator Kinbote. Aside from those two old specimens in Paris, the species remains virtually unknown, appearing in no modern collections, not even the vast Peruvian holdings of Gerardo Lamas at the national museum in Lima.

By the 1990s these old museums had undergone profound changes since their days of glory. Their grandeur and the exalted stature of their one or two curators, the lofty Herr Professor or Herr Doktor, had faded as rapid social-scientific changes and persistent financial difficulties undermined the status of the natural sciences, so redolent anyway of a bygone era. A visible result was that the biology collections at such institutions had lost many of the trappings they had once been afforded. The entomological collections at Vienna, for example, had been moved since Bálint's first visits there. They were no longer in the imposing sister building opposite the fine arts museums on the most symmetrical square in Vienna's famous Ring, but had become part of the public library. Lost in the move were the enormous, somberly lighted rooms of the kaiser's era, with their ornate painted ceilings, Rococo-ornamented appointments, and lovely blue-gray-finished display cabinets. The new collection area is a clean, well-lighted place, the new cabinets of the modern supermarket variety — safe, fireproof, but dull and spiritless. Gone too was the elderly curator Bálint had first met there, Friedrich Kasy, at the time the grand old man of Austrian lepidoptery, with his pure white hair and a short white beard, a man who in turn had inherited the spirit of an earlier era, when the famous Hans Rebel, a close colleague of Otto Staudinger — and mentioned with reverence in Nabokov's short story "The Aurelian" — had been Vienna's most prominent lepidopterist.

Kasy had died in 1990. Fortunately, the new curator, Martin Lödl, had lost none of the cordiality that has always marked this famous institution, and after two visits Bálint was able to locate some invaluable material there. This included not only Latin American Blues but what he considered a precious look at surviving specimens from the eighteenth and nineteenth centuries, collected in habitats in and around Vienna itself, that have now been extinct for well over a hundred years.

It was much the same at the Zoologische Staatssammlung in Munich, once housed in the old castle of Nymphenburg and surrounded by a magnificent park and canals filled with swans. When Bálint had first climbed the imposing stone steps for a visit there in 1984, the curator was Walter Forster, a pioneer worker on Blue butterflies. Bálint found him on a high ladder, peering into glass-topped drawers pulled from a fine bank of cabinets, all full of magnificent Blues.

Forster had begun his career shortly before World War II and, in 1936, published a study of *Lycaeides argyrognomon*, a species on which Nabokov also became an expert in the next decade. As was so typical in the careers of many German entomologists, the war interrupted Forster's work, but he began publishing again in earnest in 1951. In part because of the different eras in which the men worked, Forster's views of Blues differed significantly from those of Bálint and other younger European students of Lepidoptera. In particular, his taxonomic views were distinctly Germanocentric. It was what non-Germans, like Bálint, in an exercise of dry humor, called "the horizontally extended view." Forster seemed to lump everything into a small number of omnibus species spreading out every which way from Germany.

Ever the gentleman, Forster would courteously remind Bálint that every species Bálint was speaking of was really a mere subspecies of some other, more centrally located, European species. It was rare for such a view as Forster's to embrace the distinctiveness of lesser-known populations of Blues in far-off places like Kurdistan or the Urals, and certainly not in locales with barely pronounceable names in the wilds of Siberia or the Himalayas. It was a point of view that annoyed Nabokov, who was hard-pressed to agree with Forster even when he appeared to be right. In his 1944 "Forms of *Lycaeides*" paper, Nabokov wrote that a report by Forster of a certain species from Siberia would have been "fairly plausible had not Forster's work been full of the most preposterous blunders."

In fact, Nabokov might have taken double offense, not only as a taxonomist but as a Russian, for the majority of names that Forster merged into the oblivion of his favorite Blue species, *pylaon*, were those of Emerich Frivaldszky, a great Balkan lepidopterist whose publications also embraced many of the East Asian regions like Amur and Transbaikal traveled by Fyodor's father in *The Gift*. Even the author of *pylaon*, Gotthelf Fischer von Waldheim, was a favorite of Nabokov's, mentioned in *The Gift* along with Fyodor's fictional father as among the greatest of lepidopterists who worked in Russia, along with Eduard Eversmann and Edouard Ménétriés.

But for Bálint, aside from the usual competitive frisson associated with the clash of old and new science, there were no practical consequences to disagreement. Forster was the consummate mentor and created a welcoming environment for all younger workers at this grand museum. He took no offense that Bálint appeared to be in Munich as a champion of Nabokov.

When Bálint returned in 1993, however, the landscape had changed in more ways than one. Most of the Staatssammlung's lepidopterological collection had been moved to a new building in the western part of the city. As Bálint was finding the place, it seemed to him that the local people of whom he asked directions were hostile; later he learned that because the new institute had been built underground, many believed it actually housed a secret military laboratory rather than a collection of zoological specimens. And the faces in the neighborhood were not the only unfriendly ones. Forster had been replaced, and his successor, Wolfgang Dierl, who has since died himself, had gained a reputation for cantankerousness, which Bálint chalked up to old age. Warned that it was hard to get a response to written inquiries, Bálint made the opposite mistake of arriving unannounced. He had met the new curator before, in the company of Forster, and was sure he would be remembered.

That, however, was not the case, and Bálint found himself standing outside the institute's locked door being chided from a window for having shown up without permission. When he said his business was a desire to examine the collection's Polyommatini, Bálint was told that there was nothing to be done for him in any case, since "no one here knows those bugs." To this Bálint replied, "I don't need help, because I am, in fact, the one who does know them," and he began to recite the drawer numbers of the specimens he wanted to see. Such precision immediately melted the ice, and Herr Dierl apologized for not having understood Bálint's purpose and called for his assistant to bring the drawers. To his dismay Bálint was still not allowed into the main collection, but he was able to examine the appropriate trays in a separate room. His persistence paid off, and he discovered among the trays a new Argentine species of Nabokov's genus *Pseudolucia,* for which D. Barton Johnson, a Nabokov scholar at the University of California at Santa Barbara, later suggested the name *tamara,* after Nabokov's first love. "Tamara is a name with deep Nabokovian resonance," he wrote.

> Tamara, with its echo of the Russian word *tam* ("there" — as opposed to the "here" of his lifelong exile), signified many things to Nabokov, among them the idea of a transcendent world. But most obviously it evokes Tamara, his first love, described in Chapter 12 of *Speak, Memory.* Separated by whim and then by revolution and exile, Tamara became the theme of Nabokov's first novel, *Mashenka.*

The old European museums, which had concealed their treasures of Blues for so many years, were finally yielding the fruits of collecting that had begun with the great Age of Exploration. But in some cases these "new" discoveries had arguably been made just in time, as the museums themselves were in the throes of profound cultural change. Particularly after the world recessions in the 1970s and late 1980s, scientific institutions faced pressure to be more self-supportive and to provide an economic rationale for their activities. Budget cuts meant smaller staffs. Many museums stopped curating new specimens into their permanent collections, and some could no longer adequately protect their old ones.

In London, for example, secretaries disappeared, bevies of departmental assistants shrank to one or two. The curators lamented that if not for the historical value of their old collections in light of the biodiversity crisis, they might have been hard-pressed to make their case for continuing to exist at any appreciable level of activity. Their identification services now had price tags, and use of their collections required bench fees. New collection donations could no longer be curated and were, instead, made available to visitors on an as-is basis. It was all understandable, of course, in terms of modern economic and cultural priorities, but it was not the culture to which so many taxonomists of earlier generations in both the Old and New Worlds had been accustomed. Moreover, the culture of lepidoptery was changing. With the swing away from basic taxonomy and toward theoretical analysis requiring computer technology more than specimens, far fewer of the elite scientists in lepidoptery's new order bothered to visit these collections anymore.

By 1993 there was still much work to be done on Nabokov's Neotropical Blues. Bálint and Johnson knew, as they continued to assemble the pieces for their great jigsaw puzzle, that there was a great deal of fieldwork to do, and they had already begun to turn their attention to South America. The Blue butterflies that had spent decades in the great European museums had now given up many of their secrets; in all, eleven new species of Nabokov's Blues, including ten given Nabokovian names, were discovered there. Yet those discoveries came not because of any scientific advances since the days of Nabokov but merely from a modicum of diligence, application, and interest. At last, in the early 1990s, someone had simply made the effort to do the research. It was nothing that Nabokov himself might not easily have done had he found a way to remain in Europe during and after the war or had he had a way to return there during the crucial stages of his research. Then these new species, too, would certainly have found a place in his seminal classification for New World Blue butterflies.

When a lepidopterist thinks of Nabokov in his later years, painstakingly making the rounds of the very same European cities in search of painted specimens for his uncompleted "Butterflies in Art" project, it is impossible not to imagine this diligence transferred to a search for the real thing. But Nabokov, not wishing to be drawn back into the bright well of his microscope, had consciously forsaken formal taxonomy, so those discoveries were left to Bálint and Johnson.

7

The Incorrigible Continent

In my dreams I saw the winding road, the caravan, the many-hued
mountains, and envied my father madly, agonizingly, to the point of
tears — hot and violent tears that would suddenly gush out of me at table
as we discussed his letters from the road or even at the simple mention of
a far, far place.

— *The Gift*

SOUTH AMERICA is the fourth largest of the world's continents, with
an area of nearly 7 million square miles, 12 percent of the earth's total land surface. On a globe South America stands out first in its isolation, surrounded by ocean except for the narrow neck of land at the
Isthmus of Panama, a mere 70 miles wide at its narrowest point, that con-
nects it tenuously with the North American continent. Even this slender
link has not always existed. Scientists believe it has been built at least
twice, each time by the region's persistent volcanism, with fragments of
the earlier breakup in the age of the dinosaurs supplying the crustal blocks
that now form the West Indies. The present bridge has been in place only
for the last 2.5 to 10.0 million years, depending on geological estimate.

Two other features of South America are striking: its drastic tapering to
the south as it nears Antarctica, and the way the outline of its eastern shore
seems to be an uncanny fit with that of the western coast of Africa, some
two thousand miles away across the Atlantic Ocean. This nearly puzzle-
perfect interlocking shape intrigued generations of schoolchildren, and
geologists too, long before scientists came to accept that the two had indeed been contiguous landmasses, which along with India, Australia,
Antarctica, and other smaller pieces of the earth's crust helped make up
the ancient southern supercontinent Gondwanaland. But Africa and South

America, long divided by continental drift, have occupied their present relative positions for the last 65 million years, the age of mammals.

Biologically, many people think of South America in terms of the tropical rain forests of the Amazon Basin, but the continent has another vast and dramatically different face — the temperate zones of the Andes Mountains and Patagonia. Paradoxically, despite the unparalleled profusion of tropical species of all kinds in the rain forests of South America and the rest of the world, Blue butterflies in South America are predominately dwellers of temperate regions.

Stretching unbroken for a length of 4,500 miles, with many peaks that rise higher than 20,000 feet above sea level, the Andes are built on a spectacular scale. But their breathtaking bulk is only part of the reason for their rank among the great natural wonders of the world. They differ fundamentally from other comparably imposing ranges — the Rockies for example, or the Himalayas — in that the tropical latitudes of much of the chain have a profound effect on their climate and biological character. At the equator the tropical sun shines at vertical, summertime angles year-round. It requires impressive altitudes, 9,000 feet above sea level and more, to attenuate the tropical heat into a temperate climate approximating that of the northern latitudes. Unlike the mountains of most other parts of the globe, the Andes boast temperate zones that are in large part products of altitude, uplifted from the surrounding tropics, not of latitude. In many cases these temperate or alpine zones are like islands, totally surrounded and cut off by a sea of tropical vegetation. Collectively, these zones above the tropical level are known as the High Andes.

Similarly, the permanent snow line, which determines the upper limits of most life-forms, crosses the equatorial Andes at the astounding altitude of 15,000 to 16,000 feet, a level higher than any peak in the lower forty-eight United States. At the equivalent altitudes of Quito, Ecuador (9,350 feet), or La Paz, Bolivia (12,000 feet), both of which lie in temperate valleys surrounded by far higher mountains, travelers in much of Europe or North America would already have reached a world of permanent ice and snow. These extra thousands of feet of habitat significantly extend the range of Blue butterflies and other Andean butterfly families, part of the reason that lepidopterists and others refer to the Andes as a "vertical landscape." For scientists working at the upper levels of this unique temperate biological zone, oxygen deprivation can be a serious problem.

For much of their length, until they broaden to a more singular ridge south of Bolivia, the Andes consist of two distinct, roughly parallel ranges, the Cordillera Oriental on the east and the Cordillera Occidental to the west. Together they can be likened to a backbone extending the entire length of western South America, leaving only a narrow Pacific coastal strip. The range forms an overwhelmingly dominant feature of all the countries that fell into the Spanish half of South America when Pope Alexander VI divided the continent between rival Spain and Portugal in 1493: Venezuela, Colombia, Ecuador, Peru, Bolivia, Chile, and Argentina. The Andes reach their central height, or arch, at Mt. Aconcagua, along the border of north-central Argentina and Chile. That peak reaches 22,384 feet and is sur-rounded for some one hundred miles by clusters of other summits higher than 22,000 feet. In the north of the continent, across Colombia and Venez-uela, a short, curved neck bends into Panama; in the south, a long, lum-barlike trail of lower mountains (from 11,600-foot Mt. Tronador to Cerro Chaital, at 11,022 feet) crosses the fabled land of Patagonia to curve finally into a short tailbone around the Strait of Magellan in Tierra del Fuego, the southern tip of South America. Keeping to the metaphor, row after row of short east-west ranges protrude like ribs from the Andean spine.

Over the aeons these ribs have created conduits for titanic quantities of runoff water that has formed at their bases a vast network of alluvial plains that run the length of the Andes. For biologists the east-west chains and the attached, often intricately segmented alluvial plains offer the basis for a nearly endless litany of historical and local place-names. Only a few of these localities are accessible by road, and even fewer have been ex-plored by biologists. As incredible as it may seem, the very existence of some of these subsystems, the "hidden ranges" of Peru, was not known to Europeans until well into the twentieth century.

But this appearance of structural unity is deceptive. The Andes are not in fact a single geologic formation but rather a complex of formations, differing in age, character, and geologic origin. The Spanish Conquista-dors, the first Europeans to explore the chain, recognized this complexity and referred to the Andes in full as Los Cordilleras del los Andes — The Ranges of the Andes. The name Andes itself may have originated from the Quechuan Indian word *anti,* meaning "east," referring to the summits that rose to the east of their territory near the modern city of Cuzco, Peru; al-ternatively it may be from another word in the same language, *anta,* which means "copper," a reference either to the color of those mountains or to the metals that could be mined there. In terms of physical geography sci-entists recognize a dozen major landforms, or sectors, and twenty-two distinctive biotic provinces making up South America's montane regions. The Cordillera Occidental, in particular, as part of the Pacific Rim seismic belt, is riddled with active volcanoes, but they too are spread out in three distinct groupings, one to the north in southern Colombia and northern Ecuador, one in southern Peru and northern Chile, and another far to the south in central Chile and adjacent Patagonia.

The Andean backbone and its ribs contribute dazzling vertical and horizontal breadth to the ecosystems of South America. Climate is affected by a complex range of influences. Temperatures generally decline as the range marches southward and continue to fall as altitude increases. But areas of extreme heat — deep gorges or deserts — are sometimes only a few miles distant from the polar temperatures of extreme elevations. Moreover, at comparable altitudes and latitudes, the chain's external slopes, which face either the Pacific or the Amazon Basin, differ both from each other and from their internal counterparts. The range of altitudes, the length of the chain, the physical isolation of so many individual habitats, and multiple climatological variables — including wind patterns, proximity to the sea, and rainfall — produce extremely divergent ecological sectors, set not only amid the peaks and valleys of the system but in expansive high, mostly arid, plateaus cradled between the eastern and western cordilleras. This kind of terrain is known variously as altiplano or puna. The most notable of these plateaus, known as the Altiplano de Bolivia, extends into parts of Chile, Argentina, Bolivia, and Peru, where the Andes are at their widest. Lying at an altitude between 11,200 and 12,800 feet, it is 80 miles wide and 500 miles long, a total area nearly as large as Pennsylvania, and larger than the entire island of Hispaniola; at its northern end is Lake Titicaca, the world's highest navigable lake and a renowned name as a specimen source in old butterfly collections.

The three northern nations of the Andes — Venezuela, Colombia, and Ecuador — share closely related geologies, climates, and life-forms. In a number of places the eastern and western cordilleras are connected by small ridges and spurs that circumscribe a collection of immense intermontane basins, each one, as in so many other parts of the Andes, playing host to large and distinctive localized ecosystems and biotic communities. Here altitude, not latitude, determines the transition, often extremely abrupt, from a tropical clime to temperate. The region's situation on the equator and its spectacular elevations result in profoundly diverse conditions of climate and vegetation. Although the vertical zones of climate in much of the three countries are quite similar, the effect of the high mountains on patterns of wind and rain cause drastically varied local conditions. In the upper part of Peru, the permanent snow line disappears entirely, and as the puna becomes more humid it is known as jalca. Still farther along, in Ecuador and Colombia, at the highest levels of vegetation, where the high cordillera is cold and desolate year-round, the peaks are covered in mist, a kind of landscape known as páramo.

The high mountains of the three northern Andean nations boast a host of famous butterfly locales, names familiar from the labels on old specimens and from the pages of classic books of Lepidoptera: Monte Tolima in Colombia; La Chima, Cayambe, and Tungurahua in Ecuador; and Mérida in the Venezuelan highlands. Despite this diversity and history, however, the Blue butterflies here were poorly known in 1945; only two species from the Andes north of Peru were known to science in Nabokov's day. In fact, it is the southern two-thirds of the chain that are most important for Nabokov's Blues; some 80 percent of the species known today occur exclusively from the southern reaches of Peru southward.

In the central Andean alpine zones, the Peruvian plateau, the Bolivian altiplano, and its extensions into the northern cusp of Argentina and Chile form another distinctive region of South America's highlands. In this region occur the densest concentration of Nabokov's Blues, members of all five genuses he named in 1945. The rain forests of the Amazon region reach their southernmost point here, broken by thousands of years of Andean uplift into remnants biologists liken to individual pearls dropped from the bottom of the tropic's broad necklace. Here tropical and temperate species occur nearly side by side and offer a rare opportunity to consider questions of how species are dispersed and where they originate.

The southern, or austral, reaches of South America are as intriguing as the Andes as a whole. In contrast to North America, which broadens northward to embrace ever-widening expanses of temperate-zone climate, South America tapers dramatically from around the Tropic of Capricorn into an ever-narrowing triangle of upland and southern temperate zones packed into the so-called Southern Cone. From its northern limit the Southern Cone extends like a narrow wedge for some 2,200 miles toward Antarctica, the same distance as from Cuba to the Hudson Bay of Canada, with stark variations in climatic and ecological conditions. Extensive farm and ranch lands, so characteristic of North America and Europe, occur only in the limited area of the Argentine Pampas in the northeastern sector of the Cone. South of the Pampas, the Cone narrows sharply into Patagonia, a vast, desertlike open space that finally trickles out at Tierra del Fuego. Across this immense plateau, itself intricately divided by aeons of water runoff flowing eastward from the Andes, spreads a sparse grassland, bounded on one side by the precipitous cliffs along the Atlantic coastline and on the other by chains of lakes lying in basins carved out between the Andes and Patagonian tablelands by the glaciers of the last ice age.

Climatically, the region is shaped on the east by the cold waters of the Atlantic's Falkland Current and on the west by the formidable rain shadow of the Andes. In another contrast to the northern stretches of North America, this combination produces a climate that is inhospitable but markedly constant; while in Canada average seasonal temperatures can vary as much as sixty degrees between winter and summer, in Patagonia, where the landmass is much smaller, the moderating influence of the ocean limits those differences to as little as fifteen or twenty degrees. As far north as the Río Negro, at 41 degrees South latitude, and even across the Pampas to the northeast, summers are cool and winters mild. Only toward the northwest of Argentina, at locations like Santiago del Estero, in the Gran Chaco along the west of the tablelands, do summer temperatures often soar above one hundred degrees. Trapped between the cold Atlantic currents and the Andes, however, Patagonia is constantly buffeted by parching winds that kick up the region's loose soil and fill the air with blowing sand. Although it seldom rains, a constant covering of clouds blankets the sky; it is a region rich in Blue butterflies, but because of the clouds, and wind, good collecting days are scarce.

Along the Southern Cone's western side, the distance between the Andean divide and the Pacific Ocean rarely exceeds 150 miles and averages only about 110. The result is the narrow north-south ribbonlike strip that is Chile. Although it is about equal to Texas in land area, the resemblance ends there, unless you imagine Texas stretched like a rubber band all the way to the top of Alaska. Broadly speaking, Chile falls into three geographic divisions. Most of the population lives in the central part of the country, where the mild Mediterranean climate, quite reminiscent of California, was conducive to the agricultural development that made Chile a center of substantial European settlement. Most of the Blue butterfly specimens that Luis Peña and José Herrera had sent to Kurt Johnson had come from the upland reaches of this region, but the country has a relatively broad coastal strip that is also home to Blues.

In the less populous north lie two great deserts, the Antofagasta and the Atacama. The north and central divisions together share many characteristic

Andean features; the parallel coastal range is separated from the eastern part of the Andean backbone by long, deep valleys, each with its own characteristic ecology. Coastal climatic conditions are intensified by the continual oscillation of storm systems originating from the cold Pacific currents just offshore, subjecting many regions of northern Chile to alternating periods of drought and heavy rain; in El Niño years the rain is even heavier, resulting in yet more drastic extremes. With water at a premium through much of the nation, humankind's gradual encroachment on the natural environment has had an even more dramatic effect in Chile than in other parts of South America. Some rivers, like the Copiapó in the north, once emptied into the Pacific but now are so heavily used for irrigation that they have been essentially diverted inland.

Despite its relatively small overall area, Chile occupies more than one-half of the length of South America's western coast, nearly all of it temperate. It is unparalleled as a home for Nabokov's Blues. Members of four of Nabokov's genuses occur there and roughly half of the nearly seventy species of Nabokov's Blues that are now known from the continent.

In the southern Lake District, where the latitude affords alpine environs as low as 5,000 feet above sea level, the biotas of Chile and Argentina essentially melt together. Along the face of the Andes, the Patagonian grasslands extend some 1,800 miles north and south, their farthest reach being the western face of Tierra del Fuego. In total, the land area of this region equals the entire breadth of Central America from Panama to Mexico's Yucatan Peninsula. And it is all fertile ground for Blues.

Unsurprisingly, the High Andes and the range's other temperate zones support a wide variety of oreal, or mountainous, vegetations, but because of the disjointed nature of the chain, these ecological zones become confusingly erratic or break down completely. As a temperate home for Nabokov's Blues, a more formidable labyrinth could scarcely be imagined. The habitats of the butterflies that Nabokov studied for "Notes on Neotropical Plebejinae" were spread out like pellets from a shotgun blast across this vast region — a locality here, a locality there, with hundreds and sometimes thousands of miles in between. In 1945 formal science could speak of only nine exclusively South American species of Blue butterflies, attested from a mere handful of collecting localities. The rest of the continent's temperate zones were literally a blank.

The natural history of the temperate regions of South America has in one way or another been a puzzle to Western science from the time the

Spaniards under Francisco Pizarro, drawn by dreams of untold riches, conquered the Peruvian empire of the Incas in 1532. Pizarro, during his search for El Dorado, the rumored City of Gold, led a mere 180 men into the region around Cuzco, where the ruler, Atahualpa, had just emerged from a bloody struggle with his brother for control of the throne. The empire the Spaniards found was large, prosperous, and competently governed, covering much of the territory of modern Peru, Ecuador, and considerable parts of Colombia, Bolivia, Argentina, and Chile. When Pizarro pretended to extend the hand of friendship, Atahualpa agreed to meet in the city of Cajamarca; his reward for his naïveté was to be imprisoned by the Spaniards, who because of their guns and horses were superior to the vastly greater forces that the Incas could marshal. Despite the payment of a chamber full of gold as a ransom, he was executed, and his empire soon crumbled. Pizarro's conquest served the interest of the Spanish Crown; Lima, which Pizarro founded in 1535, eventually became the capital of most of the Spanish holdings on the continent, organized as a viceroyalty.

In 1541, having laid waste the bulk of native South American culture, Pizarro was murdered by the disillusioned son of a rival lieutenant. He had found plenty of gold in the treasuries of the conquered Incas, but not an El Dorado, although he never gave up his obsessive search. Still, among the wealth and secrets of the Incas that he had inherited, none was more important than knowledge of the Indians' ancient and secret routes that could safely be taken up and over the vast Andes. Malaria and yellow fever were scourges to both natives and Europeans, and although the diseases themselves were not understood, the routes that time had proven to offer safe passages were crucial in preserving the lives of soldiers and explorers. Centuries of trial and error had shown which routes north and south, and east and west, could be taken without succumbing to the poison in the atmosphere.

The importance of these routes for the subsequent exploration of the Andes cannot be overestimated, even though two hundred years passed before another kind of man began to explore the region in search of a quite different kind of treasure. It is a good example of how the transition through imperialistic adventurism, exploration, and science moved in virtually imperceptible stages. The Spaniards were primarily interested in gold, not knowledge, and they were at pains to protect their political and commercial interests in South America from the inquiries of other Europeans. But, they were meticulous record keepers, and in 1735 they offered a man from the world of science a glimpse of the closely guarded records of their early explorations to use as the basis of his own studies and a chance to visit their Peruvian empire. Somewhat surprisingly, that man, the first whom history recognizes as a true scientific explorer of the continent, was not even a Spaniard but a Frenchman, Charles-Marie de La Condamine, a mathematician and naturalist who belonged to the French Academy of Sciences.

Followed closely by an escort of Spanish troops, La Condamine and a colleague, Pierre Bouguer, traced the footsteps of Pizarro's Conquistadors up and over the Western Cordillera to Quito. Among the tasks assigned them by the French Academy and their Spanish hosts was the measurement of the length of a degree of meridian at the equator. Their measurement of Mt. Chimborazo (20,561 feet) made it the highest known mountain in the world at that time, a record that stood for decades until the exploration of the southern Andes and the Himalayas. Determined to study the regions lying to the east of Quito as well, La Condamine plunged into the hot, jungle-covered lowlands that Pizarro and his men had named the Green Hell. Continuing his journey by raft, La Condamine became the first scientist to navigate the vastness of the Amazon River, reaching its mouth four months after he started. By early in 1745, La Condamine was back in Paris after his decadelong journey, having brought with him two hundred natural history specimens (among them the first specimen of rubber, which the Frenchman had fashioned into a tube to protect his maps) and many notes. In 1751 these became his *Journal of a Voyage to the Equator Made by Order of the King,* the first scientific account of the Amazon.

The bulk of La Condamine's geographic observations of the Andean region, however, were kept secret by the Spanish. Out of fear of their enemies the British, La Condamine's expedition was required to submit its reports to the Spanish viceroy before leaving Quito in 1744. Later famous as the *Noticias Secretas,* these accounts were not published until 1826, and in 1745 La Condamine could report to the French Academy only information deemed purely of scientific interest.

Despite his work and his writing, La Condamine never achieved the fame that might have been his had Spain been willing fully to share its knowledge with the rest of the world. Such recognition fell instead to the next scientist-explorer allowed into Spanish realms of South America, Baron Alexander von Humboldt of Prussia. An aristocrat already distinguished in science and letters in the Weimar Coterie, an elite European scientific circle, Humboldt was fortunate enough to live under a more liberal Spanish regime, and, under the patronage of Prime Minister Mariano de Urquijo, he set sail in 1799 on the *Pizarro,* his destination the western coast of South America. There was irony in the ship's name, since Humboldt and Pizarro — the learned aristocrat and the treacherous adventurer and fortune hunter who could barely read or write and who had spent part of his youth as a swineherd — could not have been more dissimilar in background or character.

Yet, two and a half centuries after the Spanish conquest, Humboldt landed in South America in search of a wholly different sort of treasure. Over five years he and his companions achieved some of the most ambitious expeditionary and scientific goals attempted on the continent in the colonial era, and Humboldt became, after Pizarro, South America's most famous explorer. He is most famous today for his research on the Humboldt Current, the ocean current off the west coast of the continent that came to bear his name. But his South American biological collections included nearly sixty thousand specimens and thousands of unknown species. Back in Europe, where he spent twenty-one years after his return filling twenty-three volumes with his findings, not only on biology but also on geology and meteorology, Humboldt won international renown as one of the most versatile and influential scientists in history.

It was not for another half century, however, that scientists began to develop the idea that would paint their views of life in the Southern Hemisphere, and particularly in the Andes, until well into the 1980s. Since the Age of Exploration, a major question of South American biology has concerned the origin of the plants and animals of the continent's temperate zones, the labyrinthine Andes and the vast tablelands of Patagonia. Lifeforms in those regions differ dramatically from those in the tropical lowlands, in terms of both overall population and number and diversity of species. As the early explorers ascended upland or ventured into the Southern Cone, they were startled by the abrupt transition between the continent's contrasting biological zones. The burgeoning diversity of exotic life they had discovered and marveled at in the tropical lowlands gave way to biological landscapes that seemed far more familiar, with a climate and with plants and animals that reminded them much more of their European homelands. It was difficult to see any biological connection at all between the two zones. Curiously, however, as Europeans stepped up exploration of other parts of the world, they began to notice another anomaly in temperate South America: the diversity of life in the Andes and

Patagonia was small in comparison not only with the tropics but with mountainous temperate zones on other continents, such as North America and Asia, as well. Where South American temperate life-forms had come from became a compelling question from the earliest stages of the continent's exploration.

Given the early taxonomic notion that general physical similarities between organisms meant they were biologically related, European biologists readily adopted what seemed to them the obvious answer to the question of southern temperate origins, that the biotas had migrated wholesale from the north. In past centuries this idea was a natural corollary to a more generally held belief that all life in the southern continents had at one time or another come from the north, a concept that reflected a widespread prejudice in the socioreligious views of the times. Old World scientists essentially adopted a Eurocentric view — that, like "civilization," all the flora and fauna of the Southern Hemisphere derived from the north. A classic formulation of this notion is recorded by Darwin's compatriot and fellow evolutionary theorist Alfred Russel Wallace in his monumental *Geographical Distribution of Animals* in 1876: "The north-south division of modern biota represents the fact that the greater northern continents are the seat and birthplace of all higher forms of life, and the southern biota derives strictly from them."

Today, when its detractors want to ridicule this perniciously tenacious point of view, they call it the Sherwin-Williams Cover the Earth theory, a reference to that paint company's famous logo of a globe, with its great waves of thick pigment flowing over the Northern Hemisphere toward the south.

Yet there are ample reasons for biologists to view the upland biotas of South America as having primarily descended from migrants from their far vaster northern counterparts. A high percentage of the plants of the Andean uplands do have unarguable relatives to the north; botanists even place some in the same genuses. By contrast, relatively few plants occurring in the Andean uplands seem to reflect upland adaptation from the lowland flora below; that is, tropical plants do not seem to have spread and evolved in significant numbers into forms adapted to the high-altitude temperate climates, where conditions are more hostile to life than those in the lush, teeming rain forests. Moreover, the timing for a northern migration theory is right. For all their complexity the Andes as a whole are a young mountain range. They appear to have reached their present heights only in the latest mammalian era, within the last ten million years, at much the same time the Caribbean islands were rafting to their present positions. It was also a time when similar climatological and geological conditions — relatively cold temperatures and frequent cycles of glaciation — predominated there and in the north, and when the land bridge of the Panamanian isthmus seems to have existed between North and South America.

The land bridge made possible the Great American Interchange, a gradual migration of animals from one continent to another. While there was traffic in both directions, for various reasons animals from the north clearly managed to establish themselves in the south at a much higher rate than those in the south successfully moved into the north. This trend has ample support not only in the fossil record of mammals but also in anthropological data on the dispersal of early humans. For paleontologists it has been epitomized in the standard, well-documented case of camels, llamas, and their relatives, which represents the so-called camelid scenario of north-south migration. The mammalian fossil record shows that the camelid lineage originated and diversified in North America from some 40 million years ago. By about one million years ago, certain camelids, the ancestors of today's llamas, alpacas, guanacos, and vicuñas, had spread southward to South America, while others, ancestors of the familiar dromedaries and two-humped Bactrian camels, migrated westward over the Bering Strait land bridge to Asia. But camelids then died out in North America, leaving their South American and Asian relatives as relics of the great age of temperate interchange. Today the camelids of South America, known locally as *camelitos,* make up a conspicuous part of the upland and south-latitude faunas of that great continent. Most of them had long been domesticated and put to use as beasts of burden and sources for meat, milk, and clothing by the time the Conquistadors arrived in the 1500s.

The camelid scenario of northern migration, applied broadly, would neatly account for the low diversity of upland South American species. Given the narrowness of the Panamanian isthmus and the rugged and noncontiguous topography of the Andean region, only a few kinds of plants could have gradually moved southward across the upland temperate corridors, followed by other biotas — for example, butterflies — which had close relationships to those plants. Certainly for those who thought primarily in terms of such a scenario, it was easy to accept the common wisdom that there were only a handful of species of Blue butterflies in South America's temperate zones. But the camelid scenario also offered a kind of insurance policy against data on the ground that might tend to support some other origin for many South American life-forms. For example, if the South American genuses of some group of creatures seemed not to be closely related to northern genuses, that must be because the northern representatives had died out.

Modern science, of course, recognizes that such broad questions in nature can seldom be posed in terms of either-or. But it was far into the twentieth century before biologists, armed with knowledge of both continental drift and modern evolutionary theory (including the realization that superficial physical similarity is not, in fact, proof of a genealogical relationship) would entertain alternatives for the origin of some of South America's temperate biotas. In this modern context, with the idea of migration having lost its exclusive hold on biologists' thinking, two other possibilities for the origin of South America's temperate plants and animals were proposed. Andean plants and animals, or at least some of them, might have gradually evolved from lowland relatives as the mountains were uplifted over millions and millions of years during the age of mammals. In addition, some Patagonian plants and animals, which have proven increasingly intriguing as scientists have intensified their study in recent years, might be ancient survivors of South America's westward drift after the breakup of the ancient southern supercontinent of Gondwanaland.

Patagonia itself seems to suggest a nature alien from that of much of the rest of the continent. Some of the earliest and most striking evidence of its hidden geological secrets was offered to riders of the early Patagonian railroad, which by the 1890s stretched much farther southward than most Europeans had previously ventured. To workers and passengers, riding the new railroad from the Argentine Pampas deeper and deeper into the vast tablelands of the south was like entering a new world. It was a denuded landscape, dominated by rugged and immense formations of blackened rock. Early biological exploration among these wastelands uncovered extraordinary finds: amazing fossil animals, dinosaurs and gigantic mammals, many quite different from any found elsewhere in the world at the time.

Before the development of tectonic theory and the appreciation of continental drift, there seemed to be no explanation for this violent geologic transition. Modern plate tectonics, however, indicates that Antarctica and the southern tips of South America and Africa were joined during the warmer millennia of the age of the dinosaurs. The exact disposition of the early landmasses is far from certain because the icebound record of Antarctica is not readily decipherable. But, given the mysterious landforms, it is considered likely that southern Patagonia was a companion of Antarctica on its journey to its present frigid parking spot at the South Pole.

The broader Gondwanaland connection in South America could be amply illustrated in tropical flora and fauna, but temperate biological connections have been somewhat harder to prove. While plate tectonics seems to explain the mysteries of Patagonian geology, most biogeographers and lepidopterists have believed that the long exposure to the low temperatures of southern tectonic drift would have made it unlikely that much life, including butterflies, survived the journey. Recently, however, discoveries have clearly shown the continued survival of temperate Gondwanaland species.

In one classic instance, botanists, basing their conclusions in part on paleobotanic studies of ancient pollen found in drill-core soil samples from around the Pacific Rim, established that southern South American beech forests made up of a unique genus, *Nothofagus,* were Gondwanaland survivors. The research shows the previous connection of these South American forests, via the ancient supercontinent, to not only the Australian region but some more northerly parts of Eurasia, like northern China. In the insect realm a Swedish entomologist in the 1960s, Lars Brundin, had offered evidence that a group of mosquito-like flies known as midges, with close Pacific Rim taxonomic relationships of their own, also traced their South American origins to ancient Gondwanaland.

Compared with Lepidoptera, midges are primitive insects, their aquatic larvae capable of surviving in a wide variety of conditions. What about more advanced insects, specifically butterflies, tied to land and their inextricable connections with flowering plants? It seemed unlikely that the ill-fated raft of Antarctica and its companions could have acted as a Noah's Ark for a large South American butterfly fauna. However, what is apparently the continued existence of Patagonia's cold grasslands since that era offered a possibility that a highly differentiated, even if somewhat limited, southern biota might have survived and evolved there. By some curious timing individual lepidopterists, encouraged by the studies on forests and midges, were just beginning to seriously reconsider the question when Henri Descimon wrote his summary of High Andean Lepidoptera in 1986, essentially restating the traditional view of migration from the north.

In 1983 the Chilean lepidopterist José Herrera noted the number of White and Sulphur species that were unique to southern South America, suggesting they might have developed there originally, perhaps even as relicts of Gondwanian drift. Throughout the 1980s Arthur M. Shapiro, of the University of California at Davis, had been completing his own research on the Andean and austral Whites and Sulphurs, and in 1991 he published his results. He had discovered that food-plant preference of the southern species strongly supported a view of their geographic uniqueness. However, he also noted strong links between southern pierids and their northern counterparts; many of the southern Sulphurs, in fact, were being placed in the northern genus *Colias*. Shapiro was extremely curious about the contradiction between this view, which supported Descimon's traditional hypothesis of north-to-south movement, and the very different conclusions Kurt Johnson was drawing from his studies of lycaenids.

Johnson was beginning to see that many groups of Andean Elfin Hairstreaks were more closely related to their lowland counterparts than to northern Elfins, suggesting that highland species had evolved as the Andes uplifted. Johnson had discussed his findings with Descimon, but science isn't science unless it has been published, and Johnson's work on the Elfins, which began to appear in 1991, was still preliminary in 1986. Descimon noted in his acknowledgments that Johnson had suggested alternative ways of viewing the origins of southern South American Hairstreaks but could say only that his views were "novel." By now, though, Descimon realized that the Andean Lycaenidae, which included many of Nabokov's Latin American Blues, would provide another significant test of the idea of northern origins, if only their complex taxonomy could be sorted out. He despaired, however, of a general revision of Blues being carried out in satisfactory detail and within a reasonable time. After all, most of the scientists who had done work in the area were scattered around North America and Europe, historical samples of these elusive high-altitude butterflies were few, and, as attested in Nabokov's 1945 treatise, their taxonomy was extremely exacting and complex. Descimon assumed such a task would require several lifetimes.

Nabokov himself had discovered the odd anatomies that characterized the South American Blues he studied, fundamentally different from those of the north. That is why, working completely from morphology, he did not place them in northern genuses but assigned them completely new genus names. Like other scientists of his time, Nabokov accepted the traditional theory of migration from the north. Although he stated that his morphologically based conclusions were difficult to explain in terms of that theory, he said he would not be audacious enough to question the prevailing view.

Shapiro's publication of 1991, and a short commentary from 1989 aptly titled "Ignorance in High Places," had begun to focus the questions of Andean and southern South American butterflies on the lycaenids. If the Elfins did not appear to support the traditional view, what would Blue butterflies reveal when they were finally revised? Nabokov's new South American genuses, as he presented them, made the same negative point that Johnson's work on Elfins was making: that the anatomies of many Andean and austral South American butterflies did not appear to support the idea of a connection to the north. But, like other scientists, Shapiro was unwilling to accept Nabokov's taxonomic conclusions on South American Blues without some modern effort at corroboration. Moreover, because of Nabokov's tiny sample, "Notes on Neotropical Plebejinae" could not be considered definitively representative of what lepidopterists might eventually find there. Yet Shapiro realized that those same Blues were the obvious candidates to become the next major new data set for lepidopterists.

So just as Bálint and Johnson's taxonomic project was gathering steam, the big question about temperate South American Blues, the realm of Vladimir Nabokov, became not simply how many there were and where but one of significant evolutionary and biogeographical moment: what story would they have to tell about the origins of South America's temperate faunas? The work that Bálint and Johnson had carried out in the museums of Europe was but the first step in revising Nabokov's taxonomy and in beginning to look for answers to this wider biogeographical question. To advance further they would have to turn to South America itself.

The contents of "Notes on Neotropical Plebejinae," including the reliability of the early literature cited by Nabokov, and therefore to a certain extent the reliability of the work based on that material, created a body of reference that would have to be checked. Above all, the specimens Nabokov cited at second hand or studied himself would have to be reexamined, particularly to see whether their locality labels reflected reality. Since Nabokov never visited any of the locations himself, he was in most ways dependent on the sources he chose for his data. Early workers were sometimes not careful in recording their field data, especially for such specimens as lycaenids, which were generally considered of lesser interest and were of minor commercial value. Sometimes they gave only a very broad indication of the provenance of such catches, the region in which the butterflies were caught, a port of call, some town in which they had spent the night, or a place they had met native collectors who had sold them specimens that in truth might have come from anywhere. (This was a problem even with the more splendid butterflies; remember the specimens of *Anetia jaegeri* and *Battus zetides,* those rare creatures from Las Abejas that in the Natural History Museum in London were labeled merely "Haiti.")

Thus, early collecting was often an imprecise enterprise. Even if early workers had accurately recorded localities, it was possible that the old colloquial names they used might never have made their way onto maps or into the published record; it would be necessary to try to sort out those locations by talking with local lepidopterists who could perhaps make sense of them. The list of specimen localities cited by Nabokov created a kind of gazetteer of places that would have to be visited by modern researchers, to make sure not only that the species Nabokov reported actually occurred where he said they did but whether there were additional species in those localities as well. Bálint's and Johnson's fruitful work in the museums of Europe could supplement this task but could never replace it if they expected their project in any way to be called complete.

This backtracking through the work of Nabokov, in the field as well as on the printed page, crossed some impressive paths of lepidopterological history. The European museums began to assemble their great insect collections at least as early as Humboldt's expeditions, and astonishingly old specimens still exist; what is left of Humboldt's collection is reverently preserved in Paris. Nabokov was moved by such survivals: the hero of his novel *The Gift* is driven to thoughts about the meaning of mortality when he contemplates the butterflies from Linnaeus's collection still extant in London, or the showy Atlas moth in Prague once admired by Catherine the Great. But all but a handful of surviving Amazonian and Andean butterfly specimens are from the age of more recent explorers, like the eighteenth century's Joseph Banks, and Alfred Russel Wallace and Henry Walter Bates, who began their South American travels together in 1848. The older lepidopterological material has for the most part been lost to neglect and the deadly allies of Time the destroyer — occasionally war but more often rot, mold, and the dermestid beetle, a small insect found in virtually all museums. As both larva and adult it devours organic material of animal origin, and, if left alone, a few dermestid beetles can devastate an entire specimen drawer in just a few days.

The nineteenth-century collectors whose material formed much of the basis of the study groups in Nabokov's era were not world famous as Humboldt was, but they are renowned in the world of lepidoptery. As

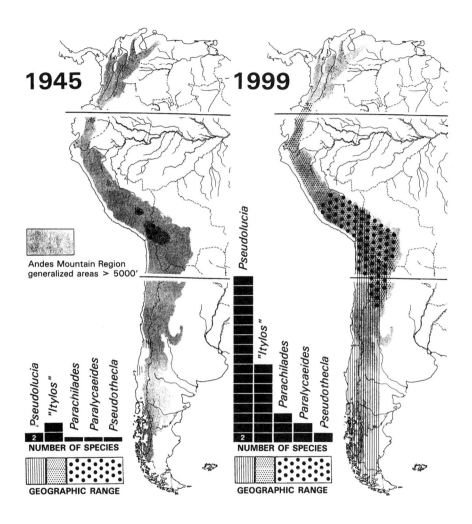

1945   **1999**

Andes Mountain Region
generalized areas > 5000'

Pseudolucia

"Itylos"

Parachilades

Paralycaeides

Pseudothecla

2

NUMBER OF SPECIES

GEOGRAPHIC RANGE

Pseudolucia

"Itylos"

Parachilades

Paralycaeides

Pseudothecla

2

NUMBER OF SPECIES

GEOGRAPHIC RANGE

Nabokov's South American Blues in 1945 and today

Simple bar graphs of numbers of species and maps of their geographic distributions, in five genuses of Nabokov's South American Blues. **Left, 1945.** A total of only nine species, from scattered localities, made up the five genuses Nabokov originally recognized and named. **Right, 1999.** Today scientists recognize over sixty species with distributions spanning the length of the Andes Mountains and Patagonia.

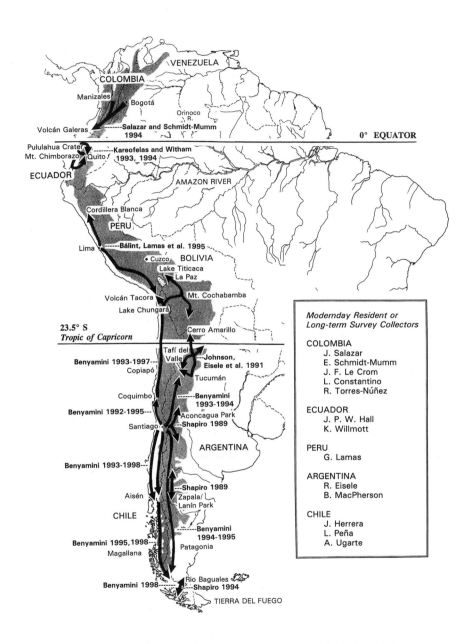

Recent expeditions to South America in search of Nabokov's Blues

Arrows indicate the general itineraries and dates of scientists' fielding expeditions in search of Nabokov's Blues, 1989–1998.

Typical examples of eight genuses of Nabokov's Latin American Blues

Top row. *Left:* the genus *Nabokovia,* some of which exhibit strange wing shapes. *Center:* a tailed Hairstreak-like species, the Cincinnatus Blue. *Right:* Krug's Zebra Blue, genus *Leptotes.* **Middle row.** *Left:* the Titicaca Blue, genus *Itylos,* showing the striped pattern Nabokov called "Ityloid." *Center:* the Charlotte Blue, genus *Pseudolucia* with the V-shaped hind wing pattern typical of the genus. *Right: Pseudolucia chilensis,* a lazy-flying orange colored Blue whose caterpillars eat toxic food plants and whose spotted pattern Nabokov termed "Catochrysopoid." **Bottom row.** *Left:* Hazel's Blue, genus *Paralycaeides.* *Center:* The Odon Blue, genus *Madeleinea.* *Right:* a typical Caribbean Blue, genus *Cyclargus,* showing the checkering that historically confused it with *Hemiargus.* *(Courtesy of Zsolt Bálint and Kurt Johnson)*

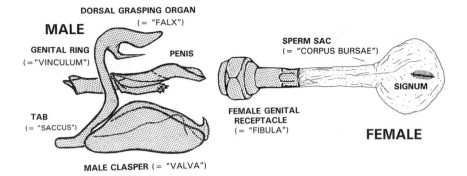

MALE

DORSAL GRASPING ORGAN
(= "FALX")

GENITAL RING
(= "VINCULUM")

PENIS

TAB
(= "SACCUS")

MALE CLASPER (= "VALVA")

SPERM SAC
(= "CORPUS BURSAE")

SIGNUM

FEMALE GENITAL
RECEPTACLE
(= "FIBULA")

FEMALE

NABOKOV'S GENITALIC DRAWINGS WITH "MAGIC TRIANGLES" INSERTED

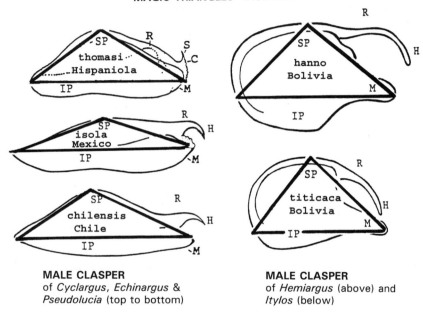

MALE CLASPER
of *Cyclargus, Echinargus* &
Pseudolucia (top to bottom)

MALE CLASPER
of *Hemiargus* (above) and
Itylos (below)

Nabokov's Terms: R (Rostellum); H (Humerulus); M (Mentum);
SP (Superior Process); IP (Inferior Process)

What Nabokov saw when he looked though the microscope

Top: a drawing of the major genital parts in lateral view (male, left; female, right) as they appear through the microscope. *Bottom:* Nabokov's innovation, the superimposition of "magic triangles" over his drawings of genitalia, allowed him to map the ground plan of species within genuses. Much admired at the time, magic triangles were an advance in morphological identification of species, deciding to which genus they belonged, and which genuses were most closely related.

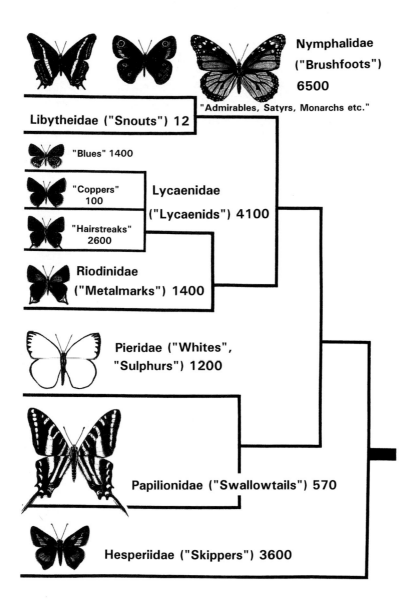

Nymphalidae ("Brushfoots") 6500

"Admirables, Satyrs, Monarchs etc."

Libytheidae ("Snouts") 12

"Blues" 1400

"Coppers" 100

Lycaenidae ("Lycaenids") 4100

"Hairstreaks" 2600

Riodinidae ("Metalmarks") 1400

Pieridae ("Whites", "Sulphurs") 1200

Papilionidae ("Swallowtails") 570

Hesperiidae ("Skippers") 3600

Family tree of butterflies

Genealogy of the butterflies expressed as the seven families preferred by most taxonomists, showing: branching family tree (starting at bottom right), scientific and common name of each family, general number of species named world-wide, and representative size, shape and wing pattern of each. The butterflies illustrated are imaginary but show the wing shapes and color patterns that would be readily recognized by lepidopterists.

The famous photograph by Philippe Halsman

Showing Nabokov with his net in a "bugs-eye view." Although the photo is arguably the most famous of Nabokov the scientist, lepidopterists often see it as too posed, the pristine white net showing no evidence of use.
(© Halsman Estate)

Nabokov collecting in the Swiss Alps, 1971

Nabokov's deep love of pine forested regions of America and Europe was rooted in cherished memories of his boyhood home near St. Petersburg, Russia. The alpine forests near Montreux, Switzerland, where he lived from 1959 until his death in 1977, were his favorite collecting grounds.
(Photograph by Dmitri Nabokov © Nabokov Estate)

The following labels appear around the mimicry ring diagram:

- ♂ & ♀ probabilis
- ♂ & ♀ bicolor
- ♂ & ♀ wagenknechti
- ♂ & ♀ atacama
- ♂ & ♀ shapiroi
- annamaria ♀
- clarea ♂ & ♀
- plumbea ♀
- zina ♀
- hazeorum ♀
- magallana
- andina ♀
- avishai ♀
- asafi ♂ & ♀
- Fidonia sp.
- Heterusia sp.
- ♀ & ♂ charlotte
- ♀ benyamini
- ♀ collina
- ♀ lyrnessa
- ♀ vera

Center labels:

Theclinae

Adesmia & Astragalus feeders
Eiseliana

Astragalus feeder
Iteoda

Adesmia & Astragalus feeder

The Model

Pseudolucia chilensis
Cuscuta feeder

Adesmia feeders
Pseudolucia plumbea group

Polyommatinae

Chortiaspe & Monijosella feeders
Pseudolucia collina/humbea group

P. andina group
Astragalus feeders

Day flying moths

Fidoniidae

Mimicry in Nabokov's Blues

Pictorial illustration of the mimicry ring which may surround the orange-colored *Pseudolucia chilensis* (at center) which feeds on the toxic food plant *Cuscuta,* known by its common name Dodder for its sickening effect on livestock. Two genuses of orange-marked Hairstreaks (above) and various day-flying moths (below) also show similar upper surface orange. Some of these Blues (*collina,* right and *plumbea,* left) feed on non-toxic plants; however, orange-colored Blues of the *andina* group (left center) feed on *Astragalus,* possibly also toxic. Dubi Benyamini has proposed this ring as a complex example of mimicry in Blues.

(Dubi Benyamini, courtesy of University of Wisconsin Museum Reports)

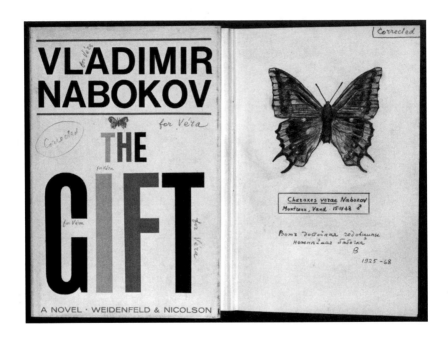

Nabokov's butterfly art

Throughout his life, Nabokov was fond of inscribing copies of his published works to his wife, Véra, and illustrating them with fanciful drawings of butter-flies. In 1999 his collection of these works was sold at auction by Glenn Horowitz Booksellers, Inc., in New York City.

(Photograph by Vladimir Nabokov, courtesy of Glenn Horowitz Booksellers, Inc.)

much as the original authors treated in Nabokov's "Notes on Neotropical Plebejinae" represented the oracles of his youth, the Staudingers and W. C. Hewitsons who had been the first to name the butterflies, these men had also been — in the realm of South America in any case — armchair scientists. The specimens themselves came from a very different brand of men, the early field collectors of the New World tropics, the real links between the European museum specimens and their remote habitats. Among them were Théophile Gaujon, who collected for nearly a decade for Paul Dognin, and Enrique Feyer, H. G. Karsten, and Richard Haensch, who worked over three decades for the wealthy German dealers. Specimens gathered by Marc de Mathan and Clarence Buckley, collectors respectively for Charles Oberthur and Hewitson, make up some of the most important material at the Natural History Museum in London.

Some of these men — like William Clarke MacIntyre, who had his own hacienda in Ecuador, and W. F. H. Rosenberg, who retired comfortably to Europe in 1897 — became reasonably well-off. But just as often they died young or returned home with broken health. For most it was a life of hardship, compensated only by living an extraordinary adventure on a raw, pristine continent. A few, too, in addition to their collecting activities were prolific writers, for example the Englishmen Edward Whymper and Richard Spruce, or the German Wolfgang von Hagen. They recorded their experiences in the popular literature of their time, leaving a lasting record in magazines or in classic books like Whymper's *Travels Amongst the Great Andes of the Equator* (1892) and Spruce's *Notes of a Botanist on the Amazon and Andes* (1908). These men came close to fulfilling Nabokov's fantasy of riding a magic carpet over the rain forest.

Remarkably, a significant number of the early collectors were missionaries, including Brother Apolinar María of Colombia and the Rev. Miles Moss, who lived for decades at the mouth of the Amazon River near Belém, Brazil. Apolinar, whose nonreligious name was Nicholas Seilus, came to South America from France. His butterfly collecting resulted in seventy-five scientific publications. Moreover, the LaSalle Institute, a scientific center he founded in Bogotá, continues to this day as a publisher of studies of Colombian butterflies. Apolinar's specimens ended up in the widely distributed collections of such well-known northern scientists as Charles Oberthur, A. H. Fassl, William Schaus, and H. G. Dyar, whose material was in turn exploited by Nabokov.

Moss was an English Protestant missionary whose interests included botany as well as entomology. Along with collections of great value now kept at the Natural History Museum in London, Moss left detailed painted records of the immature stages of tropical butterflies, their larval food plants and their adult nectar sources. Together these two men are responsible for thousands of important specimens in the world's great museums, and their published works, like Nabokov's, are yet further reminders of an era when competent self-taught scientists, even working part-time, could make lasting contributions to the advancement of biology.

Nabokov had either seen or read about some of the very specimens collected by such men, but compared with the amount of material that was now becoming available to Bálint and Johnson, it had been precious little. Along with the historic specimens they had unearthed in the museums of Europe, the new Blue butterflies the two were now receiving from Peña and Herrera in Chile, and Eisele and MacPherson in Argentina, marked a significant beginning for gathering up the pieces needed to complete the puzzle presented by the temperate regions of South America. In contrast with many other South American regions, which owe most of their butterfly names to European workers, both Argentina and Chile fostered a significant number of local entomologists who had provided scientific names for their countries' distinctive faunas over the decades. This was a fortunate situation for the Nabokov project, however, given these countries' importance as a center for Blues.

In Argentina there was a significant modern lepidopterological tradition before Eisele and MacPherson, based at some august institutions, First, Pablo Köhler, at the museum of La Plata, had assembled an impressive collection by the turn of the century and had published lists that served as a foundation for subsequent studies. Even more important was the later work of Kenneth Hayward, a resident English engineer and entomologist who since 1944 had worked out of the Instituto Miguel Lillo at the University of Tucumán, assembling a massive collection and establishing himself as Argentina's premier modern lepidopterist. Capitalizing on close relations with the government of Juan Perón in the 1950s, he had been able to produce a series of volumes on Argentina's butterflies. It was a unique work. As Phillip Ackery, one of the successors to Norman Riley at the British Museum, said in 1984, it made Argentina's fauna one of the few in South America that could, by any measure, be considered somewhat well-known at the time. But Hayward had barely touched the Hairstreaks and had done even less work on the Blues, although he was actively trying to advance those groups too before his death in 1972.

Johnson intended to use his planned 1991 research trip with Eisele and

MacPherson to visit the important collection of the Instituto Miguel Lillo, which was to serve as a host for the expedition. The prominence of Tucumán in the annals of entomology is a reflection of the time in the nineteenth century when the greater part of Argentina's population lived in the country's western half and Tucumán was a more important center of culture than Buenos Aires; even in the modern era the greatest outflow of published work defining Argentine butterflies has come from there.

Johnson's trip to Argentina was to be just the first of several expeditions on the continent. Although its initial intent had been to capture temperate Hairstreaks, those butterflies had the same territory as Nabokov's Blues, and it was easy to add them to the collecting menu. If he and Bálint could finish the studies on the Chilean and Argentine Blues, it would suggest that a run at completing Nabokov's classification for all of South America could reasonably be made. But short-term collecting expeditions by nonresident lepidopterists could not hope to ferret out all the new material that would be necessary to adequately sample Nabokov's temperate groups. Both men hoped that as more South American field researchers became aware that a fundamental taxonomy for Neotropical Blues was in place and being expanded, they would receive more material like they had from Peña and Herrera. And in fact, as word spread specimens came flooding in. But Bálint and Johnson also hoped that regional and local taxonomists would initiate their own formal work on the Blues in their areas once they saw strides being made elsewhere.

In particular, moving northward through Bolivia, Peru, Ecuador, Colombia, and Venezuela would require a great deal more help. Fortunately there were groups of resident lepidopterists in other parts of the continent, too, all ready and willing to join the project. In terms of the final disposition of Nabokov's classification, though, the most important scientist who had expressed a willingness to contribute was Gerardo Lamas, then the director of Lima, Peru's, natural history museum (which goes by the imposing name of the Museo de Historia Natural, Universidad Nacional Mayor de San Marcos). This was a museum that, aside from the austral material of Herrera and Peña, held the most extensive collections of High Andean butterflies, including a number of Blue species that Nabokov himself had been unable to obtain in 1945 and about which he could only speculate in the footnotes to "Notes on Neotropical Plebejinae." Lamas, himself one of the continent's most accomplished lepidopterists, was about to take responsibility for assembling an official list of Latin American butterflies for the Association for Tropical Lepidoptera. With butterflies promising to be one of the important "indicator groups" for the health of tropical habitats, the Association had been quickly established and expanded rapidly in the 1980s as a response to the widening biodiversity crisis in the world's tropical ecosystems. Although no one could have foreseen it in 1991, Lamas's responsibility for the Latin American butterfly list was to play a determining role in the way Nabokov's classification would be treated as a work of taxonomy.

Even with this level of international cooperation, tackling the Blue butterflies of a continent as large and diverse as South America would be no easy task. The region's intractability is a big reason that Nabokov's 1945 study was a work of such wondrous taxonomic daring. With a mere handful of specimens from a few far-flung localities in that intricate biological mosaic, he circumscribed a basic nomenclature for South American Blues. The breadth of his effort, especially in light of the modern requirements established by the taxonomic Code, made his path a difficult one to follow in any comprehensive, definitive way. For taxonomists who were to try, every corner of South America's temperate zones would add new knowledge to the outline Nabokov had established and provide a new test of the durability of his arrangement. The first such test would come within two months of Zsolt Bálint's contacting Kurt Johnson in New York, as Johnson and nine associates joined Roberto Eisele in northwestern Argentina in January 1991.

8

The Vertical Landscape

The boom of water in the gorge was enough to stun a man; head and
breast filled with an electric agitation; the water rushed with awesome
force — as smooth, however, as molten lead — then suddenly swelled out
monstrously as it reached the rapids, its varicolored waves piling up and
falling over the lustrous brows of the stones with a furious roar; and
then, crashing from a height of twenty feet, out of a rainbow and into
darkness, I ran further, now changed: seething, smoke-blue and snowlike
from the foam, it struck first one side and then the other of the con-
glomeratic canyon in such a way that it seemed the reverberating mountain fastness could never withstand it.

— *The Gift*

THE FIRST EXPEDITION to collect Nabokov's Blues in South America aimed at Argentina. Elements of the Argentine expedition left
simultaneously from New York and Chicago on January 27, 1991. It
was an intriguing group. Kurt Johnson and David and Kathleen Matusik,
veterans of Las Abejas and decades of butterfly collecting, were skilled
field entomologists. Karl Kroenlein, a high school student going on to
study science at Dartmouth College, came for his first experience in field
biology. (He and his sister Johanna, with a degree in primatology from
Princeton, have since done two stints of entomological survey work in
rural Kenya.) Their father, David Kroenlein, a New York City lawyer and
an accomplished photographer, came with both standard photo gear and
video equipment. Roberto Eisele, seasoned by years of collecting in northwestern Argentina, was guide and host. Steve Grossman, a New York financial manager, joined Eisele as the only other member of the team who
could speak Spanish.

Two additional family contingents filled out the expedition. One included

David Grae, founder of the Gotham Writers Workshop in New York City, and a writer-director of off-Broadway plays, and his brother Seth, a lawyer specializing in international law. The other included Nicholas "Nick" Pritzker, of Chicago's Pritzker family and president of the Hyatt Development Corporation, and his son Jake, at nine, the youngest member of the contingent. There was a good reason to bring so many collectors. A dozen field-workers collecting over a fifteen-day period could register a formidable number of worker-hours. Including day and night shifts, broken only by meals, total collecting time for this expedition would reach 2,500 hours.

When the group joined at Miami Airport to board a flight for Argentina, it was a curious sight indeed: ten people with outdoor paraphenalia, including various odd wraps and yellow-painted knapsacks and canteens marked MUSEUM, as required in countries that forbid the import of military gear. There were satchels full of small bottles and boxes, dozens of nets, extension handles, odd-looking insect traps, ultraviolet lights, assorted collection boxes, and photographic equipment. Johnson was carrying a set of documents in both English and Spanish explaining the purpose of all the equipment, and, spread among the eight adults, was several thousand dollars in cash (U.S. dollars and Argentine australs), since there would be no banks at their ultimate destination.

Oddest of all, perhaps, was a row of nearly twenty briefcases. Too many expeditions have returned from remote corners of the world to find their collections gone with "lost luggage," and savvy entomologists have learned that it is wise to sort the prime of their catch in advance and carry it home by hand. Even now, however, the briefcases were not empty. They carried liter bottles of New York water to tide the group over until a supply of bottled water could be found at their destination.

The outlandish paraphernalia could easily become a problem when the group switched planes in Buenos Aires for the trip to northwestern Argentina, particularly since the country was emerging from years of internal warfare. In addition, the Persian Gulf War had just gotten under way, leading to heightened security precautions everywhere.

Eisele had carefully chosen the fifteen-day window for the expedition. In his long experience of the region, those two weeks, in the middle of the Argentine summer, were often sunny; in the surrounding weeks heavy rain was common. It is an extremely important consideration. Throughout history expeditions have lived or died by the weather. It is common for field biologists to record the low points of their professional lives as times they have made the trek to some thrilling destination only to be socked in for days by rain.

On January 29, after traveling for more than thirty-six hours, including a night without sleep passing through Buenos Aires, the expedition arrived in San Salvador de Jujuy, in Argentina's northwesternmost Jujuy Province, just south of the border with Bolivia. Eisele was waiting with two vehicles, his own gas-turbine Peugeot, which could ford water up to the hood without stalling, and a hardy passenger van borrowed from local missionaries. By the time they made bivouac as guests of a Baptist mission camp outside Lozano, a forty-mile drive south from the airport, it was midmorning on a warm, sunny day. The camp, which served as a summer retreat for mission children, lay in a richly forested mountain valley, at about six thousand feet, impeccably green and fronting the Río Lozano, a river that meandered through and connected with a much wider floodplain of the Río Grande, which in the spring was full to bursting with water cascading down from the surrounding mountains. The temperature was about eighty degrees, some fifty degrees warmer than the weather they had left behind in New York and Chicago. With no time to waste a hasty decision was made to collect nearby, along the floodplain. It afforded a chance to test both the group's stamina and the collecting plan that had been designed for this mixed group of experienced and inexperienced researchers.

Like all insects, butterflies are thermodynamic machines. They warm up and cool down with the surrounding temperatures, and their activity fluctuates correspondingly. The daily flight time for many butterflies, especially in hot climates, can be very limited, often from about 10:00 A.M., when the air warms up, until 1:00 P.M., with the peak right at noon, when the sun is directly overhead. For many the heat becomes too intense by midafternoon, and they retreat to shaded perches, individually or in group roosts, only for some to reappear for a short period in the later afternoon, between 4:00 and 5:00 P.M.

Flying time is further limited by cloud cover, which in the tropics often occurs in relatively predictable daily cycles. Some upland forests are called cloud forests because much of the time they are thick with clouds, a cover that provides both moisture and a moderate temperature for the plants that thrive in them. Optimal insect activity often occurs for a brief period at midday, when the sun burns off the persistent overcast for an hour or so, only for it to return by midafternoon. The insects often fly in pulses during brief periods of optimal light and temperature conditions. A collector who misses the pulses misses everything, but with a dozen collectors in the field, the most could be made of such windows of opportunity.

The general plan for the expedition was to have the less experienced workers net the larger, easier to catch species. That would make up the "survey" part of the work, the recording of the most common and representative species from varied habitats. This is important because, with the larger butterflies thus covered, the experienced collectors and professional entomologists could concentrate completely on the smaller, more secretive and hard to net butterflies, including Blues and Hairstreaks, among which there were sure to be surprises, rare or new species.

Because an altitude acclimatization regime is necessary for anyone moving abruptly from sea level to heights above nine or ten thousand feet, a moderate mountain trek was scheduled for the next day. Time is required for the body's red-blood-cell count to reach the levels of those used to living at those higher altitudes; otherwise, the visitor's body will not receive enough oxygen, and serious illness can result. Optimally, a day per thousand feet of increased altitude is advised, but often this schedule must be accelerated. Thus, the plan for Day 3, January 31, was to collect in boggy páramo between eight and nine thousand feet, followed by transfer to a base camp for concerted collecting at ten to twelve thousand feet on Days 4 and 5. Eisele believed any problems with the weather would be negated by the verticality of the landscape; if it was raining at one elevation, the team could simply drive up above the clouds and collect in the sunshine.

Given the short acclimatization period (and the fact that butterfly hunting is much more strenuous than most people realize), all the collectors carried Dimox, a prescription drug to increase oxygen absorption by the lungs, in an attempt to nip altitude sickness at the source. Dimox is no panacea, however, and care must be taken not to overstress the heart, which at high altitudes beats at a drastically increased rate. Even in less demanding conditions the hunt and chase in butterfly collecting become arduous. The hunt requires great mental acuity, with constant visual attention to long and short distances in search of moving quarry and quick movement with little warning when prey are spotted. The chase demands running, sometimes for long distances, mixed with dodges, weaves, and sudden stops. Even when the quarry is netted, the lepist must bend over, or drop to his knees, remove the catch, and secure it in his pack. He then rises again quickly, alert for another chase. All in all, the activity might be aptly compared with the demands of basketball (and, in the Andes, at altitudes over ten thousand feet). Nabokov himself had called high-altitude collecting "a robust achievement" and reported that he lost twenty pounds in the summer of 1947 from strenuous climbing in the Rocky Mountains.

Surprisingly rested and ready to move, the group had breakfast and set out early in the morning of the thirty-first. They had packed enough food for several days, and it was good that everyone seemed fit, for in the following week they saw a bed for only a single night.

Their journey was along National Route 9 toward El Volcán, an expansive flat of High Andean grassland located at the high end of a precipitous gorge. The name, meaning "the volcano," refers to the cataclysmic outflow of water, mud, and debris that occurs each spring in this gorge — the Quebrada de Humahuaca. As part of the ambitious Pan American highway system, Route 9, with a companion railroad right-of-way, was engineered to follow the dramatic Río Grande watershed up the entire length of the Quebrada de Humahuaca gorge. This majestic gorge drops a breathtaking two thousand feet in just seven miles. At the bottom the road ends abruptly at the edge of the riverbed, a full half mile across. Strewn as far as the eye can see are piles of mammoth boulders and densely packed conglomerations of dirt, mud, chunks of broken cacti, brush, stone, and other debris. To the left, nearer the roadway, a grader had done its best to level what the deluge has left behind, but the debris is still piled up two or three times higher than a car. By midsummer of each year, February for South Americans, this and other deep valleys are total wastelands, laid bare by the spring's torrents of water and debris.

To the right, and seemingly far below, snakes a dark form looking something like the Great Wall of China. It is a dike of concrete and stone, some ten to twenty feet high, that runs the length of the valley. So violent are each spring's cataclysms that, if not protected by this dike, the railroad tracks would have to be relaid year after year.

After a drive of about ten miles, the expedition's two vehicles moved out of the top of the gorge and onto an expansive plateau of denuded, rolling grasslands, punctuated everywhere by erratically strewn piles of boulders. A startling feature of the upland temperate homes of Nabokov's Latin American Blues is the annual trauma they suffer at the hands of nature. Governed by the season, the high montane islands can capture huge amounts of rain, and the areas above them immense snowfalls, which, in the warmer months, causes a violent runoff out of the highlands. As a result Argentina's upland regions — like those of Chile, Bolivia, and southern Peru — can look at a distance like nothing so much as fields of boulders strewn in a titanic bomb blast. Yet a closer look reveals a fascinating and delicate landscape of small plants and flowers amid the boulders, peppered about like little rock gardens. In these environs even the Blues are odd. Many share a trait taxonomists call discoloration, meaning that instead of the metallic blue associated with the group, both males and females are often dull brown. The colors appear to be connected to the cold climates that pervade the regions, the brown of the wings absorbing more of the sun's radiant energy than could be gained from flashy blue tints. This extreme variety in outward appearance was one reason Nabokov had turned nearly exclusively to dissection in his "Notes on Neotropical Plebejinae."

About a mile up the road Eisele waved the convoy to the roadside, and when the group got out to take in the panorama, they found that the air had turned chilly, packing a stiff breeze. Ahead of them unfolded an endless flower garden, speckled with the familiar coin-size flashes of brilliant orange, yellow, red, and blue: butterflies were already in the air, taking advantage of the heat the sun could muster between the cold gusts.

Even here, at eight thousand feet, there was another high ridge of dark, purplish mountains along each side of this monster of a plateau, far above where no road led. It was a grand spectacle, and Johnson tried to guess the distance to the walls of those higher ridges, hoping to make out a reference — a band of trees, a rivulet or waterfall — somewhere on the slopes. The source of the cold wind was no longer a mystery. On those far ridges broad bands of snow were laid out in long, vertical strokes of white, and, fetching binoculars, Johnson could see the wind at work, picking up the snow in curls and wisps.

Eisele told how the thin air on the plateau was nothing compared with what the locals call the puna — not the upland regions of the same name but a wind that dominates the Argentine uplands in midwinter. The name, he said, refers not so much to the wind itself but to the sickness the wind brings; the puna occurs at different times of the year, depending on the altitude. In this particular area the winter winds come mainly from the north, out of the Bolivian highlands, and are extremely low in oxygen. The rarefied air is persistent and can cause severe health problems. Summer winds, however, like the one blowing that day, Eisele said, often pour out of the Humahuaca quebrada heavily saturated with oxygen from the thick vegetation below.

Eisele's cabin at Huacalera was a thirty-by-thirty-five-foot plastered adobe block, with only a few rudimentary windows, for simplified security in the months it was unoccupied and for ease of insulation during the winter. The structure was divided into two rooms along the central spine by an inner wall open at both ends. In the large back space were an open kitchen and a bathroom, the only part of the place enclosed for privacy. This humble cabin was home for a dozen people for the next three days, or rather the next three nights: everyone would be at work from dawn to well after dark, and the cabin would be little more than a place for the exhausted researchers to line up their sleeping bags. Neither of the collecting areas planned for the two days was accessible by vehicle, and reaching them would require a rough climb from the trailhead. To be sure of arriving at the highlands by late morning, when the butterflies were most likely to be flying, the group had to rise early.

As some of the expedition team prepared supper, the rest worked through logistics for sorting and labeling a day's catch. This would become a daily drill requiring both speed and precision. The first days' catches had resulted in more than a thousand glassine envelopes to sort. The less experienced entomologists were taught the basics of separating specimens at the family level, and as the sorted stacks grew Eisele circulated, reciting names to be quickly written in ink on each envelope. Specimens no one could recognize were segregated and marked for special care. Sorted specimens were placed in larger clip-lock plastic bags, one for each family of Lepidoptera, with locality and date labels firmly affixed; these bags, in turn, were loosely laid in lidded plastic tubs. Every day each tub and bag would need to be opened by someone at base camp and the contents spread out in the sun; otherwise, in the heat and humidity, the moisture locked in the bodies of the specimens could cause them to rot. Each bag was also sprinkled with some poisonous paradichlorobenzine pellets in case marauding ants or roaches discovered them.

Ordinarily, the day of a conscientious entomologist would not even now be over, and attention would turn to nighttime light trapping. At its most basic this involves spreading white sheets in convenient positions — on cars and trucks, tables, clothesline, or the side of a building — and illuminating them with ultraviolet lights. Moths, beetles, and a panoply of other insects are drawn by the hundreds or thousands, while collectors hustle around, trapping them with nets and cyanide killing jars. Researchers who trap by light or bait, an acquired skill, make up their own fraternity within entomology, and experienced trappers brag of idiosyncratic methods. Bait trappers devise recipes, often the products of trial and error, especially tailored for their chosen prey. Ingredients, usually whipped up in a blender, can include beer, molasses, fruit, and, for the daring, urine and manure — anything enticing to the denizens of the night. (Not for nothing do the wives of many trappers insist that all bait blenders be kept far away from the kitchen, in the garage, for instance.) The techniques of night trapping are one of the lessons that Fyodor's father shares with him in *The Gift*.

Many insects, including butterflies, exhibit an arresting behavior called hilltopping, in which individuals instinctively fly uphill and eventually congregate in shoals along the ridgetops and summits. This behavior, thought to have evolved as a strategy for finding mates, provided the expedition with its strategy: to collect along the high, barren ridges near Huacalera, at altitudes between 10,000 and more than 12,000 feet. Eisele had chosen two sites, readily enough accessible for a day's return journey, that he felt offered the best chance of delivering the highland Blues and Hairstreaks on the expedition's wish list. His choice for the first climb was Cerro Amarillo, a round-topped peak reaching 10,663 feet on the west side of the Río Grande about three miles northwest of Huacalera. His choice for the second climb was Abra de la Cruz, a páramo located at 12,303 feet between mountains towering just off to the east of Huacalera.

Cerro Amarillo means "Yellow Mountain" in Spanish, and it lives up to its name. From a distance its eastern façade, rising some two thousand feet above the valley floor, seems to be composed of naked, multicolored rock, mostly of hues of orange and yellow, a foreboding backdrop to the west side of Quebrada de Humahuaca at Huacalera. Its flanks are well above what might be thought of as a timberline, the only trees in the entire valley at Huacalera being domestic willows, poplars, and some conifers that have been planted in the town and along the edges of the Río Grande's course. One has literally to stand on the mountain's flanks to see any plant cover, mostly grasses, cacti, and scattered flowering scrub. According to Eisele's plan, if the party began walking from the highway west of town by 6:00 A.M., it had a chance to reach the higher reaches of the mountain, along a row of immense cliffs just below the summit, by noon. Eisele had taken this route before and had been rewarded by a dramatic noontime breakout of butterflies.

On the morning of February 1, when Eisele had pulled the vehicles off the road about two miles north of Huacalera, his finger traced the route he recommended the more experienced collectors take: an oblique path across a two-mile stretch of desert to some small foothills at the mountain's base, along a gradually rising arched ridge running up the mountain's right flank, and onto some high cliffs that ringed the area below the summit like the collar of a shirt. Eisele said that along this relatively gentle arched ridge, the alpine butterflies would be hilltopping for the better part of an hour when the sun was at its zenith. He warned the party, however, that on their five-hour walk across the barren terrain they might not see a single butterfly.

That circuit would have made unrealistic demands on nine-year-old Jake Pritzker, so he and his father planned to make a shorter loop, as far as the base of the mountain and back. This was actually an efficient division of labor, since these two would be able to take their time and thoroughly explore the intervening desert while the others hurried on to climb the mountain. Despite Eisele's advice, however, David Matusik, an experienced climber and confident of his abilities, wanted to take the more direct route, straight across the desert to the base of the mountain and then straight up the facing slope. Unable to agree on a plan, and with valuable time being wasted, the climbers agreed to split up: the Graes would go with Matusik and his wife; Johnson, Grossman, and the Kroenleins would take Eisele's longer route.

True to Eisele's prediction, only the occasional butterfly was seen along the long desert trail. But, as if in compensation, by eleven, after the steady climb up the arched ridge, the collarlike cliffs at 10,500 feet just below the peak were boiling with butterflies, all heading up the slope. The Kroenleins had been slowed by the joys of filming, but Johnson and Grossman were just below the collar when the late-morning hilltopping began, and they hurried to the top of the ridge beneath the cliffs. What filled the air was a potpourri of everything alpine — High Andean Whites and Sulphurs, orange-and-black High Andean Fritillaries, and Hairstreaks and Blues. Remarkably, at least for anyone who thinks of butterflies as delicate creatures, they were all navigating a very strong wind as they nectared from the bundles of small blue flowers covering the low bushes scattered around the area. Defying the gusts, they would gain control over their flutter as the wind slackened, using a split second of relative calm to latch onto a flower and hold tight, nectaring away as the wind kicked up again and bent the plants nearly double; in this way some butterflies manage to nectar even in the windiest weather.

It was a stroke of luck for the collectors that the butterflies were zeroing in on the flowers; when one of the creatures gave itself up to the air, it was quickly blown yards away. Chasing them at this altitude was hopelessly exhausting, and standing still hoping for a lucky catch wasn't worth the time. Collecting from the flowering plants was really the only way to catch anything. And so many butterflies were out at that magical hour that it was impossible to collect with any plan or precision, particularly with only two collectors to carry on the hunt until the Kroenleins arrived with a half hour of hilltopping to go.

The Matusiks and Graes, however, never made it. Their disembodied voices drifted up from somewhere beneath a rise where they couldn't be seen. When the butterflies first burst out, Johnson and Grossman had begun shouting to alert the others, sending echoes along the jagged faces of the yellow and orange cliffs. The invisible wanderers below, eager to find their way up and join in the sport, shouted back, but in vain. The path they had chosen was simply too steep. The only solution seemed to be to collect as fast as one could and shout at the same time. So, when the Kroenleins finally arrived along the high ridge beneath the summit, they, along with Johnson and Grossman, collected as fast as they could while shouting, "Up here! Up here," at the top of their lungs. It was an absurd picture, but the expedition would visit this site only once, and collecting time was short.

One of the biggest annoyances in high-altitude collecting, on any continent, is that you see insects flying but don't have the energy to give chase, or when you do the quarry dodges away or disappears under a pile of boulders, and all your energy has been wasted. There is also a malaise that sets in at high altitudes: will and motivation evaporate, giving way to an overwhelming lassitude. At the time this seems a perfectly legitimate reaction, probably a protective mechanism of the body. Only later comes the bitter and frustrating memory of the hours spent walking uphill — all for nothing. That is what nearly happened the next day, on Abra de la Cruz, the mountain pass ascended by the team on February 2. Reaching 12,300 feet on a high páramo wedged between two foreboding mountains towering off to the east of Huacalera — Cerro Monterrey at 13,064 feet, and Cerro Chachacomayo, at 14,028 feet — the team had arrived too late for the noonday hilltopping. In an echo of the difficult choices made by scientists for centuries, they had lingered too long on the lower slopes, captivated by two fast-flying butterflies they eventually were able to net, both Hairstreaks, both new to science.

The next day the expedition drove southward, some three hundred miles, through Argentina's Salta Province to the province of Tucumán and its capital, San Miguel de Tucumán. Leaving the mountains in early morning with temperatures barely above freezing, they arrived in midevening with the mercury hitting well over one hundred. Their major task would be to sort through fifty years' worth of backlogged lycaenids at the University of Tucumán's Instituto Miguel Lillo. Much of their itinerary after leaving Tucumán's capital city was designed to bring them to Argentina's subtropical forest remnants farther to the north, as they made their way back to the airport at San Salvador de Jujuy to return to the United States. But as they sorted through the butterflies at the institute, an enterprise that eventually led them to Blues of three of Nabokov's genuses, and several new butterfly species as well, Eisele came into the collection room with a sandy-haired young man whom he introduced as Jaime Powell of the Institute's Paleontology Department.

Powell was excited that a group of foreign scientists, with working vehicles, had landed in Tucumán City. He hadn't seen a healthy truck in some time, and he was extremely anxious to obtain the use of one, because, on a recent trip with friends through a mountain valley about forty miles west of Tucumán, he had seen what appeared to be a huge fossilized bone sticking out of a freshly graded right-of-way. He had stopped long enough to cover the protruding part of the bone with earth and rags, but he wanted to return before a heavy rain reexposed it. Argentina is famous for its dinosaur discoveries, eclipsed only by the finds in the Gobi Desert of Mongolia. The general populace is well aware of the financial rewards such discoveries can bring, so Powell was afraid if he waited too long others would dig the bone out for themselves, or it might be inadvertently damaged.

The prospect of having the expedition interrupted by the discovery of dinosaur bones reminded Johnson of a cartoon from the British humor magazine *Punch* that Nabokov had kept pinned above his workbench at the Museum of Comparative Zoology at Harvard. In it a lepidopterist is plying his net in the Gobi Desert as two tyrannosaurs attack another dinosaur in the background. "This is all very interesting," he says, "but I *must* remember I am a specialist in Lepidoptera." In this case, though, the distraction offered advantages to the lepidopterists, too. Powell's suggestion was that if the expedition could provide transport for him and an assistant and some spare hands to help with excavation for a few days, he could at least make sure the lepidopterists got to their northern Argentine destinations, and he knew of reliable accommodations along the way. Eisele stressed that Tafí del Valle was near another locality quite famous for Blues — Abra de Infiernillo, "Little Hell," a spectacularly deep canyon falling off abruptly from a mesmerizing set of mountain cliffs. Here many of Nabokov's Blues, including *Parachilades, Itylos,* and *Pseudolucia,* a number of specimens of which had been represented in the Miguel Lillo collection, had been recorded.

The route proposed to reach Tafí del Valle was the long, winding National Route 307, which runs first through deep tropical forest, then through upland cloud forest, and finally emerges from the clouds onto a vast elevated plateau surrounded on all sides by even higher mountains. Locally, Route 307 is known as the Refrigerator. The road, much of it in frightfully poor condition, is treacherously narrow and weaving, presenting drivers with curl after curl of hairpin turns, sharp inclines, and precipitous drop-offs. According to Eisele, the curves explain the road's nickname, mimicking the looped coolant tubing that covers the back of an icebox. Whatever the origin of its name, the Refrigerator was the only way to Tafí del Valle, and for entomologists it afforded an unbelievably complex gradient of biological habitat as they maneuvered its long, near-thirty-mile course. As Eisele often said of Argentina, both its land and its people — "Everything is an extreme."

On February 5 the expedition, with the paleontologists onboard, set out from San Miguel de Tucumán up the Refrigerator, happy to leave the hundred-degree heat of Tucumán and enter the cool Andes once again. It was not exactly the American Museum of Natural History's near-mythical 1920s expeditions to the Gobi with Roy Chapman Andrews and his Pierce-Arrow convoy of gun-toting fossil diggers in broad-brimmed hats, but the group projected a suitable profile for a respectable adventure-romance of natural history. The two vehicles carried, in addition to fourteen bodies and the original heaps of entomological equipment, all the paleontologists' gear as well: shovels, picks, large brushes, small brushes, dental tools, wire-mesh boxes for sifting soil, bags of plaster of paris, and jerry cans of water.

Nearly ten hours later, after a grueling drive happily broken by regular collecting stops in the lush forests along the way, the vehicles arrived at the chaletlike hotel of the Argentine Automobile Association at Tafí del Valle, perched in a murky twilight in an immense mountain valley surrounded by snowy peaks. A light breeze was blowing, and, with a temperature near seventy degrees, the basin was a vision of paradise. For as far as the eye could see, the cradling mountains were steeped in an almost liquid blue that seemed to mask any sense of distance. Here and there, at indiscernible intervals, lights from surrounding villages appeared and then vanished in eerie, intermittent rhythms, perhaps caused by the movement of the air, clouds, or trees. Taking Eisele's Peugeot and flashlights in case the deep night set in, Powell and Johnson went immediately to the site where weeks before Powell had concealed the huge bone. To the paleonotologist's relief, it was still safely tucked away.

Powell could not sleep that night. He stayed awake preparing gear for the big passenger van that would be his for the next three days; he didn't even change his clothes. With the sunrise the group set off in both vehicles, headed west toward the bones. Once arrived, half of them — the Graes, Grossman, and the Pritzkers — stayed to work with Powell. The others continued on to collect butterflies in the deep canyon along the road. The expedition's itinerary allowed only three days at Tafí del Valle. On the last day Powell told the lepidopterists that the huge hipbone was not that of a dinosaur after all but, equally exciting — at least to him — that of a giant sloth, a huge mammal that lived much later than the dinosaurs. The find appeared to be a new discovery within the giant sloth genus *Megatherium,* and it was the largest Powell had ever seen. But, Powell feared, there was going to be hardly enough time to complete unearthing it.

The Americans were reluctant to leave their Argentine colleague in the lurch, but they also wanted to be faithful to their own schedule. The solution they sought lay in the power of U.S. currency during that time of hyperinflation in Argentina. Taking heed of Nabokov's cartoon — to remember what they were there for — the Americans decided to make an academic grant to Powell on the spot, enough money for him to repair his truck in Tucumán and return with his students to complete the dig. Disguising the bone once again, in fact nearly burying it, the Americans and Argentines returned to Tucumán on February 9. Half their number then returned to the United States, as they had planned.

Johnson, with Eisele, the Matusiks, and the Kroenleins, continued for another week — northward in another long loop toward Jujuy. Powell repaired his truck and set out once again for Tafí del Valle with his students. As the ultimate result "Meg" stands today as one of the largest and most complete skeletons of *Megatherium* in existence, on full display and available for research at the Instituto Miguel Lillo.

A week later, on February 15, Johnson and the rest of the American expedition returned to the ice and snow of North America with a collection of well over ten thousand butterflies and moths. They had succeeded in netting, or borrowing from local collections, representatives of every genus of South American Blues identified by Nabokov.

Over the next months Johnson shared reams of patiently excised data and illustrations with Zsolt Bálint in Budapest as they sought to complete the basic work on the large samples now available from both Chile and Argentina. Bálint punctuated his schedule with the work necessary in the major European museums, which now included a regular schedule in London and Paris, trips to the museums in Basel and at Oxford University, an additional trip to Vienna, and letters requesting loans of material from the museums in Stockholm, Copenhagen, and Berlin. He and Johnson were laboring under the illusion that, having exhausted the specimens now in their domain, their work on Nabokov's Blues might be over. But this was not to be. They were about to be introduced to the next major scientist who would enter the project on Nabokov's Blues.

His name was Dubi Benyamini, and he was, among other things, the president of the Lepidopterists Society of Israel. An engineer by trade, he was about to go on assignment to Chile and, having been in contact with Luis Peña and his co-worker Alfredo Ugarte, had learned of the work of Bálint and Johnson in the north. He contacted them at once. Benyamini brought a range of knowledge and expertise to the project that had previously been absent. Much of his published research concerned what is called the biology of butterflies — the study of their life cycles, where they live, what they eat — the "brass tacks" of biology, particularly crucial to understanding the temperate zones of South America, where so little research has been done in these areas. One of his specialties was the rearing of butterflies from eggs through adulthood, a difficult task but one crucial to assessing the validity of species designations. Stopping in New York to visit Johnson, Benyamini immediately agreed to turn his expertise to the Chilean Blues.

Benyamini settled with his family in Santiago in 1992 and was quick to log over a month of concerted collecting across the entire central region of Chile, visiting nearly fifty localities and quickly turning up a half dozen of the Blues Bálint and Johnson had already identified for their Chilean colleagues. However, by early in the Chilean spring of 1993, Benyamini soon began to realize that to locate all the Blues Peña and Herrera had furnished Bálint and Johnson, and possibly go beyond this number to new discoveries, he would have to begin collecting with a methodical geographic plan. Nearly all previous collecting, whether by the early collector-dealers or by the modern lepidopterists of the region, had been haphazard, mostly because of the lack of a taxonomy. Five of the genuses Nabokov named from South America occur from the central Andes southward into Patagonia and include the most diverse of his groups. If he was going to provide substantial help in closing the gap in the knowledge of Nabokov's Latin American Blues, Benyamini realized he would have to explore the entire Cone — not just Chile but Bolivia and Argentina as well.

To accomplish this task he began in 1993 a strategy that Johnson came to call the Yellow Brick Road. After reviewing the specimen labels in every Chilean collection available to him, he marked with yellow pen on a regional map each location that was still unexplored. He then added two other bits of data: locations where previous collectors had taken extremely rare species, and the recorded localities of the old historical type material. For Benyamini this map represented a distinct lepidopterological frontier.

His initial plan was to leave Santiago in January. That is midsummer in the Southern Hemisphere, which would allow him to collect along the entire Chilean coast northward some 1,200 miles to Arica, at the border with Peru. Then he planned to turn east, head upland, and meet two of his Chilean engineer-friends at Putre, a locale in the country's Tarapacá region from which no fewer than twenty species of butterflies had been named. When he had collected there he could proceed with his friends over the Andean divide into Bolivia. Then, on a subsequent expedition, he would turn north from Putre instead of east and drive toward the Peruvian border to collect on Volcán Tacora, from where the nineteenth-century lepidopterist Gustav Weymer had named a number of rare Blues.

The trip from Santiago northward and then into Bolivia, as Benyamini planned it, approached five thousand miles, almost all on unpaved roads. Since he did not want to make the journey to Bolivia alone, and because he could not be sure that his friends would stick to the plans they had made, he decided to take his family — his wife, Lea, her mother, Ora, and their three children — enticing them by promising that they could attend the annual Carnaval de Río in Oruro, in southern Bolivia, which they could enjoy without Río's usual mad complement of tourists.

He did so with some misgivings, since Benyamini's Chilean friends had warned him about the hazards of travel in the Bolivian highlands. Even as summer grips the continent of South America, the months of January to March on Bolivia's altiplano, the notorious "Bolivian winter," can suddenly dump freezing rain or even snow upon an unwary visitor. High-waymen are also a danger. Not only might they steal your car and your property as you camp by the road at night but they also have the habit of pulling drivers over under pretense of being law officials, forcing them from their cars at gunpoint, and simply driving away with everything. Benyamini installed two hidden switches in his four-wheel-drive Subaru station wagon that would cut off gas to the engine if someone started the car without turning them on in sequence. He also took other precautions simply to protect himself against being stranded in the middle of no-where — a winch on his bumper for pulling the car through mud and water, enough spare tubes to assure that he could go though a number of tires without being stranded, and a three-foot vertical snorkel on his tailpipe so that submerging the car in water would not kill the engine. By the time the 4 x 4 was ready to go, it was so heavily loaded with tents, sleeping bags, heavy rescue equipment, winter clothing, food, water, extra gasoline, and seven people that the tires had to be overinflated to allow a safe clearance over the rocks and river fords he had been told to expect.

Of Chile's three geographic divisions, the north is usually defined as the area between Coquimbo, at about 30 degrees south latitude, and the Peru-vian border. It is dominated by the Atacama desert along the coast and, abutting the Andean divide, two sets of highlands, Tarapacá in the North and Antofagasta in the South.

Because of the general lack of water, the northern division of Chile has always been more a crossroads than a center of settlement. But this had never been an impediment to research. Even in the colonial era collectors visited the narrow belt of vegetation, the puna, that separates the inhos-pitable coastal desert from the high barren uplands to the east. A number of butterflies, including some of Nabokov's Blues, are native to the puna, even though they are only vaguely labeled with the notations of old village names like Putre or Belén. Antofagasta had also yielded some of its secrets to biologists, though not so much to the colonial workers as to Emilio Ureta Rojas, who had preceded José Herrera at the Metropolitan Univer-sity in Santiago. During the 1950s Ureta had named several lycaenids from that region, some of which had seldom been seen since. In fact, for decades Ureta's work was so poorly known to scientists outside Chile that, before being corrected by Johnson, bibliographies often credited the puna lycaenids to two authors — a Dr. Rojas and a Dr. Ureta. As for the desert, it was possibly even more poorly known than the uplands, but with the work of the recent Chilean and international scientists, it was to produce a number of surprises among Nabokov's groups of Blues.

Entering Tarapacá, Benyamini first crossed the broad salt flats along the Pampa del Tamarugal, covered in that season with vast flocks of flamingos. Then, at Tintados, he cut west, aiming toward the smoking Volcán Lascar along the border with Boliva. Lascar's entire peak had blown off a few years before, causing catastrophic damage to the surrounding area. But the local people had benefited from a government rebuilding project, and the region was now far more prosperous than it had been before the eruption. One development that was not good for Blues, however, was the huge numbers of rabbits that had been turned loose to be shot at will for food. Benyamini was all too familiar with their ability, along with sheep, goats, mules, and the local camelitos, to denude the mountain grasslands where Blues usually thrived.

As Benyamini neared the Bolivian border, he decided to leave his family at a pleasant spot in the foothills and drive on with Lea to check the condition of roads leading upland and eastward. His day's destination was Salar de Huasco, a high mountain flat figuring prominently on his yellow-marked map just east of Pica, Chile. Leaving the boys and his mother-in-law in Pica's pretty village park, he and Lea continued east toward the salar along the Bolivian border. At this time of year Salar de Huasco, at about ten thousand feet altitude, is not only home to flocks of flamingos but surrounded with teeming meadows of wildflowers. Here Benyamini netted the rare Andean *Phulia* Sulphurs, Whites of the high mountain *Tatochila* and *Hysochila* groups, the fiery-colored Skippers known as *Hylephila,* and the little Titicaca Blues Nabokov had placed in his genus *Parachilades* — a bountiful catch by most measures. Benyamini left Pica convinced that, despite the regional drought, he must continue northward. After all, these were his only years in Chile. Given the rugged conditions of the roads, however, he was a little nervous about his car.

Leaving Salar de Huasco, he got his first taste of the Bolivian winter, a cloudburst that came out of nowhere, covering the road with so much mud it was nearly impossible to distinguish it from the surrounding flats. Benyamini knew this was cause for concern; he knew of more than one car that had been completely submerged in a "soft salar" when an unwary driver had ventured off the road; the same had almost happened to him once in Argentina. After picking up the rest of the family at Pica, he headed to Iquique, back along the Pacific coast. Here, as an extra precaution, Benyamini bought a complete set of tires, put his old ones in reserve, and headed north to Arica. He then turned west on the deteriorating road toward Putre.

Putre, at over ten thousand feet, harbors one of the most unique life zones in Chile. Here a rare combination of year-round mild temperatures and the rains of summer combine to form a tropical isolate. Before Benyamini's work only six species of Hairstreaks and Blues were known from this restricted region. He added two new species to the list, one a Blue belonging to Nabokov's genus *Itylos,* which he named after his small daughter. He also found *faga,* in the genus Nabokov knew as *Pseudothecla,* and two other members of Nabokov's *Itylos, pelorias* and *ludicra.* These butterflies had been given species names by Gustav Weymer in 1890, but Nabokov was never able to locate any specimens. Weymer's *ludicra* had been named from Volcán Tacora, another reason Benyamini would eventually have to venture there.

Benyamini's work at Putre was planned to allow time for altitude acclimatization. However, this time, high on the plateau west of Putre and still several miles from his destination, a storm swept through with clouds so low he could barely see beyond the station wagon's hood. Within minutes the road was awash with water, rocks, and small boulders, making it nearly impossible to keep going. The family was stunned. None of them had ever seen anything like this, and Benyamini began to question his sanity for having brought them along.

They pressed on, however, and when they finally reached Putre, Benyamini was amazed to see another mud-covered 4 x 4, carrying another contingent of passengers who looked suspiciously like entomologists. In a stroke of good luck, it turned out to be Jerome Rozen's bee survey group from the American Museum of Natural History, and talk turned to mutual acquaintances. Benyamini was surprised to find that Rozen's colleague on this expedition was Johnson's office mate, Calvin Snyder. Snyder, now with the museum's Center for Biodiversity, had previously collected for Bálint and Johnson a Chilean desert Blue that was to become *Pseudolucia aureliana,* named for Nabokov's story of the Lepidoptera dealer who dreamed of hunting butterflies in the tropics.

Benyamini's spirits were dampened, however, by the report of the American scientists. They had found conditions to the east dismal and were heading back downland. And, because the rain didn't ease at all that evening or through the night, Benyamini had no idea what to do. In the end he decided to make no plans until the arrival of his Chilean engineer-friends, who had agreed to meet him at a small hotel in Putre. But as the next day wore on, there was no sign of them, no call and no explanation. Having lost a day in waiting, Benyamini decided they must have either been delayed or changed their plans. With the weather only somewhat improved, he and his family set out east of Putre, climbing slowly toward Lake Chungará in Chile's Parque Nacional Lucaca. At 14,850 feet, Chungará is some 1,650 feet higher than Lake Titicaca, and Benyamini was sure, if he could only get there in decent weather, it would have many secrets to reveal. It was, after all, near the foot of Bolivia's Mt. Sajama, from where Nabokov had reported specimens in his Harvard treatise in 1945. From Chungará it was only a short hop to the Bolivian border.

As the station wagon neared Lake Chungará, the driving rain turned into snow. Navigating around the periphery of the lake, they knew they would be unable to catch a glimpse of its most spectacular landmark, the 21,450-foot-high Volcán Parinacota, with its nearly perfectly shaped, glacier-covered cone. Of the twenty highest volcanoes in the world, eighteen lie in Chile or on its borders. Of these, Parinacota is the highest. But that day it was completely obscured by deep gray clouds and the midsummer snowstorm.

Benyamini had to wait for a second visit to take in the sight, but he did get to see another regional marvel. The station wagon had just pulled even with two large trucks that had overturned on a sharp turn and, among the vehicles alongside the road, popped up a viscacha, one of southern South America's rare chinchillas. Richly furred, rabbitlike animals, viscachas have been hunted nearly to extinction and are seldom seen in the wild. Their origins are also a puzzle; they are one of the native Andean and Patagonian animals perhaps suggesting an old relationship, via continental drift, with Australia and Antarctica. The pictures Benyamini took of the viscacha were the only prize he could claim that day from Lake Chungará.

At the Bolivian border station at Tambo Qemada, the snow had turned back into rain, and it was finally feeling warmer. Benyamini's station wagon was the only passenger car among a sea of trucks about to pass through the checkpoint. As he waited in line Benyamini tried to question the drivers about conditions ahead. All he was able to learn, while the drivers snickered at his overloaded vehicle, was that at least part of the road to Oruro was under water. When the Subaru finally pulled up to the border gate, a wry smile on the face of the young immigration officer tipped Benyamini off that he was being viewed as the tourist catch of the day. The guard demanded twenty-five dollars per person to let them into Bolivia. In

Spanish, Benyamini told him that he had contacted the Bolivian embassy in Santiago on precisely this point and had learned that no border taxes existed in Bolivia. When Benyamini refused to pay the bribe, the guard took another tack, threatening not to allow the children over the border unless he had special papers confirming that they were his. Benyamini indignantly pointed out that while they were standing there arguing, the line of trucks was simply passing around the gate as the drivers pleased.

The confrontation went nowhere until Benyamini spotted a Bolivian Army jeep with a driver and three officers nearing the station. Although they took his side in the argument, the border guard remained adamant that the crossing was his jurisdiction, not theirs. Finally, the senior Army officer insisted that the young border guard settle for ten dollars for each adult, which Benyamini reluctantly agreed to pay. Hoping to exact some small revenge, however, Benyamini insisted on a receipt, which the border guard grudgingly wrote up on a scrap of paper under the eyes of the Army officers. Sixty miles farther down the road, at another police checkpoint, Benyamini used the receipt to report the corrupt border guard's name, but, of course, he had no idea if anything would be done.

This was part of the Benyaminis' welcome to Bolivia. Another was one of the worst roads they had ever seen, swimming in mud and clogged with rocks half again as big as their tires. Every few miles the roadbed was completely submerged in pools of water, some narrow enough to allow careful passage, others so wide that it was impossible to judge their depth. Watching some of the trucks wading across two-hundred-foot pools, the water halfway up their huge tires, Benyamini would have given up and turned back had not a small Indian boy who was sitting by the roadway enjoying the spectacle revealed a trick: he showed Benyamini's two sons how to wade the waters in the car's path and, little by little, find some circuitous track shallow enough to allow them to pass. In this way the Benyaminis were able to reach Cosapa and gained some satisfaction when the truckers who had treated them rudely at the border crossing were obviously surprised that they had arrived so soon.

East of Cosapa, however, with the rain still making any thought of collecting impossible, Benyamini finally met the washout that was to be his Waterloo. Approaching the back of a long line of trucks, he could see a huge crowd of villagers watching as the trucks, one at a time, struggled to cross what seemed to be a stretch of unsurpassable floodwater, occasionally joining in with a helpful push. When Benyamini saw two trucks halfway across and completely mired in the mud, he knew the little station wagon would never be able to get past.

From speaking with one of the villagers, he learned that a few miles upstream was another village where the ford might be easier. A small track to the right of the main road led in that direction, and he decided to take it. In about twenty minutes they reached the village, where yet another large crowd had gathered by the floodway to watch the spectacle of trucks on an alternate route to the main road trying to get across. Because it was now late afternoon, Benyamini was becoming more anxious to move. So, when his sons found a shallow spot, he put the 4 x 4 into full power and roared quickly across. On the other side he had not driven twenty minutes before the road again became impassable, cut by a stream so deep that Benyamini was sure the current would wash them away.

With little choice except to drive overland, he left the road and began picking his away through boulders, sandy rises, and giant clumps of bunchgrass. There was no trace of any kind of track, and Benyamini soon had no real idea of where he was going. Spying an Indian woman with a bright hat and a basket walking with two children, he asked the way to Oruro. She did not answer but, it seemed to Benyamini, looked into the distance, where far ahead there appeared the outline of a small village, which took about fifteen minutes to reach. Although the village was utterly deserted, Benyamini was pleased to see the semblance of a road cutting through it — perhaps the road to Oruro.

At the edge of a cluster of empty mud houses, however, he could see that the way was once again blocked by floodwaters. Then he caught sight of something that astounded him: in the middle of the deluge two trucks floundered in the mud as, on the far side of the waters, a crowd stood watching and helping to push other trucks in and out of the water. Benyamini realized that in the entire afternoon he had succeeded only in making a complete circle, to the other side of where he had seen those same two trucks stuck and begun his detour.

It was still raining, nearly dark, and the Benyaminis had no choice but to sleep in what they hoped were the abandoned houses of the ghostly village. The latch on the sheet-metal door of one of the huts had been shot off; perhaps they were not the first to be marooned here. Though cold and anxious the family got through the night undisturbed, and the next day, when Benyamini's boys found an abandoned church and began ringing its bell, the researcher packed and left the village as quickly as he could. The rain had finally stopped. Returning the way they had come the day before, Benyamini met two men on bicycles who showed him the right road to Turco. They drove another five miles and were stopped in their tracks by still another washout — only about twenty-five feet wide but impossibly deep. But the sun was finally shining. Benyamini had had enough and decided to collect butterflies then and there. He remembers it as one of his most productive days on the Bolivian highlands — his collecting pouch bulging with High Andean Fritillaries and Sulphurs, and Blues of Nabokov's genuses *Paralycaeides* and *Parachilades*.

When he returned to the station wagon, he found that his sons had spent the afternoon building a dam with big rocks, which gave him an idea about how they might overcome the current. If they diverted the water enough to make it shallower, they could drive through. Three hours later they were halfway across and continuing to make headway when a local trucker, evidently admiring their ingenuity, winched them the rest of the way. No more than thirty minutes later they were in Turco, halfway to Oruro, only to find another line of about a hundred trucks. Up ahead, Benyamini learned, a bulldozer was dragging the trucks one by one across a broad washout. He was afraid they could be stuck there for days.

But having a smaller and lighter vehicle for once worked to Benyamini's advantage. He drove overland downstream from the washout until he finally found a place shallow enough to cross. Then he doubled back to the road on the other side. Within a few hours he was in Oruro. From there the next stop would be the capital city, La Paz, and all the collecting areas for Blues he had originally planned. Before leaving La Paz, however, Benyamini drove his mud-caked station wagon to the Subaru dealer and repair shop — the largest in Bolivia. His electrical circuits were in a shambles from all the water. When they saw the car and its Chilean license, the owner and his mechanics were incredulous. They photographed the car, its plates, Benyamini and his Chilean papers, and refused to accept payment for the repairs. They said the photographs would be priceless in the local war against their competitor, Toyota.

Benyamini had gambled and won. His final tally for Bolivian catches included five species of rare High Andean Sulphurs and Whites, along with their larval food plants complete with munching caterpillars, an array of Andean Fritillaries and metallic-colored Elfin butterflies, and, in the Blues, species of Scudder's *Leptotes* and Nabokov's *Itylos, Paralycaeides,* and *Parachilades.* His greatest pride was in the Blues: he had discovered not only the previously unknown food plants and larvae of five species of

Nabokov's Blues but two species new to science as well. Just as Bálint and Johnson were naming a species after Nabokov's wife, Véra, Benyamini was naming another, captured on the tumultuous Bolivian crossing, after his own wife, Lea.

In all, between 1994 and 1998 Benyamini made the circuitous journey to Bolivia three times, traveling a total of more than ten thousand miles. These expeditions, though perilous, allowed him to sample not only the uplands of Tarapacá in Chile but the important areas for Blues surrounding Bolivia's La Paz region and the historical localities of Copacabana, Cochabamba, Chulamani, Potosí, Oruro, and the region around Lake Titicaca. Without his journeys there would be no updated records for Weymer's Blues, *ludicra* and *pelorias,* named in 1890, or Draudt's *pacis,* named from old material in 1921. All were names that in 1945 Nabokov could only note as unknown to him, and give no account of whatsoever. Nor would science know the Blues Benyamini himself discovered — *lea,* the butterfly named for his wife, and *sigal,* named for his daughter, who, at only four years old, had also made the journey.

9 ❧

Finding the Frontiers

Unmindful of the mosquitoes that furred my forearms, I stooped with a grunt of delight to snuff out the life of some silver-studded lepidopteron throbbing in the folds of my net. Through the smells of the bog, I caught the subtle perfume of butterfly wings on my fingers, a perfume which varies with the species — vanilla, or lemon, or musk, or a musty, sweetish odor difficult to define. Still unsated, I pressed forward.

— *Speak, Memory*

FOR HIS HIGH ANDEAN studies published in "Notes on Neotropical Plebejinae," Nabokov could locate specimens only from Peru and central Chile. These regions were well within the general latitudes explored by Kurt Johnson's 1991 Argentine expedition and Dubi Benyamini's subsequent ventures into northern Chile, Bolivia, and Peru. The distributions and species names of Blues north and south of these territories remained a mystery. Nabokov had noted nineteenth-century reports of Blues as far north as Ecuador (a mere two specimens) and, to the south, a single specimen from Punta Arenas, near the southern tip of South America. By 1993 the publications of Zsolt Bálint and Kurt Johnson based on the Blues from José Herrera, Luis Peña, and the old European museums, had pushed the frontiers for Nabokov's Blues south as far as 38 degrees south latitude, in southern Chile's Valdivian region. Here, from specimens collected on the slopes of Volcán Lonquimay, Bálint and Johnson had named the vividly orange-and-black species *Pseudolucia vera*, after Nabokov's beloved wife. They had also located specimens in the old European collections filling some of the void northward into Ecuador. What was needed now, however, was for modern-day lepidopterists to learn exactly how far north and how far south Nabokov's Blues occurred — and whether these frontiers would represent only range extensions of known species or harbor new surprises and species still unknown to science.

At the southern end of the continent, Dubi Benyamini had already proven himself a remarkable field-worker; he would only need to change his focus from northern and central Chile to the regions that stretch southward. In northern South America a coalition of Colombian and Venezuelan lepidopterists was already working with Johnson on Hairstreaks, and in Ecuador not only were two University of Florida graduate students, Jason Hall and Keith Willmott, beginning a concerted survey of Ecuadorian butterflies but Arthur Shapiro had introduced Bálint and Johnson to two other Ecuadorian collectors, Greg Kareofelas and Carol Witham. All were willing to help.

Colombian lepidopterists wasted no time responding to the call to explore the north for Blues. Four university-based scientists — Julián Salazar, Jesús Velez, Rodrigo Torres-Núñez, and Luis Constantino — had already been collecting in diverse areas of Colombia with the support of two accomplished amateurs, the businessmen Ernesto Schmidt-Mumm and Jean François Le Crom. Hitherto their quarry had been mostly the larger, showier butterflies for which basic taxonomies already existed. Their eagerness to turn their emphasis toward little-known Blues was an invaluable commitment.

Colombia offers more than its fair share of hardships and dangers to researchers working in remote areas. By Salazar's account, the least of these are the snakes and legionnaire ants that have always intrigued readers of popular adventure writing; at the other end of the scale, with a distinct twentieth-century ring, are the mobile guerrilla bands, insurgent groups, and others involved in the growing and trafficking of drugs. These dangers were far from abstract. On March 23, 1998, four Americans, amateur ornithologists who had visited Colombia several times before to study its native birds, were kidnapped in the mountains near Bogotá by members of an insurgent group calling itself the Revolutionary Armed Forces of Colombia. One victim escaped after a week, managing to bring international authorities news of what had happened to his companions. But the others were hustled around the Colombian jungles until one, a sixty-three-year old woman, slipped on the trail and plummeted off a 120-foot cliff. Her injuries were serious, and the rebels approached the International Red Cross for help. Eventually all the hostages were released after having been in captivity for over a month.

Whatever the risks, the Colombian lepidopterists were intrigued by stories they had heard of a mysterious Blue on Volcán Galeras, an ancient volcano to the west of Pasto City, along the country's southwestern border with Ecuador. Although details were sketchy and the origin of the stories obscure, all had heard of an unknown Blue, seen and perhaps even caught, but never examined by any scientific specialist. Some recollected reports that it was perhaps *Leptotes cassius,* a Zebra-striped lowland Blue whose presence at this altitude would be inexplicable. Others had heard it was more like one of the High Andean Zebra Blues, *Leptotes andicola* or *callanga,* the former known from Ecuador south to Peru, the latter restricted to Peru and Bolivia.

If the Colombians wanted to make an immediate contribution to the knowledge of Latin American Blues, this was a good place to start. A quick check of their schedules, and favorable times known for high páramo butterflies, led to a decision to dispatch Salazar, with the support of Ernesto Schmidt-Mumm and two associates, to Volcán Galeras at the end of July 1994. Schmidt-Mumm and Salazar had both visited the volcano before, but neither had ever encountered the Blue. If it existed, it would push the limits of Nabokov's Blues farther north than had ever been recorded.

From a small hotel in San Juan de Pasto City, just at the foot of the volcano, Salazar and his team settled in for seven ascents of the mountain, beginning on the last day of July. From a distance the mountain projects a distinctive profile, its 13,350 foot peak sporting a flattened top where some long-forgotten explosion had collapsed the cone from its former, indeterminate height.

The Jeep trails of Volcán Galeras seldom reach the 8,500- to 9,000-foot mark; so each day, after making an ascent by Jeep for about an hour, the collectors had to start climbing on foot. Their first stop on the way to the high uplands was an area well-known to all tropical lepidopterists — the *ceja de la montaña* or "eyebrow of the forest." Here, where upland forests first give way to páramo, butterfly diversity can be spectacular.

On August 7, with the end of the expedition drawing near and little of note to show for their efforts, Salazar found himself alone well above ten thousand feet, collecting a number of seldom-seen High Andean Whites whose sudden presence suggested a unique collecting spot. He had just netted a great rarity — a Red Catasticta, whose white wings are audaciously lined with crimson — when his eyes caught a flash of blue; he froze in his tracks. What followed was an instant familiar to all lepists. Guided by what Nabokov called in *Speak, Memory* an instinct for "gratification admitted of no compromise or exception," the mind and body somehow integrate, instantly and involuntarily, into the split-second moves that will capture a treasured but elusive prey, or end in failure.

A quick flick and the little butterfly was in Salazar's net. He pinched its thorax and transferred the prize to a small envelope in his collection pouch. He had been spared the moment of failure, the moment Nabokov had also recorded in his memoirs, when, "muffing an easy shot" at a rarity he overwhelmingly desired, he had been overtaken by a dejection he likened to that "of the word-famous grandmaster Wilhelm Edmundson when . . . he lost his rook, by an absurd oversight, to the local amateur." Suspecting he may have netted a treasure, Salazar lingered at the site for nearly an hour, traipsing back and forth across what, in late day, was becoming a cold and continually more windswept grassland. To avoid the singular catch — what scientists often call the onesie — he was willing to risk both the worry of his colleagues and the dangers of a late-day descent from the steep flanks of the volcano. But he was to have no further luck.

Salazar's Blue was a new species indeed, duller than the Andes' prized *Leptotes* species, *callanga* and *andicola,* and (when examined in the laboratory) showing a unique spur on the tip of its male genital clasper. Bálint and Johnson asked the Nabokov scholar and translator Dieter Zimmer to propose a name for it. When told of the circumstances of its solitary capture, Zimmer exclaimed, "Alas, it is poor Krug." He referred to Professor Adam Krug, the lonely protagonist of Nabokov's novel *Bend Sinister,* whose fate Zimmer believed so horrible — madness and an executioner's bullet in a prison — that it might be a comfort to his tormented spirit to have this isolated butterfly, *Leptotes krug,* named in his memory.

In addition to the quests of the Colombians for new Blues, the northern uplands were receiving attention from a Polish specialist, Tomasz Pyrcz. A pioneer in studies of Venezuelan Satyr butterflies, Pyrcz was also eager to collaborate with the search for Nabokov's Blues. When the survey first drew his attention, he dispatched a letter to Johnson. It not only aptly characterized the biological promise and perils linking South America's three northern nations but spoke highly of the promise of Ecuador.

"All High Andean areas in the north are extremely important for conservation," Pyrcz wrote.

> Among them, Colombia's situation is the most desperate. The only regions with large areas of cloud forest are the western slopes of the Western Cordillera, and even there they are shrinking extremely fast. Elsewhere, the forests are patchy and concentrated in the National

Parks. But, because these are guaranteed virtually no effective protection whatsoever, there is serious pressure from the local populace. Colombia is fortunate to have a fine contingent of lepidopterists. It is only unfortunate that Jason Hall and Keith Willmott do not seem to have a similar contingent in Ecuador, where active Lepidoptera professionals in the last decades seem peculiarly lacking. Ecuador must be overflowing with species that need to be named.

Pyrcz's assessment of Ecuador was extremely accurate. Shortly after the appearance of Bálint and Johnson's 1993 papers naming new Blues from Argentina and Chile, Shapiro introduced Johnson to the two lepidopterists from California, Greg Kareofelas and Carol Witham, working in Ecuador. They had been pursuing a butterfly survey of the biological preserve at Pululahua Crater in Pichincha Province, as part of a developing plan for ecotourism in the country. Like Volcán Galeras, visited by Salazar and Schmidt-Mumm, much of Pululahua Crater has now been taken over for agriculture, although the crater's steep flanks retain some remnants of the region's original cloud forest. In an effort to protect them, the government of Ecuador had established the Zona de Reserva Geobotánica — Cráter del Volcán Pululahua.

Although Bálint and Johnson did not receive the Pululahua butterfly collections until mid-1993, Kareofelas and Witham arrived at the Pululahua Crater in mid-January 1992 for a six-week survey of the caldera and the forests that still graced its upper slopes. On the two-hour journey north from Quito, by the modern road that ran through small towns surrounded by agricultural holdings, they saw not a single patch of unaltered natural habitat and began to wonder if there had been some misunderstanding. But after crossing the equator at the small village of San Antonio del Pichincha, locally called Mitad del Mundo, or the Middle of the World, they turned up a narrow dirt track that ascends a steep mountain pass up and over the rim of Pululahua Crater. In contrast to the monotonous sights on their trip to that point, the vista from the pass was spellbinding. Even though they were familiar with the mountains of California, here they felt on top of the world. Along the floor of the expansive crater they could see a broad network of small farms worked by Indians. But along the steep slopes of the crater, it was obvious that many patches of the native vegetation, including cloud forest and precipitous grassland, had survived, the rugged extremes of the topography having prevented their conversion to agriculture.

In a small house provided by their Ecuadorian hosts, the two Californians would be within walking distance of the swaths of lush vegetation that they had been able to see so clearly from above. As far as anybody knows, they were the first lepidopterists ever to collect in the area.

Life in the remote crater was primitive. There was no electricity, and aside from the car that had dropped them off, they did not see a single car, truck, or tractor. Oxen pulled plows in the patchwork fields, which covered the floor of the crater almost entirely, leaving it essentially devoid of native vegetation. The few small vestiges of what may have been original plant cover at the lower altitudes inside the crater suggested it might once have been a chaparral-like landscape — dry grassland with a mix of wooded brush. Upland, however, the situation was very different. The lower interior walls of the crater supported a dense, moist shrub cover that blended farther up into a more classic cloud forest, thick with bamboo, ferns, and orchids and other epiphytes.

Moving into the lush uplands, however, Kareofelas and Witham found that the steep slopes and capricious weather made collecting difficult. Around Pululahua, currents driven from the Pacific Ocean encounter the intermontane Andean air, a collision that results in a tumultuous daily mix of sun, mist, and fog that can change within minutes. The Californians, who joked that they had come to the tropics to catch butterflies where it was warm, often found their hikes smothered in a cold, dripping fog. On good hunting days, however, if they were patient enough, the sun would suddenly burn through the clouds, for a while transforming their surroundings into a hothouse. Insect activity during these brief periods came in startling bursts, in which the lepidopterists could not catch specimens fast enough. After just a few days, given the mix of the peculiar habitats and the fact that no one had collected in Pululahua before, Kareofelas and Witham were confident that their collections were at least unusual if not of unique scientific interest.

On January 17, 1992, after a two-hour climb to a spot just above an acrid-smelling hot spring known as the Yellow Mud, they stopped above an area of dense vegetation for lunch. There Witham caught a single specimen of an unusual-looking Blue, odd enough for the two to note it specially in their field log as "Carol's Blue." Its undersurface had the banded pattern of silverish sheen that was characteristic of the genus Nabokov called *Parachilades,* but its thumbnail-size wingspread made it far too large for that genus. The habitat was also too lush — far more tropical than the barren uplands of the altiplano where true *Parachilades* are usually found. In the usual tropical pattern of high diversity and low density, it was the only individual they saw, and they tucked this treasure away for eventual referral to a specialist.

In December 1993, Kareofelas and Witham returned to Ecuador for lowland tropical fieldwork along the Río Cuyabeno, but when they visited friends in Quito once again, the owner of the cabin at Pululahua offered to take them back. When they arrived, although less than two years had passed since their last visit, they were astounded at the changes they saw. A new road had brought electricity and trucks into the region, and while oxen still plowed the fields, Kareofelas and Witham could sense that the place was on the cusp of a profound transformation.

On December 22, 1993, they visited one of their favorite collecting sites from their previous visit. At about nine in the morning, along an opening in the trail at 8,850 feet, Kareofelas saw a small Blue butterfly flit from the edge of a moist shrub forest and into an open area. Luckily, its flight path was downhill, and he was able to catch it. Again, as with the Blue Witham had taken on their previous trip, there were no other individuals on the wing. This butterfly, with bright silver striping along its ventral hind wings, went straight into the pouch for referral to Johnson in New York.

Kareofelas's catch later became the species *nodo* in Nabokov's *Itylos*. Its silvery pattern varied in only a few details from a very different (genitalically) Nabokovian Blue from Ecuador — the new species *odon*. Bálint and Johnson took their names from the half brothers Nodo and Odon in Nabokov's *Pale Fire*, the former a famous actor and Zemblan patriot, the latter a cardsharp and "despicable traitor."

In southern South America the question of the frontiers of Nabokov's Blues was primarily in Dubi Benyamini's hands. In 1993, after journeying over thirty thousand miles to one hundred localities in Bolivia, Argentina, and northern Chile, Benyamini began moving into South America's lower latitudes. Southern Chile's best-known city, the port of Valdivia, enjoys a climate that American visitors liken to that of Vancouver Island and Puget Sound. After Valdivia the western coastline fragments into the scattered Archipiélago de los Chonos, and eventually winds southward to the Strait of Magellan, where Chile and Argentina melt together and share the wedge-shaped island at the tip of the continent, Tierra del Fuego.

Benyamini first moved into Chile's southern Los Lagos and Aisén regions in 1993. By 1994 the southern regions were regularly on his collecting itinerary, from the volcanic regions of Osorno and Lonquimay in the east to the broken Valdivian coastline along the west, 3,500 miles south of

Santiago. Here, José Herrera and Luis Peña before him had collected some of the southernmost known species of Nabokov's Blues, including Bálint and Johnson's Nabokovian species, *Pseudolucia vera, charlotte,* and *hazeorum.* Benyamini had been doubly successful, not only in locating them all but, with tremendous patience and field acumen, discovering their food plants and life cycles as well. These were crucial data not only in support of their status as species but in evaluating possible environmental threats to their continued existence.

By the end of 1994, Benyamini was collecting on Cerro Castillo, at Las Trancas, and at remote Termas de Chillán in Chile's southernmost region. South of these haunts one cannot go that much farther without reaching the southern tip of South America. In this region, lurking behind every journey, was the key question that remained: what was the southern frontier of Nabokov's Blues? Although Benyamini had been seeking this answer in earnest for two years, it was to fall to Arthur M. Shapiro, who in 1994 was exploring the continent from its south, around the Strait of Magellan.

Ironically, Shapiro's intended quarry wasn't primarily Nabokov's Blues but yet another nearly legendary group that traced its place in history to a butterfly that had eluded and confused lepidopterists since 1860, a grand Sulphur named *Colias ponteni.* This species had been named by the Scandinavian Hans Daniel Johan Wallengren, ostensibly from specimens gathered on the Swedish ship *Eugenie*'s expedition to the Sandwich Islands, today Hawaii, in 1851. In nearly a century and a half, no one has ever seen a living example of this butterfly, in Hawaii or elsewhere.

As fascinating a lepidopterological puzzle as *Colias ponteni* presented, it would not have been of interest to the story of Nabokov's Blues had it not been discovered to be the same species the Englishman Arthur Gardiner Butler named *Colias imperialis* in 1871. That the two species were the same was confirmed by taxonomists who examined original specimens of both in the 1960s. Intriguingly, *C. imperialis* bore the type locality Port Famine, an important nineteenth-century port for sailing ships on the Brunswick Peninsula, across from Tierra del Fuego in Chile.

Tierra del Fuego is generally wedge-shaped, its southeastern tip washed by the Drake Passage, which separates South America from the Antarctic Peninsula. The eastern half of the island belongs to Argentina; the western side is part of Chile. Tierra del Fuego itself its cold and damp year-round, except for a small section along its northeast coast, which, adjacent the mainland, shares a piece of the Patagonian Steppe, which crosses the

Argentine border north of the island and extends, as the Magellanic Steppe, southward into Chile toward the modern mainland town of Punta Arenas. Tierra del Fuego is separated from the southern mainland by the twenty- to thirty-mile-wide Strait of Magellan.

The old Port Famine was located on the mainland side of the strait and traces its foreboding name to the English pirate Thomas Cavendish. In 1787 Cavendish planned to raid the original Spanish colony at this site, the City of King Philip, for supplies. When he arrived he found a town inhabited only by corpses. The name Port Famine may reflect Cavendish's view of the fate of this lost colony, but the fact that he found one body hanging from a gibbet has always heightened the mystery.

Butler's specimen source for his Imperial Sulphur was supposedly the material collected by naturalists of the British ship *Adventure,* which called at Port Famine — as did nearly every vessel that made the Atlantic Pacific passage around the tip of South America — in 1826–27. The *imperialis* specimens were with other material labeled from Port Famine discovered in Sir Joseph Banks's collections in London. However, since Banks himself died in 1820, it has always been a mystery how the material got there, a circumstance casting further uncertainty on the validity of the labels.

The conundrum for modern biologists is that these handsome yellow-orange butterflies are not simply of casual interest. Their anatomy appears to be the most ancient of all the world's Sulphur butterflies. Indeed, if *Colias ponteni* is actually a native of South America, the species is perhaps a key not only to the age and origin of pierid butterflies but to the existence of an entire ancient southern South American butterfly fauna as well — the one that may have come from Gondwanaland.

For students of South American biology, the question of the exact origin of *Colias ponteni/imperialis* was given new life when a Spanish translation of the *Eugenie*'s ship logs became available in 1942. The logs recorded that, before proceeding to Hawaii, the expedition had put in at Port Famine, a fact somehow overlooked by historians of the Swedish edition. This news prompted Gerardo Lamas to contact Shapiro and suggest that the likely collection locality for *C. ponteni,* given the sometimes vague labeling conventions of early biologists, was Cerro Tarn, a mountain along the South American coast near Port Famine. Cerro Tarn (named after the *Adventure*'s surgeon) had been recorded as an exploration site in the logs of both the *Eugenie* and *Adventure* expeditions.

Cerro Tarn was a locality with its own legacy. Among other British explorers of the mountain was Charles Darwin, who put into Port Famine on the historic *Beagle* expedition in February 1834. Like the authors of the logs for the *Eugenie* and the *Adventure,* Darwin described the place as dismally wet and freezing: "So gloomy, cold and wet was every part," he wrote, "that not even the fungi, mosses or ferns could flourish [above the tree line]. In the valleys it was scarcely possible to crawl along, [they were] so completely barricaded by the great mouldering trunks."

Hardly a place for butterflies, no matter how hardy, which Lamas might have realized had he ever visited. Its dense, humid forests, which support none of the food plants known to be used by pierids, and its wretched year-round climate led Shapiro to speculate that neither that hill nor any locality directly along the southern Magellanic Strait had been the true origin of *Colias ponteni,* even though it was one of several butterfly species among the old museum material with the Port Famine label. The British Museum contained other Port Famine specimens, some donated by Darwin himself from the *Beagle* voyage. Like *C. ponteni,* some of these butterflies have also never been seen in the region since. To students of Darwin's legacy, they have become known as Darwin's missing butterflies.

Then, in 1989, nearly a century and a half after Darwin's *Beagle* voyage, Santiago's José Herrera and a colleague, Don Vincente Pérez d'Angello, reported in the Chilean museum's entomological journal, *Acta Entomologica Chilena,* that they had collected one of Darwin's missing butterflies — a small brown Satyr that Butler had named *Stuardosatyrus williamsianus* — in open steppe grasslands near Punta Delgada, Chile, a ferry dock on the mainland side of the Strait of Magellan directly across from the northernmost tip of Tierra del Fuego.

Herrera and Pérez d'Angello's disclosure occurred nearly simultaneously with Shapiro's notice of the book *Darwin's Insects,* published in 1987 by K. G. V. Smith. Smith's book included notes by Darwin indicating that his Port Famine collections had been made not at Cerro Tarn but at nearby Cape Negro, at the southernmost extent of the Magellanic Steppe on the South American mainland.

These developments, and the importance of the anatomy of *Colias ponteni* in understanding the origin of austral butterflies, led Shapiro to publish his hypothesis on the Magellanic Steppe origin of *C. ponteni* in *Acta Entomologica Chilena* in 1993 and to petition the National Geographic Society for support to explore the region in search of the long-lost Imperial Sulphur.

Although the most prolific writer on Andean and austral pierid butterflies and their enigmatic origins, Shapiro is also a veteran of years of remote fieldwork in southern South America, much of it paid for out of his own pocket. Henri Descimon, who had once worked with Shapiro in boggy páramo in Peru, jokingly told Johnson that Shapiro took his collecting so seriously that after several days his muddied clothes "could stand up on their own." He and Shapiro, he said, mastered not only the art of concealed starter switches for their car but also how to bolt their suitcases from inside to the floor of the car's trunk. Indeed, in field gear, Shapiro, savvy in the native language, culture, and even street politics, wouldn't stand out much in a crowd of Fuegian lumbermen or oilriggers, and he took pride in his ability to blend in.

In a recent letter to Johnson, he said of his Magellanic fieldwork, "I wander in and out, a mysterious and perhaps not altogether savory figure . . . if you know *The X-Files,* a veritable Cigarette Smoking Man of the Southern Cone." Then he was quick to remind Johnson that all travel writers are liars. Liar or not, in the search for something as elusive as *Colias ponteni,* Shapiro might well be the collector to hit pay dirt.

After securing his grant, Shapiro traveled to Punta Arenas. With a population of 110,000, the seaport city is situated along the narrow neck of the Brunswick Peninsula, some one hundred miles southwest of Punta Delgada, at the point where the lowlands give way to more mountainous terrain to the south. Working out of the town between January 12 and February 10, 1994, Shapiro's collection strategy was to trek up and down the mainland side of the strait, from Cape Dungeness to the region near Froward Cape, over and over again. His local host was Don Vincente Pérez d'Angello, Herrera's coauthor in the article about the discovery of *Stuardosatyrus williamsianus* and also the head of environmental protection for Chile's national petroleum company.

Particular care was needed in these daily forays because the native steppe, which used to extend southward into the Brunswick Peninsula near Punta Arenas, has been widely obliterated near the city, with only scattered relics of open land still surviving. Originally it was quite a different habitat than that just to the north, harboring legumes like *Vicia* (vetch) and *Lathyrus* (wild sweet pea), food plants of both Whites and Blues. But the construction of a huge duty-free shopping area — the Zona Franca, near Punta Arenas, aimed at the crews of ships rounding Cape Horn — destroyed much of what steppe the development of the city itself had spared.

One of the ironies of the situation is that its native plants can now be most readily studied not in their natural habitats but as dried specimens at the herbarium of the University of Magallanes's Patagonian Institute, just across the highway from the shopping area. And nearby a wood-chip mill has been built to process Tierra del Fuego's virgin beech forests. Shapiro wrote to Johnson that it was a depressing spectacle, even more so when he imagined that the trees were going for nothing more than "pornographic comic books for Japanese businessmen to read on the subway."

Shapiro also visited Port Famine (Puerto del Hambre in Spanish) and carefully surveyed that region as well, coming away confirmed in his belief that its dank, cold forests could not have been the home of any of the original Port Famine butterflies. As might have been expected, there was no sign of *Colias ponteni.* But, much more disappointingly, Shapiro also failed to find the elusive Imperial Sulphur on the northern steppes. He could only comfort himself with the fact that his collecting time had been quite short and that even Pérez, who had been collecting in the region for decades, had failed to turn up any specimens.

With his grant money exhausted and his personally financed "commutes" from California to southern South America becoming fewer with the years, there was only one solid reason for Shapiro to return to Punta Arenas: a single specimen of a rarely seen austral White, *Hypsochila argyodice,* that he had noticed in Pérez's collection, recently captured along the nearby Río Baguales. Shapiro had sought this species for twenty years but had caught the butterfly only once, despite having allowed himself time away from his *Colias* itinerary to search the nearby Cerro Guido–Sierra Baguales region for it. He was determined, therefore, that while on a speaking engagement to the Chilean National Congress of Entomology scheduled for the following austral spring, he would return again to the southern steppes for one more try at *argyrodice.*

On December 2, 1994, Shapiro arrived in Puerto Natales from Punta Arenas and hired a local driver to whisk him to the site where Pérez had made his discovery. In a single frantic day of collecting, he found three of the four species of Whites reported from there, but *argyrodice* was missing. As if in recompense, though, Fortune rewarded him with something as good — or better from the point of view of the Nabokov project. On the Río Baguales floodplain, Shapiro came upon an unusual Blue butterfly sitting on an *Astragalus* plant. His notes speak to the singularity of the event: "The Blue, which is grayish above and white below with dark markings, is new to me (and probably to science). . . . I spent more than two hours on the floodplain but never saw another."

Shapiro's catch became *Pseudolucia magellana,* the southernmost species of Nabokov's Blues. The *magellana* also appears to be the southernmost record of any Blue in the New World, since, when Lamas and Bálint located the specimens Nabokov had cited from "Punta Arena" in his 1945 work, they turned out to be from farther north in Patagonia.

Shapiro and later botanist colleagues identified the plant on which he had captured *magellana* as *Astragalus patagonicus.* In 1998 Dubi Benyamini visited Río Baguales and documented *A. patagonicus* as the larval food plant. The plant may play a crucial role in the survival of this Blue, confined to inhospitable southern climes. Its large, thick, and seedy pods are perfect for the burrows of small caterpillars, providing the larvae with not only a long-lasting supply of food but also protection from the elements. Benyamini collected the butterfly's larvae a day after a fierce sleet storm. The caterpillars flew with him back to Tel Aviv, and so dedicated was Benyamini to completing the life history that, when the *Astragalus* pods began to rot, he flew back to Chile and drove to Baguales for replacements. Shapiro now considers the region of the Río Baguales one of the most promising sites for studying the remaining Magellanic biota. Perhaps one day *Colias ponteni* will be rediscovered here or somewhere near.

Like many other biologists working in South America, Shapiro has found the continuing destruction of habitats impossible to ignore, and it has been the subject of much of his recent writing. His struggle to make sense of the constant assault on the already severely depleted resources of the Southern Cone has lent a note of sardonic humor to some of the entries in his Baguales journals: remarking on the overcompetition for grassland forage, he asks, "By the way, why did God bother to make both hares and viscachas?"

One day Shapiro hoped to go to Río Baguales, but poor weather limited him to a short hike near Punta Arenas. With his usual beard, swathed in his muddied collecting clothes and laden with a large net and other paraphernalia, he came upon a mystic meditating on the top of a barren hillock. Embittered perhaps by his recent disappointments with *Colias ponteni* and *Hypsochila argyrodice,* Shapiro fell into conversation with the mystic but soon found himself toying with him. After a discussion of the Alpha and the Omega and other such metaphysical matters, the mystic eventually asked the age-old question, "Who are you?" To this Shapiro replied with a straight face, in Spanish, "I am Number 224."

The discussion, now bolstered by Shapiro's numerical authority, moved on to the age of the world, the contact between worlds, and especially how

Shapiro had ascertained his number. The source, Shapiro replied, was an oracle in Salta, in northwest Argentina, a man who spoke through the authority of his ancient books of Jewish magic. Eventually the fun wore thin and Shapiro went on his way.

Contrasts at this edge of the world border on the absurd — ancient habitats destroyed for sprawling shopping malls, an herbarium sitting next door to hungry wood-chipping mills, the discovery of a new Blue butterfly about which few are ever likely to care, and the maundering of a would-be holy man of even less interest to the world. In the same spirit, perhaps, in the mystic lore of the Southern Cone the story might someday be told of the wandering holy man who, on his solitary mountaintop, met with a mysterious bearded man, of profound spiritual insight and with a large net, who identified himself only as Number 224 before vanishing again. If so, let posterity know that he was none other than Arthur M. Shapiro, distinguished professor of ecology and evolution at the University of California, Davis, who collected the southernmost of Vladimir Nabokov's Blues.

After the Colombians' discoveries in the north and Shapiro's and Benyamini's in the south, only one frontier stood between Bálint and Johnson and the possible completion of their Nabokov project — Peru. Peru is a vast, mountain-covered country wedged between Ecuador and Colombia to the north, Brazil to the east, and Chile and Bolivia to the south. Fortunately for lepidoptery, it has long been the focus of one of South America's most active lepidopterists, Gerardo Lamas of Peru's national museum in Lima. He and Bálint had become acquainted as soon as Bálint sent his letters requesting help for the Nabokov project in 1991. By 1993 not only were the two preparing for publication a work on the unnamed Blues in the collections at Lima but Bálint, who had never been to South America, was making plans to visit the region for firsthand fieldwork. The opening of Peru provided the last piece of the puzzle in developing a comprehensive view of Nabokov's Blues across the continent.

Bálint's wish to visit Peru was fulfilled on January 28, 1995, when he touched down at the Aeropuerto Jorge Chavez in Lima. He was met by Lamas, then vice director of the Lima museum — Museo de Historia Natural, Universidad Mayor de San Marcos. Bálint knew only a few words of Spanish, so the two spoke English.

It was a hot summer night, reminding Bálint of Budapest in July or August, when the city's inhabitants try to escape to the country. Lamas drove him from the airport through the city, first along the seaside, one of the fashionable areas, and then downtown, where a hotel room had been reserved for him two blocks from the museum. Lima also made Bálint, who had traveled widely in Eastern Europe, think of Bucharest, with its sharp contrasts of old and new, and rich and poor, and with buildings that were nondescript from the outside but inside showed an idiosyncratic charm and elegance.

Bálint's hotel, the Columbus, and other buildings in the neighborhood had just such old-style grandeur beneath a genteel exterior shabbiness. Spacious interiors, high ceilings, and Baroque details compensated, to some extent, for the inadequacy of the window screening and air circulation. But after a night and morning of deep, jet-lagged sleep, Bálint awoke the next afternoon conspicuously covered with mosquito bites, which brought a laugh from Lamas when he arrived to take his Hungarian guest to the nearby museum.

Because of the terrorist activity that has become rife in the country, some of the most sensitive neighborhoods are guarded around the clock by soldiers and tanks. The natural history museum is located in Jesús Maria, the central district of Lima, an upscale and relatively safe area, which is also the home of many government buildings and embassies. Surrounded by a spacious lawn and well-kept flower gardens, the central, and oldest, part of the museum holds the public exhibitions and library. The biological collections, brought to world-class stature by Lamas and others, are housed in newer, air-conditioned annexes behind the older structure.

Lamas's office immediately brought Bálint back to a familiar world — microscopes, dissection equipment, spreading boards, cabinets filled with drawers and myriad books. Hundreds of drawers of specimens ensured there would be much work to do in the six days before the two men set out for collecting in the Peruvian highlands; many of the Blues in Lima's magnificent collection remained unnamed and unstudied, and it was the museum's policy that its material be examined only on the premises.

Unexpected problems with his accommodations added significantly to the hours Bálint chose to spend at the museum. After three days he decided that he couldn't afford the hotel on his meager wages and moved to a cheaper one, where he found himself assigned to a dark annex so infested with big, noisy cockroaches that it offended even an entomologist. ("You can see them in the insectarium of the Budapest Zoo", he wrote later, "breeding in legions behind the glass.") As a result Bálint, who had a key to Lamas's office, wound up staying in that secluded world from early in the morning until well after midnight, too proud to let Lamas know about his predicament and his finances. When forced to return to his hotel for a few hours, he slept on the table. In this way Bálint completed his studies at the museum. The cockroaches, after a fashion, performed a great service to the study of their nation's Blue butterflies.

The root of his troubles was later exposed, thanks to an apology from a hotel manager. Since Bálint was from Hungary, the right-wing hotel management had at first assumed he was a Communist and suspected he was in Lima to do some kind of undercover work for the Sendero Luminoso, Peru's notorious Shining Path guerrillas. Finally, an inquiry to the police persuaded them that Bálint had, in fact, come to study Peruvian butterflies. What was done was done, and the researcher, rather than being angry, pitied the hotel manager for his fear and thought the situation sad and funny. Trying to make amends, the manager invited Bálint to dinner, and the two spent the evening discussing the ills and evils of Communism.

On February 3, Bálint and Lamas, with Lamas's son Nicholás and a graduate student, Juan Grados, left Lima for the Río Rímac valley. At last Bálint would be hunting not in the Hungarian countryside and the Carpathian Mountains, where he had done much of his own fieldwork both as a youth and as a professional entomologist, but in the exotic new world staked out (if only taxonomically) by Vladimir Nabokov. It was only one of several ironies surrounding his research that he was helping to complete a major scientific project of a man whose literature had long been vilified by Communist regimes such as the one that had ruled his native Hungary.

Moreover, while his taxonomy for the Latin American Blues involved responsibility for far more names than resulted from his research in either North America or Europe, Nabokov, the consummate butterfly hunter, had never had the opportunity to search for any of those species in the field. It was up to Bálint, after fifty years, to make the transition from specimen trays to the haunts of the living butterflies, to appreciate them as complete organisms in their own environments. It was little less than the fulfillment of the dream of Pilgram in "The Aurelian." Bálint's destination, the High Andes of Peru, was the center of Nabokov's domain. Nearly a third of the localities represented by specimens in Nabokov's original study were Peruvian, including those for two-thirds of his new mainland genuses.

Peruvian centrality in northern South America is literal as well, with Bolivia on the south, Brazil on the east and Colombia and Ecuador on the north. Except for its narrow but long strip of Pacific coastline, the nation is dominated completely by the Andes and a densely forested eastern frontier, where arise many of the headwaters of the Amazon River Basin. At Peru's southern border with Bolivia, at the phenomenal altitude of 12,500 feet, lies Lake Titicaca, the highest freshwater lake of significant size in the world. Its location, size, and altitude attest to the characterization of Peru as a sustained high-level surface — a gigantic elevated plateau, slightly tilted to the north. From a base altitude of 10,000 feet or more, its major physical features are the mountain ranges that jut above this plane or from basins cut deeply within it. The highest altitudes, exceeding 20,000 feet, occur in the Cordillera Blanca, the lowest — aside from the strip of pacific shoreline — in the eastern forests bordering the Amazon, a mere 1,000 feet above sea level.

The vegetation of Peru reflects multiple north-south climatic belts, which become increasingly irregular toward the west. Nearer the coast unpredictable El Niño weather patterns become more and more instrumental in determining the climate. Because of these capricious cycles, annual rainfall can range from almost none to near deluge proportions. But, as is typical of much of the Andes, it is in the high mountain areas that altitude and tropical latitude combine to produce a relatively constant climate, and Peru, more than any other Andean country, is known for its rich and diverse native upland vegetation, which was skillfully exploited by the Incas. Here, below the snow line, the original grass cover ranged from various tall-grass páramo to puna and wetter jalca. The species of Satyrs, Elfins, and Blues that today inhabit these areas attest to this original diversity, often varying dramatically in numbers of unique species within the various regions of the country.

Lamas's Jeep wove its way north along the coast toward Huascar National Park in the Ancash Department, where Bálint and Grados were to be dropped off for collecting in the Cordillera Blanca. They had already collected a new species of Blue on the way, along the canyons of the Río Rímac. Bálint and Grados spend the next six days in concerted fieldwork. They were in spectacular country, an expansive panorama juxtaposing wide grasslands and precipitous green and golden brown gorges against the dizzyingly sheer peaks of Mt. Huascarán and Huandoy, lead-colored at their bases and streaked white with snow across their heights. There was a profusion of discoveries. Bálint's captures included Blues belonging to the genuses *Pseudothecla, Itylos, Hemiargus,* and *Leptotes.* He also found Elfins and the rare Hairstreak-like Blues he and Johnson had named *Polytheclus* in 1993. A new *Madeleinea* from the region became the species *huascarana,* and another was named *ardisensis,* celebrating Ardis Park, a name Nabokov had devised from the word *paradise* in his novel *Ada.*

Bálint and Grados returned to Lima on February 3, only to leave again the next day, this time with Lamas and his son, for the mountains of Peru's southern administrative departments Ica, Ayacucho, Arequipa, Moquegua, and Tacna. There they collected through the mountains at altitudes from sea level upward to 18,000 feet on the flanks of the volcanoes Coropuna and Tacora. Tacora was the nineteenth-century locale from which had come all of the German Gustav Weymer's Blues. In 1945 Nabokov had mentioned two of Weymer's species, *ludicra* and *pelorias,* but been unable to find any specimens. Bálint and Grados came to Tacora from the Peruvian side. Benyamini, on his collecting forays north from Chile, had ascended Tacora five times from its southern flank.

In Ica, along the coastal dunes, they caught species of *Hemiargus* and *Leptotes,* and, as they reached the higher altitudes first of Ayacucho and then of other departments, found members of the other genuses they had expected to find eventually — Nabokov's *Paralycaeides, Parachilades* and *Itylos.*

The expedition was memorable in another way too: an incident occurred that made Bálint fear it might be the last he or Lamas ever took. With just a slight twist of events, Peru might have lost its foremost lepidopterist, and the Nabokov project might have been shelved indefinitely.

In recent years Peru had been torn by a guerilla insurgency that at times reaches into the capital, most spectacularly with the occupation of the Japanese embassy by the Tupac Amaru guerillas in 1997. Experience had taught that not only were some Peruvians not welcome in certain regions of their own country but foreigners, particularly of European appearance, were especially at risk. Because of these dangers, although they always carried camping equipment for emergencies, Lamas and his colleagues seldom stayed out of doors at night while doing their field work. Although doing so was time-consuming and sometimes took them far from their collecting localities, they had learned to retreat at night to the safety of larger towns and secure hotels.

In Ayacucho Department on February 16, however, after collecting in a number of páramo habitats south and southeast of the town of Puquio, between 11,300 and 12,460 feet, Lamas, Bálint, and their party found themselves running unusually late in the high mountains. They had just had the startling luck of finding a new species of Nabokov's *Itylos,* a butterfly so blue it would eventually take the Nabokovian name *tintarrona,* after the blue glass of the mountains of Zembla in *Pale Fire.*

Some years earlier the area around Puquio had been heavily infiltrated by Shining Path guerrillas, and it was known that some of the local inhabitants actively supported them. As a result Lamas was unsure of finding safe accommodations in the vicinity, and they decided that at the end of the day they would move on to Incuyo, the next sizable town, near Peru's second large freshwater lake, Parinacochas. After lingering in their upland collecting spots until the mountains were swimming in a violet- and rose-colored twilight, they had driven for about an hour before the blackness of the Andean night set in. Still at 11,800 feet, they were only an hour from safety at Incuyo when they noticed the smell of gasoline.

They pulled the Jeep to the side of the road, and under a jet black sky filled with brilliant stars, their flashlights revealed that the fuel line had ruptured, and, as long as the engine was running, it spewed out gasoline. No one wanted to stop, but there was no choice except to turn off the engine and try to find a way to patch the line. Unfortunately, an hour's worth of tinkering by Lamas and Grados brought no result; when the engine was switched on again, the line still leaked badly.

Bálint meanwhile had been catching moths by the light that hung inside the hood, but as time dragged on and the situation became more serious, he decided that this distraction was probably not helpful. Having made no progress in stopping the gasoline's hemorrhaging and watching the night grow ever deeper, the group agreed that their only alternative was to leave the motor off as long as they could and to coast, hoping to make it to some village farther down. The rising of a bright moon cheered them.

The grade downhill continued for a considerable distance, and after innumerable twists and turns they found themselves in the central square of a little village, where they rolled to a stop. It was about midnight, and Lamas got out of the Jeep and began walking around the square, lightly knocking at doors. Not a single light came on in response. With no help from the villagers and nowhere else to go, Lamas decided that the safest place to stay, as long as they were forced to sleep outside, was right where they were, in the middle of the village square. After some discussion about whether they should all stay awake in the Jeep until the townspeople awoke the next morning or whether they should try to sleep, Lamas opted for sleep: he and Grados would put up with the discomfort of the Jeep while Nicholás, his son, and Bálint, stretched out in one of their tents.

Once the tent was pitched, Bálint fell asleep almost at once, only to be awoken before long by loud shouting. Lamas's son was still asleep beside him, but outside there was plenty of commotion. He stuck his head out and froze in shock. Three agitated men in civilian clothes had Lamas and Grados, their hands in the air, pushed up against a nearby house wall with guns pointed at them. When two of the gunmen aimed their weapons at Bálint, Lamas told him in Spanish to bring Niki and join them at the wall, which they did. One of the gunmen held the four of them there while the other two began searching the Jeep. With only a single guard watching them — and he was also interested in what his companions might find in the Jeep — Lamas had a chance to whisper to Bálint, "Don't speak English. They don't like Yankees here, and I have no idea who these people are."

After they had gone through the Jeep, the gunmen turned their attention to the lepidopterists' wallets, studying their papers and identification, and asking them questions one by one in Spanish: Who were they? Where had they come from? When it came Bálint's turn, his Peruvian companions were terrified that he might inadvertently say something that would endanger them even further. The gunman who appeared to be in charge asked Bálint if he spoke Spanish.

"*Poco*," (a little), he replied.

"Aymara?" (an Indian language).

"No."

"Quechua?" (another Indian language).

"No."

The gunmen were becoming irritated. Tired of Bálint's repeated nos, their leader turned angrily to Lamas and Grados and asked them, "What language does this guy speak?" But before his colleagues could answer, Bálint put enough words together in Spanish to say, "I speak Hungarian." The gunman, looking baffled, turned to his companions and, after a moment, inexplicably said simply, "OK," and the tension melted.

No one believed that the gunman had understood what Bálint meant by "Hungarian." Perhaps unwilling to let his fellow gunmen think he didn't know, or maybe satisfied that the other three were Peruvians, they let the matter pass, ordering them to strike the tent, sit in the car until dawn, and then, as soon as it was daylight, leave for Incuyo. With that the three gunmen disappeared.

At dawn Lamas looked and, seeing signs of the village coming to life, was more than happy to do as he had been told. Turning the engine on just long enough to get out of the village, they resumed coasting the few remaining miles to Incuyo. There they managed to have the fuel line repaired, and, after a hot meal at the local cantina, they were again on their way. It was then that Lamas explained to Bálint that he had learned that the three gunmen weren't Shining Path guerrillas, as they had all feared, but civil guards from the village where they had pitched their tent. The Army had provided the villagers with weapons to defend themselves against the guerrillas, and that was who they thought they had caught. The confrontation had been one of mutual misconception.

Despite the harrowing night, Bálint judged his Peruvian odyssey by his success in the field. Of fourteen lycaenid species he collected, five were new to science, including three new species of Blues. In addition, his work with Lamas in the Lima collection added not only specimens of many of these but seven more new species of Blues as well. Although in 1945 over a third of the species included by Nabokov in his original study occurred in Peru, he could scarcely have dreamed of the bounty in Blues this Andean nation would eventually produce. Their diversity was yet another testimony to the far-reaching importance of his pioneering work. He had, in fact, once told an interviewer that he planned to collect in Peru before he died ("pupated" was the word he used in jest), but he was never able to pursue that dream. If he had, one can imagine he would have pursued the Blues of the High Andes with the same zeal that characterized his many field trips to America's Rocky Mountains and the Alps of Europe. It is likely, even considering the relative inaccessibility of many areas of Peru until very recent times, that Nabokov would himself have collected a number of the new Blues now known from that fascinating nation.

Boarding a plane at the same airport where he had landed six weeks before, Bálint could leave Peru assured that the final links were in place to complete Nabokov's dream of a classification for Latin America Blue butterflies. If Johnson could continue to process the specimens constantly flowing through New York, preparing the needed dissections and drafting the basic texts for diagnoses and descriptions, the publications needed to bring Nabokov's saga to closure would be possible within a year.

10 ⸏

Dancing with Fire

> He had more difficulty in imagining the tropics, but experienced still keener pangs when he did, for never would he catch the loftily flapping Brazilian morphos, so ample and radiant that they cast an azure reflection upon one's hand, never come upon those crowds of African butterflies closely stuck like innumerable fancy flags into the rich black mud and rising in a colored cloud when his shadow approached.
>
> — *"The Aurelian"*

FOR BOTH BÁLINT AND JOHNSON as taxonomic systematists, the attempt to complete a comprehensive classification of a group like Nabokov's Latin American Blues was its own justification. For both, as for Nabokov before them, taxonomic knowledge about their subjects governed its own self-sufficient aesthetic. But science seldom operates in a vacuum, and it is subject to and informed by the cultural circumstances in which it takes place. As chance had it, because of both the timing of the new research and the extensive geographic range of Nabokov's Blues, the primary cultural force looming behind the project was the growing awareness of what appeared to be a die-off, on a scale never encountered before, among the world's plant and animal species. This phenomenon, which has become widely known as the biodiversity crisis, is of particular importance in the tropical regions, where 90 percent of the Earth's species dwell; for them, it is a crisis of survival.

In some ways the biodiversity crisis was a driving force behind the Nabokov project. Surveys that were meant to gauge biodiversity in the temperate zones of South America, though overshadowed by similar activities in the lowlands, were the sources of many of the specimens from the field that first came into Bálint's and Johnson's hands. The crisis not only lent a wider perspective to the pair's project but also contributed to it a sense of urgency and moment.

The Earth's fossil record reveals that since life appeared on the planet more than three billion years ago, five great waves of extinction, relatively short periods with extinction rates many times greater than normal, have wiped out large proportions of the species that existed at the time. Because speciation — the constant branching development of new species from the old — is a dynamic process, the damage was eventually made up, but in each instance the rebuilding process took something on the order of ten million years. The best-known of these biological disruptions occurred sixty-five million years ago, when the dinosaurs perished. That cataclysm, many scientists have come to believe, was caused by a bolide, a large meteor or comet, colliding with the Earth with such force that it destabilized the planetary environment and destroyed along with much else a race of impressively large and diverse creatures so successful in their adaptation that they are said to have ruled the Earth.

Now, much evidence suggests that the world is in the first stages of a sixth great extinction, this one caused not by cosmic events but by human beings and their devastation of vast areas of the natural habitat necessary for the survival of so many species. Estimates of the number of species of living things worldwide vary from around an extremely conservative 10 million to more than 100 million; whichever number is closer to the truth, a mere 1.5 million have been studied enough to have scientific names. It can be only an educated guess, but by one calculation the current extinction rate is 30,000 species per year and is expected to accelerate. Some scientists predict that half the species on Earth will cease to exist in the next thirty years.

The destruction is hardly limited to the world's tropical rain forests, but because they teem with so much life — and so little of it has been studied — the situation there is the most critical. For reasons that aren't completely understood but are clearly bound up with the abundance of solar energy and the evenness of climate, the tropical rain forests of Asia, Africa, and South America are extremely conducive to the diversification of life. While they make up only about 6 percent of the Earth's land area, they are host, by a necessarily inexact estimate, to more than 50 percent of its plant and animal species. Butterflies are particularly well-represented in the rain forests. Gerardo Lamas and others have recorded a total of 1,234 species within the Tambopata Reserve, an area slightly less than a square mile, in southeastern Peru. In the sixteen square miles of the Cacaulândia area of western Rondônia, including the Fautron reserve in western Brazil, George T. Austin and Thomas C. Emmel have listed 1,863 butterfly species, but they note that many others are still unnamed or unidentified. E. O. Wilson, in his widely read book *The Diversity of Life,* cites a particularly striking instance of tropical diversity in Jaru, also in Brazil, where one entomologist recorded 429 species of butterflies from a twelve-hour collecting period in 1975. (The site was later cleared for agriculture.) For some perspective on these numbers, there are only 169 species of butterflies in the entire temperate country of Chile, 750 species reported in North America, but 4,000 in Peru.

Not only because of the huge numbers of species that live in the multiple stories of the rain forests but also because so many of them are restricted to small areas, the destruction of tropical habitats means a corresponding destruction of species — irreplaceable units of biological knowledge. Tropical rain forests covered about 10 percent of the Earth's surface in prehistoric times; in 1979 only 56 percent of the original cover was left, and by 1989 that figure was reduced to about half the original, some 2.75 million square miles. Today the forests are disappearing at an estimated rate of 88,000 square miles a year, meaning that by the year 2032, unless something is done, the world's rain forests may no longer exist, except perhaps for a few isolated reserves.

Human activity is responsible for most of this destruction, predominately wholesale clearing by earthmover or fire for ranching and agriculture on every scale, or for lumber. While the destruction represents profits or livelihoods for a relatively few people, consideration of the potential treasures the rain forests harbor — from undiscovered drugs and chemicals to new food crops and the raw materials of genetic engineering — reveal it for astounding economic folly on the part of the human race.

Knowing what is happening today in the Amazon Basin, it is sobering to think of how overwhelmingly intractable the area once appeared to Europeans. In 1540, after the Spanish had invaded the Incan city-states of the High Andes in search of gold, Francisco de Orellana, a lieutenant of Francisco Pizarro's half brother Gonzalo, was ordered to proceed down the Río Napo in Ecuador to find provisions. Advancing southeastward in a hastily fashioned wooden galley, Orellana found it impossible to reverse his course and ended up in the uncharted Amazon. Unwittingly, he became the first European to descend the Amazon to the sea, arriving on what is now the Brazilian coast two years later, after a calamitous journey of more than two thousand miles. (Orellana's reports of women warriors —

probably long-haired tribesmen — were the source of the river's name.) It took nearly another century for a European to navigate the river in the opposite direction. Father Domingo de Brieva, with over forty canoes and a thousand men, many of whom died on the way, managed to make the journey in 1621, rowing the entire length of the river so his seventy-year-old commander, Pedro Teixeira, could claim the region in the name of Portuguese Brazil. The trip took eight months.

It was another century still before Charles-Marie de La Condamine made his scientific voyage down the river, and others, like Alexander von Humboldt and the Englishmen Henry Walter Bates and Alfred Russel Wallace, followed in his footsteps. Bates and Wallace sailed to Brazil in 1848, a mere half century before Nabokov's birth, hoping to support research on the origin of species by the sale of duplicate specimens. In a decade of work in the Amazon Basin, Bates discovered nearly eight thousand new species of insects and wrote the first treatises on protective mimicry. He became assistant secretary of the Royal Geographic Society and wrote the famous book *The Naturalist on the River Amazons,* published in 1863 with an introduction by Charles Darwin. Wallace, better known today than Bates because of his work on evolution, published his *A Narrative of Travels on the Amazon and Rio Negro* in 1853 and with Darwin in 1858 presented the historic joint paper before the Linnaean Society in London proposing the theory of evolution by natural selection. Shortly before his death in 1913, he received the Distinguished Order of Merit from the British Crown.

The activities of La Condamine, Humboldt, Wallace, Bates, and other such explorers touched on only the tiniest fraction of the vastness of a world so expansive as to seem impervious to harm. But today the Amazon River Basin, occupying more than 2.7 million square miles, is at our fingertips and is considered one of the most ecologically threatened regions of the world. The ability of humans to destroy the native rain forests has far outstripped the abilities of the successors of the early scientists to discover, catalog, and exploit the possibilities of the species they harbor. By most measures the age of technology is in full flower, but biological exploration is by comparison a science still in its infancy. In terms of the history of that exploration and of the fruit it has yielded, the biodiversity crisis has arrived with stunning suddenness.

For taxonomists there is a particular irony to the crisis: that organisms are disappearing far faster than they can be named, something that comes as a surprise to many ordinary people. Despite the higher public profile the biodiversity crisis has received since E. O. Wilson's *Diversity of Life* was published in 1992, most people still do not understand its urgency. According to a Harris Poll conducted recently for the American Museum of Natural History, American biologists recognize that a mass extinction, primarily attributable to human activity, is under way. They consider population growth and the loss of biodiversity — which are in fact interrelated phenomena — the greatest threats to the Earth. The poll found, however, that the wider public for the most part did not believe in the reality of the mass extinction. To most of them pollution loomed as the greatest threat to the planet, partly a measure of the success antipollution advocates have had in spreading their message and partly a reflection of the immediacy of pollution in the lives of most Americans. In contrast, the threatened ecosystems most often heard about — in Africa, in Asia, and in Latin America — seem unimaginably remote, almost an abstract world of dreams.

There is a corollary to this incomprehension, an unconsidered popular assumption that the natural world is essentially understood, that for every obscure group of organisms there are somewhere experts with all the essential knowledge about it. Nothing could be further from the truth. The sketchy state of knowledge about Nabokov's Latin American Blues up until the 1990s makes a telling illustration of the situation.

In terms of taxonomic and general interest, butterflies are the undisputed favorites of the insect world. Yet they too are little known by objective measures, even at the fundamental level of how many species exist. Biodiversity studies — like those being conducted on lycaenids by Kurt Johnson and on wider groups of butterflies by researchers like Keith Brown and Olaf Mielke in southeastern Brazil and Robert Robbins, Donald Harvey, and Gerardo Lamas in tropical Peru — suggest that hundreds or perhaps thousands of lycaenid species alone remain to be described. Under current conditions projects in these regions have to be measured in terms of many scientist's lifetimes.

By contrast, Nabokov's Latin American Blues are a relatively small group. But they would have been too much for any one taxonomist to tackle under the ordinary conditions of research. Until the work of Bálint and Johnson, Nabokov's skeletal taxonomy essentially represented the sum of the technically accumulated scientific knowledge about the group. In contrast with many lowland butterflies, museum collections in general are even today notoriously lacking in High Andean and austral representatives among Latin American lycaenids. As Johnson, José Herrera, and

Lee D. Miller suggested in their studies of Andean and austral Hairstreaks, one could hope to have representative series of butterflies only by combining the collections of nearly every available museum plus the material from recent collectors in Chile and Argentina.

By any estimate the numbers of the world's organisms that remain undiscovered are so indisputably large that taxonomists refer to this gap in knowledge as a black hole. There no doubt remain a small number of mammals and birds to be discovered, but it is among the organisms that represent the far vaster diversity and numbers on the globe — like the huge groups of invertebrates, of which insects are only one part — that the black holes of knowledge become truly awesome.

Human beings almost reflexively despise such animals, but according to the rules of biodiversity it is precisely on such creatures that human life ultimately depends. Ecosystems are structured like pyramids, reflecting both numbers of species and individuals, and the food-dependency relationships that inexorably bind them. At the base of any pyramid are vast numbers of microorganisms, and higher up come the plants. As one reaches higher levels still, those made up of various plant eaters and finally meat eaters, overall numbers of species and individuals become successively fewer. Biologists form a sort of pyramid, too, but on an opposite principle. For the ever-larger study groups located further down the pyramid of life, predominately undiscovered and unclassified, there are proportionately fewer and fewer taxonomic specialists. Insects are a case in point, so diverse worldwide as nearly to defy imagination but, institution to institution, with a tiny number of taxonomists equipped to wrestle with their numbers.

Naming an organism might seem simple enough, but it is only a first step toward something much larger. When the Natural History Museum in London inaugurated its World Map project, which projected a method of plotting the locations of organisms worldwide and designating the "hot spots" where certain species were threatened, they chose owls as one of their trial groups. Taxonomically, owls are relatively well-known, many with long-established colloquial names. This is because the comparatively low diversity of predators near the top of the food pyramid causes them to stand out in local and regional faunas; there was therefore enough available data on owls to make a World Map model possible. The number of groups for which such data exist, however, is small. What superficially appears to be relatively strong knowledge at the level of local, regional, or national lists can be miles wide but only inches deep. That is, such lists may feature only a record of species reported in a given geographic area. Accuracy is a problem because of poor taxonomy, lack of reference to definitive type specimens, or reliance on misleading secondary sources or colloquial usage. Even if the lists of existing creatures might be quite complete for any given nation or region, knowledge about their life histories — what they eat, how they reproduce, precisely where they live, or the extent to which they share living spaces and resources with their fellow creatures — can be scarce or nonexistent.

While simple lists can sometimes help persuade politicians to draw boundary lines around a park or preserve, it is research that produces information on lifestyles that, theoretically at least, can help preserve organisms from extinction. That is why the tropical biological community was so stunned in 1993, when Alwyn Gentry, a botanist who was the senior curator at the Missouri Botanical Garden, and Theodore A. Parker III, an ornithologist who was senior scientist with Conservation International, were both killed in the same plane crash while performing "rapid assessment" biodiversity studies in Ecuador. Russell Mittermeier, president of Conservation International, was quoted in *The New York Times* as saying the two men "carried two-thirds of the unpublished knowledge of neotropical biodiversity, especially the tropical Andes, in their heads."

The complexity of the lives of many creatures, butterflies among them, often confounds even the best-intentioned efforts to save them. This holds true not just for tropical exotics but for the butterflies we see in our own backyards. The Monarch, large and majestic in its striking orange, brown, and cream cloak, is the most popular and beloved butterfly in North America. Its equally dazzling caterpillars eat milkweed, from which they absorb a toxin that makes them unpalatable to most birds, even after they have metamorphosed into adults. Another butterfly, the Viceroy, has evolved to look extremely similar to the Monarch, thus gaining the advantage of the birds' revulsion for Monarchs. This relationship is probably the most widely known example of such mimicry in nature (known as Batesian, after the Amazonian explorer).

Anyone who has seen flocks of these tough butterflies, with a wingspread of 3.5 to 4.0 inches, headed south in the fall understands why they are so beloved. It is then that the Monarch populations east of the Rockies migrate as far as the two thousand miles from southern Canada and the Great Lakes region to roosts in the Oyamel fir forests in central Mexico, ten thousand feet up in the volcanic mountains west of Mexico City. There they overwinter in great clusters, clinging to every branch and bough and huddled together in thick layers for protection against the wind, freezing rain, and occasional snow. The clustering butterflies, in the millions, make one of nature's most breathtakingly beautiful sights. The family to which the Monarchs belong, the danaids, are a warm-weather group, and none of them can survive winters in the north. But only the Monarch has developed this birdlike migratory strategy to extend its range. After surviving the much milder Mexican winter on fat they have stored in their bodies, they fly north again in spring, producing several generations along the way. Finally, the great-grandchildren of last year's migrators, guided by instinct alone — for none of them made the outward journey — renew the age-old cycle and return to Mexico.

As familiar and commonplace as the Monarchs seem to be, their roosts in Mexico were discovered only on January 2, 1975, a treasured date in lepidopterological history, by Kenneth C. Brugger, an American textile engineer who was also an amateur naturalist. The Mexican government eventually set up preserves meant to protect them, but these, along with efforts by scientists to be secretive about site locations, have not curtailed their gradual destruction. At the time of their discovery they had already undergone long-term attrition. Firewood gathering and logging have progressively thinned the trees in and around reserves to the point where they offer insufficient protection against the elements. It was a shock to the scientific world when, over the last decade, site monitors witnessed firsthand the devastating effects of winter snowstorms on the thinned Oyamel forests. Monarch die-offs were so massive (approaching 80 percent at one colony in 1982) that experts suggested continued winter snows might destroy the Mexican Monarch colonies by the early twenty-first century. It was a disturbing specter.

It had not helped matters that when reserves were established no compensation was offered to the people, many impoverished, who had come to depend not only on the forests for firewood but on Monarchs as food for livestock. (They had learned, long before Brugger's discovery in 1975, that smoke sent into the trees caused the huge butterflies to fall helplessly to the ground.) Innovative efforts, supported by the Mexican government and private groups, are now under way to replant forested tracts as alternative sources of fuel and lumber to use or sell. But it is a fragile peace, without a guarantee of permanent success.

It is easy to criticize Mexico for the situation there, but in California, where the sites of wintering colonies of North America's western Monarch populations have been known for years, it was also a tortuous journey to today's uneasy, and closely monitored, truce between humans and Monarchs. California's wintering grounds are, by and large, already disturbed habitats. Host trees are a mix of native pines and planted domestics distributed intermittently in a megalopolis where prosperity, not poverty, is the perennial force driving environmental degradation. Today's protected sites, like the often-photographed colonies at Santa Cruz, are a source of solace and wonder to many Americans. But the scattered locations of the colonies have always made them vulnerable to abuse and locked their fate in a constant battle between the uses of private and public land. Americans may take some comfort in the efforts to protect California's Monarchs, but the situation is far from stable. Since 1996 there have been steep population declines, followed by mysterious rebounds. Scientists link these drastic fluctuations to parasitic infections but are unsure whether the cycles are normal or a danger signal. In addition, recent research has suggested that California sites ultimately receive some individuals from the Mexican flyways. If so, the future of the Mexican and Californian overwintering sites may be precariously linked.

Lincoln P. Brower, one of the foremost authorities on Monarchs and protective mimicry, was instrumental in developing science's knowledge of the Mexican Monarch wintering sites. Stunned at their apparent fragility, he took to the road about a decade ago to promote the argument that world citizenry must learn to imbue natural wonders with the same inherent value they have somehow learned to accord human art. In his compelling presentations, Brower notes that while most people would be incensed by destruction of the Mona Lisa, the Pietà, or Chartres Cathedral, they are somehow unable to transfer this outrage to the destruction of natural objects — miles of Amazon rain forest or remote overwintering sites of Monarch butterflies in Mexico. As Brower says, the idea that Amazon forests or Monarch butterflies have some inherent, unarguable value seems odd to people until you ask them about art. Brower believes it is a matter of long-term education, since where else could a sense of value in art have come from?

This view of nature's inherent value, sometimes referred to by conservationists as the aesthetic argument, is being increasingly applied to the concept of biodiversity as a whole. As Niles Eldredge, the chief curator of the American Museum of Natural History's Hall of Biodiversity, a permanent exhibit that opened there in 1998, told *The New York Times:* "We want people to say, 'My goodness, life is beautiful, and you mean it's under dire threat?'"

The idea of a biological cultural heritage hasn't been fast to catch on. Countries may have particularly beloved parks, like Yellowstone in the United States, or fauna that have become national symbols, like the bald eagle. But the plight of the Monarch butterfly, almost universally loved in this country, belies even the first part of the Senegalese conservationist Baba Dioum's well-known preservation dictum: "In the end, we will conserve only what we love, we will love only what we understand, we will understand only what we are taught." If the Monarch is to die, what is likely to be saved for love alone?

The Monarchs of Mexico make it clear that simply setting aside reserves is not necessarily enough to save a species because of the complexities of nature or the intricacies of human involvement. Other examples of such natural complexity abound, and that fact has created an immense challenge to conservation and the maintenance of parks and reserves. Over millennia free from human interference, many organisms become finely attuned to cycles of localized natural events — even catastrophe, like flooding or fire — and if these events are disrupted, disaster can result. In regions where natural fires are commonplace, for example, the destruction of a local population is mitigated by eventual repopulation from the overall metapopulation, most of which will be unaffected by localized destruction at any given time. But if a metapopulation no longer exists, local populations become unique, and their destruction irreversible.

To complicate matters further, localized members of a metapopulation may actually need catastrophic change to maintain their lifestyles; for example, clearing fires set the stage for optimal growth of food plants. This phenomenon is widespread and has been one of the great challenges in maintaining national parks and preserves, most famously perhaps in Yellowstone National Park. In a case ripe with Nabokovian coincidence, the butterfly that has become the cause célèbre of metapopulation collapse, the much-loved Karner Blue, *Lycaeides melissa samuelis,* is actually one of Nabokov's North American Blues, named by the author himself during his work on museum specimens for his 1943 study of the northern *Lycaeides.* As Robert Dirig, a botanical curator and lepidopterist at Cornell University who has devoted much of his life to the Karner Blue, has maintained, it is the most famous of Nabokov's Blues both because Nabokov named it and because of the mystique that has come to surround its endangered status and the protracted efforts to protect it. The butterfly was an early project of the Xerces Society, formed in 1971 to preserve rare insects through the protection of their unique habitats around the world; the group was named after the Xerces Blue, driven extinct in 1943 when the expansion of a military base near San Francisco claimed the land on which the last colony lived.

The Karner Blue, whose common name comes from the hamlet of Karner in the Albany Pine Bush of New York State, is a striking butterfly, one reason it has become a poster child for conservationists' efforts to maintain its disappearing habitats. The wing undersurfaces of both sexes are gray marked with black spots circled in white; a continuous band of orange crescents emblazons the lower edges. The upper wing surfaces of the male are dark blue with hard black margins on the edges; females show grayish brown and blue on the topside, with irregular bands of orange crescents inside the narrow black edges. The wingspread is a mere inch or so, framing a dark body. In the 1980s a contingent of state lawmakers tried to make the Karner the official insect of New York, but it lost out in favor of the ladybug, a beneficent creature without the ignominy of extinction hanging over its head.

For many years the Karner Blue was confused with the more northern Blue *Lycaeides idas*, which occurs across the colder climes of Canada. However, Nabokov's meticulous anatomical work, which centered on distinctive structures of the butterflies' genital grasping organ, suggested that these Blues, scattered thinly among the wild lupines in the barrens and savannas of the Northeast and Great Lakes states, were actually a subspecies of *Lycaeides melissa*, a Blue whose primary range is across the Rocky Mountain region. Nabokov's recognition of the uniqueness of the Karner Blue, which he named *samuelis* after the pioneer American lepidopterist Samuel Scudder, was of considerable biological importance.

The fact that it was a member of the *melissa* group, otherwise known only from far to the west, meant two things. First, the eastern pine barren populations might be very old. After the last Ice Age, some thirteen thousand years ago, a dry gulf that is now the Great Plains region gradually divided the forested areas of the continent into two sectors. The western and eastern population of *melissa* may have been continuous before this early barrier, or perhaps the eastern population moved from west to east when this dryer and warmer period was in its infancy. Whatever the exact age of the great disjuncture, it had left a huge population of *melissa* across the Rocky Mountains but only a small remnant on the eastern side. These sparse pine barren populations, in fact, defined the scientific term for this phenomenon — they were a relict of what had been there long before.

Second, and perhaps most important, Nabokov's discovery meant that the loss of the few remaining eastern populations would be the loss of all *melissas* left in the East. In fact, Nabokov's later conviction — based on his discovery of further structural differences and differences in the larvae — that his *samuelis* was an entirely separate species, reproductively incompatible with its long-estranged relative to the west, made the Karner even more important, for its loss would mean the permanent loss of a distinct and irreplaceable biological entity. (Whether the Karner is in fact a separate species has still not been conclusively established in the scientific literature, but some of the scientists who have studied it closely are inclined to see merit in Nabokov's case.)

Nabokov developed a deep, lifelong affection for this butterfly. In 1975, when he found out that *The New York Times* had used a drawing of the Karner Blue to illustrate an article about the federal government's first listing of endangered insects, he wrote a letter to the editor: "By a nice coincidence," he said, "the so-called 'Karner Blue' illustrating Bayard Webster's note on insects needing protection is a butterfly I classified myself. It is known as *Lycaeides melissa samuelis* Nabokov or more properly *Lycaeides samuelis* Nabokov (I considered it at first to be a race of the western *melissa* Edwards, but have concluded recently that it is a distinct species)."

He also revealed that it was the butterfly he had described in a well-known passage of his novel *Pnin*, although he attached no name to it in the novel: "A score of small butterflies, all of one kind, were settled on a damp patch of sand," he wrote there, "their wings erect and closed, showing their pale undersides with dark dots and tiny orange-rimmed peacock spots along the hindwing margins; one of Pnin's shed rubbers disturbed some of them and, revealing the celestial hue of their upper surface, they fluttered around like blue snowflakes before settling again."

In 1952, reviewing Alexander B. Klots's *Field Guide to the Butterflies of North America, East of the Great Plains,* Nabokov described how he kept track of the butterfly in the Albany Pine Barrens, which is its type locality — that is, the source of the type specimen that Nabokov used to name it: "I visit the place every time I happen to drive (as I do yearly in early June) from Ithaca to Boston and can report that, despite local picnickers and the hideous garbage they leave, the lupines and *Lycaeides samuelis* Nab. are still doing as fine under those old gnarled pines along the railroad as they did ninety years ago."

But now, nearly half a century later, the Karner Blue is on the edge of extinction, and some think it is unlikely to survive. Its plight shows how complex the problems of conservation can be and why an intricate knowledge of a species's relationship with its habitat is imperative if it is not to go the way of the Xerces Blue.

The Karner Blue is adapted to live in barren-savanna ecosystems, areas of well-drained, sandy soil characterized by open spaces dominated by grasses, other herbaceous plants, and shrubs. Historically, expanses of Karner Blue habitat were measured in the tens of thousands of acres. Such regions are unsuitable for farming but have shrunk under the pressures of urbanization and industrial development. Within the barrens the caterpillars of the Karner Blue, like those of many butterflies, feed on a single food plant, in their case *Lupinus perennis,* the wild lupine mentioned in Nabokov's review of Klots's field guide. The lupine, in turn, is what is known as a fire plant. It depends on the intermittent lightning-ignited wildfires that swept the barrens before the encroachment of humankind to burn off the herbaceous plants that otherwise crowd it out; it is one of the first plants to spring up after a fire. Thus, the Karner Blue is perilously dependent on what John A. Shuey of the Nature Conservancy, an expert on the ecology of Karner Blue habitats, aptly calls "dancing with fire."

As a pine barren butterfly, the Karner Blue had adapted over the millennia to these natural fire cycles. When the fires swept one region of the barrens, Karner Blues, none of whose stages appear to be resistant to destruction by fire, were destroyed. Still, with other *samuelis* populations nearby untouched by the flames, and with the understory of the burnt area cleared of undergrowth, allowing lupines to thrive, the metapopulation of Karner Blues would soon restock the burned area in renewed profusion. The Karner is thus a "fugitive" species, driven from place to place by the unpredictably unstable conditions within its habitat but always surviving as a metapopulation.

However, when human beings began to encroach, the barrens shrank and were broken into isolated patches. Within the last decades fifty or more United States populations of Karner Blues have been identified, but some of them are tiny; as Robert Dirig has put it, eight small populations he and his fellow Karner Blue researcher John F. Cryan saw in eastern New York could very easily be destroyed by an hour's bulldozing. Now, if fire burns a reduced patch of habitat, there is not likely to be another group of Karners close enough (about half a mile seems to be the maximum distance) to repopulate the area; tiny, isolated swaths of territory aren't enough to support populations of Karner Blues, which in this way fall victim to patch dynamics. And if the barrens are simply "preserved," which often also entails misguided protection from fire, the unchecked undergrowth is likely to choke off the lupines to unsustainable levels. Karner Blues have disappeared from the Oak Openings oak barrens ecosystem in Ohio, near the Toledo suburbs, despite the "preservation" of nine thousand acres; with the fires suppressed the area has largely converted to oak woodland. Although lupines may persist in the denser oak woodlands, without the intermittent sunny areas, Karner Blues cannot.

The Albany Pine Bush, so fatefully near the city of Albany, now covers barely 1 percent of its former territory. Originally there were some small fenced patches, set aside as Karner Blue reserves under the terms of development agreements, but eventually government and private groups contributed to the support of a larger Wildlife Preserve and Park, which grew at the beginning of 1999 from 500 to 2,600 acres. The establishment of the park reflects the affection with which a large part of the area's residents view the butterfly. But the Pine Bush as a whole is largely overgrown, and the metapopulation of Karner Blues is near collapse; it has been estimated that the Karner's numbers there have plummeted by 90 percent over the last decade. (Ironically, this vulnerability has given the butterfly a reputation as "fragile," although in terms of individuals nothing could be further from the truth. Dirig has pointed out that in areas where the environment is conducive, they thrive prolifically.)

Thus, the difference between "preservation" and "conservation" forms the crux of studies being carried out by modern researchers like Shuey, Dirig, Cryan, and Ann Swengel on measures necessary to save the Karner Blue and other plains-prairie-savanna butterflies that dance with fire. The only hope — evidently a slim one — seems to be a regimen of carefully managed burning in what's left of the butterflies' habitat. If such efforts bear fruit, it will be both because the butterfly is beloved enough to inspire widespread support for its survival and because enough is known about its lifestyle to make its preservation possible.

Nabokov's connection with the Karner Blue may well have had a positive effect on efforts to preserve the butterfly; Robert Dirig believes it has. But while it is impossible to know what he might have said about the biodiversity crisis or the destruction of the rain forests, issues that came to prominence only after his death, it is hard to paint Nabokov as a vigorous conservationist or to recruit him as a vehement spokesman for environmentalism in the terms of his own time. He may well have seen his letter to *The New York Times* in 1975 explaining his authorship of the Karner Blue and its appearance in *Pnin* as tacit support for the butterfly's preservation, but he made no overt appeal. Similarly, according to Dirig, when he wrote Nabokov about the Karner Blue in 1975, Nabokov responded concerning how he came to name the butterfly and, although he acknowledged that Pine Bush preservation was important, he offered no personal support. Dirig adds that when he and Cryan again wrote to Nabokov shortly afterward, specifically requesting his help in the Pine Bush matter, the author did not reply.

Nabokov was extremely busy during those last years of his life. Moreover, he was not a joiner, and one suspects that his aversion to belonging to groups would have made him temperamentally ill-disposed toward the environmentalist movement as it tends to be structured today. This is not to say that he was unaware of or unconcerned about preservation issues. He clearly grasped the fundamental connection between habitat and survival, and frequently expressed indignation that farmers and others were altering the landscape, often needlessly, in ways that made survival for butterflies impossible. But as one might expect from the Karner episode, he seldom advocated any specific actions to preserve Lepidoptera, and when he did it could be couched in such a whimsical context as to deprive it of any practical meaning. For example, when he was asked in a BBC interview in 1969, "If you ruled any modern industrial state absolutely, what would you abolish?" he answered: "I would abolish trucks and transistors, I would outlaw the diabolical roar of motorcycles, I would wring the neck of soft music to public places. I would banish the *bidet* from hotel bathrooms so as to make more room for a longer bathtub. I would forbid farmers the use of insecticides and allow them to mow their meadows only once a year, in late August when everyone has safely pupated." Contrary to what the average reader might gather from the context, Nabokov's imaginary strictures on mowing are quite sound and show considerable insight into the subtle mechanisms of ecology. After the disastrous agricultural dust bowls of the 1930s, prominent botanists, among them J. E. Weaver, F. W. Albertson, and H. H. Hopkins, vehemently championed annual versus regular mowing, stressing that regular mowing not only destroys the insect life of prairie and farm ecosystems but kills plants at midgrowth, breaking the critical cycle of foliage replacement that protects grassland soils from water and wind erosion. One annual mowing, late in the year as Nabokov advocated, approximates the natural timing of autumn, leaving the ecosystem far more intact.

Despite Nabokov's unwillingness to act as public advocate for Lepidoptera, his fundamental sentiment was clearly heartfelt, finding expression, for example, in his diary on June 21, 1971: "Collected between 11:30 and 2:00 at Martigny above Plan Cerisier [about one and a half miles west of Montreux at an elevation of about 650 meters, 2,100 feet] in little flowery niches near little vineyards. Below c. 650 no flowers, no butterflies, only pesticide-treated vineyards down to the village of Plan Cerisier." It also made its way into his fiction. In a passage of his novel *Ada,* in which a rare mosquito is feasting on the title character's blood, the narrator observes of the tormenting creature, "Nowadays it seems to be getting extinct, what with the cooler climate and the moronic draining of the lovely rich marshes in the Ladore region as well as near Kaluga, Conn., and Lugano, Pa."

His observations of environmental degradation were also coupled with, apparently, even more strongly felt objections to the sometimes senseless restrictions that government preservation efforts placed on scientific collectors. In this he was (and is) in the mainstream of field researchers, who complain about the same thing to this day. The letter he wrote in 1953 to *The Lepidopterists' News,* excerpted in Chapter 3, might have been the model for John Heppner of the Florida State Collection of Arthropods, writing for a similar lepidopterists' newsletter forty-five years later. Heppner noted that in Florida's protected areas "visitors can step on, kill and maim countless insects while just walking through the park, or, during a picnic . . . kill any number with a fly swatter or buy spray, yet . . . if you collected a mosquito for a scientific collection it would be illegal without a permit." (The irritation aside, no serious scientist or enthusiast questions the value of laws protecting endangered habitats or preventing illegal collecting of endangered organisms for profit — a business that annually nets $5 billion worldwide. As recent cases of illegal poaching in United States national parks have shown, there is a strong market for endangered butterflies, as there was in Nabokov's day.)

In an interview on French television with Bernard Pivot in 1975, Nabokov said,

> It seems to me that the protection of certain rare animals is an excellent thing. But it becomes absurd when ignorance or pedantry intrude. It's all very well if they prosecute those curio-dealers who, in order to sell them to amateurs, collect the French race of the Spanish species whose scattered colonies risk extinction in the Durance valley. But it's absurd when a warden prevents a naturalist, with his old net full of holes, from

wandering in a certain place where this butterfly — which eats only a bladder-senna, something the warden doesn't realize — often lives in the vicinity of vineyards wherever there's a bush, there's a butterfly. So it is the bush they should protect! A million hunters couldn't destroy the insect, which is as big as this — the big, blue sky. Only the vineyard keepers can destroy it, by destroying, for some mysterious reason, the bladder-senna in their vineyards along the Rhône. It's a shame! It's a shame! . . . The farmers, with their infernal pesticides, their road construction, the cretins who burn tires and mattresses in vacant lots — the smell! Those are the real guilty ones, and not the scientists without whom the policeman couldn't distinguish a butterfly from an angel or from a bat.

At such times Nabokov seems to have been less concerned with preventing the destruction of butterflies, though it clearly angered him, than with shifting public blame away from scientific collectors, whose activities hardly put a dent into butterfly populations, and onto the truly guilty. In most of these passages it is hard to see much of what might pass today as significant environmental advocacy. In an interview in 1976, not long before his death, Nabokov also revealed an optimism about the future of butterflies in general that those who worked to complete his major project only a few years later found very difficult to share. "One sees Skippers and Blues relish black filth near country garages and camping grounds," he said.

In the case of very local species whose numbers are not kept up by wide-wandering impregnated females, the destruction of an uncommon food plant by some idiot vineyardist can of course wipe out a habitat. But nature is hardy and certain delicate semitransparent little larvae are known to have outmaneuvered the most modern pesticides. It is wonderful to pick out on the crazy quilt of an agricultural area as seen from an airplane the number of green holes where a lovely insect can safely breed. The gloomiest lepidopterist perks up when he thinks that butterflies have survived millenniums of reckless farming, overgrazing and deforestation.

Nabokov was perfectly right about the damage caused by the vintners' unthinking and unnecessary clearance of what they regarded as weeds. (The butterfly he was thinking of in these quotations was the Old World Iolas Blue.) But his conception of habitat destruction shows how suddenly and with what force the biodiversity crisis has arrived. The obliteration of vast swaths of the tropics by earthmovers and slash-and-burn clearing is on an entirely different scale from anything Nabokov could have conceived. Had he been aware of what is happening, he could hardly have been so sanguine about the chances for some butterflies, those rarities in Las Abejas, for instance, and their cousins across much of South America. Nabokov's modern-day colleagues making their way around the continent, not inherently gloomy men and women, found little there to perk them up.

Yet Nabokov clearly has had an impact on efforts to preserve the Karner Blue. Although it is impossible to say what effect his celebrity has had, it cannot have hurt the Karner's chances that it was discovered and named by a legendary writer. But, more important, had Nabokov (or somebody like him) not recognized the butterfly's true character as a unique and biogeographically significant entity — that is, performed the basic work of taxonomic identification — the natural history of the Karner Blue would never have been understood and it might have joined the Xerces before its significance was even comprehended.

In 1972, when Robert Dirig began his long association with the Karner, the first step in acquainting himself with the insect was to refer to the foundation work, particularly that of Nabokov. From there Dirig built a precious portfolio of knowledge about the historic distribution and lifestyle and history of the Karner and its food plant, the wild blue lupine. That knowledge in turn, passed on to a well-disposed public, has arguably helped win support for government and private measures to preserve the Karner Blue and its habitat. And there is still hope that the same knowledge will provide scientists and preservationists with the practical tools to effect the butterfly's survival. Nabokov's research was an essential part of that chain. (Dirig, incidentally, is another informed lepidopterist with high regard for Nabokov's work.)

Nabokov's research on the Karner Blue marvelously parallels, on a small scale, his work on the Neotropical genuses. In each case, basing his studies on museum holdings that had long been at hand, Nabokov looked at specimens more closely than had anyone before him. Using his skill and knowledge of morphology, he saw relationships his predecessors had missed and was able to accurately classify his subjects. His own successors, in their turn, were able to confirm his judgments and to build on his observations, advancing natural science in ways that are intrinsically valuable in terms of human knowledge and that, with luck, might also prove useful in preserving the butterflies and their habitats for the future.

Whatever the fate of the Monarch or the Karner Blue — and it has been estimated that legal protection gives any endangered species only a fifty-

fifty chance of surviving — their futures are closely tied to a relatively intricate knowledge about their lifestyles. Multiply these two cases by millions and you have the best picture of the challenge that faces biology in the next century. It amounts to nothing less than E. O. Wilson's proposed response to the biodiversity crisis in *The Diversity of Life:* a concerted, long-term, interdisciplinary effort to save and use in perpetuity as much of the Earth's diversity as possible. As a first step in this broad plan, Wilson calls for a multifaceted worldwide survey of fauna and flora, which would mean the eventual cataloging of at least 10 million species, perhaps 100 million. (In fact, Wilson's goal is not much different from that of Linnaeus, the father of taxonomy, when he devised a classification for the ten thousand or so species known to him in the mideighteenth century, creating the flexible framework that has expanded to accommodate every subsequent biological discovery. But somewhere between Linnaeus and Wilson's plea, the effort stalled.) This sort of cataloging is precisely the realm of systematic taxonomy — Nabokov's line of work, what he did for the Karner and for the Neotropical Blues.

According to Wilson, an effort to classify every organism on Earth would require the lifetime work of 25,000 professional systematists, calculated on a forty-year working life and a total caseload of ten million new species. It is ironic then that, just as systematic taxonomy is being summoned to a higher role by the biodiversity crisis, the scientific establishment finds itself unprepared to respond to the call, a logjam for which modern cultural and political trends are in large part responsible. Such trends have always affected the course of science and the lives of individual scientists. In the Age of Exploration, biological discovery was a path to fame and fortune because the Old World was hungry for new products to exploit, from new food sources like potatoes, tomatoes, and maize to ornamental trees and exotic flowers like orchids. One might argue that, for much of more recent times, broad-based study and research and support of basic biological science had been the order of the day. But after midcentury science became increasingly oriented toward specific goals, usually with potential for immediate economic payoff, and the shine was taken off something so apparently unremunerative as taxonomy. Within the specific field of entomology, for example, there has long been a strong sustained level of financial support, but a great majority of the money is destined for research with clear and immediate medical or agricultural benefits.

In addition, available resources have been more and more aimed at projects that reflected short-term political or popular interests — the scientific one-night stands, as skeptics say. For more refined sophistication, the quest to define and be on the cutting edge, became a prevalent route to generating the interest needed to attract money. Over the past decades the cutting edge in biological science has been molecular biology, with cell biology and genetics not far behind. In light of the enormous benefits to humanity that these fields have provided, it would be ludicrous for anyone to argue that support for them is in the least unwarranted. But at the same time it is imperative to understand that a consequence of these trends has been a drastic decline in academic opportunities for systematists. In universities today systematists are usually the have-nots at the bottom of the pecking order, often holding the part-time and temporary positions that have come to characterize much of academia as a whole. Or they are forced to find other work as some universities have abandoned a commitment to systematics altogether.

The consequences are becoming increasingly clear and are attracting more attention in some intellectual and academic circles. As Ian Stewart and Jack Cohen put it recently in their 1997 book *Figments of Reality: The Evolution of the Curious Mind*, "Not so long ago, most of the world's biology departments got rid of all the old fogies doing things like zoology, botany, and taxonomy because they *knew* that the only important biology in the world was molecular. Now that environmental problems such as algal blooms, depleted fish stocks, and loss of biodiversity in rain forests are on the agenda, they are trying desperately to reconstitute the [kind of expertise] that resided in those old fogies, which is not so easy."

A related trend is evident at the world's museums — the traditional refuge of systematists, Nabokov among them — which shed many of their collections-based researchers during the economic slowdowns that followed the Vietnam War. Some museums, for example, cut back all their entomological programs, aside from those supported by agricultural or medical projects, and replaced their collections-based scientists with lower-paid, nonscientist "collection managers." Others shifted emphasis away from collections-based research and hired scientists whose focus was theory; in such cases not only did the theorists corner much of the job market but museums sometimes became top-heavy with scientists who typically might be familiar with only the few organisms they had studied during their doctoral programs.

Sophisticated methods and specialization sometimes complicated efforts to publish basic research. Papers were rejected if not accompanied by complex mathematical analysis; regional taxonomy was discouraged and authors told to wait until they had the "big picture." Taxonomists pursuing biodiversity surveys in distant places on small budgets often felt the pinch; as George Austin complained to Kurt Johnson concerning the ever-dwindling outlets for basic descriptions of new species — "I get so tired of this work being impeded by young theoreticians who think publication of basic taxonomy is not prestigious enough for their institution. They are often the same fellows who, when they go to a museum case, don't know one organism from another." Austin also despaired at the double standard that appeared in the academic journals — "The journals tell us they have to have the 'big picture' before they'll publish anything regional; meantime, E. O. Wilson's 'bioregionalism' tells us if we don't proceed regionally, we'll run out of time. What do we do?"

In fact, biological researchers who concentrate on describing new species and completing taxonomic groupings — that is, bringing the embryonic work of Linnaeus closer to its logical conclusion and essentially filling the role called for by Wilson — are often held in low esteem by their more specialized colleagues. Taxonomy is descriptive rather than experimental, and can in a sense be branded with something akin to the "stamp collecting" stigma that professional lepidopterists often attach to amateur collectors. Some even consider the taxonomic aspects of systematics not "real science" at all. This attitude undoubtedly lies behind many of the dismissive assessments of Nabokov's scientific career.

Today researchers who work to name and publish new insect species are caught in a paradox. Despite the legions of undescribed organisms and the urgent need for classification, taxonomy lacks glitter in the wider world of professional biology, and there are few avenues of financial support for publication. Workers without influence over their institutions' budgets may not be able to get a paper published under the auspices of that institution; independent journals often demand page charges — page-by-page fees to pay for publication costs — that may be unaffordable. In the field of High Andean and South American austral butterflies, for example, many important projects, like those of Arthur M. Shapiro on pierid butterflies, have been to a large degree personally financed. As a result some competent researchers are never able to publish new names in the extensive format required by the International Code for Zoological Nomenclature, falling back instead on brief entries in general lists or in museum collections as rudimentary as "new species 1" "new species 2," and so forth. While useful to a specific collection, such notations have little value in the wider scientific scheme of things. Another odd result of the financial constraints of systematics is that some professionals advocate not publishing new names at all. For them it is enough that an ad hoc knowledge of particular groups exists among a small circle of specialists. This arrangement leads to confusion when other workers, departing from the ad hoc system, step in and begin applying Latin names under the criteria of the Code.

Much of the basic work of systematics can be advanced with a good eye, diligent application, and little more equipment than a calipers and a microscope. This is as true today as it was in the 1940s, but since then the sociology of science has changed radically. Then it was possible for a self-trained and highly motivated naturalist, like Nabokov himself, to compete on a more or less level playing field with more highly trained professionals. Systematics had not yet entered the era in which, absent a recent Ph.D., one would be lost in all the mathematics and jargon-laden theory that dominates the science today. The requirement for success then was only that one produce published results and that those results be of quality.

In many respects the situation is no different than elsewhere in the world of academia. Trends come and go. In literature, philology is out, deconstructionism in; some specialties flourish and others flounder; some individuals prosper while others struggle. In literature one might argue that future generations, tired of last year's trends, can return to the shelf, and if the librarians have done their job, the old books, though dusty and a little damp, will still be there. In biology, however, the books of life are burning before they can be cataloged, let alone read and studied. And just when science needs an army of systematists to confront the biodiversity crisis, the foot soldiers are missing. More often than not basic descriptive work is simply not getting done.

Despite the overall popularity of butterflies, the story has been the same in lepidoptery as in other taxonomic fields. The long neglect of Nabokov's Neotropical Blues reflected all the chronic syndromes of the postwar years: a shortage of people to do the work, a certain complacency about what was already known, and the low prestige of taxonomy. The only differences were the names and the characters. Had this not been so, the study of Nabokov's Blues would likely have been completed decades earlier, biogeographers would not have fallen into the erroneous belief that the vast expanse of Latin America held an "impoverished" diversity of

Blue butterflies, and Vladimir Nabokov might have been accorded some of the respect he deserved for his pioneering work before his death in 1977.

But even in 1991, when Zsolt Bálint wrote Kurt Johnson urging that Nabokov's work somehow be finished, there was no well-prepared army just needing a few essential arms and ammunition to go into battle. Rather, at best, the whole project had from the beginning an ad hoc aura, and Bálint, Johnson, and the others who determined to carry it out were in many respects themselves considered more among the have-nots of systematics than among the scientific establishment. Like many productive taxonomists, Johnson, at the time a research associate at the American Museum of Natural History, did not hold a paid entomological position but worked instead in commercial aircraft finance; Bálint had only recently been named a collections manager at the Hungarian Museum of Natural History, a respectable but by no means dazzlingly prestigious position in the world of academia; Dubi Benyamini, Roberto Eisele, and Bruce MacPherson had all made impressive, lifelong contributions to lepidoptery while supporting themselves in other careers. Luis Peña, modeling himself on the old nineteenth-century explorers, had managed to make a good living selling biological specimens from Chile. Only José Herrera and Gerardo Lamas were full-time academics.

As has been pointed out, Blues occupy a somewhat odd position in the hierarchy of taxonomy. Although they are not the showiest of butterflies, they are still butterflies, and butterflies in general are taxonomically the flagship of the insect world. If the insects of a given locality are at all well-known, butterflies, in part because of their beauty and psychological allure, are likely to attract the most attention. Moreover, the Neotropical Blues not only represent a vast and intriguing biological homeland but potentially hold the key to answers to some of the most sweeping questions about the region's biological history. And unlike an overwhelming majority of the Earth's creatures, they are connected with the name of a world celebrity, Vladimir Nabokov. That Nabokov's Latin American Blues went unstudied for so long is in part a strong reflection on the inactivity in basic biological science since 1945.

As the status of taxonomy has changed since Nabokov's day, the terms of the environmental debate have shifted as well, and the participants have become more sophisticated, better organized, and better funded. Not a year goes by without most Americans' hearing from one of the major conservation organizations, among them the Nature Conservancy, the Sierra Club, the Wilderness Society, the Environmental Defense Fund, the World Wildlife Fund, the National Wildlife Federation, Conservation International, and Greenpeace. Around the world there are six hundred environmental organizations with annual budgets large enough to allow significant on-site projects; these groups now administer nine thousand areas, exceeding a total area of 22.3 billion acres, that are at least in name protected. Many nations have turned to legal protections, for both habitats and species, and many also require closely scrutinized permits for collecting.

Obviously, the only sure way to preserve such habitats as those of Nabokov's Latin American Blues and their lowland relatives would be to close off great tracts of territory from human exploitation, an option that is in virtually every case impossible, particularly in those places where people depend on the land to survive. As easy as it is to polarize the world's conservation concerns into two opposite camps, the exploiters and the preservationists, the examples of the Monarch and the Karner Blue suggest that conservation is increasingly a matter not of such dichotomies but of necessarily more complex responses like graded development, management, and sustainable use. Even some of the best-known names in the environmental movement in recent years are advocates of this approach, people like Chico Mendes, the Brazilian rubber tapper and crusader for renewable forest management whose murder in 1988 lit a fire under a generation of environmentalists, or the ecological campaigner Sylvia Mitraud, who crisscrosses the Amazon region advocating ecologically sustainable land use and livelihoods with the zeal of a revolutionary. The same attitude pervades E. O. Wilson's formulation of the very meaning of biodiversity studies — a conscious rejection of science for science's sake — as the systematic study of the full array of organic diversity, together with the methods by which it can be maintained and used for the benefit of humanity.

On yet another side of the environmental issue are formidable voices from industry and commerce, supported by their own contingent of scientists, who maintain that environmentalists often poison the terms of honest debate. They compare the most outspoken leaders of the environmental movement — people like Paul Ehrlich, a prominent lepidopterist at Stanford University, Lester Brown, or the late Carl Sagan — to old-time millenarians, who feed an arbitrary belief in world-ending catastrophe to a gullible public through masterfully orchestrated media and public-relations campaigns. The major, politically explosive documents of the environmental movement, the "Big Three" — Rachel Carson's *Silent Spring*

(1962); Ehrlich's *Population Bomb* (1968); and *The Limits of Growth* (1972) by Donella Meadows and others — come in for particular criticism. In this view dire predictions about pollution, world hunger, the population explosion, the fuel crisis, nuclear winter, the hole in the ozone layer, and global warming follow upon one another as fast as public attention shifts, and the biodiversity crisis is merely the latest ploy. The doubters note that few if any of the catastrophic predictions of the environmental movement have come to pass. Environmentalists, in turn, give their warnings credit for staving off disaster.

In this war of words, who can blame the ordinary person for feeling baffled? But one must judge by what one sees. Undoubtedly the circumstances of Nabokov's life and his individual character kept him from being an outspoken environmentalist, even by the standards of his own day. But, like him, biologists are often temperamentally reluctant to become overtly involved in political issues, even in serious matters of conservation. Robert Dirig, whose attitude is typical of many, told Kurt Johnson that when he first became involved with the Xerces Society's Karner Blue project, he saw himself as a Lepidoptera specialist "who was dragged, sometimes kicking and screaming, into the preservationist arena (which is not my natural element), but recognizing the necessity of these efforts." Similarly, many of the scientists involved in the Nabokov project had no political ax to grind. But as they traveled South America and the Caribbean, they were often stunned by what they saw — destruction of forests, overgrazing, and the bulldozing of vast areas of habitat. The devastation was most overwhelming in the tropics, where Johnson was involved in the study of lowland Hairstreaks. But everywhere Nabokov's Blues can be studied it was much the same, with the destruction increasing exponentially each time the researchers returned. This was the experience of Albert Schwartz, David Matusik, and Johnson in Las Abejas, Dubi Benyamini throughout temperate South America, the collectors of the Colombian and Ecuadorian highlands, and Arthur Shapiro as he trekked through the Patagonian Steppe and Tierra del Fuego's dank marine forests. Because most of Nabokov's South American butterflies are relatively widespread, none may appear as immediately threatened as the rare butterflies of the Las Abejas forest or even the Karner Blue. But so relentless is the destruction and so unpredictable its consequences, it is impossible to say how many species once limited to much smaller environmental pockets are already gone or how safe the others will be even over the short term.

Benyamini, with his specialty in butterfly life cycles, became increasingly troubled by the threats he saw to habitats in Chile as his fieldwork advanced there. More than once he had returned to the type locality of a new species a year after it had been discovered and found it grazed completely bare and devoid of butterflies. In much of the Andes butterflies face competition from other herbivores, both natural and domestic. The grazing of livestock is of particular environmental concern in Chile, where it is still unrestricted on public land, even in the national parks. The country lacks the climate and land area needed for the wide cultivation of the grain crops often used to feed sheep, cattle, and mules. Corn in particular, the livestock staple in the Northern Hemisphere, cannot be grown in Chile's cool, dry climate. As a result, with no winter feed source herders fall back on a diet of alfalfa, an easy crop to grow in Chile, and in the summer simply let the animals loose in the upland and austral grasslands. Throwing in the traditional camelitos, goats, and, increasingly, rabbits, the total environmental pressure from grazing is immense. As Benyamini realized, the loss of Blue butterflies, many no larger than a thumbnail, makes no difference to the overall panoramic beauty of these regions' national parks — the absence of butterflies may go quite unnoticed. Yet, while grazing might appear to cause no damage, a silent catastrophe may already be under way among the plants and insects basic to the temperate grassland ecosystems.

Many of the Blue butterfly species thus affected are reasonably widespread, but so once was the Karner Blue. They may long survive in places where people and their livestock are absent, but those places are becoming fewer and probably more fragmented, even in the vastness of Chile. And Benyamini discovered what may be another metapopulation phenomenon at work. He knew that in some places, like the deserts of the Middle East, Blue butterflies had evolved to survive bad weather — drought or prolonged freezing temperatures — by "skipping" a season, remaining in the chrysalis to emerge in a more favorable year. But Blues in the Andes and the Southern Cone of South America do not have that ability; in bad-weather seasons they either die in the chrysalis stage or emerge on schedule into the teeth of harsh weather. In the past local populations wiped out this way were restocked from the regional metapopulation — but this cannot continue once it has been destroyed as well.

Preservation strategy development and implementation in temperate grassland habitats in High Andean and austral regions of South America is in its infancy. Of the thirty-one projects in the Nature Conservancy's Parks in Peril program on the continent, not a single one includes grassland habitats in Chile or Argentina. And farther south only recently has an important effort by the World Wildlife Fund's Global 2000 Ecoregions program included some remaining temperate forest fragments in Chile.

Although its author could never have intended it, Kurt Johnson's thoughts always turned to the plight of the tropics when he read Nabokov's short story "The Aurelian," a work that in many ways represents his most straightforward and transparent treatment of lepidopterological themes. *Aurelian* is an old term for a lepidopterist, a collector and breeder of butterflies, a usage that *The Oxford English Dictionary* dates to the year 1778. It derives from the word *aurelia,* which means "chrysalis" and comes from the Latin for "gold." As many lepidopterists who rear butterflies know, some chrysalises attain a deep, rich, golden color just before the butterfly emerges, unfolds its wings, and flies away.

"The Aurelian," written in 1930, is the tale of a man who fantasizes about collecting rare butterflies in the tropics but dies before he can fulfill even the shadow of his dreams. The aurelian of the title is a world-weary German butterfly dealer, Paul Pilgram, a man of some scientific acumen but trapped in a humdrum existence, battling feelings of monotony, verging on disgust, as day after day he shifts the specimen boxes on his shelves. There is undoubtedly something here of that feeling of perplexity that all lepidopterists, particularly taxonomists, have experienced when, in moments of self-doubt, they find themselves wondering why they go to all this trouble — an existential instant in which their world of butterflies seems terribly small and empty. Pilgram's response is to dream of the tropics, whose wonders might transcend the deracinated banality of the commercial specimens in his collection.

When he gets a little money Pilgram decides to leave his uncomprehending wife behind and go on a lepping trip to Spain. While dragging out his suitcase, however, he suffers a heart attack, and his wife finds him dead on the kitchen floor. But in fact, Nabokov explains, Pilgram's life and death represented a kind of transcendence. "Yes, Pilgram had gone far, very far. Most probably he visited Granada and Murcia and Albarracín, and then traveled farther still, to Surinam or Taprobane; and one can hardly doubt that he saw all the glorious bugs he had longed to see — velvety black butterflies soaring over the jungles, and a tiny moth in Tasmania, and. . . ." In Nabokov's story this idea of transcendence can be understood on several levels: the transcendence of dreams in even the most drab of lives or the ultimate human transcendence that consists of death itself.

As Johnson became more familiar with Nabokov's work, he was amused by what he felt were unintended links between "The Aurelian" and Nabokov's career. In his interviews and letters the author sometimes conjured up visions of butterfly expeditions to exotic locales. Often such expressions seem to carry connotations of the impossibly remote, although it can be hard to discern Nabokov's exact intention. Even when he had the means Nabokov seems to have been happy to collect in North America and Europe; it is touching that his most lastingly significant work and his only work based on butterflies of exotic areas, "Notes on Neotropical Plebejinae," was carried out with borrowed museum specimens in decidedly unexotic Cambridge, Massachusetts. And many of Nabokov's own Latin American Blues, despite the misleading all-purpose label "Neotropical," were in fact from South America's temperate zones — the terrain lifted high above the continent's tropical climes by the Andes Mountains and the vaster, low-latitude steppes that characterize its Southern Cone.

Still, in taking on this venture Nabokov stepped out of the familiar realm of North American Blues, in which he had invested so many years of meticulous research, and moved briefly into the study of Latin American fauna. Pilgram's journey into the tropics was imaginary, Nabokov's was vicarious; for Nabokov, at least, that first journey also proved to be the last. It would obviously not have been apparent to the author of "The Aurelian" in 1930, but the same pallor of death that pervades the story seems to hang over many Latin American biotas, Nabokov's Blues among them. Indeed, one cannot be sure that the death of Pilgram, whose dreams are survived only by the dead butterflies in his specimen boxes, does not foreshadow the fate of tropical America.

PART III

NABOKOV'S BLUES

11 ⸎

The Code

As happens in zoological nomenclature when a string of obsolete, syn-
onymous, or misapplied names keeps following the correct designation
of a creature throughout the years and not only cannot be shaken off, or
ignored, or obliterated within the brackets but actually grows on with
time, so in literary history, the vague terms "classicism," "sentimental-
ism," "romanticism," "realism," and the like straggle on and on, from textbook to textbook.

— *Commentary on Eugene Onegin*

I N 1945 Nabokov published "Notes on Neotropical Plebejinae" on the
basis of 120 specimens of Blue butterflies from the Museum of Comparative Zoology at Harvard and the American Museum of Natural
History in New York. Although the small number of specimens he studied
paled in comparison with the thousands cataloged in his studies of northern Blues, the geographic breadth of Latin America made this Neotropical
study the most far-reaching in scientific implication of any work Nabokov
attempted. His laboratory-based expedition into Latin America, amounting to some sixty pages of dense type, involved a few months of solitary research spread over late 1944 and early 1945. Nabokov evaluated the status
of twenty-eight species names, eventually grouping a mere eighteen of
them into his new genus-level classification, in addition to one species he
discovered himself but did not immediately name.

Half a century later it required a near constant flow of scientific publications to communicate the results of the worldwide study that grew from
his work. Up until 1993 the scientific literature made only the barest reference to "Notes on Neotropical Plebejinae." Today nearly forty articles on
Nabokov's groups of Latin American Blue butterflies have appeared in a
half dozen scientific journals, written by various combinations of eight

scientists, including Zsolt Bálint, Kurt Johnson, Dubi Benyamini, Gerardo Lamas, and other scientists from Colombia, Italy, and Germany.

As Bálint and Johnson's initial work on Chilean and Argentine Blues came to fruition, there were obstacles to publication. Because of financial problems the American Museum of Natural History had placed a moratorium on manuscripts from its associates; at the Hungarian museum Bálint's support allowed a mere two publications per year. Thus, in an effort to keep all the first technical papers in one volume, in 1993 Bálint and Johnson turned to the Museum of Natural History at the University of Wisconsin at Stevens Point. This somewhat out-of-the-way branch of a large state university system had long been dedicated to natural resources topics, and in February of 1993 it had been host to a conference called by Secretary of the Interior Bruce Babbitt to discuss the fate of America's temperate grasslands, plains, and prairie ecosystems. This was a topic of moment among midwestern scientific institutions; Johnson had been a speaker at a similar conference in Iowa in the mid-1980s.

In March 1993 the official journal of Wisconsin's natural history museum published the results of Bálint and Johnson's studies of Chilean and Argentine Blues, the first edition of Bálint's catalog of Polyommatini from the old European museums, and other related studies. Some of the specimens treated had been added at the last minute, after the work was already in proof, as other researchers found out about it and asked to contribute. A comparable trove of information on Latin American Blues had not appeared in one place since "Notes on Neotropical Plebejinae" in 1945. From its beginnings with the Las Abejas expedition, and continuing for the better part of a decade, Nabokov's bare taxonomic framework had evolved into a full-blown, worldwide study encompassing a topic that, as recently as 1986, Henri Descimon had believed could not be completed in several lifetimes' research.

The most immediately striking result of these labors was an explosion of species discoveries. Instead of the nineteen species that Nabokov ultimately arranged in his nine genuses of Neotropical Polyommatini, science now recognizes nearly eighty. The sheer volume of new species has overturned a long-held belief in the low diversity of Andean Blues and raises questions about the distribution of life in and out of the rain forests of South America, the world's great furnaces of biology.

It is the job — and the privilege — of taxonomists to name new species. For Nabokov's new Blues over a dozen names from his fiction, including *lolita, luzhin, sirin,* and *shade,* were suggested to Bálint and Johnson by the

Nabokov devotee Warren Whitaker in 1993 for some of the forgotten butterflies Bálint had discovered in European museums. More followed in
1995, recommended by Whitaker and Nabokov scholars such as Brian
Boyd, D. Barton Johnson, Stephen Jan Parker, and Dieter E. Zimmer. Particular care was taken in the case of the new species *humbert,* to ensure
that in nature, if not in literature, Lolita would live eternally free from the
monstrous Humbert Humbert. The scientists made certain to place *humbert* in a separate genus and assigned to that name a species with a limited
range living some fifteen hundred miles from where *lolita* might ever be
found roaming.

All the new species names were meant to honor Nabokov as the single
most important pioneer in South American Blue butterflies, and also to
reflect Bálint's and Johnson's recognition of the acumen and skill of their
predecessor. While Nabokov was not, of course, directly responsible for
everything that evolved from his study, as the first reviser he had forged
the pivotal part of the chain of research that created the modern picture of
the Latin American Blues. All the basic taxonomy rests on the foundation
he laid, a fact reflected at every level of the subsequent work. For instance,
Bálint's catalog of Polyommatini in European museums, addressing matters obligated under the rules of modern taxonomy, required 143 references to details of Nabokov's 1945 treatise. Nabokov, who was wonderfully
sensitive to history, was very conscious of being part of a long and noble
tradition of lepidoptery. He had lamented to Edmund Wilson in 1944 that
he expected the value of his work on the subspecies of *Lycaeides* to last
only twenty-five years or so. He fully expected that his work would be developed by his successors and would no doubt have relished this evolution
of his 1945 study.

Part of any such evolution is the correction of errors committed in earlier work, and this was also true of the Nabokov project. The publication
of March 1993 provided the first opportunity to correct some of Nabokov's
original mistakes and those of various others who had subsequently mis-
interpreted his work. In most cases these were the first corrections to
"Notes on Neotropical Plebejinae" since its publication. It is unsurprising
that errors would crop up in such a study, and friends and supporters of
Nabokov have long feared that closer examination would actually vitiate
Nabokov's work. As his colleague and friend Charles Remington told *The
New York Times* in 1997, "A lot of people have been uneasy about how well
his work would stand up under the scrutiny of good professionals."

Bálint and Johnson, however, found that Nabokov's work stood up exceptionally well, and to see why this is so it is important to understand the nature of the errors he committed. None of them reflected badly on Nabokov as a scientist. Rather, the major problems with "Notes on Neotropical Plebejinae" were due to circumstances beyond his control. One was his inevitably small sample of specimens. Another was his inability, given the wartime conditions under which he worked and the more primitive state of communications of that era, to get his hands on some of the pertinent literature.

A third involved a trick of time. Nabokov understood that he was part of a continuous tradition in taxonomy that reached back beyond Linnaeus and continues today. But that tradition has undergone many adjustments over time, the most important being the institution of a uniform set of rules regularized in 1961 under the International Code of Zoological Nomenclature. This is the Code under which Bálint and Johnson and all other modern taxonomists determine new species and assign new names to them; in fact, while there are many complex aspects of the Code, the simplest way to think of it is as a mechanism that controls what an organism can be named. This is the bottom-line function of taxonomy.

The formal part of Nabokov's career was over before the Code was introduced, so he did not work directly under its regulations. His taxonomy is not, however, exempt from the Code's jurisdiction, for the Code was designed to govern the validity not only of new taxonomic names but also of those proposed before it was issued. In fact, the Code is strongly rooted in the widespread taxonomic conventions that preceded it, the conventions that Nabokov for the most part followed. But with the Code's formal adoption, the claims of older works came into question. It mandated that modern taxonomists review the work of their predecessors and, if necessary, revise it in conformity with the Code's provisions. Depending on the caliber of work performed by a taxonomist before the institution of the Code, his or her legacy may, after revision and in the eyes of posterity, fare well or very poorly. While there are rules within the Code that turn on the quality of a scientist's work, others merely declare blindly how something will be done thereafter. Sometimes these rules determine whose names will stand and whose will fall. In this light, and historical perspective, the Code is a grim reaper. In determining a taxonomist's eventual legacy, it may truly be said, with some trepidation, "The Code giveth but the Code also taketh away." The modern fate of Nabokov's taxonomy cannot be properly understood without some knowledge of the Code itself.

What eventually became the International Commission on Zoological

Nomenclature, made up of distinguished scientists who would review the works of others and make arbitrative decisions, was envisaged by the international scientific community before World War II. By 1942, even as war engulfed the globe, the commission was beginning to issue official opinions on the status of zoological names. But it was not until 1961, more than fifteen years after World War II and twenty years after Nabokov came to America, that the organization published the Code, which has had two subsequent editions, in 1964 and 1985. The current version of the Code, published in English and French, is 338 pages long and includes eighty-eight articles organized in eighteen chapters, each addressing various aspects of taxonomic procedure. It is a document with a legalistic flavor and is more concerned with the technicalities of nomenclatorial rules than with analytical science. The Code is not a guide to scientific theory or method. Its goal is rather to keep straight what had become through the years a tangle of confusion over the taxonomic names of the world's organisms.

The confusion was largely the result of two common problems. In the age before computers, fax machines, and other modern means of communication, when taxonomists were isolated from one another by geography, different researchers often unknowingly proposed entirely different names for the same organism. This is known as synonymy, and the various duplicate names are called synonyms. Conversely, different researchers might, by chance, attribute the same name to different organisms — this is known as homonymy, and the identical names are called homonyms. Synonymy and homonymy are most common at the species level but they also occur with genuses. Although mostly inadvertent, such coincidences had always caused trouble and confusion in lepidoptery, and vigilant researchers like Nabokov often tried to point such cases out when they discovered them, lending the weight of their authority to the name they considered valid by the rule of priority — that is, it was generally accepted that whatever name was properly proposed for an organism first would become the "official" name until there was sufficient scientific reason for it to be supplanted by another.

Sorting out the synonyms and homonyms of earlier scientists was in fact one of the major tasks Nabokov faced in his classification of Latin American Polyommatini. While this sounds straightforward enough, imagine being handed a group of old hand-drawn illustrations, of varying quality, together with a list of sometimes vague physical descriptions, and being asked to determine which are descriptions of the same butterfly and which are not. The difficulties grow exponentially in a group of butterflies like the Blues, many species of which vary little from one another externally and must be identified mainly by microscopic dissection of their genitalia.

For every species Nabokov placed in his classification, he suspected and listed from one to four synonyms. In most cases he had no access to the original type specimens of the species he was attempting to sort out. Often he had no representative specimens at all, only the short and sometimes confusing original published descriptions, some as old as the eighteenth century. He was in effect judging the work of his predecessors on a best-guess basis.

This process, practiced by all taxonomists of Nabokov's era, was risky and inexact, and dependent as much on the artistic skill and descriptive powers of others as on taxonomic acuity. In the worst cases such revisions served only to deepen existing confusion. To prevent this, the criteria of the Code governing evaluation of previously existing names are much more rigorous than they were in Nabokov's day. Today such work must be based on type specimens or accepted substitutes, and the priority of all names is sorted out through the many official rulings — known as opinions — issued by the International Commission on Zoological Nomenclature.

In addition, since the Code was designed to govern names that already existed, it mandated that modern taxonomists scrutinize earlier work in light of its regulations. This created a problem with the validity of Nabokov's use of scientific names. There was no problem with the types that Nabokov himself had first identified and named since, according to subsequent rules, these became the standards. As a taxonomist, however, Nabokov made many judgments about the meaning and status of scientific names proposed by others before the Code had mandated a standard for the usage of types. When Nabokov, or any other taxonomist before the Code, identified species based on examination of specimens other than those eventually recognized as the types — or on mere references in the published technical literature — these usages could, in retrospect, be judged technically incorrect. Among its many other provisions the Code requires that for formal revisionary work a modern researcher locate and identify the original specimens used by the original author to establish names. So not only did Nabokov's specimens have to be tracked down but so did the specimens from the work of others that he cited. In the end, Bálint and Johnson were obligated to establish new type specimens for seventeen species of Latin American Blues whose authors did not follow the conventions later officialized by the Code. Thereafter, regardless of the views of Nabokov or other former researchers, these became the standard for proper identification.

It is in this context that the errors in Nabokov's 1945 treatise must be considered. At one level some of the problems are illustrated perfectly in Nabokov's *Pseudolucia,* the first South American genus taken up in depth by Bálint and Johnson and the one in which the largest number of new species was discovered. Nabokov, who knew of only two species, would probably have been astounded by the variety that Bálint and Johnson were able to assemble by 1993, working from a sample of more than two hundred specimens. Today there are nearly forty known specimens, some still unnamed, many with wing patterns quite unlike anything Nabokov had considered in setting up the genus.

Pseudolucia was an ideal group to cover in a regional study. Generally occurring only south of Peru, its natural geographic range fit well into the parameters of both the guide to Chilean butterflies proposed by José Herrera and Luis Peña and the work on the Argentine fauna that had been begun by Johnson, Roberto Eisele, and Bruce MacPherson. Combining the Greco-Latin prefix meaning "false" with *Lucia,* the name of a well-known genus of copper-colored Blues from Australia, Nabokov had named this genus *Pseudolucia* for good reason. He no doubt recognized that, by Old World standards, the Blues he was assigning to *Pseudolucia,* like those in *Lucia,* did often look much like some Coppers. In fact, the species he placed in *Pseudolucia* had been assigned by their original authors to the European Copper genus *Lycaena,* a group introduced in 1807 by Johann Christian Fabricius, one of the first naturalists to adopt Linnaeus's system of binomial nomenclature. This mislabeling is forgivable, given the often ornate orange appearance of those species, quite unlike European Blues. In 1992, when the prominent American lepidopterist Charles Covell, author of the Peterson field guide to Eastern American moths, was casually shown one of the boxes of Peña and Herrera's material at the American Museum of Natural History, he exclaimed in disbelief, "Those are *Blues?*"

Nabokov's view of *Pseudolucia* was severely restricted by his tiny sample. Of the two species he knew, one, *chilensis,* was his type species, of which he had only four specimens. (Just as a type specimen defines a species, a type species defines a genus — in the most modern sense by limiting its membership to the genealogical relatives of that species.) This quarter-size, mottled orange-and-brown butterfly had been named in 1852 by the Frenchman Emile Blanchard, in a classic but now extremely rare multivolume work on the natural history of Chile, Claudio Gay's monumental *Historia física y política de Chile* privately published in Paris and Santiago. Nabokov's other *Pseudolucia* species, from a sample of only two specimens, was named *collina*, Latin for "of the hills," probably a reference to its mountain habitats. Typical of the taxonomic irregularities before the Code, *collina*'s author, Rudolph Amando Philippi, actually published its name twice, first in 1859 in the *Annales de la Universidad de Chile*, a journal seldom seen outside that country, and again in 1860 for a wider audience, in another rare journal, *Linnaea Entomologica*, published from 1846 to 1866 in Leipzig.

Both sexes of *chilensis* have an undersurface wing pattern of blackish spots forming a line across each wing, over a whitish to beige ground color. This is what Nabokov called the catachrysopoid pattern — one that is quite common in Blues outside South America. *Pseudolucia collina* was very different, nickel-sized, with a band of black spots on the forewing but on the hind wing a vivid black, V-shaped mark across the entire surface, its zenith pointing to the outer margin. On the upper surfaces males and females of *chilensis* were not blue at all but basically brownish orange, females with a vivid burst of orange across the forewing. By contrast, males of *collina* were a lovely sky blue with a vivid white fringe; females of *collina*, however, were completely different, a vivid yellow-orange or brighter orange outlined by striking black margins. Apparently considering this pattern unique, Nabokov did not assign a special name to it. Given the radically different markings of the two species, he found the unity of *Pseudolucia* in the genitalia, the male clasper with a prominently hooked end and the female with a simple tubular ductal tract. In his original description Nabokov conveyed the anatomical characteristics of his new genus with flair and inventiveness: The allulae of the male genitalia were "shrugged" and the falx differed from those of other genuses "as a beckoning index [finger] does from a warning one."

Nabokov specifically excluded a number of previously described Latin American Blue butterflies from his new genus. First, he listed three as synonyms of either *chilensis* or *collina:* identical species given different names by other researchers. In every case he lacked actual specimens to work with and was forced to rely on the descriptions in the old literature, which were based exclusively on wing pattern. In two of the three he turned out to be wrong. When Bálint and Johnson later examined these butterflies, two species — *sibylla* and *lyrnessa* — clearly shared the distinctive genitalic features of the genus *Pseudolucia,* just as Nabokov had described them. But they were also just as clearly distinct from *chilensis* and *collina.*

In two other cases, again with no specimens available, Nabokov accepted the judgments of his predecessors and left what turned out to be two species of *Pseudolucia* in other genuses. One of these had been named by the British Museum's assistant keeper of entomology Arthur Gardiner Butler in 1881 as *Scolitantides plumbea.* The species name, *plumbea,* means "leaden" and refers to a row of blackish blotches across the lower edge of the hind-wing undersurface; the genus *Scolitantides* is a well-known group of northern Blue butterflies, and the common assumption was that their South American members had filtered down from the Northern Hemisphere. The other species Nabokov excluded from *Pseudolucia* in this way turned out to be one of the most common in southern South America. It had been named *Scolitantides andina* — of the Andes — in 1894 by another pioneer in Chilean entomology, William Bartlett-Calvert. On its hind-wing undersurface it sported an arched row of vivid black, crescentlike marks, so much like the arrowhead markings of Old World *Scolitantides* that both Nabokov and Butler were fooled.

The undersurface patterns of both these butterflies were very different from those of either *chilensis* or *collina,* and without specimens for dissection Nabokov was unable to examine their genitalia. For that reason, and because he, like other lepidopterists of his day, believed that most of the South American fauna had come originally from the north, he accepted these species as *Scolitantides.* Since his study covered only Polyommatini that occurred exclusively in Latin America, he was content to leave it at that. But again, when Bálint and Johnson followed up Nabokov's research these butterflies were clearly seen as belonging to *Pseudolucia* as well.

Pseudolucia is a fascinatingly complex genus. In all five of the recorded species that Nabokov excluded, there were not only variations on the genitalic structures that he had seen but additional components as well. To complicate matters further, these odd structures are not always distributed consistently with the color patterns expressed externally by the wings. Instead, they cut across the general categories of wing patterns, suggesting that many of these species might be quite ancient, with ample time for adaptive convergence to work. Had Nabokov been able to examine specimens himself, these taxonomic intricacies might have given him some brief pause. He might even have lost a little sleep over them. But there is no doubt that ultimately he would have placed them in his

Pseudolucia. Despite having worked with only two species, Nabokov formulated a solid genitalic ground plan for the genus, one that easily accommodates even the species he was unable to see for himself.

As for the wings, Bálint and Johnson now knew that there were five variations of underwing patterns in *Pseudolucia,* not just the two that Nabokov had recognized, and each pattern was shared by several species, a striking display of the hidden diversity so typical of the South American Blues. That was in part what had misled lepidopterists into thinking there were so few species of South American Blues and to the surprising jump in the number of species discovered by Bálint and Johnson. In addition to patterns like that of the spotted *chilensis* and the V-marked *collina,* which Nabokov had recognized, there were various leaden-orbed species that closely resembled *plumbea,* crescent-marked species related to *andina,* and intricately patched species of the *sibylla* group, which was so poorly known that even Peña and Herrera's samples contained fewer than ten specimens.

Clearly, in one sense Nabokov's picture of his genus *Pseudolucia,* which he set up on the basis of only two species, differed drastically from the modern one, which recognizes nearly forty. He turned out to have been wrong about a number of species he excluded from the genus, either by erroneously categorizing them as synonyms of other species or by accepting the judgments of earlier lepidopterists that they belonged to a genus completely outside the purview of "Notes on Neotropical Plebejinae." But in every case both the shortcomings and the errors were attributable to his severely restricted specimen sample and his lack of access to type specimens combined with the general taxonomic unreliability of the literature. These are risks inherent in the necessarily limited kind of study Nabokov undertook. Given the constraints of his resources and the restrictions on his time, it is remarkable how few errors of this sort he made. Had he had the specimens in hand, there is no question that he would have made the same discoveries as the researchers who took up his work fifty years later.

Species, however, were not the main thrust of Nabokov's study, except insofar as they were used to define his genuses; he was certainly not primarily concerned with naming species; rather he was concerned with taking species, most of them already named by others, and arranging them in an innovative scheme at the genus level. In fact the same sampling error that affected Nabokov's understanding of the species in *Pseudolucia* ramified to his genus classifications, but less often than might have been expected.

From references in the historical literature, Nabokov was aware of the existence of a lovely group of Latin American Blue butterflies with tails on their wings like Hairstreaks; because of this resemblance the one species known at the time had been placed in a Hairstreak genus in 1921 and named *Thecla sylphis*. Like other lepidopterists Nabokov realized these were actually Blues, and he entertained the reasonable suspicion that the species might be allied in some way to his more dull-colored genus *Pseudothecla*, represented in his day by a single species, also with tails. But even today rare and spectacularly colored purple, blue, and golden butterflies like *sylphis* are represented in the European collections by only a handful of specimens, and Nabokov was unable to find any to study. Therefore he chose to go no further than to refer to the existing literature in a footnote.

In 1991 Bálint found a single specimen of *sylphis* in the Natural History Museum in London, a beautiful Blue epiphany. Next to it were two equally gorgeous specimens of an obvious relative, violaceous silvery blue over the entire upper wing surface except for its ornately checked yellow and brown marginal borders. Those two butterflies were labeled "Gen.?, sp. n.," museum shorthand to signify that they represented a new species of a doubtful or unknown genus; the species had never been published, but the butterflies that represented it had been dissected at some time in the past. It was impossible to say when, because preserved dissections at the Natural History Museum bear only location numbers and no direct notation to indicate the dissector and date of dissection. Bálint was unaware that in this case he was following in the tracks of someone else, a fact that returned to haunt the entire Nabokov project with startling complications in the taxonomy of Latin American Blues.

But when Bálint studied the dissections it was obvious they represented a distinct genus that had been known to Nabokov. Bálint and Johnson called this new genus *Polytheclus;* it was the only genus that they added to Nabokov's classification. For the new species in the Natural History Museum they chose the name *cincinnatus,* after the tormented prisoner in Nabokov's dystopian fable *Invitation to a Beheading.* Later it thrilled Bálint to capture members of *Polytheclus* himself in the Peruvian Andes.

Anyone who names a genus, or any other taxonomic group for that matter, must go some way to demonstrate that it reflects an underlying natural group, with members more closely related to one another than to anything outside the group. That is, the author must establish a convincing and defendable ground plan for the new genus. If in the eyes of other taxonomists a genus does not accurately reflect such a relationship, it can be superseded by another grouping or groupings, with someone else's name attached, and the old grouping, along with its author's name, becomes just more flotsam and jetsam in the obscure history of lepidoptery. Thus the survival of a name, in this case that of a genus, represents to some degree the validation of the underlying science.

Despite the large number of specimens of Latin American Blues that Bálint and Johnson studied, and the large number of new species they discovered, they found no reason to add further genuses to the Andean Polyommatini identified by Nabokov. Nor did they see grounds to lump any of his genuses together or to split any. Because of Nabokov's analytical skill, together with a little luck, from a strictly scientific point of view, the generic framework of Latin American Blue butterflies that he created was corroborated and validated by Bálint and Johnson's expansive, meticulous study. In their view, with the exception of their genus *Polytheclus*, the generic ground plans Nabokov had created accommodated every new-species discovery.

But there are also purely technical reasons that a genus name might be judged invalid under the rules that govern modern taxonomy, reasons that do not reflect scientific acumen. While this makes no difference to science, the technical invalidation of names can affect the reputations of individual lepidopterists as much as can the disappearance of names because of bad science. It is not always a fair gauge of scientific ability, but a claim to a reputation in lepidoptery has a better chance of lasting if it has as a foundation a claim to a taxonomic grouping.

Although Norman Riley's field guide obscured "Notes on Neotropical Plebejinae" for decades, all the genus names that Nabokov adopted for Caribbean Blue butterflies survive today, and his name is therefore formally associated with those genuses, as in *Cyclargus* Nabokov. In books like *The Butterflies of the West Indies and South Florida,* by David Spencer Smith, Lee D. Miller, and Jacqueline Y. Miller, that name appears in full above the column that describes the various species within the genus, not only as an identifier but as a kind monument to Nabokov and his work. Moreover, every newly discovered species that fits satisfactorily into one of Nabokov's genuses will automatically have a Nabokovian genus name as part of its two-part scientific name, *Cyclargus kathleena*, for instance, or the single species Nabokov himself added to that genus — *erembis* in 1948.

In South America, however, not all of Nabokov's genus names have survived. In every case this is the result not of any scientific failing but of technical reasons connected with the rules that govern taxonomy according to the 1961 Code. To appreciate Nabokov's science it is necessary to understand how this happened.

In the first half of the century, many people were becoming concerned about the increasing levels of confusion in taxonomy because of rampant synonymy and homonymy, and one of the most prominent was the British lepidopterist and systematist Francis Hemming. Hemming, who was the secretary to the International Commission on Zoological Nomenclature from 1937 to 1958, took it upon himself to sort out the tangle of butterfly genuses, eliminating synonyms and homonyms and ensuring that each genus had an official type species. The result of this important work was a posthumous five-hundred-page monograph entitled *The Generic Names of the Butterflies and Their Type Species,* published in 1967. The need for this volume and the fact that a scholar like Hemming had devoted much of his life to it suggests how thorny the taxonomic thickets had become. In 1959, during the course of his research, Hemming discovered that the name of one of Nabokov's South American genuses, *Pseudothecla,* had already been used for a group of Hairstreak butterflies by the Norwegian lepidopterist Embrik Strand, in 1910. Under the conventions of taxonomy, later standardized by the Code, that meant that Nabokov's name was a homonym, technically unavailable for use and in need of what the Code calls a replacement name.

Hemming wrote Nabokov to inform him of this and advised him to replace his name as soon as it was convenient for him to do so, which Nabokov might easily have done even with his busy schedule. But instead he replied saying he would prefer that Hemming provide a replacement name. Nabokov himself was meticulous about nomenclatorial precision, and one of his specialties was the almost lexicographical task of sorting out confused tangles of genuses and other groups; his unselfish gesture probably reflected his appreciation of the work Hemming was doing. Hemming, in turn, renamed the genus *Nabokovia.* "I have much pleasure in naming this genus for Dr. V. Nabokov," he wrote, "who has done so much to increase our knowledge of the subfamily Plebejinae." Nabokov was no doubt pleased with this choice, since his own strong preference was for preoccupied names to be replaced with new ones in some way based on the names of the authors of the first names.

In this way one of Nabokov's genus names was invalidated before the Code was even formally adopted. But it is important to realize that that is not a reflection on the quality of Nabokov's lepidoptery. In fact, between

1945 and the early 1990s no one, with the possible exception of Norman Riley, subjected Nabokov's taxonomic judgments about Neotropical butterflies to exacting analysis; rather, "Notes on Neotropical Plebejinae" was simply ignored. Hemming wasn't concerned with the strictly scientific aspects of Nabokov's work. He was concerned with what in taxonomy is known as housekeeping. He was for the most part simply compiling lists of all the names of butterfly genuses to make sure that there were no duplicates and that each genus had a proper type species. The group known first as *Pseudothecla* Nabokov and now as *Nabokovia* Hemming is perfectly sound as a genus, and Nabokov described its ground plan — what makes a specimen a member of that group and not another — carefully, exactingly, and accurately. Nabokov's mistake was that he was unaware of the Hairstreak genus already known as *Pseudothecla*. Taxonomic convention recognized it as trivial and offered Nabokov a chance to replace the name with another for which he would have received credit.

Hemming readily resolved the nomenclatorial problem posed by *Pseudothecla* in 1960, but until the 1990s no one had dealt decisively with related difficulties in two other genuses that Nabokov used in his classification of South American Blues: *Parachilades,* which he had named himself, and *Itylos,* which the lepidopterist Max Draudt had proposed for a wide group of Andean Blues in 1921. But without the compulsion of the rules enforced today by the Code, Draudt had not listed a definitive type species for his *Itylos.* The confusion that resulted from this case is a perfect example of why such a rule is necessary.

In 1929 the same Francis Hemming who named *Nabokovia,* on his pre-Code mission to ensure that every genus was properly represented with a type species, arbitrarily designated a species called *speciosa* to define the genus *Itylos,* as convention allowed him to do. But in 1945, still with no international rules in place, Nabokov recognized a very different *Itylos* type species, called *moza,* based on a sort of law of priority of his own — the view that Draudt mentioned *moza* as a member of *Itylos* on page 818 of his text, whereas *speciosa* was not mentioned until page 821. Under the taxonomic rules of the time, Nabokov was not compelled to adopt Hemming's designated type species. He had a perfect right to designate his own, and the way he based his choice on page numbers is a good example of how meticulous Nabokov could be. When the Code was published, however, it did not recognize such a procedure, and its law of priority theoretically officialized Hemming's original type designation, simply because it had been published first.

This would have proved unproblematic had both species, *moza* and *speciosa,* belonged in the same genus. But like many early taxonomists Draudt was unfamiliar with genital dissection and the concept of hidden diversity. Indeed, guided merely by the similar appearance of wing surfaces, he had placed many species into his *Itylos* that in fact fell more naturally into other genuses. To make birds of these little butterflies, *speciosa* was a crow and *moza* was a woodpecker. Nabokov realized this and thus decided to restrict Draudt's *Itylos,* using *moza* as the type species, in the same way he restricted Hübner's *Hemiargus* in the Caribbean. As a result, between 1945 and 1961 the genus name *Itylos* had two usages, one going back to Hemming and the other to Nabokov. With no serious scientific work being done on Nabokov's Blues, all those who might have been interested in some way — museum curators, active amateurs, and publishers of popular books, who establish what science calls common usage — would have been thoroughly confused.

When the Code came into effect, however, and recognized Hemming's concept of *Itylos,* with the type species *speciosa,* over Nabokov's, there was another ramification. Nabokov had used *speciosa* as the type species of his new genus *Parachilades.* But since the genus defined by *speciosa* had to be called *Itylos, Parachilades* became a synonym and was technically invalid. The Code required subsequent researchers to publish the necessary taxonomic changes in order to make them binding in light of the Code's rules. Yet no one ever undertook this task for Nabokov's Neotropical genuses; thus, between "Notes on Neotropical Plebejinae" in 1945 and Bálint and Johnson's publications in 1993, Nabokov's position on *Parachilades* and *Itylos* was technically wrong, although the work went uncorrected and the errors remained unrecognized. In 1986, for example, Henri Descimon was unaware of the changes in Nabokov's work required by the Code and referred to both his *Parachilades* and *Itylos* as if they remained valid names. Few such errors in major zoological groups went uncorrected for so long, yet another indication of the general scientific neglect of both Nabokov's seminal taxonomic work on Neotropical Blues and the group itself.

By associating the name *Itylos* with the *moza* group, Nabokov effectively lost his chance to name what would have been a new genus. It fell to Zsolt Bálint, nearly fifty years later, to confer the new generic name, *Madeleinea,* chosen out of respect for William D. Field, a former curator at the Smithsonian Institution. Field had studied South American Blues for a time, but ill health prevented him from completing his work. Gerardo Lamas, who as curator at the Peruvian national museum in Lima has always kept tabs on what is going on in Neotropical lepidoptery, told Bálint that Field had been aware of the technical problem and had intended to rename Nabokov's *Itylos* group himself, after his wife, Madelein. Accordingly, Bálint followed Field's wish. Today *Madeleinea* is the genus that includes *lolita, cobaltana,* and three other names chosen from *Pale Fire: odon* and *nodo;* and *tintarrona,* from tintarron, the precious deep-blue-stained Zemblan glass, produced in Bokay, a medieval place in the kingdom's mountains.

As in the case of the invalidated *Pseudothecla,* there was nothing wrong with Nabokov's taxonomic science. In fact, he had a far more sophisticated understanding of the butterflies involved than did either Draudt or Hemming. Moreover, the Code granted Nabokov himself the right to rename the *moza* group, which he had wrongly called *Itylos.* Doing so would not have been difficult even for the busiest novelist. The Code would have required Nabokov merely to publish two sentences, something along the lines of "Under the rules of the recently implemented International Code of Zoological Nomenclature, the *moza* group of Neotropical Blues is without a valid generic name. Therefore, I propose the new genus name *X.*"

But it is unclear how much Nabokov, in the years after 1961, thought about the Code or knew about its ramifications for his Latin American nomenclatures. There appears to be no evidence that he ever discussed the situation with anyone. Even John Downey, who maintained correspondence with Nabokov in the 1960s and '70s in connection with Downey's work on Doubleday's *Butterflies of North America,* had no recollection of his ever mentioning the status of his South American Blues. Perhaps, like Descimon, Nabokov remained unaware of the implications of the Code for his 1945 treatise or perhaps he was merely unconcerned and content to leave such work to others, as he had been with *Nabokovia.* Brian Boyd has suggested that since Nabokov had never been in a position to collect them himself, he simply never developed the proprietary interest in his Latin American Blues that he felt for their northern counterparts. In any case these are errors in the technical sense only and no reflection on Nabokov's lepidoptery. When his work depended on the specimens he had before his eyes and under his microscope, he seldom made mistakes.

Remedying the technical problem of the names of Nabokov's invalidated genuses — in the end a simple matter of housekeeping — was far from the only taxonomic result of Bálint and Johnson's publications. There was a deeper, potentially more significant difficulty with three Latin

American Blues genuses. In the Caribbean, it will be remembered, Nabokov set up his genus *Pseudochrysops* on the basis of a single species, which created something of a taxonomic anomaly. Taxonomists, especially modern ones who recognize the process of evolution as dichotomous branching, hesitate to recognize the validity of single-species genuses. *Pseudochrysops* still holds only one species, but it has subspecies on several Caribbean islands and thus is at least a branched lineage.

But Nabokov, who was very confident of his morphology, did the same for three of his South American genuses. *Itylos* Hemming, *Paralycaeides,* and *Nabokovia* were all established to hold only a single species. Thus, one of the major thrusts of Bálint and Johnson's research, and one of the motives for the itineraries of both Johnson's 1991 expedition and Benyamini's journeys to the classic Bolivian localities like Lake Titicaca, Volcán Tacora, and Mt. Sajama was to discover what actual diversity those groups might represent.

Answers came quickly. Bálint's own discoveries in London very early laid to rest the concerns over *Itylos.* In addition to Hemming's chosen type species, *speciosa,* the genus contained at least three species: *luzhin, pnin,* and *mashenka,* named after the Russian title of Nabokov's first novel, translated into English as *Mary.* Though published in Russian in 1926, *Mashenka* did not appear in English until 1970; until then it was an unknown quantity for most non-Russian readers. Similarly, *mashenka* the butterfly had long sat unappreciated in the Natural History Museum in London as part of a long series of brown-colored Blues, but, as Bálint noted in his catalog, it had obviously never been turned upside down for a full read. In that position *mashenka* looked nothing like the Blues with which it had been placed.

On its underwing surfaces it sported fantastic silver-white lateral stripes, which were not precisely like those of any other Blue but were similar to those that typify *Madeleinea.* The butterfly Bálint found was missing its abdomen, as some old specimens do. Unable to carry out a dissection, he placed it in *Madeleinea* solely on the basis of the stripes. Later, however, Lamas found *mashenka* in nature, and dissection confirmed that it belonged to *Itylos,* another cornerstone in proving that the genus was taxonomically safe and sound as a diverse and broadly distributed South American entity. Likewise, the genus *Paralycaeides,* which Nabokov erected for Draudt's species *conspicua,* was filled out with other species, including *shade* and *hazelea,* and was rescued from the danger of sinking, as taxonomists say.

Bálint and Johnson laid to rest the analogous doubts regarding *Nabokovia* in a technical paper that they had drafted as they prepared the 1993 Wisconsin publications but that did not appear until 1994 in the *Annals* of the Hungarian Museum of Natural History. *Nabokovia*'s single known species had been *faga*, a dull brown, curiously tailed species named by the Frenchman Paul Dognin in 1895 and known only from Ecuador south to northern Chile. Had *faga* remained alone, *Nabokovia* might also have been doomed to disappear from the taxonomic map. But Bálint and Johnson found a second species among Peña and Herrera's unknowns, collected by Rudolfo Wagenknecht in 1952 along the Totoralillo coast in what was then south Huasco Province, Chile. They named this species *ada*, after the heroine of Nabokov's novel of the same name, who was a formidable lepidopterist herself. Later Lamas discovered additional new species of *Nabokovia* in Peru, which he and Bálint named from sources other than Nabokov's life and works, the last of them as late as 1998.

By the end of Bálint and Johnson's comprehensive study, one new genus — *Polytheclus* — had been added to Nabokov's Andean classification and two of the seven genuses named by Nabokov himself had been invalidated and replaced by others, which are now officially *Nabokovia* and *Madeleinea*. Nabokov missed *Polytheclus* only because he lacked specimens to examine. As for the two others, he erred in the former because he lacked the pertinent literature and in the latter because of the enforcement of a retroactive rule that he could not have foreseen, both technicalities. Moreover, had he made the effort during his lifetime, he would have had the right to rename both *Nabokovia* and *Madeleinea*. As for scientific judgment, Bálint and Johnson saw little or nothing to alter. By any measure Nabokov's classification was a remarkable achievement given the time and circumstances under which he worked.

As should be clear by now, however, there is a certain element of subjectivity in taxonomy, and in February of 1993, twenty-eight days before the appearance of Bálint and Johnson's first extensive papers in the United States, a radically different view of Nabokov's Latin American Blues was published in Europe, one that introduced no fewer than five generic changes in his work. The sudden appearance of two competing nomenclatures for Latin American Blues after a lapse of fifty years took the small world of Lepidoptera systematics by surprise and threw a shadow of doubt on Nabokov's ultimate legacy.

12 ⟳

The Race to Name Nabokov's Blues

> Entomologists are the most gentle people on earth — until a taxonomic
> problem crops up; it then transforms them into tigers.
>
> — *Letter to Michael Walter, 1971*

FOR BETTER OR WORSE, as Nabokov explicitly recognized in his list
of the joys of lepidoptery, competition is as intrinsic to science as it is
to any other human endeavor. In fact, it is probably a necessary condition for continued discovery and advancement. The history of science
and exploration is peppered with spectacular, sometimes bitter rivalries. In
1909 Admiral Robert Peary, having been the first Western explorer to reach
the North Pole, had to defend his achievement against the rival claims of
Frederick Cook, who maintained he'd reached the pole a year earlier.
When the Royal Geographical Society demanded of each man that he submit his astronomical readings (presumably taken at the pole) for scrutiny,
it became obvious that Cook was a fraud; more recently, doubt has been cast
on Peary's claim as well. A few years later Roald Amundsen and Robert
Falcon Scott raced to be the first to the South Pole. Scott reached the goal
nineteen days after Amundsen and perished just a few miles from safety
on his way back. For decades climbers competed to ascend the world's
highest mountain, 29,028-foot Mt. Everest, until, in 1953, it was conquered
by New Zealand's Edmund Hillary and his Sherpa guide Tenzing Norgay.
But even Hillary's record is not certain. In May 1999 climbers discovered
the body of Sir George Mallory partially buried in snow at 27,000 feet, on
the Tibetan side of Everest. Mallory, who when asked why he would climb
Everest famously quipped, "Because it is there," disappeared in his summit
attempt in 1924. Some now believe from the evidence that he may have
succeeded, and died in a night storm on his way back down.

Races for biological discovery during the Age of Exploration became no less legendary, bestowing fame and fortune on some — like Baron Alexander von Humboldt, Sir Joseph Banks, and Charles Darwin — and claiming the lives of others. After two famous expeditions to the South Seas, Captain James Cook was killed by natives in Hawaii. John Hanning Speke, the British explorer and adventurer, was found shot to death on the very day he was to defend before British university colleagues his claims of having discovered the source of the Nile, at Lake Victoria.

In the nineteenth century's tumultuous era of dinosaur discoveries across the American West, hired hands of the competing pioneer paleontologists Othniel Charles Marsh and Edward Drinker Cope exchanged fisticuffs, and some say even carbine shots, over their rival finds in areas of Wyoming and Colorado that became famous as Como Bluff and the Robber's Roost.

Consistent with its public reputation as a relatively placid pursuit, butterfly collecting, whether practiced as specialized science or as quaint preoccupation, has never attained these violent extremes. A popular "Far Side" cartoon by the humorist Gary Larson depicts an effervescent lepidopterist bragging of his prize new catch. Wined and dined by jealous colleagues into a drunken stupor, he is then mugged and summarily relieved of his specimen. The cartoon is fantasy, of course, but it reveals Larson's insight into the worst impulses that taxonomic competition can engender. For lepidoptery has certainly had its share of bitter rivalries, simmering feuds, and disputes over the custodianship of specimens and the ownership of names. Moreover, particularly in the tropics, vigorous commercial collecting was long part of the heritage behind the great museums, and specimens of rare or unknown species commanded exorbitant prices. Since even today many butterflies are valuable commercially as well as scientifically, outright theft, particularly from museum collections, has been an enduring problem.

The world's most notorious butterfly thief was no common hoodlum but one of the field's elite, the nineteenth-century lepidopterist Ferdinand Heinrich Herman Strecker, author of classic works like *Butterflies and Moths of North America* (1878). Strecker was a familiar sight in the museums of this country, decked out in the best of clothes and a tall top hat. Inside, the hat was fitted with a false top equipped with a cork pad into which he pinned the prize specimens of some of his competitors. After Strecker's death, when his collection was obtained by the Field Museum of Natural History in Chicago, any number of American collectors claimed to see missing specimens of theirs there.

Strecker has his modern successors. Among others Nabokov's mentor, William P. Comstock, was a victim. Specimens of a new and rare species reported in print in 1941 but not officially named disappeared from the American Museum of Natural History in New York soon afterward. Fifty years later Kurt Johnson and David Spencer Smith of Oxford University gave the species a name so its one remaining female could gain the protection of New York's closely monitored Type Collection.

In most cases the museums involved have preferred to keep such episodes quiet, perhaps to avoid embarrassment, perhaps in fear of copy-cat crimes. But sometimes local authorities believe the publicity of a prosecution may prevent similar abuses. In the mid-1980s, officials at the Natural History Museum in Los Angeles noticed that a number of conspicuously collectible insect specimens were missing and increased security measures. In 1987 a twenty-year-old amateur entomologist from El Segundo, California, a frequent visitor to the entomological collections, was stopped at the exit with more than $500 worth of museum property, mostly specimens from the research collections with a high market value because of their rarity or desirability to private collectors. (Specimens included a $300 Longhorn beetle and a very rare Paradise Birdwing butterfly worth some $75.) Later that year the collector pleaded guilty to misdemeanor theft and was sentenced to twenty-four months of summary probation and ordered to pay a fine of $150 and perform a hundred hours of community service.

Early in the history of butterfly larceny, the motives of the thieves could be based on a desire for scientific recognition, as in Strecker's case, but most theft today is aimed at profit in the commercial market for rare species. This is also true in the growing field of butterfly poaching, the capture of protected insects for commercial sale, often in American national or state parks. Two recent and well-publicized cases, one involving three men in California in 1995 and another an Italian collector in 1997, have focused attention on what has apparently become a minor industry. (In an article in *Outdoor* magazine, one of the men accused in the 1995 case was quoted as saying that he had chosen not to study entomology formally, believing that doing so would spoil the enjoyment of lepidoptery. "I had seen enough entomologists driving rusty old cars," he said. "Very few people are able to make a living in this profession.")

In contrast, most lepidopterological controversies stop well short of criminality. Unsurprisingly, many revolve around disputes over authorship and discovery. The very conventions of taxonomy, institutionalized in the Code, encourage rivalry by recognizing the validity of names published first. This has been true in every era of lepidoptery, and there is a wonderful passage in Nabokov's novel *The Gift* reflecting the frustrations that naturally arose. Konstantin Godunov-Cherdynstev has come home to St. Petersburg from Siberia with a new species of moth, only to find, on the first day after his return, while on a walk with his wife and son, Fyodor, the exact same species in the garden near his house. But the coincidence doesn't stop there, because a few days later Fyodor's father "learned that this new moth had just been described from St. Petersburg specimens by a fellow scientist, and Fyodor cried all night long: they had beaten Father to it!"

Under this inexorable law of priority, the temptation to rush to tag one's name onto something first — a somewhat discreditable practice known in lepidoptery as scooping — has been irresistible to many taxonomists. In some particularly confusing cases, before the International Commission for Zoological Nomenclature was inaugurated as the official last-resort arbiter, competing claims of priority had endured for years. Unsurprisingly, such disputed claims were the subjects of many of the first binding opinions issued by the commission when it began convening in the early 1940s.

One of the commission's early cases, in fact, involved Blue butterflies and reached back to 1807, when Johann Christian Fabricius named the original genus *Lycaena,* into which nearly all the known Blues later associated with Nabokov were first placed. Following the method of binomial nomenclature originated by Carolus Linnaeus, Fabricius produced a now-famous work called *Systema Glossatorum.* However, at the time it was published as part of a larger work by another author, Johann Carl Wilhelm Illiger, entitled "Die neueste Gattungs-Eintheilung der Schmetterlinge aus den Linnéischen Gattungen *Papilio* und *Sphinx.*" For nearly 150 years the question of who deserved credit for the names in Fabricius's contribution to Illiger's work perplexed taxonomists and bibliographers. It created an almost unbelievably hostile rivalry among the followers of both taxonomists. Was it *Lycaena* Fabricius or *Lycaena* Illiger? Each group accused the other's champion of out-and-out plagiarism.

When the commission published its "Official List of Works Approved as Available for Zoological Nomenclature, for the year 1958," authorship of the names was credited to Fabricius and the matter finally laid to rest. As a result, while nearly every lepidopterist has heard of Fabricius, few today can recall Illiger's name. It is an interesting illustration of how a lasting reputation is more easily built on a foundation of names above the species level. In Nabokov's case, because it dealt with organization at the genus level, his ultimate legacy in lepidoptery arguably hung on the eventual reputation of "Notes on Neotropical Plebejinae."

The idea that Nabokov's group — Nabokov's Blues — was one gap that could be plugged in the Latin American biodiversity crisis brought lepidopterists from eight countries to work together on the project. In 1991, however, when Zsolt Bálint was working on the Blues at the Natural History Museum in London, he had the first inkling that another researcher was working independently on Latin American Blues. Bálint had been compiling data on the museum's Blues, preparing a working list of the material there to share with Bernard D'Abrera, a noted Australian lepidopterist and photographer who had, with the cooperation of the museum, been publishing a series of picture books of butterflies in its collections. As Bálint went through the collections of Latin American Blues to be sure D'Abrera didn't miss any, he began noticing specimens whose lack of abdomens suggested someone had been dissecting them.

When he asked the curator, Phillip Ackery, about this, Bálint learned that Emilio Balletto of the University of Turin in Italy had also spent some time looking at the Latin American Blues. There was a record of a loan returned to the museum by Balletto, but since he had not attached labels, the collections contained no indication of what material he had studied. At least initially, since the matter seemed to have little to do with his catalog, Bálint let it drop. It was to come up again, however, when he contacted Kurt Johnson about broadening his plan to complete the study of Nabokov's Latin American Blues.

Bálint, of course, learned that Chile's premier lepidopterists, José Herrera and Luis Peña, had been sending their Chilean Blues to Kurt Johnson for identification. In their search for someone to turn to concerning South American Blues, Balletto's name had somehow never come up. Instead, due most probably to Herrera's already working with Johnson on Chilean Hairstreaks and Peña's long-term associate position with the American Museum of Natural History, they had turned to Johnson. Only in early 1991, when Johnson first received Patagonian Hairstreaks from Arthur Shapiro and informed him of the new research on South American Blues, did Johnson and Bálint learn that Shapiro had previously been sending his Argentine Blues to Balletto. The effort to study Nabokov's Blues organized in New York and Budapest had put Shapiro in a quandary. Would he continue to send his Blues to Balletto or turn to this new group, which, because of its international composition, appeared finally to have all the ingredients necessary for a complete and thorough study of the Latin American Polyommatini?

Shapiro decided to help Bálint and informed Balletto of his decision. Having thus learned of the whereabouts of Shapiro's early Patagonian catches of Blues, Bálint first wrote to Balletto in 1991 inquiring about the specimens and inviting the Italian lepidopterist to consider joining the other scientists in the larger study. He received no reply. In late 1992, his catalog completed and having submitted papers coauthored with Johnson on the Peña and Herrera material, Bálint wrote his Italian colleague again. This time he offered an account of the studies on Nabokov's Blues that he and Johnson had submitted for publication and suggested that since he, Johnson, and Balletto had all received material from Shapiro, they might cooperate in the future.

Now Balletto replied, in English: "Prof. Shapiro's Andean and Chilean materials have been studied completely, for what I can judge, and I have had a paper in the press, also dealing with a few other South American groups." Although Balletto was somewhat imprecise about his own studies, it seemed clear that it was suddenly too late to stave off an unexpected clash of papers, already submitted and simply waiting to see which would appear first.

There was a scientific danger in such a predicament. As Nabokov's own work had shown so well, taxonomic conclusions can vary depending on factors such as sample size and the makeup of samples and of specific specimens studied. It was not so much a question of the competition — which is healthy to science — but of the confusion that might result from two very different sets of results. Indeed, with none of the authors able to control the publication dates of their papers, the major misfortune of competing published nomenclatures for Nabokov's Blues occurred in February 1993. Just twenty-eight days before Bálint and Johnson's first volume of publications came out in the United States, a short paper on Latin American Blues by Balletto appeared in the *Bulletin of the Italian Entomological Society,* published in Genoa. It was entitled "On Some New Genus-Group and Species-Group Names of Andean Polyommatini." On March 28, 1993, Bálint and Johnson's studies of Peña and Herrera's Blues, their evaluation of the Hairstreak-like Blues Nabokov had been unable to locate, and the first edition of Bálint's extensive catalog of Latin American Blues also appeared in print.

Under the conventions of the Code, the major implication of Balletto's Genoa publication was that any valid taxonomic names he published would become the official ones by the law of priority. Depending on one's point of view, either Balletto had prevented being scooped by Bálint and Johnson, or Bálint and Johnson had been scooped by Balletto. Bálint and Johnson's work, however, was much longer, and dealt with many groups of Blues that Balletto had never seen, so what had happened was really less a scoop than an inopportunely timed duplication of data subsets.

In fact, rather than being a question of who had scooped whom, the situation simply reflected the general neglect into which the Latin American Blues had fallen. These two early 1993 publications combined did not come close to covering all Nabokov's Latin American Blues; this was the group of butterflies that Henri Descimon had feared would take the lifetimes of several scientists to complete. Monopolizing the remaining undiscovered Latin American Blues after Nabokov would have been an impossibility; there were far too many for any single worker to study or name.

It was not as if people did not suggest a scoop, however. In fact, Balletto wrote to Johnson shortly after the competing papers appeared, clearly expressing this view. As the elder of the scientists involved, he felt it was appropriate that his results be published first, and he was quite satisfied that they had been. Yet a question remained concerning Shapiro's specimens. Balletto's letter to Bálint had stated that the study of Shapiro's material was complete. But although Shapiro had been acknowledged in Balletto's paper, not a single one of his specimens had been listed. Balletto had also credited his assistants for his dissections and drawings. Such methods led Bálint to conjecture that the taxonomist had been in a great rush.

In any case, Johnson replied to Balletto that, although the nearly simultaneous publication would cause complications according to the international Code, there was really no argument about who had published first. This was simply a fact of life. He and Bálint would be going on to a much larger set of studies of the remaining Latin American Blues, and the problems of these first missteps would either be worked out in time or not. To his younger associate, Bálint, Johnson offered the comfort that at least someone in the rapidly shrinking world of lepidoptery still had access to a bevy of assistants. Balletto was a distinguished European lepidopterist and a leader in conservation causes; the collision had been unfortunate but would not happen again. It was unlikely, Johnson suggested (and he turned out to be right) that, having worked almost solely from the European museum specimens available to him, Balletto would go on with further studies of Latin American Blues.

Nevertheless, the sudden appearance of competing nomenclatures for Neotropical Blues after a lapse of fifty years in scientific work in this area caused a stir in the small world of Lepidoptera systematics. In light of the international Code, the taxonomic questions were major. The difficulties with the near-simultaneous publications by Balletto and Bálint and Johnson were to prove profound — not only for the study of the Latin American Blues but for the scientific legacy of Vladimir Nabokov.

In sum, this is what Balletto did. Working from a sample of fewer than ten species, and specifically listing only some dozen study specimens, he proposed five significant revisions at the genus level to Nabokov's original taxonomy. In contrast, Bálint and Johnson had examined more than fifty species and cited hundreds of specimens and dissections. From this large data set they recognized only two generic changes from those identified by Nabokov, and these were based only on technicalities the Code had introduced after Nabokov's 1945 work.

Balletto proposed splitting Nabokov's *Paralycaeides* into two genuses, each with only a single species. Bálint and Johnson considered these species to be each other's closest relatives within the single genus. How could each be put in a separate genus?

Balletto proposed splitting Nabokov's *Pseudolucia* into four genuses. One would retain the name *Pseudolucia,* two would each contain a single species, and the fourth would hold a few species that Nabokov, having seen no specimens, had speculated were most likely a species group under his original name. Bálint and Johnson noted that Balletto had drawn his conclusions from examining only nine of the then-known twenty-four species of *Pseudolucia.* They suggested that he had recognized generic gaps between species that simply didn't exist when you considered the larger sample. Also, because Balletto had been unable to secure type specimens, two of his critical identifications in new genuses were incorrect, and one of his new species was not new at all.

For the genus Nabokov had mistakenly called *Itylos* in 1945, Balletto proposed the new name *Nivalis.* Bálint, in his 1993 catalog, had proposed the name *Madeleinea* for the same group. And for the real *Itylos,* which Nabokov had called *Parachilades,* Balletto proposed two genuses, the new one to contain a single new species, the same butterfly to which Bálint had given the Nabokovian name *Itylos luzhin*. Here again Bálint and Johnson suggested Balletto was seeing genus gaps that did not exist — *Itylos* had not just two species but upwards of a half dozen, all waiting to be named from collections in South America.

Last, simultaneous with Bálint and Johnson's naming of the Hairstreak-like Blues, Balletto added his own name, not as an independent genus but as a subgenus of *Nabokovia* (just as Nabokov had suggested in his foot-notes). Here, however, both Balletto and Nabokov, who had seen no spec-imens, were wrong. Balletto's name, *Eldoradina,* was elevated to genus status by Bálint and Johnson and recognized by them as replacing, by pri-ority, their own name for these spectacularly colored Blues, *Polytheclus.*

On the most superficial level these disagreements can be understood as a basic conflict between lumpers, taxonomists who are temperamentally inclined to distinguish relatively few groups as genuses, and splitters, who happily admit more. Balletto with his new genuses, many containing only a single species, was the splitter, while Bálint and Johnson, following the lead of Nabokov himself, were (relatively speaking) lumpers.

There were some delicious ironies in this situation, for Johnson, certainly, but more important for the legacy of Vladimir Nabokov. Among some of his colleagues Johnson was known as a splitter, so in a way he was amused to see his confirmation of Nabokov's work challenged on the ground that his splitting hadn't gone far enough. No doubt Nabokov, who also had a reputation as a splitter, would have felt the same way. In his lifetime a joke was current that he wanted to see butterflies declared a separate phylum; this is lepidopterist humor to suggest that Nabokov was an extreme split-ter. Similarly, in 1995 when Charles Remington discussed Nabokov's scien-tific legacy for *The Garland Companion to Vladimir Nabokov,* he realized that insufficient follow-up work had been done on "Notes on Neotropical Plebejinae" to allow meaningful evaluation. But he suggested that it would eventually hinge on whether Nabokov's "elevating traditional subgeneric units to full genera" would be confirmed by subsequent study. Like most of Nabokov's contemporaries, Remington would have been astonished to learn that even as he was composing his *Garland Companion* contribu-tion, a respected authority was undermining Nabokov's classification on the grounds that he had been too much the lumper.

In principle, Nabokov would have felt some sympathy for Balletto's penchant for splitting. He realized better than many of his contempo-raries that splitting — the tendency to divide organisms into ever-smaller groups — is in some ways a natural consequence of intimate knowledge of those organisms. The more one examines a group of organisms, the more distinctions one is likely to see. At the same time Nabokov was also aware that genuses, and most groups with the exception of biological species, are arbitrary constructs. In general he was concerned less about what label was attached to his groups of related butterflies than about the recognition of the evolutionary relationships he was trying to establish. "Views may differ in regard to the hierarchic element in the classification I adopt," he once wrote, "but no one has questioned so far the fact of the structural relationship and phylogenetic circumstances I mean it to reflect."

Nevertheless, there were serious implications in Balletto's classification for Nabokov's eventual place in lepidoptery. At bottom Bálint and Johnson's changes to Nabokov's taxonomy for the Latin American Blues were technicalities necessitated by the introduction of the Code and did not reflect badly on Nabokov's skill as a taxonomist. Balletto's revisions, by contrast, clearly questioned Nabokov's analytical judgments.

Although there was still much work to be done on the groups Nabokov had pioneered, by 1993 two major questions had suddenly arisen. Would the five genuses he had employed for the South American Blues (six if one included *Echinargus,* which also had representatives outside the continent) be upheld as scientifically sound, or would they be contradicted by Balletto's proposed new schema? And would the new species names Bálint and Johnson had created from characters in Nabokov's life and writings survive, or would they be replaced as well?

The second question, albeit scientifically superficial, was significant as a professional homage to Nabokov's work and a recognition of its quality. While a large percentage of the new species names proposed by Bálint and Johnson were based on Nabokov's life or writings, Balletto's proposed names were all derived from distinctive traits of the butterflies themselves or from the surnames of various of his scientific colleagues. That is a time-honored and perfectly conventional way of naming new species, but both Bálint and Johnson had come to see their own names as a justified tribute to Nabokov and his work.

Since Balletto's names, all else being equal, would be validated by the law of priority, much of Nabokov's classification was in danger of being supplanted. The only thing likely to prevent this would be scientific or technical errors in Balletto's work blatant enough to prevent its adoption by other taxonomists. Among many specialists on butterflies and taxonomy in early 1993, questions on these matters were circulating rapidly, in letters, personal discussions, and taxonomic meetings. The world of Nabokov's

Blues, an unregarded backwater for some fifty years, was suddenly alive with controversy. Fortunately, the matter was to receive almost immediate attention in the professional literature. An official list of Neotropical butterflies was being prepared by the Association for Tropical Lepidoptera, and the editor that organization had chosen, Gerardo Lamas, could be relied upon to resolve the matter to the satisfaction of most lepidopterists. If not, the international commission could be a court of last resort.

As for the sections of Balletto's work that could immediately be evaluated according to the Code, his valid species names clearly took priority over those proposed twenty-eight days later by Bálint and Johnson. By the law of priority *argentina* Balletto superseded *sirin* Bálint (named for Nabokov's Russian nom de plume); *scintilla* Balletto had priority over *kinbote* Bálint and Johnson; *fumosus* Balletto had priority over *luzhin* Bálint, and *cyanea* Balletto superseded *cincinnatus* Bálint and Johnson. The remaining matter, a grittier one concerning the validity of Balletto's seven new genuses, hung in the balance, awaiting the decision of the broader scientific community.

That the attention of other capable lepidopterists would come soon gave Bálint, Johnson, and Dubi Benyamini considerable comfort. Their chief interest was pushing ahead with their studies of the remaining Nabokov's Blues, and for this purpose they had assembled an enormous amount of material from their multitude of sources.

As Bálint and Johnson worked with Benyamini throughout 1994 toward the next set of scientific publications on Nabokov's Blues, they turned their attention to coordinating their work with Lamas's list of South American butterflies. To avoid taxonomic confusion there would have to be agreement not only on the revised status of the old names but on the names for newly discovered species, which needed to be assigned in a timely way. Bálint also decided to prepare a full commentary on Balletto's positions in light of all the discoveries on Latin American Blues that had been made by the international team. This commentary could then be shared with other taxonomists who would need to weigh in with their eventual judgments. Bálint and Johnson had promised the Association for Tropical Lepidoptera's director, John Heppner, that they would come to an agreement with Lamas on the status of names. The eventual list would affect names at both the genus and species levels. As a part of this effort it would be important to resolve the problems caused by the duplicative publications of Balletto and the international team and move on.

Among lepidopterists there had been almost immediate controversy about the status of many of Balletto's names. This resulted not from the quality of his work but from certain technicalities within the Code. The central question hung on a point of language, which Nabokov the scientist, no less than Nabokov the novelist, would have relished. It concerned the validity of the new genuses Balletto proposed by splitting Nabokov's existing groups. Several taxonomists who contacted Bálint and Johnson noticed that some of Balletto's genus names were explicitly described as *adjectives.* The Code, in Article 11g, requires that genuses be *nouns,* whose grammatical gender is specifically declared masculine, feminine, or neuter. (This is so Latinate species names, which are gender-specific, can be made to conform.) Balletto's adjectival names clearly violated the letter of the Code. Ultimately, if there was no general agreement among taxonomists concerning the implications of these technical violations, the international commission could be asked to decide whether the names violating Article 11g would be ruled invalid. This is a time-consuming process that requires a formal application for a decision to "suppress" certain names. Such a proposal is authored by one or more taxonomists citing the ruling they seek and their reasons. It is then reviewed by a board after being sent out for comment from other experts. After a decision by the board, the final ruling is published by the commission (in English and French) and is considered authoritative. However, all this is unnecessary if lepidopterists can agree without an official arbiter and adopt their usage unanimously into their common published usage. This is, in fact, what had happened in the general ignorance of Nabokov's nomenclature for Blues after 1945.

To be fair, Johnson wondered if it was significant that Balletto had published in English and not Italian. Perhaps his error with respect to Article 11g had simply been the mistake of a nonnative speaker. The consideration of intent can be used to mitigate the rules of the Code, and Balletto's linguistic error may have been pardonable on those grounds. With this in mind Johnson wrote to Balletto, alerting him to the technical problem of Article 11g in case he might want to plead his case with Lamas. Balletto sent Johnson a reply, acknowledging his error and saying it had been inadvertent. Johnson forwarded the reply to Lamas for his consideration.

Lamas's reply amply illustrates the depth of technical and legalistic hairsplitting that is a central aspect of professional taxonomy. Indeed, the language of the Code itself suggests the exactness of taxonomic legality — it reads like a complicated book of recondite law. Interpreting the meaning of the various sections and articles of the Code is a process as fastidious as that applied by lawyers and judges to the statutes, sections, and clauses of the legal code.

First, Lamas addressed Balletto's action to replace a generic name attributed to Nabokov with one of his own. The language is typical of how taxonomists address issues to each other, in the jargon of their trade. "I believe," he wrote,

> Balletto is totally wrong in assuming that Nabokov (1945) created a junior primary homonym of *Itylos* Draudt. What Nabokov actually did was to designate a type-species for *Itylos* Draudt (*Cupido moza*), simply being unaware that Hemming (1929) had designated *Cupido speciosa* sixteen years before! It is just because of that ignorance that Nabokov proposed *Parachilades*, with *Lycaena titicaca* as type. . . . So *Parachilades* is a junior subjective synonym of *Itylos* Draudt, and the assemblage of species placed under *Itylos sensu* Nabokov (*not* a primary homonym!!!) did not have an available generic name until Balletto proposed *Nivalis* and Bálint *Madeleinea*. Balletto proposed *Nivalis* as a new replacement name for *Itylos sensu* Nabokov . . . , but that is erroneous because *Itylos sensu* Nabokov was *not* an already established name. *Nivalis* is properly a new scientific name (cf. Glossary in the Code, pp. 258–9). I certainly cannot accept the view expressed by Balletto. . . . For me, it is crystal clear that Nabokov simply committed the mistake of ignoring Hemming's 1929 type-selection: he did *not* introduce a junior homonym.

In the complex thicket of this language is the clear opinion that Balletto's actions were invalid. Then Lamas turned to the status of names that Balletto had explicitly etymologized as adjectives. "It doesn't matter what he *meant* to do," Lamas wrote, "but what he *did*. The Code refers to an adjective used as a substantive in the genitive case . . . as an acceptable specific name, not generic. Strictly speaking, to me there is no evidence at all in Balletto's paper that the names . . . should be considered . . . as nouns in the nominative singular, as mandated (by Art. 11g and further recommended by Appendix D4) of the Code.

"Now, to be honest," he continued, "I believe all this is just mere nomenclatorial hair-splitting. I don't care much if either *Nivalis* or *Madeleinea* are used for *koa* and relatives by others, but as long as the present Code is extant, I'll follow its rules, and will use *Madeleinea* Bálint."

Thus, Bálint's name for Nabokov's *Itylos* got the nod in light of the Code, and the butterflies of Nabokov's *Itylos* became known as the genus *Madeleinea*. Because of Lamas's application of Article 11g of the Code, when the list of Latin American butterflies sponsored by the Association for Tropical Lepidoptera is published, Nabokov's genuses will not be superseded by the larger number proposed by Balletto. The majority of the Nabokovian names proposed by Bálint and Johnson will survive. It is a fitting irony that the fate of those names, and of much of Nabokov's seminal taxonomy for Latin American Blue butterflies, was ultimately decided on a point of grammar.

However, this would not have prevented Balletto, or someone else, from simply republishing Balletto's genuses with new names in the nominative. To forestall this possibility Bálint formally published arguments concerning the Code and Balletto's names in 1995. This paper, "A Review of Recent Literature and Taxonomic Synonymy in the Neotropical Polyommatinae," included not only Lamas's views of the relevance of Article 11g but assessments that Bálint and other taxonomists had made of Balletto's highly split nomenclature based on many other taxonomic criteria. In their view not only had Balletto's small sample led him to recognize generic gaps where none existed but his genuses were sometimes so finely drawn that they required males and females of the same species to be placed in separate genuses. Nabokov could have made the same errors in 1945 with his sample of barely 120 specimens, but his acumen with anatomy and his conservative sense of nomenclature saved him from that fate.

Taxonomists use the phrase "a good eye" in speaking of early researchers whose care and discrimination allowed them, even at a time of relatively unsophisticated methods of classification, to recognize taxonomic distinctions between groups of organisms that are eventually confirmed by more advanced methods. Nabokov possessed such an eye, and his strict adherence to anatomy in distinguishing taxonomic characteristics further reinforced his ability to recognize what scientists now call natural groups, that is, actual relatives. His good eye had brought him to a level of taxonomic sophistication beyond that of many of his contemporaries, but in a sense it also made it easier for his work to be overlooked or misunderstood by those who weren't disposed to look as deeply.

In the context of the more than eighty species of South American Blues now known, Nabokov's six genuses for the region are a marvel of economy. It is the extent of their diversity, geographic distributions, and unique taxonomic characters that distinguishes Nabokov's work from the maudlin level of simple, anecdotal retrospective assessment of whether his taxonomy was good or bad. It is the breadth of the groups he originally recognized and named, and their significance to major biological questions, that ends up making his Blues "big science."

13 ✑

Literature and Lepidoptera

Does there not exist a high ridge where the mountainside of "scientific"
knowledge joins the opposite slope of "artistic" imagination?
— *The New York Times Book Review, December 28, 1952*

I N RETROSPECT it was inevitable that the Nabokov project would
eventually catch the attention of literary scholars, although none of
the scientists involved anticipated anything of the sort in the early
stages of their work. When Warren Whitaker, the lawyer who had proposed so many of the project's Nabokovian species names, saw the first
published results in 1993, he suggested that the literary community be
clued in on what was going on. The eventual result was a 1996 article about
Nabokov and his Latin American Blues in the journal *Nabokov Studies*,
written by Johnson, Whitaker, and Bálint. D. Barton Johnson, an editor of
the journal and the man who had named *Pseudolucia tamara*, was interested in organizing literary scholars to participate in choosing additional
Nabokovian names for new butterflies, and he formed a committee of
the International Vladimir Nabokov Society for the purpose. Since then
Johnson and his successor as the editor of *Nabokov Studies*, Zoran Kuzmanovich, along with Brian Boyd, Stephen Jan Parker, Simon Karlinsky,
Dieter E. Zimmer, and Ellendea Proffer, have suggested names.

In the meantime, however, scholars like Boyd and Zimmer had learned
about the project independently and had begun to consult with Johnson
on their own books relating to Nabokov's Lepidoptera. Zimmer is the author of *A Guide to Nabokov's Butterflies and Moths*, a reference manual on
many aspects of Nabokov's lepidoptery but focusing on allusions in
literature. Boyd, along with Robert Michael Pyle, the lepidopterist who

founded the Xerces Society, was editing *Nabokov's Butterflies,* a collection of Nabokov's writings on Lepidoptera, from formal science to fiction, college lectures to personal correspondence. Both books reflected the increasing appreciation of Nabokov's science in the 1990s, and both Boyd and Zimmer were delighted to find a scientific contact who was not only a lepidopterist but an expert on Blue butterflies and had closely studied Nabokov's formal papers.

The specialist assessment of his lepidoptery is important to Nabokov scholars for a number of reasons beyond simple biographical accuracy. Above all it inevitably reflects on the tenor of the many references to butterflies and lepidoptery in his fiction. Nabokov engaged the subject as a complex literary element, so pervasive that it is a recognizable personal stamp, not unlike the fanciful little butterflies he was fond of inscribing in copies of his works presented to those near him. Nabokov wrote a great deal of poetry involving Lepidoptera, particularly in his earlier years but later in life too. Butterflies appear in one way or another in all his novels and many of his other works, with particularly strong motifs in *Speak, Memory,* the short story "The Aurelian," and the novels *The Gift* and *Ada.* Far from a clever but facile literary affectation, the lepidoptery of Nabokov the gifted scientist reflects a deeper understanding of the natural world by Nabokov the writer. His scientific acumen makes a difference in the way the informed reader approaches his literature.

In describing Nabokov's use of butterflies in his fiction, one should first put the matter in this perspective: lepidoptery, while pervasive, is by no means an overriding motif. It is more prominent than another of Nabokov's loves, chess, but it is of an entirely different order from his true principal themes — sacred and profane love, isolation, exile, tyranny, and marital and familial relationships. There are hints, too, that Nabokov took pains to keep lepidoptery in its place. While he was working on *King, Queen, Knave* in 1928, he wrote to his mother saying that he found it boring without any Russian characters and that he was tempted to introduce a lepidopterist. He gave in to that impulse only forty years later, when he revised the novel in English. But the letter suggests that he saw lepidoptery in some ways as a facile way out of difficulties and that he wanted to avoid employing it unthinkingly. (His early biographer Andrew Field's apparent mistranslation of this letter introduces such an error in the matter of Nabokov's entomological career that it is worth mentioning here: he took the letter to mean that Nabokov was so discouraged by the writing that he was contemplating giving up literature for lepidoptery, which was never the case.)

Nabokov was famously scrupulous about the accuracy and historical coherence of the elements that went into his fiction. In this sense lepidoptery offered him a valuable literary palette, always available, the Nabokovian equivalent of "writing what you know." But just as he refused to overuse it, Nabokov took pains to vary his presentation of lepidoptery, in both prose and poetry, throughout his career. It never became a predictable mannerism. Perhaps, too, he believed he was filling a gap. In *Speak, Memory,* he lamented that he could find few fine images of butterflies in Russian or English poetry.

Beyond that, because of the strength of two prevalent literary traditions, both of which thrive today, it is necessary to characterize Nabokov's use of Lepidoptera by what it is not, or usually not. These conventions make of insects something unsettling, ominous, and sinister, a one-dimensional use to which entomology has traditionally, almost reflexively, been put by most writers. First, entomological motifs are often used to suggest erotic attraction, lust, and reproduction, as in A. S. Byatt's novella *Morpho Eugenia,* the basis for the movie *Angels and Insects.* Otherwise an interest in insects, often linked to obsessive-compulsive collecting, is seen mostly as evidence of homicidal psychosis, as books and films from *The Silence of the Lambs* to John Fowles's novel *The Collector* attest. Nabokov was painfully aware of this tradition in his day. "Only Wells, Conan Doyle and Conrad have portrayed lepidopterists — all of them spies, or murderers or neurotics," he wrote in a letter to Harry Levin in 1953.

Nabokov, as we shall see, did not entirely reject either of these conventions. But in his writing the lepidopterist is never a stock character but always something more complex, an attitude that reflects in part the joyous associations of his childhood and his experiences in the real world of lepidoptery. As often as not it is majestic, benign, or a source of vital energy. This attitude is evident in all of *Speak, Memory,* for instance, and in much of *The Gift,* but for most people it remains a paradoxical literary stance, not easily assimilated. (It is amusing to think that Nabokov's exploitation of the motifs of chess, a hobby with far different popular associations, doesn't seem to perturb his readers unduly. No one asks, "Why the chess?")

The Gift, which was written between 1933 and early 1938 and has been quoted liberally throughout this book, is a good starting place to consider the scientific complexity in Nabokov's work. The second chapter of the novel is his greatest homage to lepidoptery, an extended portrait of the fictional Konstantin Godunov-Cherdyntsev, a turn-of-the-century Russian explorer of Central Asia, a legendary figure with much in common with

Alexander von Humboldt and the larger-than-life pioneers of lepidoptery. "Between 1885 and 1918," Nabokov wrote, "he covered an incredible amount of territory, making surveys of his route on a three-mile scale for a distance of many thousands of miles and forming astounding collections. . . . Tackling Asia in earnest he investigated Eastern Siberia, Altai, Fergana, the Pamirs, Western China, 'the islands of the Gobi Sea and its coasts,' Mongolia, and 'the incorrigible continent' of Tibet — and described his travels in precise, weighty words."

The tale is told through the eyes of the man's son, Fyodor, a Russian exile in Berlin, an aspiring poet and writer who learned lepidoptery from his father. (If the biographical detail sounds close to home, Nabokov insisted that he pictured himself, not his own father, in the guise of the elder Godunov-Cherdyntsev, as a kind of stand-in for the trip to Central Asia he had planned as a wealthy teenager, a dream destroyed by the Russian Revolution.) Nabokov based his portrait of the fictional Godunov-Cherdyntsev in large part on the celebrated Nikolay Przhevalsky, a real explorer-naturalist, decked him out with an impressive and authentic list of publications and career of travels, and, using his own thorough knowledge of natural history and lepidoptery, planted his fictional creation firmly in the real world of lepidoptery.

"Write to Avinov, to Verity," Fyodor's mother advises when she learns he has decided to compose his father's biography, "write to that German who used to visit us before the war, Benhaas? Banhaas? Write to Stuttgart, to London, to Tring, in Oxford, everywhere, *débrouille-toi* [see what you can do] because I know nothing of these matters and all these names merely sing in my ears, but how certain I am that you will manage, my darling."

The significance of some of the place-names is perhaps obvious by now. The personal names are those of real lepidopterists. Avinov is Andrey Avinoff, like Nabokov an aristocratic Russian who lost his extensive collection in 1917. He was an expert in Central Asian butterflies (an apt connection for Godunov-Cherdyntsev) who eventually became director of the Carnegie Museum in Pittsburgh. When Nabokov himself moved to America in 1941, Avinoff was among the first people he contacted. Verity is Ruggero Verity, an Italian physician and lepidopterist who in the early 1940s wrote *Le Farfalle diurne d'Italia (The Day-Flying Butterflies of Italy)*, a book that Nabokov called in 1969 "the greatest work on butterflies published in the last thirty years. . . . Owing to that sumptuous and exhaustive work the Italian butterflies are remarkably well known." Fyodor's mother couldn't quite come up with the name of Andreas Bang-Haas, senior partner in the renowned insect dealer firm Staudinger & Bang-Haas, Dresden-Blasewitz.

This is only a small taste of Nabokov's technique in fictional lepidoptery so evident in *The Gift*. Among the many other scientific treats in the novel are Fyodor's explanation of the entrancing biological wonders of lepidoptery as learned from his father, and a splendid re-creation of an exotic and heroic journey in search of butterflies that Brian Boyd has described as a voyage "through territory that in sheer wonder outdoes all previous literary landscapes — eerily strange and beautiful, but observed with the trained eye of the naturalist." In a smaller register are insights into such arcana as the paraphernalia of collecting and specimen mounting. Its texture is so rich that *The Gift* could in some ways serve as a commentary on the history of lepidoptery.

Yet Nabokov's intent, or at least his principal intent, was not to teach about butterflies. Rather, behind the mask of the lepidoptery his deeper theme is the elder Godunov-Cherdyntsev's obsession and its consequences for Fyodor, the real hero of the novel. To further his researches Godunov-Cherdyntsev left his bride and son on their own much of the time, instilling in each an emptiness that could not ultimately be filled. In a crucial scene the father's interminable absences and his refusal to take Fyodor on one of his journeys causes the son to burst into helpless tears. Godunov-Cherdyntsev's obsession seems literally to have destroyed him — he disappeared on his last journey. Whether he was alive or dead his family never learned, and Fyodor was left to struggle with the phantom hope that he might one day fling open the door and join their lives again. It was only when Fyodor reached adulthood that he came to suspect that Godunov-Cherdyntsev undertook his journeys out of a mysterious restlessness, "not so much to seek something as to flee something," and to realize what a toll his father's obsession had taken on his mother and himself. Part of the majesty of *The Gift* is how thoroughly an expansive and majestic treatment of the golden age of lepidoptery is made to serve Nabokov's larger artistic purposes.

On a different scale, there are similar motifs in Nabokov's 1930 short story "The Aurelian," about Paul Pilgram, the frustrated Berlin insect dealer and "first-class entomologist." Hans Rebel, the well-known Viennese lepidopterist, had named a moth for Pilgram, and Pilgram himself had published several descriptions. A bored shopkeeper, Pilgram sees his wife, through no obvious fault of her own, as part of the enforced dreariness of a life away from exploration and collecting. The couple were childless because Pilgram believed that "children would be merely a hindrance to the realization of what had been in his youth a delightfully exciting plan but had now gradually become a dark, passionate obsession." Before the end of the story, Pilgram not only is ready to abandon his wife to the burdens of their shop while he embarks on his long-dreamed-of expedition but fantasizes about splitting her head open with an ax. Yet his death by heart attack, and the apparent journey of his soul across all the exotic locales he had longed to explore, caps, as Brian Boyd has said, a wealth of perfectly blended themes: "the outwardly ordinary person who carries his special secret within; the excitement of discovery; the dream of perfect happiness, unattainable in this life; the terrible exclusiveness our dreams can have; and death, which will cut off all our dreams or perhaps make them come true."

Godunov-Cherdyntsev was much more accomplished than Pilgram, but the two share fundamental similarities. Along with Nabokov himself, both felt the strange power of lepidoptery — all three belonged to that special breed of dreamers who dream of things that are unintelligible to most people. Throughout his life Nabokov described his own interest in butterflies as an obsession, a mania, a sickness. It was mostly tongue-in-cheek, a habitual way of speaking. Yet perhaps his attitude was also a reflection of a kind of reverence toward the latent power of his second calling. Nabokov bore a professional admiration for Fyodor's father and respect for Pilgram's much more modest scientific attainments as well. But unlike their creator, for whom lepidoptery was an integral part of a joyous family, the two are overwhelmed by their passion.

In this sense the scientific motif — with its own internal complexities — is subsumed into the larger themes of Nabokov's work: the concern for the human being twisted into grotesque shape by an obsession of one kind or another, and the meaning of love between husband and wife and children and parents. These themes are so typically Nabokovian and so evident in both *The Gift* and "The Aurelian" that it seems strange that critics still feel they must probe deeper, to find that symbolic something behind mere butterflies, what Nabokov "really" meant.

One writer who has done so is Joann Karges, in her book *Nabokov's Lepidoptera: Genres and Genera*. Basing her interpretation of *The Gift* largely on the sexual activities of some of the Lepidoptera that brought Fyodor to tears as he thought of his father, she suggests that the real object of Godunov-Cherdyntsev's journeys to the East was to be with a second, clandestine family. Although Karges appreciated the profound importance of lepidoptery in Nabokov's work long before many others, she cannot bring herself to accept the power of butterflies as butterflies. Fyodor's mother, by contrast, learned early. On their honeymoon her husband became engrossed in the pursuit of an alluring specimen near the couple's resort and disappeared for so long that his bride feared he might be dead. When he finally returned his hat was gone and his jacket torn. "I expect you have already guessed what had happened," she explains years later to her son. "Thank God at least that he finally caught it after all — in his handkerchief, on a sheer cliff — if not he would have spent the night in the mountains, as he coolly explained to me."

Karges represents one end of a critical spectrum about the textual significance of butterflies in Nabokov's fiction. "Every Lepidoptera allusion, or trope," she writes, "and each named or unnamed species is distinctly purposeful to its text." In the same spirit the search for symbols — the desire to find some profounder generalized meaning behind mere insects — has been in the forefront of critical efforts by Karges and others to explain the butterflies in Nabokov's literature. Karges herself draws some general conclusions about butterflies of varying colors and their contexts: "Many of Nabokov's butterflies, particularly pale and white ones, carry the traditional ageless symbol of the *anima,* psyche, or soul," and "Nabokov's blue butterflies represent for the most part various degrees of ethereal happiness." Indeed, as we shall see, they sometimes do.

On several levels, though, whatever one makes of it, this is a general approach to interpretation that Nabokov himself always despised, and one that was alien to his artistic principles. In 1970, discussing his planned project "Butterflies in Art" with Alfred Appel, Jr., he said, "That in some cases the butterfly symbolizes something (e.g., Psyche) lies utterly outside my area of interest." He believed that the unrelenting pursuit of symbols, whether by critics or by his students at Cornell, was counterproductive and inimical to the understanding of literature. "Ask yourself if the symbol you have detected is not your own footprint," he wrote in a characteristic passage. John Shade, Nabokov's poet alter ego in *Pale Fire,* lists the failings he will not tolerate in his students' papers: "Not having read the required book. Having read it like an idiot. Looking in it for symbols: example: "The author uses the striking image *green leaves* because green is the symbol of happiness and frustration."

Another association made a certain kind of symbol anathema. In his own happy childhood and sublime concord with both his parents, Nabokov saw the complete refutation of Freud, the "Viennese quack," a favorite target of his derision. For similar reasons, and because he believed that as an author he was in despotic control of his characters and their actions, he hated interpretations of his work that relied heavily on notions of Freud's "standardized symbols" or subconscious associations.

"I happen to remember the essay by a young lady who attempted to find entomological symbols in my fiction," he told an interviewer. "The essay might have been amusing had she known something about Lepidoptera. Alas, she revealed complete ignorance and the muddle of terms she employed proved to be only jarring and absurd." The article, "Lolita Lepidoptera," written in 1960 by Diana Butler, found parallels between Humbert Humbert's passion for Lolita and Nabokov's hunt for the female of *Lycaeides sublivens,* one of his North American Blues, in southwestern Colorado. Privately, Nabokov called the piece "pretentious nonsense from beginning to end." He remained so annoyed that he appears to have tweaked its writer, disguised as the Roman goddess of hunting, years later in his novel *Ada.* There the title character invokes her old nature teacher, Krolik: "Knickerbockered, panama-hatted, lusting for his *babochka* [Russian for lepidopteron]. A passion, a sickness. What could Diana know about *that* chase?"

Influenced by such vehement expressions of distaste, some Nabokov commentators take a course opposite to Karges and maintain that butterflies bear little or no symbolic, representative, or interpretive force in his literature, an idea put most succinctly by Dieter E. Zimmer: "Butterflies are butterflies." In this view one of the greatest glories of Nabokov's use of lepidoptery in his writing is its unerring accuracy. Zimmer maintains that Nabokov would never have taken the trouble to match symbolic butterfly to context, rather, "thinking like a naturalist, he would have asked himself only what butterfly would be the right one in a given habitat, and what behavior it would display." Nabokov would never muddle his terms or hatch his butterflies out of season, or be guilty of the sort of error the uninformed were likely to commit. He once complained of Edgar Allan Poe's symbolic employment of the Death's-Head Moth: "Not only did he not visualize the Death's Head Moth, but he was also under the completely erroneous impression that it occurs in America."

But Karges was right not to take all of Nabokov's pronouncements even on this subject completely at face value. Nabokov is known for operating on several literary levels at once, for structuring his fiction in layers of meaning. It would be odd if butterflies were somehow sacrosanct, exempt from literary manipulation. As part of his multifaceted handling of Lepidoptera, Nabokov was perfectly capable of using butterflies and moths as what would ordinarily be called symbols. In an early story, "Christmas," the hatching of an Attacus moth that was part of a dead youth's collection clearly bears the resurrectional significance that is so easy to attach to metamorphosis. Toward the other end of his career, in *Ada,* an enraged Van Veen provokes a duel with a stranger. "At the moment his foot touched the pine-needle strewn earth of the forest road, a transparent white butterfly floated past, and with utter certainty Van knew that he had only a few minutes to live." He was mistaken; Nabokov, in his playful way, invalidated Van's ominous symbol. But this game can be played in reverse, as Joann Karges pointed out. Later in the novel, after a separation of twelve years, Van eagerly awaits a reunion with his lover, Ada, who has married Andrey Vinelander. In a pub near her hotel, Van noticed, "a dead and dry hummingbird moth lay on the window ledge of the lavatory. Thank goodness, symbols did not exist either in dreams or in the life in between." But this time the omen proves accurate, at least for the short run: Ada refuses to abandon Andrey for Van.

More strikingly, the nymphalid butterfly *Vanessa atalanta* (one of Nabokov's favorites — he was horrified that its noble vernacular name Red Admirable had been degraded to Red Admiral) appears in his work at a particularly ominous moment: in *Pale Fire* an exuberantly friendly specimen settles on the sleeve of John Shade as he walks up the garden path near his house on his way to meet a bullet meant for another man. Discussing the Red Admirable in an interview with Alfred Appel, Jr., in 1970, Nabokov noted that in northern Russia it was known as "the Butter-fly of Doom" because it was particularly plentiful in 1881, the year Czar Alexander II was assassinated, and because the markings on the underside of its wings seemed to bear the date 1881.

These are a few obvious examples. In addition to this sort of thing, there are many looser associations and suggestive juxtapositions in Nabo-kov's work that arguably rise at times to the level of the symbolic, some of the most memorable of them erotic. In *Speak, Memory* he recalls an ex-pedition with one of his tutors, a man he called Ordo, on which he dis-covered "two freshly emerged specimens of the Amur hawkmoth, rare in our region — lovely, velvety, purplish-gray creatures — in tranquil copula-tion, clinging with chinchilla-coated legs to the grass at the foot of the tree." Before the end of the paragraph Nabokov reveals that a flame had been kindled in poor Ordo: "I seem to remember a door ajar into a drawing room, and there, in the middle of the floor, Ordo, our Ordo, crouching on his knees and wringing his hands in front of my young, beautiful, and dumbfounded mother."

Nabokov also describes how on another occasion he followed a *Parnassius mnemosyne* — the tutelary butterfly of *Speak, Memory* — into some dense underbrush and came upon Polenka, a sweetheart, splashing naked with some other children in the ruins of an old bathhouse. Again, he says he once pedaled his bicycle through the fields near Vyra and near the river came upon the scattered clothes of peasant girls who romped naked in the water, "heeding me as little as if I were the discarnate carrier of my present reminiscences." Meanwhile, on the other side of the river, "a dense crowd of small, bright blue male butterflies that had been tippling on the rich, trampled mud and cow dung through which I trudged rose all together into the spangled air and settled again as soon as I had passed." The mildly erotic associations of these Blue butterflies are intensified in *Ada,* in which Ada and Van meet for their first assignation as lovers in a park, surrounded by clouds of them. (These are the same Iolas Blues, incidentally, that Nabokov saw threatened by the vintners in southern France.)

The question should not be whether Nabokov used butterflies as symbols — to use the word in a broad, non-technical sense — because at times he clearly did. The question is, whose symbols? It was the off-the-rack associations of butterflies in general that Nabokov viewed with distaste and consciously avoided in scientific as well as literary writing. In 1965 the lepidopterist William H. Howe sent him a copy of his fulsomely titled book *Our Butterflies and Moths: a True-to-Life Adventure into the Wonderland of the Butterfly World and Its Related Insect Kingdom as Seen Through Fact and Fancy, Fable and Folklore.* Nabokov was very impressed with Howe's painted illustrations but found the book objectionable in most other ways, as he explained to Howe in a letter. "I also cannot imagine," he wrote, "what or who induced you to insert all those stale anecdotes, pseudo-Indian legends and samples of third-rate poetry." Nabokov wanted no part of standard folkloric or "Freudian" symbols that took off on their own wings and flew out of the control of the all-powerful author. His own emblematic creatures, which reveal themselves only in his chosen contexts and under his careful direction, were quite another matter.

Yet, where even these associations can be found, they form only a part of Nabokov's fertile scientific repertory, and a fixation on the symbolism of butterflies is just more proof of the gulf of incomprehension between lovers of Lepidoptera and lovers of literature, a crevasse Nabokov could bridge easily but most others still cannot. Through the dwelling on symbols, as fascinating as they are, many other aspects of Nabokov's lepidoptery — even the epic journeys of Godunov-Cherdyntsev or the psychological complexities of Paul Pilgram — are given short shrift.

The same is true of Nabokov's use of lepidoptery in erotic contexts, which is at its most provocative and sexually suggestive in *Ada*, his most complex, ambitious, and most thoroughly playful, deliberately over-the-top novel. Published in 1969, *Ada* deals with some of Nabokov's favorite themes: the nature of love and time and personal morality. The setting is a bizarre world that is a disjunct version of our own, identical with the earth in physical geography but shaped by a divergent history. Consequently, its Lepidoptera too are an imaginative mixture of the real and the invented. The novel's main characters, the lifelong lovers Van and Ada Veen, are putative cousins, but they learn that they are in fact full brother and sister — Nabokov's well-known venture into incest. In typically Nabokovian fashion, though, incest is anything but the be-all and end-all of the novel, as it would be in the work of a more pedestrian author; it is rather, in large part, a metaphor for narcissistic self-absorption.

Ada is also a botanist and an entomologist ("I'm crazy about everything that crawls," she says), and it is largely through her that Nabokov introduces his varied butterfly motifs. On one plane entomology represents just a single facet of a brilliant polymath mind that is also thoroughly versed in literature and art. But unsurprisingly her own personality, including her strong sexual appetites, is reflected in her entomological interests. She is particularly interested in reproduction and the mating habits of butterflies and, at one point in her life, the nurturing of larvae. Her fondest childhood entomological dreams involved the creation of an elaborate larvarium, a place to rear caterpillars; as she matures she prefers to film adult butterflies.

Sex and butterflies are linked in many smaller, more specific ways in the novel, too. For instance, Ada loves the feel of various kinds of caterpillars. In a passage with comically prominent phallic symbolism, she laments, "I think Marina would stop scolding me for my hobby . . . if I could persuade her to overcome her old-fashioned squeamishness and place simultaneously on palm and pulse (the hand alone would not be roomy enough!) the noble larva of the Cattleya Hawkmoth (mauve shades of Monsieur Proust), a seven-inch-long colossus, flesh colored, with turquoise arabesques, rearing its hyacinth head in a stiff 'Sphinxian' attitude." (The Cattleya Hawkmoth is an invention, a taxonomic crossing of an orchid and a moth, or perhaps a reference to a putative food plant. But

Nabokov also called it the Odettian Sphinx, and Dieter E. Zimmer has pointed out that in Proust's *Swann's Way,* a Cattleya orchid is Odette's favorite flower, and that "to play Cattleya" becomes a private synonym for Swann and Odette's lovemaking.)

In another elaborately ribald joke, Nabokov used the name of one of his beloved butterflies to suggest the sexual specialty of one of Van's paramours, "a part-time model (you have seen her fondling a virile lipstick in Fellata ads), aptly nicknamed Swallowtail by the patrons of a Norfolk Broads floramor." The location of the sex club is also a reference to the last remaining haunts of the Swallowtail *Papilio machaon* in England.

In a different register, Van's reaction to catching a view between young Ada's legs, accidentally exposed as they climb a tree, is compared with that of someone watching "a moth's shocking metamorphosis."

This is all wonderful fun, as Nabokov intended. But, it is tempting to critics to belabor the significance of these and other butterfly motifs and to exaggerate what they "reveal" about Nabokov's lepidoptery. It is no secret, for instance, that *Ada* is much about sex; Nabokov was not using Lepidoptera to convey otherwise "hidden" themes in his novel. Rather, his profound knowledge of butterflies and moths was a minor motif to reinforce themes — in this case, sex and sexuality — that are in many ways obvious in reading the book, or that have been adequately highlighted in criticism that does not focus on Lepidoptera. It is significant that Brian Boyd, in his main discussion of the novel in his biography, does not feel it necessary to mention that Ada is an entomologist at all.

This is part of what Nabokov resented about superficial readers' banal, symbol-obsessed considerations of butterflies in his writing — the presumption, together with the inevitable Freudian smirk, of having found psychological "insight," usually pruriently discreditable, into the author's fascination with Lepidoptera. It is no doubt one of the reasons that Nabokov was distinctly reluctant to talk a great deal about the role butterflies played in his literature, since he knew what a field day writers would have with such trifles as a naïve character's realization that *insect* is an anagram of *incest.* In the meantime many other aspects of Lepidoptera in his literature would go unremarked.

The quotations that have been used throughout this book should go some way to suggest the thematic breadth of the lepidopterological motifs in Nabokov's non-scientific writings. For more specific examples of other facets of his technique, one might begin with the inherent ease with which he habitually applied brief metaphors or similes from lepidoptery to many aspects of his wider life, both informally and in literature. One of the most powerful of these, his words to his son shortly before his death about the butterfly of life, has already been discussed. But there are many other examples, both striking and charming, and they easily found a place in formal literature as well. After writing his first version of *Speak, Memory*, Nabokov adapted it into Russian; years later, in his English revision of the same work, he used his Russian version as a guide. As he explained in his foreword: "This re-Englishing of a Russian re-version of what had been an English re-telling of Russian memories in the first place, proved to be a diabolical task, but some consolation was given me by the thought that such multiple metamorphosis, familiar to butterflies, had not been tried by any human before."

Also in *Speak, Memory*, Nabokov worries about the letters his sweetheart, unaware that he and his family have been driven from Russia by the Bolsheviks, will keep sending to their old refuge in Crimea: "The sense of leaving Russia was totally eclipsed by the agonizing thought that Reds or no Reds, letters from Tamara would be still coming, miraculously needlessly, to southern Crimea, and would search there for a fugitive addressee, and weakly flap about like bewildered butterflies set loose in an alien zone, at the wrong altitude, among an unfamiliar flora." And in the 1999 Knopf edition of *Speak, Memory*, which contained an additional chapter, he meditated in the third person on his artistic strategy in the work:

> He is out to prove that his childhood contained, on a much reduced scale, the main components of his creative maturity; this, through the thin sheath of a ripe chrysalis one can see, in its small wing cases, the dawning of color and pattern, a miniature revelation of the butterfly that will soon emerge and let its flushed and diced wings expand to many times their pupal size.

All these examples are more poignant when the reader realizes that Nabokov was a serious lepidopterist, not just a novelist searching for a striking simile.

Not surprisingly, perhaps, when Nabokov the author enters his own narratives, as he sometimes does, he chooses the guise of a lepidopterist — a more substantial version of his authorial stamp or a ghostly shadow of the omniscient creator fallen across the page. In *Bend Sinister*, his World War II–era political tragedy-farce, Nabokov, speaking in the first person, eventually emerges as the omnipotent deity pulling the levers behind the fictional actions. At its conclusion the curtain is pulled back on the writer amid the literary drafts in his study, distracted by the twanging sound of moths striking against his window screen: "As I had thought, a big moth was clinging with furry feet to the netting, on the night's side; its marbled wings kept vibrating, its eyes glowed like two miniature coals. I had just time to make out its streamlined brownish-pink body and a twinned spot of color, and then it let go and swung back into the warm damp darkness." And the novel ends with a strangely haunting line: "Twang. A good night for mothing."

Similarly, in his revised version of *King, Queen, Knave,* published in 1968, Nabokov and Véra show up amid the proceedings, their marital happiness in marked contrast to the moral misery of the adulterers who are the story's main characters; the husband's avocation is revealed by his butterfly net, an accoutrement absent in the original Russian. ("Oh, it must be good sport," one character says when he realizes the Nabokov figure is a lepidopterist. "In fact, I think to have a passion for something is the greatest happiness on earth.")

Not that the lepidopterist character in such cases is always a hero. In *Pnin* the narrator, one Vladimir Vladimirovich, turns out to be a lepidopterist and an academic, as was Nabokov. But in his indifference to the suffering of the title character, he is a slightly warped and certainly more selfish and unfeeling version of the author.

As a final example, Nabokov wrote himself into a scene, never filmed, in the screenplay for Stanley Kubrick's *Lolita.* Humbert Humbert and Lolita are lost on a dirt road through a canyon. (Their car's radiator grill is plastered with dead butterflies.) Lolita spots Vladimir Nabokov, who has just caught a butterfly:

LOLITA: Ask that nut with the net over there.
HUMBERT: Is that a rare specimen?
NABOKOV: A specimen cannot be common or rare, it can only be poor or perfect.
HUMBERT: Could you direct me —
NABOKOV: You meant "rare species." This is a good specimen of a rather scarce subspecies.
HUMBERT: I see. Could you please tell me if this road leads to Dympleton?
NABOKOV: I haven't the vaguest idea. I saw some loggers (pointing) up there. They might know.

Sometimes, the intersection of lepidoptery and literature seems to be a sort of private Nabokovian joke, a cryptic adaptation of Nabokov's stamp, and nowhere more so than in *Lolita.* If, along with Nabokov, the reader dismisses the notion that Lolita is a little-girl version of a butterfly and

Humbert Humbert a monstrous lepidopterist, there are many delightfully amusing covert references to taxonomy and lepidoptery in the text, a number of which Nabokov pointed out to Alfred Appel for his *Annotated Lolita*.

They begin with the fictional author of the introduction to the novel, Nabokov's parody of academic sociology: the name is John Ray, Jr., a descendant, no doubt, of the well-known English systematist of the seventeenth century, a predecessor to Linnaeus. Within the story many incidental characters and places recall butterflies: Avis Chapman comes from Chapman's Hairstreak, whose full scientific name is *Callophrys avis* Chapman. Vanessa van Ness is just a doubling of the name of the beautiful nymphalid that Nabokov mentioned so often in his fiction. "Miss Phalen's name attracted me because *phalène* means moth in French," Nabokov told Appel. Edusa Gold, he said, was named for *Colias edusa,* an old appellation for the Clouded Yellow. Her sister, Electra Gold, was named for "a close ally" of that species, which Zsolt Bálint has suggested is *Colias electo.* Other names, Schmetterling and Falter, are simply German words for "butterfly." The little town of Lepingville is meant to suggest not leprosy, as one recent writer has it, but Nabokov's favorite sport.

No amount of ingenuity can make much more of this than what Nabokov himself said it was: a private mnemonic handle on his characters that provided him with great fun. He explained that other names in the novel, too, were borrowings or adaptations, in the Nabokovian mode, from other literary and cultural realms. (For the benefit of the butterfly stalkers, he also pointed out that there were fewer mentions of Lepidoptera in *Lolita* than of dogs and birds.) The allusion to the entomological term *nymph* in Nabokov's famous coinage *nymphet* was discussed in Chapter 2; at most it is a commentary on Lolita's immaturity. Its primary force is in its reference to the spritelike and elusive deities of the Greek countryside. (Lolita's male counterparts, after all, are "faunlets.") The setting in which Nabokov composed *Lolita,* the motor lodge landscape of the West on his lepping expiditions, is far and away more meaningful in a wider sense to the creation of *Lolita* than any direct lepidopterological references in the novel itself.

Another hallmark of Nabokov's literary use of Lepidoptera is its intentionally allusive quality. That is, he very often avoided precisely naming his butterfly of the moment, particularly by its scientific name, referring instead to some characteristic physical feature or lifestyle trait and leaving it at that. This choice was to some degree aesthetic: part of Nabokov's success in incorporating Lepidoptera into literature was that he was careful to keep it in bounds. While he understood the connections between science and art as well as anyone, he was also well aware of the distinctions between writing a novel and drafting an article for *Psyche.*

But the allusiveness also reflected another particularly Nabokovian trait: the practice of hiding little gems of discovery for the pleasure of particularly careful readers or for those in the know in some arcane area of cultural knowledge. In the case of butterflies Nabokov came close to spelling his attitude out in a letter to Alfred Appel in 1975 in which he thanked Appel for having sent him a copy of the *New York Times* article on endangered butterflies illustrated with the Karner Blue. "But what must tickle some of my best readers an iridescent pink," he wrote, "is that it is precisely the butterfly which settles on damp sand at the feet at Pnin and Chateau!" in a scene from the novel *Pnin.* He revealed this secret to a wider audience in a letter to the editor of the *Times* at about the same time.

This propensity is evident in many of the passages that have been cited in this book; some sections of *The Gift,* for instance, provide example after fertile example. In such cases recognition of specific butterflies is usually not essential to the understanding of the literature, but it adds another layer for interested readers and sometimes provides literary ironies. In "The Aurelian," Paul Pilgram mentions a beauty from Madagascar, which, he is careful to note, is not a butterfly at all but a radiant green moth. Nabokov did not, however, disclose that the creature is a Sunset Moth — arguably more beautiful than any known butterfly — whose name perhaps bears metaphorical significance within the story. Such instances explain the value of cross-referenced lists — the most elaborate and up-to-date produced by Dieter E. Zimmer — of the scientific names of the butterflies and moths found in the novels and stories.

Beyond the specific detail of his use of Lepidoptera in literature, though, it is natural for many of those interested primarily in his literature to ask whether there is a deeper connection between Nabokov's science and Nabokov's art. Writing and writers enjoy a much wider appreciation than lepidoptery, so the normal formulation of the question assumes that lepidoptery must in some way be the handmaiden of literature. (Lepidopterists, of course, will debate this.) But it is easy to think of parallels between the skills needed to excel in butterfly taxonomy and those required to write the kind of literature that made Nabokov great. Both necessitate an attention to details and a recognition of how those details fit into larger overall patterns ("In high art and pure science detail is everything.") Nabokov often explained that his fiction rested on the drive to exalt the specific over the general, and taxonomy satisfied this need as well. It also gave him another field in which to delight in the choice and rare. His dismissal of a drearily common butterfly, recorded in Robert H. Boyle's *Sports Illustrated* article in 1959, as a "winged cliché" says a great deal about Nabokov's attitude to both fiction and lepidoptery.

In any case the question of the relationship between literature and science, or art and science, or — more straightforward — literature and lepidoptery has become part of the stock of Nabokovian commentary. And as might be expected of a writer famous for his literary masks, mirrors, and sleight of hand, as well as his sense of humor, many of Nabokov's own pronouncements on the matter were enigmatic rather than clarifying. When asked directly about connections between literature and lepidoptery, he tended to deny they existed or to evade the question. In 1962, an interviewer's question ("Is there any connection with your writing?") drew a classic Nabokovian formulation: "There is in a general way, because I think that in a work of art there is a kind of merging between the two things, between the precision of poetry and the excitement of pure science." He was fond of this deliberate paradox, and one former student has said he would use it several times a term to provoke his students into thought. Another characteristic statement was "There is no science without fancy, no art without facts."

In such cases — and this is very much in keeping with his personality — Nabokov was not being merely provocative, he was also serious. Unlike most other people he understood both fields and sincerely found a beauty in science that is most often associated with art. Yet Nabokov seemed to be habitually evasive with journalists on the matter. As a result many commentators have treated the whole question as a tantalizing mystery.

In this context it is amusing to note that when Nabokov spoke of uniting science and art in lepidoptery, which he did more than once, he often meant by "art" not literature at all but art in the ordinary sense of pictorial representation. For this there were literal, historical reasons. Even today, in the age of advanced photography, colored drawings of specimens are by far the best means of accurately conveying the appearance of many biological organisms, butterflies included. For this reason early biologists in particular were of necessity artists as well. In part because of the strong impression made on him in his youth by those illustrated volumes of biology from Vyra's attic, Nabokov developed a profound admiration for nature drawing. When he was a child, his family arranged for him to have drawing lessons from Mistislav Dobuzhinsky, one of Russia's foremost artists. As he noted in *Speak, Memory,* those lessons stood him in good stead as a scientist; he was a very competent illustrator of butterflies and their anatomies.

One of Nabokov's most eloquent calls for a unity of art and science serves as the epigraph for this chapter. As here it is often tantalizingly and misleadingly quoted, quite out of context, when broader questions about art and science drift in the rarefied air. But the expression comes from a review of a book written around some drawings by John James Audubon, the well-known ornithologist and illustrator; Nabokov felt unqualified to judge Audubon's other fauna but found his butterflies inept burlesques of the real things and posed the question "Can anyone draw something he knows nothing about?"

Nabokov was thinking of art in a most concrete sense here. He used the same language in his 1965 letter in response to the lepidopterist William H. Howe's gift of a copy of his guide to butterflies and moths. Nabokov was disdainful of many aspects of Howe's book but much admired his illustrations of butterflies. Advising Howe to steer clear of a portfolio he had planned on feeding habits, migrations, and so forth, Nabokov wrote that "your gifts entitle you to concentrate on something where art and science really meet, such as an illustrated monograph on *Polygonia* or on the various races (both sexes and undersides) of *Papilio indra.*" And it was respect for masterful pictorial representation that drew him to his unfinished "Butterflies in Art" project.

This is not to say that Nabokov never thought seriously about the link between science and his own art, literature, because he clearly did. It was, however, before he became famous, in the 1940s, when he was a lecturer at Wellesley College, that he formulated his most direct and unvarnished expression of what he thought of the matter, for the benefit not of journalists or of his fans but, tellingly, of his students.

In an introductory lecture to his Russian literature students, few of whom probably knew that he was a serious lepidopterist, he explained:

> Whichever subject you have chosen, you must realize that knowledge in it is limitless. Every subject brims with mysteries and thrills, and no two students of the same subject discover a like amount of delight, accumulate exactly the same amount of knowledge. . . . Suppose a schoolchild picks up the study of butterflies for a hobby. He will learn a few things about the general structure. He will be able to tell you that a butterfly has always six feet and never eight or twenty. That there are innumerable patterns of butterfly wings and that according to those patterns they are divided into generic and specific groups. This is a fair amount of knowl-

edge for a schoolchild. But of course he has not even come near the fascinating and incredible intricacies invented by nature in the fashioning of this group of insects alone. He will not even suspect the fascinating variety of inner organs, the varying shapes of which allow the scientist not only unerringly to classify them, often giving the lie to the seeming resemblance of wing patterns, but also to trace the origin and development and relationship of the genera and species, the history of the migration of their ancestors, the varying influence of the environments on the developments of the species and forms, etc. etc. etc.; and he will not have even touched upon other mysterious fields, limitless in themselves, of for instance mimicry, or symbiosis. This example applies to every field of knowledge, and it is very apt in the case of literature.

Years later in a far different climate, in an interview in 1962, Nabokov returned to this theme and used the same lines of explanation. But this time he picked lilies as his illustrative example. His choice of the flowers suggests something else about his attitude: for Nabokov the deepest connection between literature and science involved not the specific knowledge of any one field and certainly not the application of any personal or universal system of butterfly symbolism to writing. It was rather a habitual way of looking at the world that is as conducive to the study of science, natural science as Nabokov practiced it, as it is for the practice of literature. For this reason the most careful lists of the butterflies mentioned by Nabokov and the most minute passage-by-passage studies will inevitably miss a central point in his work.

Nabokov considered an interest in natural science — not necessarily butterflies — an essential part of a cultured and healthy mind receptive to the wonders of the world around it. As a child he was disdainful of the tutor who dismissed a species he had inquired about as "just a bird," and as an adult he was shocked that his students at Cornell couldn't identify an American elm that grew outside his lecture hall. In this sense the eternal question Why the butterflies? is particularly otiose. Lepidoptery found Nabokov early in his life and for various reasons never let him from its grasp, but he viewed it not as a uniquely elevating field of study in itself but merely as one corner of the broad world of specialized knowledge. He realized that other pursuits could adequately fill the role for others that butterflies filled for him.

Of his son, Dmitri, Nabokov once wrote to his sister, "He can forget everything in the world to immerge in an aviation magazine — airplanes, to him, are what butterflies are to me; he can unerringly identify types of aircraft by a distant silhouette in the sky or even by a buzz, and loves to assemble and glue together various models." Moreover, Nabokov clearly linked his mother's interest in mushrooms to his own interest in lepidoptery; his cousin Yuri knew the uniforms of the tin soldiers he collected "as well as I did different butterflies."

In literature, among many other examples, a scientific specialty in seashells becomes part of an antic portrait of an ideal monarch in *Pale Fire*: "How often is it that kings engage in some special research? Conchologists among them can be counted on the fingers of one maimed hand." In the same novel John Shade's father was an amateur ornithologist who had a bird named after him; the son inherited a love for nature, including butterflies. This penchant irritates Shade's unhinged hanger-on, Kinbote, who might be speaking for many tunnel-visioned literary admirers of Nabokov when he says, "As most literary celebrities, Shade did not seem to realize that a humble admirer who has cornered at last and has at last to himself the inaccessible man of genius, is considerably more interested in discussing with him literature and life than in being told that the 'diana' (presumably a flower) occurs in New Wye together with the 'atlantis' (presumably another flower), and things of that sort."

Kinbote does not know that the Diana and the Atlantis are both Fritillary butterflies, members of the nymphalid family. (It is impossible for a lepidopterist to resist mentioning here that the Diana, one of the most beautiful eastern butterflies, as Nabokov noted — the females deep blue and the males vivid orange — is now very rare in most of its former range because of the cutting of the eastern forests.) Similarly, one of Nabokov's most disturbed characters, Humbert Humbert in *Lolita,* is notoriously ignorant and dismissive of nature. He can't distinguish a butterfly from a moth, or a hawkmoth from a hummingbird.

As Nabokov understood the relation between his literature and his science, he also enforced certain boundaries between them. It may seem obvious that fiction isn't science, but the distinction is sometimes lost in discussions of Nabokov's butterfly writing. He actually worked in several distinct modes. His fictional treatments of lepidopterological themes, which were aimed at a literary audience, clearly profited from his scientific knowledge while sidestepping scientific technicalities. But the exchange seldom worked the other way: his technical scientific writing, with a few exceptions, is devoid of literary influence. Here and there is a memorable turn of phrase, even a descriptive gem, but on the whole his major taxonomic treatises are extremely dry. The distinction is, of course, not a reflection on Nabokov's literary skill but rather an indication of the integrity of his formal science. When he sat behind the microscope, he intentionally left the influence of literature behind and was all scientist.

But he also worked in a third mode, seen to some degree in a handful of reviews of Lepidoptera books for *The New York Times* and *The Times* of London but above all in articles such as "Butterfly Collecting in Wyoming, 1952" and "The Female of *Lycaeides Argyrognomon sublivens*." These articles, both published in the early 1950s, after Nabokov's formal scientific career had ended, appeared in the Lepidopterists' Society's *Lepidopterists' News,* the kind of chatty, informal journal, of a sort common not so many years ago, that appealed to advanced amateurs as well as to professionals and offered a field for literary charm and grace along with more technical considerations. (Another such was *The Entomologist,* the journal that Nabokov loved from his boyhood and that published his first paper on butterflies.) In this context Nabokov felt free to relax the constraints he had imposed on his technical prose — which meant that the natural literary exuberance found everywhere else in his work could flood back in — and managed to turn the vocabulary of fieldwork into a kind of elegant and unexpected poetry. Lepidopterists, who recognize the conventions — the geography, the descriptions of butterflies, the elevations, the lists of food plants — may be inclined to appreciate these pieces as much as Nabokov's fiction. Explicitly recognizing their literary merit, Nabokov himself later included them in his collection *Strong Opinions.*

Here is a lovely passage from "The Female of *Lycaeides sublivens*":

Owing to rains and floods, especially noticeable in Kansas, most of the drive from New York State to Colorado was entomologically uneventful. When reached at last, Telluride turned out to be a damp, unfrequented, but very spectacular cul-de-sac (which a prodigious rainbow straddled every evening) at the end of two converging roads, one from Placerville, the other from Dolores, both atrocious. There is one motel, the optimistic and excellent Valley View Court where my wife and I stayed, at 9,000 feet altitude, from the 3rd to the 29th of July, walking up daily to at least 12,000 feet along various more or less steep trails in search of *sublivens.* . . . Every morning the sky would be of an impeccable blue at 6 A.M. when I set out. The first innocent cloudlet would scud across at 7:30 A.M. Bigger fellows with darker bellies would start tampering with the sun around 9 A.M., just as we emerged from the shadow of the cliffs and trees onto good hunting grounds.

Alas, with the gulf between amateur and professional growing wider, and with serious "hobbies," as Nabokov understood them, having been replaced by packaged entertainment, the kinds of informal journals that welcomed such writing have gone out of fashion. *The Lepidopterists' News* has been replaced by the more academic *Journal of the Lepidopterists' Society*. As for Nabokov's favorite journal, dwindling submissions and a disappearing readership put *The Entomologist* out of business in 1997. In the modern world of ultrasophisticated specialization, this melting pot of the amateur and professional communities, with papers on local and regional faunas, ecological and behavioral notes, and descriptions of new species, simply had no audience. A format in which Vladimir Nabokov produced eloquent and vital prose about one of the great loves of his life has essentially ceased to exist.

Whether writing for *The Lepidopterists' News* or *The New Yorker,* in the complexity and sophistication of his presentation, the breadth of his range, and the utter conviction with which he transformed lepidoptery into literature, Nabokov has no equal. And as the specialized worlds of science and art continue to hurtle relentlessly away from each other, it is hard to imagine his achievement ever being matched. In fact, it is hard to think of any branch of science that can boast the kind of literary representative Nabokov is for lepidoptery. For those lepidopterists who are touched by that fact, it is surprising that so many of their colleagues treat his writing with studied indifference. For years it has been clear to many students of literature that they need to know something about lepidoptery to fully appreciate some of his work, and some of them, at least, have made efforts to learn more about his butterflies. In the same spirit some of the scientists who worked on the Nabokov project came to hope that more lepidopterists would come to see his literature as a precious link between their world and the world of letters.

Among other things they would find that in some choice cases Nabokov's works not only form a commentary on the study of butterflies, but also stimulate reflections on its long history. In works like *The Gift* and "The Aurelian," we have seen how references to the history of lepidoptery lend a realistic power and air of authenticity to the stories. But the depth of the connections between real scientific history and both the grand expeditions of Konstantin Godunov-Cherdyntsev and the world of Paul Pilgram are such that they might even elude lepidopterists not immediately familiar with old imperial collections and the specimens they contained. For material in both works reflects arcane details of the old label data that recorded famous collecting localities, information Nabokov must have read of as a youth or gathered from the material of the European insect dealers.

When Pilgram is discussing some choice specimens with a sophisticated customer, the name Eisner crops up, though as was his fashion Nabokov did not tell everything he knew. Eisner is undoubtedly Curt Eisner, Europe's prolific namer of Parnassian butterflies — large Swallowtails of a solid white or often a mixture of red, yellow, and white that grace Eurasia's mountainous regions. Because they are so widespread, they fracture into so many disjunct populations that they can be given myriad names, and those from little-explored recesses of Mongolia or Tibet fetch extremely high prices on the commercial market. According to Pilgram, the labels say that the specimens were "taken by the native collectors of Father Déjean" — the Roman Catholic missionary Léonard-Louis Déjean — in Tatsienlu, East Tibet, a famous missionary source for many nineteenth-century specimens, prominent in Europe's great museums. Pilgram longed for discovery, and all along, trapped as he was in Berlin, he was perhaps not far from it. He did not know (and perhaps neither did Nabokov) that among the specimens attributed to Father Déjean were many species new to science, some named only as recently as 1992.

The old typeset labels in museums and among the dealers' stocks were copied from the original handwritten ink labels made by those who bought the specimens from their native collectors. Common labels in the old Asiatic collections began with regional names typifying nineteenth-century geography, like Tibet and Tashkent, and the famous mountain ranges that were the haunts of the early dealer-collectors — Altai, Nanshan, Tyan-shan, all in *The Gift*. Occasionally the labels also bore the names of specific towns or villages, like Tatsienlu, which is cited in *The Gift* as well as "The Aurelian."

Like many lepidopterists, Nabokov shared Pilgram's capacity to conjure up an alternative universe from such names. "Out of localities cited in entomological works [Pilgram] had built up a special world of his own, to which his science was a most detailed guidebook." Tatsienlu is a name with great resonance in nineteenth-century lepidoptery. The old European collections were full of unusual, and often unnamed, butterflies bearing that label, or versions of it, specimens acquired from local collectors by the British explorer-dealer A. E. Pratt. Pratt was responsible for much of the exotic Asian material that reached the dealers' markets in the late nineteenth century, destined for the big aristocratic collections and, subsequently, the various national museums.

Reflecting the nationalities of the dealers who handled the material, London specimens read, "Tibet, Tatsien-lu, native collectors." In Paris it was transcribed as "Tibet, Tat-sien-lu, Chasseurs indigènes"; there are also examples in the Fournier collection there with the same labels in Russian, which appear to have been bought by Madame Fournier from aristocratic Russian collectors.

In science Tatsienlu was the type locality of large numbers of exotic species, including seven of lycaenid butterflies. Many of these were made famous by John Henry Leech in his classic work *Butterflies from Japan, China, and Corea.* Published in sections between 1893 and 1894, this book eventually totaled 681 pages, with copious color illustrations and, for a limited number of the old European museums, was bound in presentation copies by the London printing firm R. H. Porter. Today it is rare, but it was clearly familiar to Nabokov, who mentioned Leech several times in *The Gift.*

In the realm of Nabokov's literary imagination (and Fyodor's) Tatsienlu was transformed into a place where shaven-headed lamas in narrow streets suspected that the Westerners were not collecting butterflies but stealing children. But it is one of history's tricks (Nabokov would have appreciated the slip of the scribal hand) that Tatsienlu was not in Tibet. The village, known today as Kangding, lies four hundred miles from the Tibetan border on the Yunnan Plateau, on the border between Sichuan and Yunnan Provinces in western China. Biologists know the plateau as one of the most hospitable climates in the world, famous for its mild temperatures and brilliant blue skies dotted for a great part of the year with fair-weather cumulus clouds. The village sits at an altitude of about nine thousand feet, and its site is a far cry from the high-altitude Tibetan plateau, barren and snow-strewn, upon which Nabokov's fiction placed it.

The error somehow crept into history when dealers processed Pratt's collection, because Pratt himself, in his little-known account of his expeditions, *To the Snows of Tibet Through China,* published in 1892, clearly marked its correct location. It was Kurt Johnson who discovered and pointed out the error in 1991, as he labored to finish Leech's uncompleted work on Chinese lycaenids. At the time Johnson had no idea that Nabokov had celebrated the small village in *The Gift* and "The Aurelian." Like most lepidopterists, he had never read either.

14

Darwin's Finches — Nabokov's Blues

He told me about these magic masks of mimicry . . . about the curious harem of that famous African swallowtail, whose variously disguised females copy in color, shape and even flight half a dozen different species (apparently inedible), which are also the models of numerous other mimics.

— *The Gift*

IN 1996 Dmitri Nabokov spoke at the Mercantile Library in New York City as part of a lecture series sponsored by the Nabokovian Society. In response to a question during his presentation, "The Lolita Legacy: Life with Nabokov's Art," he revealed that his father had felt considerable anxiety over his place in the world of science and whether it would ever come near his fame in literature. The son suggested that this concern might to some extent explain why his father, so outspoken about his literary opinions, was relatively self-effacing in personal relationships with his scientific colleagues.

There can be no doubt that the author of *The Gift* was stirred by the notion of lepidopterological fame in its heroic guise or that the author of "On Discovering a Butterfly" was proud to claim for himself a reasonable share of glory. Yet Nabokov remained modest about his taxonomic achievements throughout his life. "Let us not exaggerate," he responded in a 1996 interview, when Dieter E. Zimmer suggested he might be described as a "lepidopterist of renown." On occasion there was a tone of regret about the dreams he did not manage to fulfill, as in an interview published in *Esquire* magazine in 1975: "If any goal has eluded me, it must be sought in another domain, that of lepidoptery. . . . I have not, and probably never shall, accomplish the greater part of the entrancing research work I had imagined in my young mirages, such as 'A Monograph of the Eurasian and American *machaon* Group,' or 'The *Eupithecias* of the World.' "

Nabokov was well aware of the trade-offs he had made for the sake of his writing. As Charles Remington recognized, his achievements must to some degree be judged against the broader circumstances of his life. There is no question that, had he devoted himself exclusively to lepidoptery, he would have produced monographs such as those he dreamed of and much, much more, including, most likely, works like his "Butterflies of Europe" and "Butterflies in Art." The former, after all, came close to becoming reality despite the demands of his primary career. Nabokov also perhaps understood, with mixed emotions, the paradoxical effect that his writing, and the celebrity it brought, had on the perception of his lepidoptery. While literary fame always kept the question of Nabokov's place in science in play, it was also one of the factors that helped obscure the answers. Celebrity encourages myth, and myth creates confusion that resists penetration.

Robert Dirig, who because of his work on the Karner Blue is one of the relatively few lepidopterists to have closely scrutinized Nabokov's work, once remarked to Kurt Johnson, "It is always difficult to sort the legends from the facts that surround a person of Vladimir Nabokov's prominence," an observation illustrated with his story of "Nabokov's butterfly net," a sacred relic preserved in the Entomology Department at Cornell University, where Dirig teaches. "It has a twelve-foot handle and a bag of heavy fabric like canvas," Dirig said, "too heavy for butterflies, with a handle so long as to be unwieldy. It looks like an aquatic dip net or sweeping net to me, and is probably misattributed. I have not been able to discover the origin of this story. Perhaps VN handled it at one point?"

The aura of myth around Nabokov's lepidoptery, of which the apparently spurious net is beautifully emblematic, is one of the reasons that his scientific legacy was never defined, neither by scientists nor by his literary enthusiasts, in his own lifetime. But it is also hard to know what Nabokov himself thought his eventual standing in lepidoptery would be. While he was modest about his ability, his acknowledged intelligence, his devotion and excellence as a field collector, and his "good eye" in taxonomy clearly brought him respect among his peers, men like William Comstock, Cyril dos Passos, Alexander B. Klots, J. H. McDunnough, John Downey, and Charles Remington, to name just a few. And this respect has been shared by subsequent lepidopterists who had occasion, because of their careers, to look closely into his work, not only Bálint and Johnson and their collaborators but also Dirig and Robert Pyle.

Excluding Latin American Blues named during the Nabokov project, the esteem in which Nabokov was held is reflected in the many butterflies that have been named in his honor over the years, with both scientific and common names, some still valid or in common use, others not. Nabokov's Pug, Nabokov's Blue, Nabokov's Fritillary, Nabokov's Brown, Nabokov's Satyr, and Nabokov's Wood Nymph are all common names that have at various times been applied by lepidopterists to particular butterflies and moths. There are a comparable number of scientific names in honor of Nabokov. Some were given by lepidopterist friends in token of affection or some favor. But others, applied quite recently, were in recognition of the importance of his work, like Francis Hemming's designation of the genus *Nabokovia* in 1960. In 1972, to cite a later example, John Masters, continuing Nabokov's work on the northern Blue genus *Lycaeides,* named a Minnesota subspecies *Lycaeides idas nabokovi,* for "Dr. Nabokov, who first recognized its distinctness and whose papers on Nearctic *Lycaeides* . . . have provided a background to make this description possible." In 1984 Paul Opler and George Krizek gave this butterfly the common name Nabokov's Blue, which is still in general use. And in 1974 Lee D. Miller named a subspecies of a Satyr butterfly *Cyllopsis pyracmon nabokovi,* pointing out that Nabokov's work on the genus *Cyllopsis,* which he knew as *Neonympha,* "too long has been ignored."

The collective judgment of so many of his peers paints a considerably different picture of Nabokov and his work than the rather dismissive accounts that have been available in the most accessible published assessments, certainly until the work of Brian Boyd in the early 1990s. And this is entirely without reference to Nabokov's most important work, "Notes on Neotropical Plebejinae." In this one concrete sense he was incontrovertibly ahead of his time: nothing like a final judgment on his career has been possible until now because it has taken science so long to follow up on his fundamental work. But now that that work is essentially finished, most of the seminal names he gave to the vast array of Latin American Blues still stand. His groups are the same natural groups recognized by modern science, so he has literally succeeded in putting a personal stamp on all of them. Moreover, they are diverse and widespread enough to serve as a database for big questions about evolution and biogeography.

While Nabokov listed "Notes on Neotropical Plebejinae" as one of his favorite lepidopterological works, there is no evidence that he thought it more important than many of his other papers. It is in fact likely that he himself had no comprehension of the actual size and geographic spread of the groups he pioneered and their centrality to major scientific questions.

Since the research is recent, many of those questions have yet to begin to be answered. As late as 1990 Arthur Shapiro and others lamented that broad studies of temperate organisms in the Andes were being hampered because so little in-depth work had been done on any of them. Shapiro sought to remedy the situation in part through his own pioneering work on High Andean and austral Whites and Sulphurs. Now Nabokov's groups, elaborated by Bálint and Johnson and others, can take their place alongside Shapiro's. Shapiro himself, in the introduction to Luis Peña and Alfredo Ugarte's book *The Butterflies of Chile,* noted that the questions posed by Nabokov South American Blues carve out large areas for fertile new research:

> Thanks to Kurt Johnson and Zsolt Bálint, we now know there are plenty of endemic Chilean butterflies! Actually, many or most of these inconspicuous little butterflies may also occur in Argentine Patagonia. The discovery that at least one lineage has speciated explosively in the region raises all sorts of questions. For example, do Blues speciate more rapidly than other butterflies? Does their population biology predispose them to this? Their low vagility? . . . Is host specialization a factor in speciation? In this lineage many species have symbiotic relationships with ants. Is ant association a factor? Suddenly the butterfly fauna of Chile has an entirely new dimension.

It is a new dimension built squarely on the foundation laid by Nabokov, and any lepidopterist who seeks to answer any of the questions formulated by Shapiro will view Nabokov as a kind of founding father. In fact, the process is already well under way, thanks largely to Dubi Benyamini, whose many discoveries about the southern Andean and austral Blues represent a quantum leap in knowledge about their lifestyles, and not only a natural extension of Nabokov's pioneering work but one central to the historical vindication of his emphasis on anatomical study. Detailed study of butterfly life cycles has settled, once and for all, the issue of whether Nabokov's attention to genitalic detail had been worth it, or whether he was simply a taxonomic splitter dividing Blues of similar wing pattern into many species based on minor differences in their anatomy. It was a dimension of the project that Bálint and Johnson could not have explored alone. In a remarkable turn of events one of Benyamini's most important discoveries came in an area that might at once represent Nabokov's deepest fascination with nature, and also the one facet of his science that has most often been held against him — his understanding of mimicry.

Benyamini owes part of his particular success to his skill at raising butterflies in the laboratory. For some groups this is easy, but for others it reaches the level of an art, as Nabokov, who raised caterpillars in his youth and was proud of his skill, understood very well. The lepidopterist heroine of the novel *Ada* shares a dream of an elaborate butterfly-breeding system with her nature teacher: "Our fondest dream . . . , Krolik's and my fondest dream," she relates, "was to describe and depict the early stages, from ova to pupa, of all the known Fritillaries, Greater and Lesser, beginning with those of the New World. I would have been responsible for building an argynninarium (a pestproof breeding house, with temperature patterns, and other refinements — such as background night smells and night-animal calls to create a natural atmosphere in certain difficult cases) — a caterpillar needs exquisite care!"

Outside a few hardy groups a small variation in any environmental factor — humidity, light, temperature, or in any pulses or rhythms involving any combination of these — can lead to the failure of the experiment. A particular problem in the laboratory is the possible breaking of the diapause, or period of hibernation. Getting the chrysalises in and out of hibernation without their dying involves putting them into a freezer at the right time with precise temperature, humidity, and duration. Benyamini is a master of the art.

Before his work virtually nothing was known about the life cycles of South America's Blues. Nothing, for example, had ever been documented about Neotropical Blues and their relationships with ants, which Shapiro had so eagerly noted. In March 1994 Benyamini was the first to describe ant-lycaenid symbiosis in the New World tropics. Typical of such relationships, adult ants tend the caterpillars of Nabokov's Blues like battalions of bodyguards, swarming around them, even sheltering them in their nests. They aggressively protect the caterpillars from predators, not only overt predators that might enter the ants' nest but far more insidious threats, such as parasitic wasps and flies, which, like something out of science fiction, seek to use the Blues' larvae as living hosts for their own. In turn, the caterpillars offer the ants an exudation — "honeydew" the scientists call it — from a gland behind the caterpillars' head capsules. The ants drink it with relish. So coveted are the larvae of some Blues that even ant larvae are served up in exchange for the honey from their Blues' glands. In turn, so fixated are the ants on their larval cows, as scientists have also come to call them, that when an adult Blue emerges from a chrysalis within the ants' nest, and is no longer recognizable by its hosts, it must dash to the entrance and run or fly away quickly lest it be devoured by its former protectors.

By the end of 1995 Benyamini's list of ant-related lycaenid species in South America had reached seventeen, and his list of the attendant ants totaled seven species in six genuses. The butterfly list included Nabokov's only species of *Nabokovia,* eleven species of *Pseudolucia,* one species of his *Paralycaeides,* and four species of *Madeleinea.*

Between 1992 and 1995 Benyamini had also documented food plants, mostly varieties of legumes, for thirty of the thirty-six species of Nabokov's Blues he had located and studied in Chile, Argentina, and Bolivia, rearing nearly all of these species in the laboratory. Testifying to the overall distinctness of South American Blues from their worldwide counterparts, many species fed on plant species that had never before been documented as hosts to Lycaenidae. However, for all the excitement of these discoveries, Benyamini counted the detection of the food plant of the species *Pseudolucia chilensis* the most fulfilling. *P. chilensis* was one of a group of Blues — all of which have bright orange females and males with orange wing suffusions or patches — that particularly intrigued Benyamini. These butterflies in turn share physical characteristics and behavior traits with certain orange-patched Hairstreak butterflies, those belonging to the appropriately named bicolor complex — their wing upper surfaces a striking contrast of brown ground and vivid orange patches.

For one thing, both groups have a peculiar defensive habit of playing dead. When faced with predatory surprise — the sweeping of a net in their direction, for example — they plummet to the ground. An experienced lepidopterist usually thinks he has knocked them down. Putting the net aside and looking to the ground, if his eyesight is sharp, he may discover the quarry lying there, to all appearances stunned and insensible. Against a background of stones, old leaves, or soil, however, the butterfly's tawny, cryptically mottled hind wings, crossed by a confusingly ruptive blackish wing band, are nearly invisible. Thinking he has stunned the poor creature, the lepidopterist reaches down, only to have the butterfly dart away, leaving him empty-handed and completely humiliated. When he first encountered these species, Benyamini was fooled this way time and time again. He was always reminding himself, so he reported to Johnson, not to swear in front of his children.

Benyamini had also noticed that among orange-colored Blues that dominated the southern Andes and austral tablelands, it was not the wary, cryptically marked species that were the most common but the orange-and-brown *chilensis,* its underwings covered with a simple pattern of blackish spots. When he first came to Chile, he had noticed that *chilensis* was the most common Blue in collections there. On his expeditions he found it locally common from sandy dunes along the coast up into the meadows of the Precordillera as high as 7,220 feet. This, he thought, was possibly the reason that Nabokov had chosen it as the type species for his genus *Pseudolucia.* But Benyamini also observed that it was in many ways an unrepresentative choice. For a *Pseudolucia* it is oddly colored. Neither sex is actually blue; the males are brown and yellowish orange, and the females are brown with brighter orange markings. Both sexes show a wing under-surface with simple spots, differing starkly from the genus's more common venter — cryptically colored and with a black or brown V-shaped band.

In its habitat *chilensis* is usually the first lycaenid in the air in the spring, and it remains on the wing through three or four broods until fall. Often it seemed as if *chilensis* could be found almost anywhere at any time. Sometimes, at the extremes of season, it is the only butterfly flying. The other *Pseudolucia* are far more restricted, in both habitat and flight pe-riod. Both sexes of *chilensis,* especially the females, also behave differently from other *Pseudolucia.* They are docile compared with other Blues, par-ticularly the females, which will sit on plants for long periods, wings open at a forty-five-degree angle to show the prominent orange forewings. They will remain motionless, as if listening or waiting for something. A careful collector can occasionally grasp a sitting female with his fingers.

Despite the ubiquity of *chilensis,* Benyamini's many attempts to dis-cover its life cycle had always ended in failure. His first expedition in search of its immature stages was to Parque Nacional El Morado in Chile. In broad, green-banded meadows between 5,900 and 7,200 feet, he re-corded every plant on which the females landed and then searched each one for eggs or larvae. The list of plants was made up mostly of the flow-ers commonly called composites — the family Asteraceae, but also a few legumes, family Fabaceae, and plants of the much less well-known Hydro-fyllaceae, Santalaceae, and Berberidaceae. He never found eggs or larvae on any of them. Most frustrating was Asteraceae, the plant the butterflies seemed to like the most. Its abundance forced Benyamini to examine it again and again, often with the patient help of his sons, even though he knew that it was not a known larval food plant for any butterfly.

Yet, trusting the females, as he characterized it, he turned to the laboratory in Santiago, having collected plants of five genuses of Asteraceae, two of Santalaceae, and one each of Fabaceae and Hydrofyllaceae. In glass aquariums, under the proper light, heat, and other conditions, he confined *chilensis* females with all these plants, and still achieved no result.

His failure drove him to more elaborate measures. He considered the possibility that the butterflies might be so dependent on ants that the females would not lay eggs without their ant attendants. Since the ant *Dorymyrex tener* was always quite common on the plants *chilensis* flocked around, Benyamini also introduced that species to the aquarium. He even checked for eggs under the rocks and in the soil, because he knew that certain Old World Blues place their eggs to make sure ants will find the caterpillars, sometimes even on the ants' nest. It was all to no avail. The failure of this second elaborate laboratory attempt left Benyamini completely baffled. He decided, in the interest of other urgent collecting priorities, to put aside this problem and leave its solution to serendipity.

Then, on February 2, 1995, as Benyamini followed a female *chilensis* through the dunes along the Chilean Pacific coast south of Constitución, in the Maule Region, she came to rest on an unlikely composite of the genus *Ambrosia*. Benyamini was watching the butterfly with what had almost become distaste when suddenly it began walking up the *Ambrosia* and then off onto a common parasitic plant of the region, *Cuscuta racemosa*. Members of this genus form a web over plants of the family Covolvulaceae and Euphorbiaceae. As farmers across the southern region of South America are well aware, when unwary cattle consume *Cuscuta*, especially those on Euphorbs, they become violently ill. The resulting staggering behavior gives the plant its common name, dodder.

To Benyamini's amazement, the *chilensis* female laid an egg among the *Cuscuta* flowers. It is easy to spot a butterfly in egg-laying position. She will sit still or walk very slowly, all the while arching her abdomen to place a gluey egg, which eventually pops out and attaches to the food plant, often under a leaf or flower petal. As far as Benyamini knew, there was no record of dodders being butterfly food plants. But he had never before seen a *chilensis* female lay an egg on anything, particularly galling since he had watched countless of the less common Blues do it nearly every day he spent in the field. As he watched, the little Blue deposited another egg on the stem of the *Cuscuta* and then two more, each on a leaf and a spiny fruit of the noxious plant; rather than laying eggs in large clusters, lycaenid butterflies tend to spread them around a plant or several plants, to increase the odds of their survival.

Armed with this information, Benyamini began religiously checking for *chilensis* in other places where he knew dodders were common. He soon learned that if he patiently waited among stands of *Cuscuta,* he could observe as often as he liked the oviposition that had so long eluded him. Finally able to rear *chilensis* in the laboratory, he could easily pick out its eggs and larvae and would not mistake them if he happened to see them on any plant other than *Cuscuta,* but he never did.

Almost seven weeks later, as the austral summer was beginning to turn to fall, Benyamini traveled to higher altitudes in the Parque El Morado. Here, he knew, stands of dodders remained in the late summer, at some 7,200 feet in an area of soda springs (the Aguas Panimavidas). The place was of special interest to him for two reasons. First, the dodder there was a different species — *Cuscuta micrantha,* easily recognized by its elongated fruit. Second, as summer fades dodders began to dry and shrivel. Knowing well the flight period of *chilensis,* Benyamini remembered that on earlier trips he had seen the upland *micrantha* at the soda spring still with fresh late-summer foliage. Downslope, *Cuscuta* was by now completely desiccated. Would it be possible to find *chilensis* breeding this late in the season high upland where the dodders were still relatively fresh?

On *micrantha* at the soda springs Benyamini found both *chilensis* eggs and larvae, the latter feeding at the far edges of the plant that were still green. This observation confirmed his suspicion that the flight period of *chilensis* were synchronized with the growth cycle of *Cuscuta.* Its late-summer refuge in the uplands also reflected what Benyamini had documented in other Blues, an "upslope shift" — upland migration of populations as each season progressed. It was the same strategy the local Chilean farmers and herders had used with their livestock for centuries. Livestock had become the Blues' biggest natural competitor; whereas their attendant ants could protect them from the plagues of parasitic wasps and flies, they could do very little against cattle, sheep, goats, rabbits, viscachas, and camelitos. But the dodders appeared to be long entrenched as the natural food plant of *chilensis,* and that entrenchment gives the species protection against their most aggressive competitors, and perhaps an edge over other Blues.

In 1995 Benyamini went on to propose that *chilensis* might be a model for an elaborate mimicry phenomenon. If true, this would be an eye-opening development in the world of lepidoptery — an intriguing explanation for the hidden diversity among South American Blues that Nabokov himself had detected by meticulous study of their genitalia. It was also a particularly happy coincidence that such mimicry might occur in Nabokov's groups, for he was fascinated with the subject. "The question of mimicry is one that has passionately interested him all his life," Véra wrote on his behalf to a publisher in 1952, "and one of his pet projects has always been the compilation of a work that would comprise all known examples of mimicry in the animal kingdom. This would make a voluminous work and the research alone would take two or three years."

In literature he touched on his ideas about mimicry as early as *The Gift*, and soon after his arrival at Wellesley College in 1941 he began to prepare a "rather ambitious" article on the subject, with "furious refutations of 'natural selection' and 'the struggle for life.'" Like the book suggested in Véra's letter, the article was never published and nothing of it survives except, apparently, a short passage that became part of *Speak, Memory*, although Nabokov gave several talks on the subject.

Today the wonders of mimicry are widely appreciated, but Nabokov, with his incomparable power of language, conveyed its fascination perhaps better than anyone else. In *Speak, Memory* he wrote:

> Consider the imitation of oozing poison by bubblelike macules on a wing (complete with pseudo-refraction) or by glossy yellow knobs on a chrysalis ("Don't eat me — I have already been squashed, sampled and rejected"). Consider the tricks of an acrobatic caterpillar (of the Lobster Moth) which in infancy looks like bird's dung, but after molting develops scrabbly hymenopteroid appendages and baroque characteristics, allowing the extraordinary fellow to play two parts at once (like the actor in Oriental shows who becomes a pair of intertwisted wrestlers): that of a writhing larva and that of a big ant seemingly harrowing it. When a certain moth resembles a certain wasp in shape and color, it also walks and moves its antennae in a waspish, unmothlike manner. When a butterfly has to look like a leaf, not only are all the details of a leaf beautifully rendered but markings mimicking grub-bored holes are generously thrown in.

As he did here, Nabokov and many others have loosely used the term *mimicry* to describe an incredibly diverse range of imitative survival strategies in nature — butterflies that look like leaves, butterflies with large spots on their wings that suggest the eyes of a large predator, and butterflies like Hairstreaks with deceptive "false heads" are only a few. Many of these strategies are better described as the sort of protective adaptation known as object resemblance. In its proper sense, mimicry is restricted to relationships that involve toxicity or unpalatability to predators in one or more of the members of the mimicry relationship. (Nabokov was well aware of the difference in these strategies; the use of the word *mimicry* to cover them all was clearly a literary concession, another example of his boundaries between literature and science.)

One kind of true mimicry is Batesian mimicry, described by Henry Walter Bates in 1861. Here the model, but not the mimic, is noxious or distasteful to predators, which quickly learn to avoid the colors of the offender; the palatable mimic species gain protection through the adoption of the model's colors, fooling the predator. Historically, the best-known example of Batesian mimicry is the relationship between the Monarch, which because of its consumption of milkweed most predators find inedible, and its mimic, the perfectly palatable Viceroy. But in 1878 the German Fritz Müller noted another type of mimicry, which occurs more commonly in the tropics; in Müllerian mimicry, all the organisms displaying a particular warning color are noxious themselves. The members of such a ring gain a survival advantage by sharing the same set of warning signals, which thereby become far more widely recognized by predators. In general, if there is one toxic model and one or many nontoxic mimics, that is Batesian mimicry; when there are more than one toxic model, and a ring or complex of mimics, that is Müllerian mimicry. Interestingly, in 1991 Lincoln Brower and his associates published data showing a degree of distastefulness in Viceroys. This suggested either that its mimicry of the Monarch might not be classically Batesian or that the lines recognized by science between the two categories of mimicry might actually blur.

If a mimicry ring or mimicry complex of one sort or the other indeed exists for *Pseudolucia chilensis,* not only the other orange-colored Blues in the region but orange Hairstreaks, Satyrs, and perhaps even the yellow or orange day-flying moths might be mimics as well. There aren't that many well-documented mimicry rings in the world of lepidoptery — particularly complex ones that can be worked out in sophisticated detail — and the best-known examples involve the larger butterflies, the Batesian Monarch-Viceroy relationship, for example, or the Müllerian complexes built around the Heliconian Longwing butterflies of the American tropics and the Dardanus Swallowtail, "that famous African swallowtail" cited by Nabokov in the epigraph for this chapter. If Benyamini's hypothesis turns out to be right, any ring centered on *P. chilensis* could well be a large and complex one, involving at least twenty species belonging to five genuses of moths and butterflies. Such a ring among the lowly lycaenid butterflies would be an exciting and unexpected discovery.

Moreover, the group could be so complex as not to conform completely to the Müllerian-Batesian dichotomy. It seems unlikely on the face of it that the hypothetical *chilensis* mimicry ring would be purely of the Müllerian sort: ten species of Blues involved feed on plants that are not known to impart toxicity to butterflies that feed on them. And *Pseudolucia chilensis* — if it does indeed soak up toxins from dodders — seems an obviously toxic model: its "don't have a care" behavior (a sign of reliance on defenses other than elusiveness) starkly contrasts with the wariness and rapid flight in the possible mimics.

But as Benyamini pointed out, four species of Blues and at least five of the orange-patched Hairstreaks feed on the legume genus *Astragalus*, a plant with its own record of toxicity. It is possible that the ring, if it exists, is a combination of Batesian and Müllerian mimicry in the same complex. Thus, Benyamini was at least able to present lepidopterists with a new puzzle. From a quantity of meticulous data, he showed that his hypothesis fit the circumstantial evidence: the hypothetical model and its mimics coexisted in shared habitats, and the model was overridingly common. Still needed, however, are autopsies of the species in question, both adults and caterpillars. Although *Pseudolucia chilensis* larvae feed on a toxic parasite of a toxic plant, it is possible that no toxins are absorbed by the caterpillars or, even if they are, that they are not present in its orange-colored adults. If *chilensis* adults are not noxious, then imitating them would serve no evolutional advantage to any other butterfly, and all the distributional, color, and behavioral coincidences observed over the years among these austral Blues, Hairstreaks, and day-flying moths are simply that — coincidences.

This final piece of evidence is crucial for the formal demonstration of the mimicry ring. But such sophisticated tests, if carried out with the proper controls, can be prohibitively expensive. Often the toxins under examination are chemically arcane, and an entire chemical protocol may have to be created to test for them. In yet another reminder of the poverty of the Nabokov project, Benyamini has not yet been able to obtain access to the facilities needed for such tests. At a conference at Yale University in 1997, Johnson presented a report on Benyamini's theory of this possible lycaenid mimicry ring. Lincoln Brower, who carried out the pioneer work on the Batesian mimicry of the Monarch-Viceroy relationship, remarked to Johnson in passing, "It's possible they're poisonous."

Benyamini's hypothesis represents a frontier still to be explored, but the subject of mimicry is profoundly relevant to Nabokov's work and reputation in another way: his observations on the matter have often been used to suggest that his science was inadequate. Nabokov strongly believed that the Darwinian mechanisms of evolution, as he understood them, were insufficient to explain cases in which nature had created mimics that were far and away more sophisticated than could possibly be needed to delude a predator. " 'Natural selection,' in the Darwinian sense," he wrote in *Speak Memory*, "could not explain the miraculous coincidence of imitative aspect and imitative behavior, nor could one appeal to the theory of 'the struggle for life' when a protective device was carried to a point of mimetic subtlety, exuberance, and luxury far in excess of a predator's power of appreciation."

Beyond these objections Nabokov, at least in any surviving scientific document, did not attempt to explain these aspects of mimicry in his own scientific terms, but his language seems to appeal to the metaphysical: "Its phenomena showed an artistic perfection usually associated with man-wrought things," he wrote in *Speak, Memory*. "I discovered in nature the nonutilitarian delights that I sought in art. Both were a form of magic, both were a game of intricate enchantment and deception." Likewise in *The Gift* he suggested (or at least his hero, Fyodor, suggested) that mimicry "seemed to have been invented by some waggish artist precisely for the intelligent eyes of man." These passages, with their appeals to magic and enchantment and their intimations of a conscious design behind nature have played a significant role in the dismissal of Nabokov in some quarters as a "scientific naïf," despite their distinctly literary — as opposed to scientific — settings. As expressed by Deane Bowers, at the time the curator of Lepidoptera at the Museum of Comparative Zoology, quoted in a 1998 *Boston Globe* article, Nabokov in such instances "contradicts the known genetic basis of marvelous coincidences of mimicry."

But it should be remembered that these judgments come from workers privy to modern science's elaborate understanding of genetics. Today knowledge of the principles of population genetics is required of all students of biological science. Their elegant and mathematically robust explanations of how actions of genes in specific populations drive evolution toward sometimes fantastic but still mechanistic external resemblances are part of the common property of biologists. But it wasn't until these concepts of modern genetics were married to the broader Darwinian notions of evolution by natural selection — the so-called neo-Darwinian synthesis — that Darwin's concepts could be held to explain the intricacies of mimicry. (The development can be seen as the natural but hard-won convergence of macroevolution — natural selection, fossils, biogeography, and so forth — with microevolution — the intricacies of genetics and cell biology.)

Darwin himself, after all, could not understand the precise workings of natural selection without the fundamental knowledge of how genes act in populations. The groundwork for the neo-Darwinian synthesis was being laid while Nabokov was at Harvard, and his objections to a Darwinian explanation of such phenomena were not uncommon at the time. Even then the synthesis was just beginning to take on a general form. There was simply not enough statistical understanding of how genes work in populations for it to provide a completely satisfactory "Darwinian" explanation for mimicry.

Stephen Jay Gould, writing in *Véra's Butterflies,* a book produced in conjunction with a recent sale of books from Nabokov's personal library by Glenn Horowitz Bookseller in New York, is among those who recognize that Nabokov's stance was not unusual for his time: "When Nabokov wrote his technical papers in the 1940's, the modern Darwinian orthodoxy had not yet congealed, and a Nabokovian style of doubt remained quite common among evolutionary biologists, particularly among taxonomists immersed in the study of anatomical detail and geographic variation."

It was really not until the 1950s, and even later, that the neo-Darwinian synthesis began to take anything like its final form. This was in particular the decade for the most important work in population genetics, crucial for the complex conception of mimicry as it is understood today. By then Nabokov had for all practical purposes abandoned significant work in the laboratory and he understandably seems not to have made significant efforts to keep up with theoretical developments in his field.

It is important to realize that Nabokov fully accepted the concept of evolution per se. He was simply honest enough to admit that he could not understand how the theory as it was developed in his day could account for phenomena like mimicry. Contemporary scientists who were more confident than Nabokov in a Darwinian explanation for mimicry didn't necessarily have one in hand: they simply assumed that the mechanism would be discovered, and of course they were right.

In the *Garland Companion,* the Yale lepidopterist Charles Lee Remington cites work by V. E. Alexandrov attempting to link Nabokov's mimicry themes with the ideas of the metaphysician P. D. Uspensky and the playwright N. N. Evreinov, Russians whose works were peaking in public acclaim when Nabokov came to Harvard. These writers are known today as vitalists, who nourished the Aristotelian belief that there is a driving intelligence behind nature and that natural processes, like mimicry, are developed by this intelligence toward a desired end. This teleological (that is, goal-oriented) system of belief easily becomes metaphysical if the intelligence is attributed to God or other supernatural force. Working before a clear understanding of genetics, Uspensky, Evreinov, and their like tried to explain a complex phenomenon without the tools that would make such an explanation fully possible. Now, of course, their ideas have been discredited. Nabokov is known to have been interested in the work of another well-known vitalist, Henri Bergson, but there is no direct evidence that he read anything by Uspensky and Evreinov. While Uspensky's often magical view of the world suggests some of the layered realities Nabokov himself created in works like *Pale Fire*, it seems unlikely that Nabokov the scientist would have put much faith in Uspensky's overall worldview.

Unlike Uspensky and Evreinov, Nabokov never tried to advance his own explanation for mimicry in any kind of formal or scientific setting that can be examined today, nor did he ever openly attribute the phenomenon to supernatural causes. Rather, in his literature, which provides the standard texts for his feelings on the matter, he felt free to express his awe about mimicry in terms that had more to do with human feelings and natural wonder than with laboratory science.

Remington, who knew Nabokov well, suggested that he might have had such a strong metaphysical investment in his objections to natural selection that he could never have accepted an evolutional explanation for mimicry. But there appear to be no major biological concepts, established in his own age, in which Nabokov was not fully proficient, and given his intellect it is impossible to believe that he would not have been fascinated by many of modern science's elegant explanations of biological phenomena, or that he would not have quite easily grasped their significance, as do thousands of current graduate students of biology. Nabokov's views on mimicry and evolution were conservative, but this was an attitude he shared with many of his contemporaries; it certainly does not reduce him to the level of a scientific naïf.

The charge of unsophistication was similarly leveled during Nabokov's most public dispute with any of his colleagues during his own lifetime. In conjunction with his scale-row counting for his "Nearctic Members of the Genus *Lycaeides*" paper of 1949, he published lists and tables recording the number of wing scales and other taxonomic characteristics in various groups of Blues. But the following year in a letter to *The Lepidopterists' News,* F. Martin Brown, another successor to William Comstock at the American Museum of Natural History, pointed out that without a statistical analysis (which could simply show which of Nabokov's counts might have resulted from chance alone) the numbers were without scientific value, particularly given the small sample sizes. Brown, drawing on the discipline of biological statistics, a relatively new development at the time, stated that the scale-row counts "mean nothing until the statistical parameter of the data on each subspecies is established." Although Nabokov had been a pioneer in introducing meticulous scale-row counts and other quantitative measures of taxonomic characters, he was unfamiliar with the function of statistics and took offense. In a published response, basically defending the quantitative methods that predated statistical analysis, he ended with the bold flourish "After all, natural science is responsible to philosophy — not to statistics."

In years since some of Nabokov's champions have salvaged something from this exchange by pointing to the wit and fiery spirit of Nabokov's response to Brown's objections to his paper. But Brown was right about the statistics and the science. Nabokov's pride and apparent embarrassment led him down a path that is hard to defend. As for Brown, he was a gentleman who seems to have realized that he had put Nabokov in an uncomfortable position. In his own response to Nabokov's reply, he wrote that he had felt free to use Nabokov's paper as an example of common misuse of statistics "because in every other way it is excellent." (In 1956 Brown introduced the common name Nabokov's Blue for *Lycaeides idas sublivens,* the subspecies Nabokov had named in 1949; it has been known more recently as the Dark Blue.)

At the time of this exchange statistics were just beginning to be used in sophisticated ways to explore biological phenomena, and forward-looking entomologists like Brown were employing them in their research. Nabokov, who had adopted or devised quite innovative methods in many areas of taxonomy, was not on board with this development. Yet, again, this is a reflection more of his character and perhaps circumstances than of his intellect; as Brown suggested, this fault was widespread. The basic principles of statistics are not difficult to learn, and had Nabokov continued his academic career and developed his innovative scale-counting methods, it is reasonable to suppose that he would have learned them. During an interview for *The New York Times,* Remington said, "Nabokov was a very good lepidopterist; he would have been an even better one had he had formal training." Nabokov's exchange with Brown is perhaps the best illustration of the truth of Remington's remark, but its importance should not be exaggerated in terms of Nabokov's broader career.

Benyamini's proposal of the mimicry ring and his other explorations of South American Blue life cycles were not the only result the Nabokov project yielded beyond taxonomic classification. With the mass of data they had gathered, Bálint and Johnson were at least able to turn to the question of origins. Since biogeographers had assumed for decades that all the Andean Blues had filtered down from the North during the Great American Interchange, the two lepidopterists were particularly eager to examine genealogical relationships with Blues in the Nearctic region. They found that only two genuses, *Paralycaeides* and *Madeleinea,* showed any clear anatomical affinity to northern Blues, and those genuses also happened to have the northernmost distribution of any of the South American groups. (*Paralycaeides* proved akin to two northern genuses in which Nabokov had considerable expertise, *Plebejus* and *Agriades; Madeleinea* was a relative of the Nearctic genus *Aricia.*)

However, two of Nabokov's genuses from the High Andes of central South America, *Nabokovia* and *Itylos,* had anatomies that could be closely related only to those of other Neotropical Blue genuses, both of which have representative species in the tropical regions around the base of the Andes. *Itylos* was found to be closely related to Nabokov's restricted genus *Hemiargus,* and *Nabokovia* was a sister genus of *Echinargus.* Each of these relationships — a distinctive High Andean genus coupled with a sister genus of wider lowland distribution throughout Latin America — suggested that the upland genus evolved from lowland ancestors as the Andes began their uplift, the same pattern that Johnson had detected earlier in certain South American Hairstreaks.

Moreover, both the *Itylos-Hemiargus* and *Nabokovia-Echinargus* clusters were in evolutionary terms far more primitive than any groups of northern Blues, meaning that they could not have evolved from northern immigrants. The central Andean genus of Hairstreak-like Blues that Bálint and Johnson had named *Polytheclus,* although it did not show a clear relationship to any other known group of Blues, had a very primitive anatomy as well. Nabokov had cunningly guessed at its ancientness — simply from the features of its wings — when he suggested it might be akin to his *Pseudothecla,* what is today *Nabokovia.*

As for *Pseudolucia,* not only was it genealogically very ancient, nearly as old as *Nabokovia, Itylos,* and *Polytheclus,* but its exclusive distribution in the continent's southern reaches suggested either evolution from a temperate line going back to the supercontinent Gondwanaland or, of more recent origin, one nurtured through the millennia in the cold grasslands of Patagonia. Although no close and direct African or transoceanic relationships have as yet been detected for any of the Latin American Blues Nabokov studied, the patterns of their geographic distributions and their distinctive anatomies suggest ages comparable to *Brephidium* and *Leptotes,* genuses of Blues with members in both Africa and South America.

At this stage of research the origins of Blue butterflies in central and southern South America remain the subject of intense speculation. Pondering the many unique plants and animals from these regions, biogeographers have considered not only the possibility of Gondwanian, or early Patagonian, origin but the intriguing prospect that a complete fragment of the earth's crust may have actually disappeared — a lost continent called Pacifica. This fragment has been postulated by some geophysicists and biogeographers to have journeyed across the Pacific Ocean in ancient times, only to disappear, by remelting, beneath South America along the Andean ridge. If this were so, they speculate, it might have deposited the ancestors of animals and plants that today show very odd distributions — from the central Andes south to Patagonia but also in far-flung regions around the Pacific Rim. What is clear today is that the long-held view of origin from the north, by the Great American Interchange, can provide a viable explanation for only two of Nabokov's South American genuses, *Paralycaeides* and *Madeleinea.*

The new data from the Nabokov project upset decades of biogeographical assumptions about the origins of South America's butterfly faunas. But in retrospect they also provided some insight into Nabokov's thinking about some of the questions of the distribution of butterflies. When it came to biogeography Nabokov, like all his contemporaries, was hobbled by not understanding that the continents are mobile. The prevalent "stable earth hypothesis" of Nabokov's time required the organisms to move and, as will be remembered, in his conclusions to the Latin American treatise, this caused Nabokov some puzzlement. The only route available to him in the conventional biogeography of the day was the traditional one recognized from Asia to North America across Alaska's Bering Strait in what was guessed to have been a warmer era. Nabokov obviously recognized the problems this caused with his data, saying, "The difficulty of making them take the Bering Strait route is very great." However, he bowed to convention, deciding, he wrote, to "hang my distributional horseshoes on the nail of Nome [the town on the Alaskan side of the strait] rather than postulate transoceanic land-bridges in other parts of the world." But he was clearly unconvinced — concluding that the anatomy of many of his South American Blues must be "very ancient" and stating that it would make more sense to him if he could postulate that, somehow, the Blues got from Asia to South America first and later to North America.

Again he acceded to the dominant theory of his day, concluding that the uniqueness of his South American butterflies must be a result of their ancestors' having crossed from Asia into North America, advancing to South America and then going extinct in the north. This was precisely the camelid scenario that pervaded the biogeography of the day. Thus, Nabokov's "good eye" was clearly in play here, but he had no alternative view available by which to make sense of his data. As in his views on mimicry, Nabokov's scientific acumen needs to be considered not in relation to what scientists know today but in relation to his own time. Next to the complications caused by his celebrity, perhaps, failure to consider Nabokov's accomplishments in this light has been the biggest factor in the dismissive assessments of his competence.

The literary world has long taken it for granted that Nabokov possessed a superior intellect, was a superior abstract thinker, a genius — call it what you will. In the world of science, however, the assumptions have been quite different. As has been discussed, systematic biology is a two-tiered discipline, distinguishing taxonomy — nuts-and-bolts classification and naming — from systematics, which explores broader, more far-reaching questions of methodology, taxonomic technique, and evolutionary theory. Although intertwined in the wider perspective, taxonomy and systematics often involve different scientists, different journals, and sometimes even different academic departments or scientific institutions. This disjuncture clearly hurt Nabokov's standing among scientists, a fact amply reflected in some of the prominent assessments of his career discussed in Chapter 1, typified by Frank Carpenter's characterization of his level of interest as "that which we find in the majority of amateurs" and the observation by Deane Bowers that "his scientific contributions never rose beyond the descriptive to the synthetic."

There is a general feeling among systematic biologists that while almost anyone can do basic taxonomy, "systematic," or synthetic thinking takes place on another intellectual level. For those who hold this view, it is hard to accept that Nabokov was ultimately a taxonomist not because he lacked capacity but by personal inclination. To convince them otherwise would require evidence at the level of the synthetic.

Nabokov, who found the truth in the details, would no doubt have been as skeptical of the thinking of many systematists as he was of those writers or critics who expected great works of art to be parables of generalized social conditions. Certainly none of his writings deals in depth with the theoretical notions of systematics in any great detail. But, contrary to typical belief, Nabokov did at times think at the level of what would be considered systematics, although only a few scattered paragraphs of his published scientific work — in his brief introductions or discussion sections, for example — offer clues to his views on issues such as taxonomic method and evolutionary theory. Therefore his theoretical affiliations, such as they are, must be gleaned mostly from offhand or out-of-context remarks that bore mostly on his taxonomy.

From the time Nabokov's work was published, no systematist would take it from a shelf in search of elucidation. The workaday lepidopterist, generally lacking any interest in or knowledge of Nabokov's intellectual or literary accomplishments, would normally read Nabokov's papers, if at all, simply to locate some classificatory fact or detail required by other taxonomic work. In such review most scientists, particularly given Nabokov's uninviting formal style, are likely simply to pass over the discussion sections to reach the formal taxonomic data.

However, three themes, all of which have been examined in this book, constantly recur in Nabokov's work, and they seem to reflect crucial aspects of his thinking on three key elements of evolutionary biology and taxonomy — the definition of species, the origin of species, and the relationship of evolution to observable characteristics in living organisms. Nabokov believed that

1. species must be defined by considerations of interbreeding *and* structure

2. careful research could reconstruct the genealogical pathways of evolution and classifications should be based on these genealogies

3. the direction of evolution could be discerned through the gradual transformation of characteristics from the most primitive to the most advanced.

Nabokov's views on these issues have often been misunderstood or unrecognized. Science's concept of species was in flux when he came to Harvard. New discoveries in genetics were just beginning to be consolidated with prevailing Darwinian theory in neo-Darwinism synthesis, and the taxonomic methods of accompanying it became the evolutionary school of systematics. Its leaders were famous contemporaries of Nabokov from the American Museum of Natural History and Ivy League universities, most notably Ernst Mayr and George Gaylord Simpson.

Evolutionary systematists were intrigued by the new discoveries in genetics. Some of them envisioned that taxonomy's practice of defining species by sets of observable characteristics would ultimately be replaced by a foolproof, genetic, and reproductively based "biological" definition of species. What was lacking, however, was a perspective well-known today to all students and practitioners of taxonomy. While the biological definition of species (that they are "reproductively isolated" entities) is precisely what species *are,* this concept is not readily applicable for the workaday taxonomist. Since the collections-based taxonomist is most often dealing with dead specimens, which are not, obviously, reproducing in laboratory, she or he must make some reasoned judgment about how to categorize and name species from observable characteristics. The balanced view, that species involve both biology and structure, was precisely the one voiced by Nabokov in the 1940s. It occurs in all his Harvard publications, in his draft introduction to "Butterflies of Europe," and in notes for his speeches to the Cambridge Entomological Club.

Contrary to what some critics have stated, Nabokov never disagreed with the biological species definition. He only stressed that it should not be the *primary* definition, that biology informs structure in providing a standard for species recognition. It is true that Nabokov occasionally mentioned his more famous colleague Mayr in critiques of species definitions, but his criticisms were not of Mayr or of the new discoveries in genetics. Rather Nabokov's view was the one to which, in the end, most working taxonomists returned — knowing what species are *in nature* but also knowing that a taxonomist must still distinguish them by visible characteristics. Today graduate students are taught that this is the difference between species as a concept and species as a method.

When it came to species and their classification, Nabokov believed strongly in classifications based on branching genealogical relations — what modern science calls a phylogenetic approach. He asserted throughout his scientific papers and speeches that the pathway of descent from a common ancestor was discoverable. In "Notes on Neotropical Plebejinae" he engaged his readers to likening it to the taxonomist obtaining a "Wellesian time machine," with which to go back in time and follow the precise history of evolution. As always for Nabokov, anatomy was the key both to rediscovering this pathway and to classifying organisms.

Although the natural connection between the branching genealogy of evolution and grouping living things into a classification seems obvious to modern minds, it must be remembered that for a time following Nabokov's tenure at Harvard — a period coinciding quite exactly with the general ignorance of his work among taxonomists — this view fell completely out of fashion. Evolutionary systematics was weakened by its inability to develop a precise method for reconstructing evolutionary genealogy. Having to resort to "best guess" views of its adherents, the discipline became authority-driven and criticized for a lack of scientific objectivity. Consequently, by the 1960s a new method was sweeping systematics — phenetics, a technique based on the sophisticated mathematics made possible by a new invention, the computer. Pheneticists believed their computers, which totaled the sums of multitudes of similarities and differences between organisms, could provide the objectivity that evolutionary taxonomy had lacked. Quite befitting the era of JFK, RFK, and LBJ, pheneticists' computer programs determined not species but OTU's — operational taxonomic units.

The dominance of phenetics was short-lived, however. It was, as Nabokov had stated in his own taxonomic discussions, a "horizontal" method, concerned only with the sums of pluses and minuses, not the vertical branching of evolution. When systematists realized that phenetics was taking them farther and farther away from their original goal, discovering the pathways of evolution, they by and large returned to that search. By the 1970s and '80s systematics was again pursuing a genealogical method. The conundrum of Nabokov's *Cyclargus* versus Riley's *Hemiargus* was almost an icon of this transition. The inability of phenetics to distinguish the important characters, as Nabokov had pointed to in the anatomy, had been its downfall.

The renewed quest for a genealogical method was the same one that Nabokov had firmly been on forty years before. As he had said in "Notes on Neotropical Plebejinae": "A 'polytypic' genus [that is, a genus with several different species] is determined by structural characters which are common to all the species it includes and the particular combination of which, more than the presence of some particular detail, no matter how striking, distinguishes the group from any other. . . . Hence the conviction that there is *some* phylogenetic link where there is a recurrence of similar genitalic characters and that certain groupings — the new genera to which we must now turn — may be so devised as to reflect the natural affiliations of the species." And, as he had said in his theses on *Lycaeides,* the direction of evolution can be understood by recognizing the transition from primitive to advanced features — the direction not only in the features themselves but in groups of organisms as well.

It was because of a clear view of evolutionary process, and its relation to patterns in taxonomic characteristics, that Nabokov was confident in his ability to discover the real, or natural groups even among the small samples of Blues available to him in the tropical study. This attitude has some bearing on notions of Nabokov's sophistication as a scientist.

The fundamental goal of modern systematics is to reconstruct biological lineages, to ascertain the genealogy of evolution. It is important to realize that Nabokov also sought this goal. In "Notes on Neotropical Plebejinae," he explicitly stated that he sought genealogical relations and that he believed morphological data could predict these. From his own detailed research on Blues, he knew that internal anatomy was key to disentangling a complex group of look-alike butterlifes and insisted that sound anatomical work was the way to understanding the path of evolution. In this his views are very close to the current phylogenetic school of taxonomy. This doesn't make him a great biological innovator, but his views here are much more similar to modern notions of systematics than were those of many of his contemporaries.

Moreover, in the 1970s and 1980s, the German scientist Willi Hennig and his followers consolidated the genealogically based method of taxonomy known as phylogenetics, or cladistics. They earned wide and admiring recognition for articulating a breakthrough system for reconstructing a map of evolution based on recognizing a progression of physical characteristics through time, from "primitive" to "derived," in a given group of organisms. The unique sharing of such derived physical characteristics, or characters, is what allows the grouping of the organisms as relatives into a genealogy. Today this is considered the most cutting-edge, up-to-date way of looking at physical evolution, and Nabokov's language in much of his work seems to reflect the same underlying assumptions.

The view is amply illustrated in his 1944 *Lycaeides* paper, where he wrote: "I view evolution in *Lycaeides* as . . . its general graduation from the most primitive structures to the most specialized ones." That declaration reads like a basic methodological statement from today's cladistics. Nabokov's magic triangles, whimsical or archaic as they may seem today, formed the mapping technique for his genitalic studies and represent a concrete expression of what the modern method calls character transformation.

In 1945 he wrote in "Notes on Neotropical Plebejinae": "What I term species, in my department, can be defined as a phase of evolutionary structure, male and female, traversed more or less simultaneously by a number of, consequently, more or less similar organisms morphologically shading into each other in various individual or racial ways." The crucial phrase here for modern scientists is "a phase of evolutionary structure." Nabokov realized, quite remarkably for his time, that what scientists study in the laboratory is merely a momentary glimpse into a constantly changing, ongoing process of structural transformation in living organisms. In the same vein he articulated other concepts whose ring would be quite familiar to modern cladists: primitive prototypes, lost ancestral characteristics, and hypothetical ancestors.

Like the cladists, Nabokov realized the difficulties of attaching the static notion of a species to evolution, which is constantly progressing. Doing so, he said, was the "equivalent of describing a journey as a series of stops along the way." Of course Nabokov had no inkling of methods that are used by systematists today, more than half a century after he completed his most important work, any more than he could have known of the use of modern computers to group genealogical data. But since the cladists have essentially returned to the notion of species as delineated by physical structures, precisely the point upon which he insisted and the hallmark of his methodology, Nabokov's point of view has an impressively modern ring.

Philip Zaleski, in his 1986 *Harvard Magazine* article, wrote that Nabokov's "laboratory labors display great exuberance and patience, but not a glimmer of the imaginative insight that marks the scientific groundbreaker." Nabokov was not a scientific groundbreaker, at least on the synthetic level that Zaleski and his sources hold up as the gold standard, in part because he preferred other paths. But his work still unarguably displays glimmers of systematic insight and the occasional flash of intuitive brilliance concerning nature and how it works.

Nabokov's reputation in lepidoptery is secure mostly because of the acumen he demonstrated in defining his genuses of Latin American Blues in "Notes on Neotropical Plebejinae" and the fact that the methods he used in this study of far-reaching implication were consistent with those applied in all his published works on butterflies. As grandfather to a very important group of butterflies, Nabokov will continue to be associated with every step of the subsequent work, a tie made stronger by the Nabokovian names assigned to so many of his species. Yet, in considering tantalizing hints of his theoretical conceptions, the scientists of the Nabokov project were once again left to think of the brilliance of what might have been — an almost permanent state of mind in dealing with the lepidoptery of Vladimir Nabokov.

Nabokov was speaking lightheartedly when he wrote to his sister Elena Sikorski in 1945 to describe his job at the Museum of Comparative Zoology at Harvard, saying that in *The Gift* he had in a sense foretold his own destiny. He was only vicariously the kind of explorer that his fictional creation Konstantin Godunov-Cherdyntsev was. And, unlike Godunov-Cherdyntsev, his passion for exploration competed with another — literature — that proved even stronger. But on the centennial of his birth, to those scientists who have been more deeply involved in his work than anyone else, Nabokov looks remarkably different as a lepidopterist from the way he was commonly described a mere ten years ago. He should never have feared for his legacy in the field.

Only a few scientists see their names permanently associated with their discoveries in popular parlance. Darwin's Finches and the Humboldt Current come readily to mind; both of those men were celebrities in their own day, and it can be argued that it is easy to pin the label "Nabokov's Blues" on a certain significant group of Latin American Blue butterflies in large part because of celebrity gleaned from another facet of his career. Vladimir Nabokov can show many achievements in literature that will preserve his name. But Nabokov's Blues will justifiably assure his legacy in lepidoptery, a fitting monument for a man who found all the wonder of the world in the spots on a butterfly's wing.

Afterword

IN 1996 Zsolt Bálint, Kurt Johnson, and Dubi Benyamini drew their ten years of work on Nabokov's Blues to a temporary pause after submission of the scientific papers that appeared in 1997. The work will go on, eventually. The questions still to be answered on Nabokov's Blues and their origins, and the continued discovery of new species, many of which still do not have official names, demand it. But in the meantime each of these men's lives took directions that required them to turn their attention elsewhere.

Zsolt Bálint received his Ph.D. in 1996 and took time off to prepare and defend his dissertation — on Nabokov's Blues, of course. He became the collections manager for Lepidoptera at the Hungarian Museum of Natural History in Budapest.

In 1996 Kurt Johnson's position at the American Museum of Natural History was not renewed. Although continuing to live in New York, he moved on to a research associateship with the Florida State Collection of Arthropods, where the Association for Tropical Lepidoptera had been established in 1989. As of this writing, he and Bálint have never met.

By 1997 Dubi Benyamini could see an end drawing near to the work that had allowed him to reside in Chile and travel regularly to Argentina and Bolivia. Until he finally left South America for Israel in 1998, he continued to work frantically to cover the remaining 10,000 miles of field itinerary that had eluded him on that incorrigible continent.

A Glossary of Binomial and Common Nabokovian Butterfly Names

Groups Above Genus Level

Nabokovia Bálint and Johnson 1995. A section name (a section is a large number of related genuses) among the Latin American Blues, including the infratribes Pseudo-chrysopsina and Nabokovina (see next entry).

Nabokovina Bálint and Johnson 1995. An infratribe name (an infratribe is several re-lated genuses) of the Nabokovia section, including the genuses *Echinargus* Nabokov 1945, *Nabokovia* Hemming 1960, and *Eldoradina* Balletto 1993.

Genuses and Species

Genuses and species within them are listed alphabetically. Scientific names are itali-cized, followed by names of scientist-author(s) and date of publication. In species en-tries bracketed first and surnames are of the Nabokov scholars who suggested names (otherwise names were suggested by G. Warren Whitaker).

- **r:** region of occurrence and general remarks;
- **e:** etymology, a brief explanation of the name required by the nomenclatorial Code;
- **cn:** common name, a suggested common name based on general traditions in lep-idoptery (with all patronyms rendered in the possessive, as in Lolita's Blue, etc.)

Latin American Blues

Cyclargus Nabokov 1945. **r:** A valid genus of Caribbean region Blues placed, in 1975, by Britain's Norman Riley as equivalent to Hübner's *Hemiargus*. Since 1992 reinstated by Johnson, Bálint, and other scientists, who demonstrated *Hemiargus* is related to Draudt's *Itylos*, not *Cyclargus*.

Echinargus Nabokov 1945 **r:** A valid genus of Latin American Blues closely related to *Nabokovia*. Because only a single species occurs in the United States, the genus was ig-nored by North American scientists for many years.

Eldoradina Balletto 1993. **r:** The valid genus name for Hairstreak-like Blues (superseded *Polytheclus* Bálint and Johnson 1993). Species occur in the central Andes.

> *cincinnatus* Bálint and Johnson 1993
>> **e:** Cincinnatus in *Invitation to a Beheading;* **cn:** Cincinnatus Blue; **r:** Peru; a striking Hairstreak-like Blue, above silvery blue, beneath light brown strewn with vivid dark spots; *cyanea* Balletto is now the valid name.

Itylos Draudt 1921. The valid name for Blues Nabokov placed in his genus *Parachilades* (see *Parachilades*). Species occur throughout the central Andes.

> *luzhin* Bálint 1993
>> **e:** Luzhin in *The Defense;* **cn:** Luzhin's Blue; **r:** Peru; above shiny blue, beneath buff gray with indistinct wavy stripes; *fumosus* Balletto is now the valid name.

> *mira* Bálint and Lamas 1998 [Galya Diment]
>> **e:** Pnin's beloved, from *Pnin;* **cn:** Mira's Blue; **r:** central Peru; above, luminous blue, beneath, ash gray, hind wing with prominent continuous blackish band.

> *mashenka* Bálint 1993 (originally named in *Madeleinea*)
>> **e:** Mashenka (Mary) in *Mashenka;* **cn:** Mashenka's (or Mary's) Blue; **r:** Peru; oddly marked, wings angulate, above shimmering blue, beneath with alternating slashes of silver-white and deep brown.

> *pnin* Bálint 1993
>> **e:** Professor Pnin in *Pnin;* **cn:** Pnin's Blue; **r:** central Peru; above luminous blue, beneath buff-gray with emphatic wavy spot-bands.

Leptotes Scudder 1876. **r:** A group of Blues that Nabokov did not include in his 1945 study but that have since become inextricably linked with his name and legacy. Species occur in Latin America and several other parts of the world.

> *delalande* Bálint and Johnson 1995
>> **e:** Nabokov's invented philosopher alter ego; **cn:** Delalande's Blue; **r:** Peru; above deep blue, beneath brown overlaid with vivid pattern of narrowly marbled Zebra-like stripes.

> *krug* Bálint, Johnson, Salazar, and Vélez 1995 [Dieter E. Zimmer]
>> **e:** Professor Adam Krug in *Bend Sinister;* **cn:** Krug's Blue; **r:** Colombia; above dingy violet, below brown marbled with fine white and with semblance of a single Zebra stripe.

Madeleinea Bálint 1993. **r:** Because of rules of the nomenclatorial Code, Nabokov's *Itylos* (1945) still needed a name. Accordingly, *Madeleinea* became valid when proposed in 1993. Species occur throughout the northern and central Andes.

> *ardisensis* Bálint and Lamas 1996
>> **e:** suffix *-ensis* associates it with a place, the great estate Ardis Hall in Nabokov's *Ada, ardis* being a word Nabokov fashioned from *paradise;* **cn:** Paradise Blue; **r:** central Peru; above shiny blue, beneath both wings boldly spotted, the hind wing nearly checked with deep brown and brilliant white.

cobaltana Bálint and Lamas 1994
  e: after the Kobaltana mountain resort in *Pale Fire;* **cn:** Cobalt Blue; **r:** central Peru; above gleaming blue with a large black spot at edge of hind wing; beneath greatly spotted, hind wing with bold brown patches outlined in vivid silver-white.

lolita Bálint 1993
  e: after Lolita (Dolores Haze) in *Lolita;* **cn:** Lolita's Blue; **r:** northwest Peru; above dark blue with short tail-like extension on hind wing edge; beneath with odd white-and-black patchlike pattern and a black spot along hind wing edge.

nodo Bálint and Johnson 1995
  e: Nodo in *Pale Fire;* **cn:** Nodo's Blue; **r:** Ecuador, southern Colombia; above deep violet, beneath dark tawny with two vivid silver slashes crossing the hind wing.

odon Bálint and Johnson 1995
  e: Odon in *Pale Fire;* **cn:** Odon's Blue; **r:** Ecuador; above brownish, beneath brown and buff with profuse silver slashes.

tintarrona Bálint and Johnson 1995
  e: the precious blue Tintarron glass in *Pale Fire;* **cn:** Tintarron Blue; **r:** central Peru; above brilliant blue, beneath light brown and buff with interspersed deep brown and silver patches.

vokoban Bálint and Johnson 1995
  e: An anagram (mirror reversal) of Nabokov; **cn:** Nabokov's Anagramatic Blue [various North American Blue subspecies named *nabokovi* are already called Nabokov's Blue]; **r:** Ecuador; above bronze brown, beneath tawny with narrow, brown, V-shaped marking on hind wing.

Nabokovia Hemming 1960. **r:** Hemming replaced *Pseudothecla* Nabokov 1945 (invalid because the name had been used by Embrik Strand in 1910) with this patronym honoring Nabokov. Species of *Nabokovia,* which occur from Peru to northern Chile, are basically brown, with odd-shaped wings and short hind wing tails.

ada Bálint and Johnson 1994
  e: Ada Veen in *Ada;* **cn:** Ada's Blue; **r:** northern Chile; wings angulate, above brown, beneath buff with blocklike brown spots centralized on the hind wing.

Parachilades Nabokov 1945. Because of technicalities in the nomenclatorial Code, this genus is now considered the same as *Itylos* Draudt (see *Itylos*).

Paralycaeides Nabokov 1945. A valid genus of South American Blues occurring throughout the northern Andes.

hazelea Bálint and Johnson 1945 [Brian Boyd]
  e: Hazel in *Pale Fire;* **cn:** Hazel's Blue; **r:** Peru; above brown, beneath buff with various spots and a bold, elongated silver patch crossing the hind wing.

shade Bálint 1993

    e: John Shade in *Pale Fire;* **cn:** Shade's Blue; **r:** Peru; above brown with hind wing showing whitish patches, beneath with colorful combinations of gray, golden, and reddish in various spots and patches.

Pseudochrysops Nabokov 1945. A valid genus of Blues from the Caribbean islands. Because its single species, a brilliant blue with hind wing tails, is extremely unusual, for years *Pseudochrysops* was the only Nabokovian genus widely used by scientists.

Pseudolucia Nabokov 1945. A valid genus of South American Blues, extremely diverse, from Peru nearly to Tierra del Fuego.

aureliana Bálint and Johnson 1993

    e: Popular name for a lepidopterist, from "The Aurelian"; **cn:** Aurelian Blue; **r:** northern Chile; above glistening silver-blue, beneath tawny yellow with specklelike brown and white spots.

charlotte Bálint and Johnson 1993

    e: Charlotte Haze in *Lolita;* **cn:** Charlotte's Blue; **r:** Patagonia; above male blue with orange overcast, female orange and brown; beneath both with forewings orange, hind wings mottled brown with a dark, V-shaped spot-band.

clarea Bálint and Johnson 1993

    e: Clare Quilty in *Lolita;* **cn:** Clare's Blue: **r:** central Chile; above male blue with orange overcast, female dull blue with orange-brown overcast; beneath forewings bronze, hind wings with distinct white-edged brown patches forming a broad V-shaped patch.

hazeorum Bálint and Johnson 1993

    e: Charlotte and Delores (Lolita) Haze in *Lolita;* **cn:** Haze's Blue; **r:** south-central Chile; large, with males blue and females orange, forewings of both sexes with dark, hazy, marginal borders; beneath orange and tawny with broad V-shaped mark on hind wing vividly edged with white.

humbert Bálint and Johnson 1995

    e: Humbert Humbert in *Lolita;* **cn:** Humbert's Blue; **r:** above orangish, forewing with vivid black border, beneath forewing orange, hind wing dark gray-brown at base, outlined by a darker, V-shaped band and light gray and buff along the wing edges.

kinbote Bálint and Johnson 1995

    e: Kinbote, Shade's commentator in *Pale Fire;* **cn:** Kinbote's Blue; **r:** central Chile; appearing more like a *Madeleinea,* above brown, beneath buff with V-shaped hind wing mark extremely broad, like the larger patches common in *Madeleinea; scintilla* Balletto is now the valid name.

sirin Bálint 1993

    e: Sirin, Nabokov's Russian nom de plume; **cn:** Sirin Blue; **r:** southern Andes; above male vivid sky blue outlined with black, female duller bluish; beneath both sexes dark bronze-orange, hind wing with an archlike band of black; *argentina* Balletto is now the valid name.

tamara Bálint and Johnson 1995 [D. Barton Johnson]
  e: Tamara, Nabokov's first love, recounted in *Speak, Memory;* **cn:** Tamara's Blue; **r:** Patagonia; above female dark brown and buff, forewing showing a zigzagged juncture of these colors; beneath forewing orange, hind wing with cryptic, woodlike complexion formed by jagged black marks overlaying buff and gray.

vera Bálint and Johnson 1993
  e: Nabokov's beloved wife, Véra; **cn:** Véra's Blue; **r:** southern Chile; very small, above male light blue with dusty orange overcast, female brilliant orange and black; beneath both sexes with vivid, elongate, black, V-shaped marking.

zembla Bálint and Johnson 1993
  e: Zembla, the mythical kingdom in *Pale Fire;* **cn:** Zembla Blue; **r:** Chile; above male azure blue with vivid white and black checkered fringe, female vivid orange and black; beneath both sexes with bold, narrow, vivid, black V-shaped marking.

zina Bálint and Johnson 1995 [Stephen Jan Parker]
  e: Zina Mertz, Fyodor's paramour in *The Gift;* **cn:** Zina's Blue; **r:** central Chile; above male deep and vivid blue with bold black and white checkered fringe, female similar but with burst of orange on forewing; beneath both sexes with greatly contrasted light and dark areas appearing almost checkered.

Pseudothecla Nabokov 1945. Replaced by *Nabokovia* Hemming in 1960 (see *Nabokovia*).

North American and Eurasian Blues

Icaricia Nabokov 1944. **r:** Nabokov named this genus to include several North American species in a large group of Blues previously placed in the genus *Plebejus.* Various scientific works have used *Icaricia* as a genus, subgenus, or not at all. Bálint and Johnson (1997) in their classification on a worldwide basis, synonymized *Icaricia* not with *Plebejus* but with Reichenbach's *Aricia;* this change resulted because they examined more characteristics and species than had previous authors. Theirs is a lumped nomenclature; splitters might return to *Icaricia.*

Plebejus Kluk 1802. A long-standing genus of Northern Hemisphere Blues. Bálint and Johnson (1997), in their worldwide classification, placed *Lycaeides* Hübner within *Plebejus,* thus including the North American Blues Nabokov had named in *Lycaeides.*

ardis Bálint and Johnson 1997 [Ellendea Proffer]
  e: the great estate Ardis Hall in *Ada;* later the publishing house established by Carl and Ellendea Proffer that produced scholarly studies and a number of Nabokov's Russian works; **cn:** Ardis Blue; **r:** Central Asia; above male sky blue with white fringe, beneath with black spots peppered on the wings and an orange flush along the margin.

argyrognomon longinus Nabokov 1949
  r: Lepidopterists are taught to pronounce each syllable of scientific names; thus, the name of this species (perhaps the toughest to say among the Blues)

is "ar-ge-rog-no-mon," usually with emphasis on the *no*. When the butterflies of a continent become well-known, lepidopterists begin denoting those of more specific geographic areas as subspecies. Nabokov named this subspecies from northwestern Wyoming; today it is known as *Plebejus idas longinus* (Nabokov).

argyrognomon sublivens Nabokov 1949
   r: Nabokov named this subunit from southwestern Colorado. Modern taxonomists, looking beyond the United States, now consider it a subspecies of a different species — *Plebejus idas sublivens* (Nabokov).

melissa inyoensis (Nabokov) 1949
   r: Nabokov gained authorship of this subspecies through some technicalities of the Code; thus, the parentheses around his name (a convention telling taxonomists "Nabokov made a change"). This Blue, from Southern California, was originally described as a "form" by Jean Gunder. However, as this book explains, modern workers can evaluate the original "intent" of an early author and judge a name to be a valid subspecies. This is what Nabokov did.

melissa pseudosamuelis Nabokov 1949
   r: Nabokov named this subspecies from alpine areas of Colorado, choosing the name because its wing markings were reminiscent of those of his famous Karner Blue. Today the Code advises against prefixes like *pseudo-* and *sub-;* the myriad names that might begin with such combinations could become a bibliographer's nightmare. Nabokov's *pseudosamuelis* is now considered a synonym of *P. melissa melissa*, named in 1873 by W. H. Edwards.

melissa samuelis Nabokov 1943
   r: Nabokov's famous Karner Blue, whose story is detailed in this book.

pilgram Bálint and Johnson 1997 [Simon Karlinksy]
   e: Paul Pilgram, main character in "The Aurelian"; **cn:** Pilgram's Blue; **r:** Central Asia; above male sky blue with white fringe, beneath with black spots peppered on the wings and an orange flush along the margin.

Plebulina Nabokov 1944. **r:** Nabokov named this genus for a single, highly unusual species from the Mojave region of Southern California. Bálint and Johnson (1997), for reasons noted in the *Icaricia* entry and consideration of butterfly life cycles, synonymized *Plebulina* with *Plebejus*. Theirs is a lumped nomenclature; splitters might return to *Plebulina*.

Polyommatus Latreille 1804. **r:** The titular genus of the tribe Polyommatini, a genus of long standing among Northern Hemisphere Blues. It is significant here because, according to Bálint and Johnson's worldwide classification, it includes *Lysandra* Hemming, the genus in which Nabokov described his first Blue, *cormion*.

cormion Nabokov 1941
   r: from the French Alps; a Blue named while Nabokov was a volunteer at the American Museum of Natural History. It turned out to be a hybrid between two European species and today has no status under the Code.

Nabokov's Scientific Publications on Blue Butterflies

1941. *Lysandra cormion,* a new European butterfly. *Journal of the New York Entomological Society* 49: 265–267.

1944. The Nearctic forms of *Lycaeides* Hüb. (Lycaenidae, Lepidoptera). *Psyche* 50: 87–99.

1944. Notes on the morphology of the genus *Lycaeides* (Lycaenidae, Lepidoptera) *Psyche* 50: 104–138.

1945. Notes on Neotropical Plebejinae (Lycaenidae: Lepidoptera). *Psyche* 52: 1–61.

1948. A new species of *Cyclargus* Nabokov (Lycaenidae, Lepidoptera). *The Entomologist* 81: 273–280.

1949. The Nearctic members of the genus *Lycaeides* Hübner (Lycaenidae, Lepidoptera). *Bulletin of the Museum of Comparative Zoology,* Harvard College 101: 479–541.

1952. The female of *Lycaeides argyrognomon sublivens. The Lepidopterists' News* 6: 35–36.

1954. A third species of *Echinargus* Nabokov. *Pysche* 52: 193.

Principal Academic Publications Completing Nabokov's Work on Neotropical Blues

1986. Johnson, K., and D. Matusik. Five new species and one new subspecies of butterflies from the Sierra de Baoruco of Hispaniola. *Annals of the Carnegie Museum* 57: 221–254.

1992. Additions to the Hispaniolan fauna. In K. Johnson ed. "Taxonomic additions to recent studies of Neotropical butterflies. *Reports, Museum of Natural History, University of Wisconsin, Stevens Point* 23: 3–5.

1993. Bálint Zs., and K. Johnson. New species of *Pseudolucia* Nabokov from Chile and Patagonia (Lepidoptera, Lycaenidae, Polyommatini). *Reports, Museum of Natural History, University of Wisconsin, Stevens Point* 27: 1–25.

1993. A new genus of thecline-like Polyommatinae from the Andean region of South America (Lepidoptera, Lycaenidae, Polyommatinae). *Reports, Museum of Natural History, University of Wisconsin, Stevens Point* 28: 1–4.

1993. Bálint, Zs. "A catalogue of polyommatine Lycaenidae (Lepidoptera) of the xeromontane oreal biome in the Neotropics as represented in European collections. *Reports, Museum of Natural History, University of Wisconsin, Stevens Point* 29: 1–42.

1993. Balletto, E. On some new genus-group and species-group names of Andean Polyommatini (Lepidoptera). *Bollettino della Società Entomologica Italianola* 24: 231–243.

1994–1998. Bálint, Zs., K. Johnson, and G. Lamas. Polyommatine Lycaenids of the oreal biome in the Neotropics. Pts. 1–12. *Acta Zoologica Academiae Scientiarum Hungaricae* (1–4, 10); *Annales historico — naturales Museum nationalis Hungarici* (2, 9–12); *Reports, Museum of Natural History, University of Wisconsin, Stevens Point* (5–8).

1995. Bálint, Zs., K. Johnson, and D. Benyamini. *Neotropical Blue Butterflies. Reports, Museum of Natural History, University of Wisconsin, Stevens Point* 43–54.

1996. Johnson, K., G. W. Whitaker, and Zs. Bálint. Nabokov as lepidopterist, an informed appraisal. *Nabokov Studies* 3: 123–143.

1997. Bálint, Zs., and K. Johnson. Reformation of the Polyommatus section with a taxonomic and biogeographic overview (Lepidoptera, Lycaenidae, Polyommatini). *Neue entomologische Nachrichten* 40: 1–68.

General Bibliography

Alexander, Caroline. "Crimes of Passion: A Glimpse into the Covert World of Rare Butterfly Collecting." *Outside.* January, 1996.

Ackery, P. R. "Introduction." In Richard I. Vane-Wright and Phillip R. Ackery, eds. *Biology of Butterflies.* London: Academic Press, 1984.

Appel, Alfred, Jr. *The Annotated Lolita.* New York: McGraw-Hill, 1970.

—— [Interview with Vladimir Nabokov.] *Novel,* Spring 1971.

Austin, G. T., T. C. Emmel, and O. H. H. Mielke. "The Tropical Rainforest Butterfly Fauna of Rondônia, Brazil: Species Composition and Richness." *Tropical Lepidoptera,* in press.

Austin, G. T., and K. Johnson. "Theclinae of Rondônia, Brazil." *Tropical Lepidoptera* 6: 1995 31–39, 7: 1996 45–59, 9: 1998 3–13; *Insecta Mundi* 3–4: 1998 201–236, 255–272.

Bartlett-Calvert, W. "Nuevos Lepidópteros de Chile." *Anales de la Universidad de Chile* 84 (1894): 813–833.

Bates, Henry Walter. *The Naturalist on the River Amazons.* Reprint, Berkeley: University of California Press, 1863 1962.

Blanchard, C. E. "Lepidoptera." Vol. 7 of C. Gay. *Historia física y política de Chile.* Paris and Santiago: Privately printed, 1852.

Boyd, Brian. *Vladimir Nabokov: The American Years.* Princeton: Princeton University Press, 1991.

—— *Vladimir Nabokov: The Russian Years.* Princeton: Princeton University Press, 1990.

Boyd, Brian, and Robert Michael Pyle, eds. *Nabokov's Butterflies: Unpublished and Uncollected Writings.* Boston: Beacon Press, forthcoming.

Boyle, Robert [Interview with Vladimir Nabokov.] *Sports Illustrated* Sept. 15, 1959, pp. E-5 to E-8.

Bridges, Charles A. *Catalogue of the Family-Group, Genus-Group, and Species-Group Names of the Riodinidae and Lycaenidae (Lepidoptera) of the World.* Urbana, Ill: Lincoln Book Bindery, 1994.

Brower, L. P. "Monarch Migration." *Natural History,* 1977, June–July 41–52.

—— "Oyamel Forest Ecosystem Conservation in Mexico Is Necessary to Prevent the Extinction of the Migratory Phenomenon of the Monarch Butterfly in North America." In P. Canevari, ed. CMS Technical Series Publication 1. Bonn and The Hague, forthcoming.

—— "Understanding and Misunderstanding the Migration of the Monarch Butterfly

(Nymphalidae) in North America: 1857–1995." *Journal of the Lepidopterists' Society* 49 (1995): 304–385.

Brown, F. M. "Animals Above Timberline; Colorado and Ecuador." Colorado College Publication 223, 1942. 29 pp.

—— "The Origins of the West Indian Butterfly Fauna." In F. B. Gill, ed. *Zoogeography of the Caribbean.* Special Publication 13. Philadelphia: Academy of Natural Sciences of Philadelphia, 1978. Pp. 5–30.

Brown, Frederick M., and Bernard Heineman. *Jamaica and Its Butterflies.* Hampton, Middlesex: E. W. Classey, 1972.

Brown, K. S. "Paleoecology and Regional Patterns of Evolution in Neotropical Forest Butterflies." In G. T. Prance, ed. *Biological Diversification in the Tropics.* New York: Columbia University Press, 1982. Pp. 255–308.

Buskirk, R. E. "Zoogeographic Patterns and Tectonic History of Jamaica and the Northern Caribbean." *Journal of Biogeography* 12 (1985): 445–461.

Brundin, L. "Insects and the Problem of Austral Disjunctive Distribution." In *Annual Review of Entomology* 12 (1967): 149–168.

—— *Transantarctic Relationships and Their Significance, as Evidenced by Chironomid Midges, with a Monograph of the Subfamilies Podominae, Aphrotaeninae, and the Austral Heptagyiae.* Stockholm: Kungliga Svenska Vetenskaps-Akademiens Handlinger. 1966.

Butler, Arthur G. *Lepidoptera Exotica.* London: E. W. Janson, 1869–1874.

—— "List of Butterflies Collected in Chile by Thomas Edmonds, Esq." *Transactions of the Entomological Society of London* 29 (1881): 449–486.

Butler, Diana. "*Lolita* Lepidoptera." *New World Writing* 16. Philadelphia: Lippincott, 1960.

Cabrera, Angel T., and Abraham Willink. *Biogeografica de América Latina.* Washington, D.C.: Organización de los Estados Americanos, 1980.

Carson, Rachel. *Silent Spring.* Thorndike, Maine: G. K. Hall, 1962.

Clench, H. K. "A Synopsis of the West Indian Lycaenidae with Remarks of their Zoogeography." *Journal of Research on the Lepidoptera* 2 (1964): 247–270.

Clough, M. W. "Endangered and Threatened Wildlife and Plants: Determination of Endangered Status for the Karner Blue Butterfly." *Federal Register* 57 (1992): 59, 236–59, 244.

Coates, S. "Nabokov's Work, on Butterflies, Stands the Test of Time." *New York Times,* May 27, 1997.

Comstock, W. P. "Insects of Porto [sic] Rico and the Virgin Islands, Lepidoptera, Rhopalocera." *New York Academy of Sciences Scientific Survey of Porto [sic] Rico and the Virgin Islands* 12 [1944]: 421–622.

Comstock, W. P., and E. I. Huntington. "Lycaenidae of the Antilles (Lepidoptera: Rhopalocera)." *Annals of the New York Academy of Sciences* 45 (1943): 119–130.

Croizat, L., G. Nelson, and D. E. Rosen. "Centers of Origin and Related Concepts." *Systematic Zoology* 23 (1974): 265–287.

D'Abrera, Bernard. *Butterflies of the Neotropical Region.* Pt. 7, Lycaenidae. Victoria, Australia: Hill House, 1995.

Darwin, Charles. *On the Origin of Species.* 1859. Reprint, Cambridge, Mass.: Harvard University Press, 1964.

—— *Voyage of the Beagle.* Reprint, New York: Bantam, 1958.

Descimon, H. "Origins of Lepidopteran Faunas in the High Tropical Andes." In F.

Vuilleumier and M. Monasterio, eds. *High Altitude Tropical Biogeography.* London: Oxford University Press, 1986. Pp. 500–532.

Dietz, R. S., and J. C. Holden. "The Breakup of Pangaea." *Scientific American* 223 (1970): 30–41.

—— "Reconstruction of Pangaea: Breakup and Dispersion of Continents, Permian to Present." *Journal of Geophysical Research* 75 (1970): 4939–4956.

Dietz, R. S., and W. P. Sproll. "Fit Between Africa and Antarctica: A Continental Drift Reconstruction." *Science* 167 (1970): 1612–1614.

Dirig, R., and J. F. Cryan. "The Karner Blue Project: January 1973 to December 1976." *Atala* 4 (1976): 22–26.

Dobzhansky, Theodosius. *Genetics and the Origin of Species.* New York: Columbia University Press, 1937.

Dort, Wakefield, Jr., and J. Knox Jones, eds. *Pleistocene and Recent Environments on the Central Great Plains.* Lawrence, Kans.: University of Kansas Scientific Publications, 1970.

dos Passos, Cyril F. *A Synonymic List of the Nearctic Rhopalocera.* Memoir 1 of the Lepidopterists' Society. New Haven, Conn., 1964.

Downey, J. C., et al. "Variation in *Plebejus icarioides.*" *Journal of the Lepidopterists' Society* 15 (1961): 34–42; *Ecology* 45 (1964): 172–178.

Draudt, M. *"Thecla."* In A. Seitz, ed. *Die Gross-Schmetterlinge der Erde* [*Macrolepidoptera of the World/Butterflies of the World*] Vol. 5. Stuttgart: Kernan Verlag, 1919. Pp. 795–811.

—— "Polyommatinae" in A. Seitz, *Die Gross-Schmetterlinge der erde* [*Macrolepidoptera of the World/Butterflies of the World*] Vol. 5 Stuttgart: Kernan Verlag, 1917–1924. Pp. 821ff.

Druce, H. H. "On Neotropical Lycaenidae, with Descriptions of New Species." *Proceedings of the Zoological Society of London,* 1907, 566–632.

Ehrlich, Paul R. *The Population Bomb.* New York: Sierra Club–Ballantine, 1968.

Ehrlich, P. R., and P. H. Raven. "Butterflies and Plants: A Study in Coevolution." *Evolution* 18 (1965): 586–608.

Emmel, T. C., G. T. Austin, and Harald H. Schmitz. "The Tropical Rainforest Butterfly Fauna of Rondônia, Brazil: Current Status of Investigations and Conservation." *Tropical Lepidoptera,* in press.

Fabricius, Johann C. *Systema glossatorum.* 1807. Reprint, Solna, Sweden: Bryk Facsimile, 1938.

Field, Andrew. *Nabokov: His Life in Part.* New York: Viking, 1977.

Field, W. D., and J. Herrera. "The Pierid Butterflies of the Genera *Hypsochila* Ureta, *Phulia* Herrich-Schaffer, *Infraphulia* Field, *Pierphulia* Field, and *Piercolias* Staudinger." *Smithsonian Contributions to Zoology* 232 (1977): 1–64.

Fitz Roy, Robert. *Narrative of the Surveying Voyages of His Majesty's Ships Adventure and Beagle Between the Years 1826 and 1836.* 3 vols. London: H. Colburn, 1839.

Franclemont, J. G. "Remembering Nabokov." In G. Gibian and S. J. Parker, eds. *The Achievements of Vladimir Nabokov.* Ithaca, N.Y.: Cornell University, Center for International Studies, 1996. Pp. 227–228.

Funke, Sarah. *Véra's Butterflies.* New York: Glenn Horowitz Bookseller, 1999.

Godart, Jean Baptiste. *Encyclopédie méthodique.* Paris: Privately printed, 1819–1823.

Godman, Frederick, and Osbert Salvin. *Biologia Centrali-Americana: Zoology: Insecta, Lepidoptera.* 3 vols. London: Taylor and Francis, 1879–1901.

Goodman, Edward Julius. *The Explorers of South America.* New York: Macmillan, 1972.

Halsman, Yvonne. *Halsman: Portraits.* New York: McGraw-Hill, 1983.

Hayward, K. "Catálogo de los Ropaloceros Argentinos." *Opera Lilloana* 23 (1973): 1–318.

—— "Insecta Lepidoptera Rhopalocera." Vol. 3 of A. Willink, ed. *Genera et species animallium argentinorum.* Buenos Aires: Bonariae, 1964.

—— "Neuvas especies de Lycaenidae de la Argentina (Lep. Rhop.)." *Acta Zoologica Lilloana* 8 (1949): 567–581.

Hemming, F. "Establishment of the Genus *Nabokovia* gen. nov. (Lycaenidae)." *Annotationes Lepidopterologicae* 2 (1960): 41–42.

—— *The Generic Names of the Butterflies and Their Type-Species (Lepidoptera: Rhopalocera).* Supplements [9] to *Bulletin of British Museum (Natural History)*, 1967.

Hennig, Willi. *Phylogenetic Systematics.* Urbana: University of Illinois Press, 1966.

Heppner, John B. *Classification of Lepidoptera.* Supplement to *Holarctic Lepidoptera* (Association for Holarctic Lepidoptera), 1998.

Heppner, John B., ed. *Lepidoptera News* (Association for Tropical Lepidoptera) 1–4 (1996–1999).

Herrera, G. J., and R. Covarrubias. "Distribución biogeográfica del grupo *Tatocheila* [*sic*]-*Phulia* (Lepidoptera: Pieridae)." In [*Abstracts*] (Congress Latin American Zoology, Arequipa, Peru) 9 (1983): 213.

Herrera, G. J. and V. Pérez d'Angello. "Hallazgo en Chile de *Stuardosatyrus williamsianus* (Butler) 1868 y consideraciones sobre el género (Lepidoptera: Satyridae)." *Acta Entomologica Chilena* 15 (1989): 171–196.

Herrera, J., and W. D. Field. "A Revision of the Butterfly Genera *Theochila* and *Tatochila* (Lepidoptera: Pieridae)." *Proceedings of the United States National Museum* 108 (1959): 467–514.

Hewitson, William C. *Descriptions of New Species of Butterflies Collected by Mr. Buckley in Bolivia.* London: John van Voorst, 1869–1877.

—— *Descriptions of Some New Species of Lycaenidae.* London: John van Voorst, 1868.

—— *Illustrations of Diurnal Lepidoptera, Lycaenidae.* London: John van Voorst, 1863–1878.

Higgins, Lionel G., and Norman D. Riley. *A Field Guide to the Butterflies of Britain and Europe.* London: Collins, 1970.

Holland, William J. *The Butterfly Book.* Garden City, N.Y.: Doubleday, 1951.

Howe, W. H., ed. and illus. *The Butterflies of North America.* Garden City, N.Y.: Doubleday, 1975.

Hübner, Jacob. *Sammlung exotischer Schmetterlinge.* Augsburg: Privately printed, 1806–1838.

—— *Zütrage zur Sammlung exotischer Schmetterlinge.* Augsburg: Privately printed, 1818–1837.

Humboldt, Alexander von. *Personal Narrative of Travels to Equinoctial Regions of the New Continent During the Years 1799-1804.* 5 vols. Philadelphia: M. Carey, 1915.

Huxley, Julian, ed. *The New Systematics.* London: Oxford University Press, 1940.

Illiger, J. C. W. K. "Die neueste Gattungs-Eintheilung der Schmetterlinge aus den Linnéischen Gattungen *Papilio* und *Sphinx*." *Magazin Insektenkunde* 6 (1807): 277–289.

International Trust for Zoological Nomenclature. *International Code of Zoological Nomenclature.* London: International Trust for Zoological Nomenclature, 1961, 1964, 1985.

Johnson, Kurt. *Genera and Species of the Neotropical "Elfin"-like Hairstreak Butterflies (Lepidoptera, Lycaenidae, Theclinae).* 2 vols. Stevens Point: University of Wisconsin, Stevens Point, Museum of Natural History, 1992.

—— "A High Andean Species of *Terra* (Lepidoptera, Lycaenidae)." *Journal of the New York Entomological Society* 100 (1992): 522–526.

—— Letter to Editor and Photograph [Concerning Deforestation in the Sierra de Baoruco National Park]. *News of the Lepidopterists' Society* 43 (1989): 8–9.

—— *The Palaearctic "Elfin" Butterflies (Lycaenidae, Theclinae).* Neue Entomologische Nachricten, vol. 29. Markleuthen, Germany, 1992.

—— "*Penaincisalia,* a New Genus of "Elfin"-like Butterflies from the High Andes (Lepidoptera, Lycaenidae)." *Pan-Pacific Entomologist* 66 (1990): 97–125.

—— "Prairie and Plains Disclimax and Disappearing Butterflies in the Central United States." *Atala* 10–12 (1986): 20–30.

—— "Types of Neotropical Theclinae (Lycaenidae) in the Muséum Nationale d'Histoire Naturelle, Paris." *Journal of the Lepidopterists' Society* 45 (1991): 142–157.

Johnson, K., R. Eisele, and B. MacPherson. "The 'Hairstreak Butterflies' (Lycaenidae, Theclinae) of Northwestern Argentina." *Bulletin of the Allyn Museum* 123 (1988) [49 pp.] and 130 (1990) [77 pp.].

Johnson, K., and L. D. Miller. "The Genus *Ministrymon* Clench 1961 in Chile and a New Species from the Northern Desert Biotic Province (Lepidoptera, Lycaenidae)." *Acta Entomologica Chilena* 16 (1991): 183–192.

Johnson, K., L. D. Miller, and J. Herrera. "*Eiseliana* and *Heoda,* High Andean and Austral Genera of the Neotropical Eumaeini (Lepidoptera: Lycaenidae)." *Acta Entomologica Chilena* 17 (1991): 107–146.

Johnson, K., and D. S. Smith. "A Remarkable New Butterfly Species from Jamaica (Lepidoptera, Lycaenidae), with Notes on Jamaican Endemics and Their Sister Species." *Reports, Museum of Natural History, University of Wisconsin, Stevens Point* 24 (1993): 1–14.

Karges, Joann. *Nabokov's Lepidoptera: Genres and Genera.* Ann Arbor, Mich.: Ardis, 1985.

Klots, Alexander B. *A Field Guide to the Butterflies of North America, East of the Great Plains.* New York: McGraw-Hill, 1958.

Kohler, Pablo. *Catálogo de Lepidópteros Argentinos.* Buenos Aires: Publicaciones Breyer, 1928.

La Condamine, Charles M. de. *A Succinct Abridgement of a Voyage Made Within the Inland Parts of South America.* [Abridged English translation.] Paris, 1745.

Lamas, G. "La fauna de mariposas de la Reserva de Tambopata, Madre de Dios, Perú (Lepidoptera, Papilionoidea, y Hesperioidea)." *Revista de la Sociedad mexicana de Lepidopterología* 6 (1981): 23–40.

—— "Los Papilionoidea (Lepidoptera) de la Zona Reservada de Tambopata, Madre de Dios, Perú. I: Papilionidae, Pieridae y Nymphalidae (en parte)." *Revista peruana de Entomología* 27 (1985): 59–73.

Leech, John Henry. *Butterflies from China, Japan and Corea,* Part II: Lycaenidae, Papilionidae, and Hesperiidae. London: Privately printed, 1892. Pp. 115–286.

Lepidopterists' Society, *Commemorative Volume, 1945–1973*. New Haven, Conn.: Lepidopterists' Society, 1977.

Linnaeus, Carolus. *Systema naturae* [. . .]. Stockholm: Laurentii Salvii, 1758.

Mayr, Ernst. *Animal Species and Evolution*. Cambridge, Mass.: Harvard University Press, 1963.

McDunnough, J. "New North American *Eupithecias* 1 (Lepidoptera, Geometridae)." *Canadian Entomologist* 77 (1945): 168–176.

Meadows, Donella, et al., eds. *The Limits to Growth*. New York: New American Library, 1972.

Miller, Jacqueline Y., ed. *The Common Names of North American Butterflies*. Washington, D. C.: Smithsonian Institution Press, 1992.

Miller, L. D., and J. Y. Miller. "The Biogeography of West Indian Butterflies (Lepidoptera: Papilionoidea, Hesperioidea): A Vicariance model." In C. A. Woods, ed. *Biogeography of the West Indies*. London: Oxford University Press, 1989. Pp. 229–262.

Nabokov, Vladimir. *Ada or Ardor: A Family Chronicle*. New York: McGraw-Hill, 1969.

—— *Bend Sinister*. New York: Time, 1964.

—— "Butterfly Collecting in Wyoming, 1952." *Lepidopterists' News* 7 (1952): 49–52.

—— *The Defense*. New York: Vintage, 1990.

—— *Eugene Onegin*. Translated and with commentary by V. Nabokov. 4 vols. New York: Bollingen, 1964.

—— "A Few Notes on Crimean Butterflies." *The Entomologist* 53 (1920): 29–33.

—— *The Gift* Translated by Michael Schammel and Dmitri Nabokov with Vladimir Nabokov. New York: Putnam's, 1963.

—— *Invitation to a Beheading*. Translated by Dmitri Nabokov with Vladimir Nabokov. New York: Putnam's, 1963.

—— *Lolita*. New York: Putnam's, 1958.

—— *Lolita: A Screenplay*. New York: McGraw-Hill, 1974.

—— "*Lysandra cormion*, A New European Butterfly." *Journal of the New York Entomological Society* 49 (1941): 265–267.

—— *Mary*. Translated by Michael Glenny with Vladimir Nabokov. New York: McGraw-Hill, 1970.

—— *Pale Fire*. New York: Putnam's, 1962.

—— *Pnin*. Garden City, N.Y.: Doubleday, 1957.

—— *The Real Life of Sebastian Knight*. Norfolk, Conn.: New Directions, 1941.

—— *Selected Letters, 1940–1977*. Edited by Dmitri Nabokov and Matthew J. Bruccoli. New York: Harcourt Brace Jovanovich/Bruccoli Clark Layman, 1989.

—— *Speak, Memory: An Autobiography Revisited*. New York: Putnam's, 1966.

—— *Strong Opinions*. New York: McGraw-Hill, 1973. This book is a compilation of Nabokov's interviews and some book reviews and was the source for most of our quotations of such material.

Nabokov, Vladimir, and Edmund Wilson. *Nabokov-Wilson Letters*. Edited by Simon Karlinsky. New York: Harper & Row, 1979.

Peña, Luis E., and Alfredo J. Ugarte. *Las Mariposas de Chile* [*The Butterflies of Chile*]. Santiago: Editorial Universitaria, 1997.

Peterson, A. T. "New Species and New Species Limits in Birds." *The Auk* 115 (1998): 555–558.

Peterson, B. "The Male Genitalia of Some *Colias* Species." *Journal of Research on the Lepidoptera* 1 (1963): 135–156.

Pratt, A. E. *To the Snows of Tibet Through China*. London: Longmans, Green, 1892.

Pyle, Robert M. *National Audubon Field Guide to North American Butterflies*. New York: Alfred A. Knopf, 1981.

Nature Conservancy. *The Nature Conservancy in Ecuador*. Washington, D. C.: Nature Conservancy, 1997.

—— *Parks in Peril: Partnership for the Americas*. Washington, D.C.: Nature Conservancy, 1998.

Nijhout, H. F. *The Development and Evolution of Butterfly Wing Patterns*. Washington, D. C.: Smithsonian Institution Press, 1991.

Raven, R. H., and D. I. Axelrod. "Angiosperm Biogeography and Past Continental Movements." *Annals of the Missouri Botanical Gardens* 61 (1974): 540–673.

Remington, C. L. "Lepidoptera Studies." In *The Garland Companion to Vladimir Nabokov*. New York: Garland, 1995. Pp. 274–283.

Riley, N. D. *Field Guide to the Butterflies of the West Indies*. London: Collins, 1975.

Rindge, F. H., and W. P. Comstock. "An Unnamed Lycaenid from Trinidad (Lepidoptera)." *Journal of the New York Entomological Society* 61 (1953): 99–100.

Schappert, Philip, et al., eds. *News of the Lepidopterists' Society, 1–41*. Lawrence, Kans.: Allen Press, 1958–1999.

Schwanswitch, B. N. "Evolution of the Wing Pattern in the Lycaenid Butterflies." *Proceedings of the Zoological Society of London* 119 (1948): 189–263.

Schwartz, Albert. *The Butterflies of Hispaniola*. Gainesville: University of Florida Press, 1989.

—— "The Taxonomic Status of *Pseudochrysops* (Lycaenidae) on Puerto Rico." *Bulletin of the Allyn Museum* 110 (1987): 1–5.

Scott, James A. *The Butterflies of North America*. Stanford, Calif.: Stanford University Press, 1981.

Scudder, Samuel H. *The Butterflies of the Eastern United States and Canada with Special Reference to New England*. 3 vols. Cambridge, Mass.: Privately printed, 1889.

Seitz, Adalbert. *Die Gross-Schmetterlinge der Erde*. 16 vols. Stuttgart: Lehmann/Alfred Kernen, 1906–1954 [unfinished].

Shapiro, A. M. "Ignorance in High Places." *Paleobiology* 15 (1989): 61–67.

—— "The Proposed Magellanic Type-Locality of *Colias imperialis* Butler (Lepidoptera, Pieridae)." *Acta Entomologica Chilena* 18 (1993): 77–82.

—— "Why Are There So Few Butterflies in the High Andes?" *Journal of Research on the Lepidoptera* 31 (1994): 35–56.

—— "The Zoogeography and Systematics of the Argentine Andean and Patagonian Pierid Fauna." *Journal of Research on the Lepidoptera* 128, no. 3 (1989 [1991].)

Shields, O. "Fossil Butterflies and the Evolution of Lepidoptera." *Journal of Research on the Lepidoptera* 15 (1976): 132–143.

Shields, O., and S. K. Dvorak. "Butterfly Distributions and Continental Drift Between the Americas, the Caribbean, and Africa." *Journal of Natural History* 13 (1979): 221–250.

Shuey, J. "Dancing with Fire: Ecosystem Dynamics, Management, and the Karner Blue (*Lycaeides melissa samuelis* Nabokov) (Lycaenidae)." *Journal of the Lepidopterists' Society* 51 (1997): 263–269.

Smith, A. G., and A. Hallam. "The Fit of the Southern Continents." *Nature* 225 (1970): 139–144.

Smith, David S., Lee D. Miller, and Jacqueline Y. Miller. *The Butterflies of the West Indies and South Florida*. London: Oxford University Press, 1994.

Smith, Kenneth G. V. *Darwin's Insects: Charles Darwin's Entomological Notes.* Historical Series [14] to *Bulletin of the British Museum (Natural History),* 1987.

Spruce, Richard. *Notes of a Botanist on the Amazon and Andes.* 2 vols. London: Macmillan, 1908.

Staudinger, Otto. *Exotische Schmetterlinge.* Furth: Privately printed, 1884.

Stempffer, Henri. *The Genera of African Lycaenidae (Lepidoptera, Rhopalocera).* Supplements [10] to *Bulletin of the British Museum (Natural History),* 1967.

Stewart, I., and J. Cohen. *Figments of Reality: The Evolution of the Curious Mind.* Cambridge: Cambridge University Press, 1997.

Swengel, A. "Observations on the Effect of Fire on Karner Blue Butterflies." In D. A. Andow, R. J. Baker, and C. P. Lane, eds. *Karner Blue Butterfly: Symbol of a Vanishing Landscape.* St. Paul: University of Minnesota, St. Paul Agricultural Experiment Station, 1994. Pp. 81–86.

Taylor, Robert. "Nabokov Exhibition at Harvard Shows Off His Other Passion: Butterflies." *Boston Globe,* January 29, 1988. P. 73.

The Emergence of Man: Life Before Man. New York: Time-Life Books, 1972.

Tuxen, S. L. *Taxonomists' Glossary of Genitalia in Insects.* Copenhagen: Munksgaard, 1970.

Ureta, E. R. "Nuevas especies de Lycaenidae (Lep. Rhopalocera) de Chile." *Boletín Museo Nacional* 26 (1956): 261–267.

Urquhart, F. A., and N. R. Urquhart. "The Overwintering Site of the Eastern Population of the Monarch Butterfly (*Danaus p. plexippus;* Danaidae) in Southern Mexico." *Journal of the Lepidopterists' Society* 30 (1976): 153–158.

Vane-Wright, Richard I., and Phillip R. Ackery, eds. *Biology of Butterflies.* London: Academic Press, 1984.

Wallace, Alfred Russel. *The Geographic Distribution of Animals.* 2 vols. London: Macmillan, 1876.

—— *A Narrative of Travels on the Amazon and Rio Negro.* London: Ward and Locke, 1889.

Webster, B. "Butterflies to Be First Insects on U. S. Endangered List." *New York Times,* March 21, 1975.

Weymer, Gustav, and P. Maassen. *"Lepidopteran gessamelt auf einer Reise durch Colombia, Ecuador, Peru, Brasilien, Argentien, und Bolivien in den Jahren 1868–1877 von Alphons Stubel."* Berlin: Asher, 1890.

Whymper, Edward. *Travels Amongst the Great Andes of the Equator.* 2d ed. London: John Murray, 1892.

Wilson, Edward O. *The Diversity of Life.* Cambridge, Mass.: Harvard University Press, Belknap Press, 1992.

World Wildlife Fund. "Temperate Rain Forests of Chile and Argentina." *Global 200 Ecoregions Reports,* April 1998, 1–6.

Zaleski, P. "Nabokov's Blue Period," *Harvard Magazine,* July–August 1986

Zimmer, Dieter E. *Les papillons de Nabokov.* Lausanne: Litterae Zooligicae Actes du Musée Cantonal de Zoologie, 1993.

—— "Nabokov's Lepidoptera: An Annotated Multilingual Checklist." In his *Les papillons de Nabokov.* Pp. 25–171.

—— *A Guide to Nabokov's Butterflies and Moths.* Hamburg: Privately printed, 1998.

Index